MW00759504

THE COLONEL
WHO WOULD NOT REPENT

THE COLONEL WHO WOULD NOT REPENT

THE BANGLADESH WAR AND ITS UNQUIET LEGACY

———

SALIL TRIPATHI

Yale UNIVERSITY PRESS

New Haven and London

First Yale University Press edition 2016.
Preface copyright © 2016 by Salil Tripathi.
Copyright © Salil Tripathi. First published in the English
language by the Aleph Book Company 2014.

Yale University Press books may be purchased in quantity for
educational, business, or promotional use. For information,
please e-mail sales.press@yale.edu (U.S. office) or sales@
yaleup.co.uk (U.K. office).

Library of Congress Control Number: 2015956430
ISBN: 978-0-300-21818-3 (hardcover: alk. paper)
Printed in the United States of America.

A catalogue record for this book is available from the British
Library.

This paper meets the requirements of ANSI/NISO Z39.48-
1992 (Permanence of Paper).

10 9 8 7 6 5 4 3 2 1

CONTENTS

Late one evening in February 2015, Avijit Roy and his wife, Rafida Ahmed Bonya, both Americans of Bangladeshi origin, were making their way home from the annual festival of books in Dhaka, Bangladesh's capital. A group of militants wielding machetes attacked them, stunning passersby, while police officers who were standing by did nothing. Roy died almost instantly; Ahmed was severely injured. She lost a thumb and was permanently scarred.

Roy was the founder of a blog called *Mukto Mona* (Free Mind), an online space for atheist and rationalist bloggers to express their views. Ahmed met Roy through the blog and they married; she later became an editor of the blog. Roy was the author of several books that argued for reason, science, and rationality, and that challenged ignorance, superstition, and religion. In the months following that attack, three more bloggers in Bangladesh were murdered in similar fashion: Washiqur Rehman, Ananta Bijoy Das, and Niloy Neel. Two of them were frequent contributors to *Mukto Mona*.

In recent years, Bangladesh has become a crucible for religious fundamentalism and free speech, impunity and immunity, war crimes and the rule of law, tribunals and international justice—all are challenging issues that affect human rights and international law today. And yet Bangladesh's saga—so full of human drama, strategic challenges, geopolitical consequences, and developmental dilemmas—has remained largely untold.

The murders of the bloggers not only tell a story of religious bigotry and freedom of expression, though that is very much part of the narrative, but also show the conflict between two forms of identity struggling within the Bangladeshi soul—Muslim and Bengali. That conflict has deep roots in the war for Bangladesh's independence from Pakistan in 1971, in which hundreds of thousands of civilians died as Pakistan sought to crush Bengali nationalism.

The leaders of newly independent Bangladesh were determined not to let the perpetrators of those war crimes remain unaccountable. Inspired by the Nuremberg and Tokyo tribunals that prosecuted Nazi and Japanese war criminals, respectively, after World War II, and long before the International Criminal Court was set up in 1998, Bangladesh's leadership decided to prosecute their war criminals. But Sheikh Mujibur Rahman (or Mujib, as he was popularly known), Bangladesh's first elected prime minister (and later president), was assassinated in 1975, and the governments that followed did not consider prosecuting war crimes a priority. The tribunals were finally set up in 2009 after Hasina Wajed, Mujib's daughter, was elected prime minister for the second time. Some of the bloggers who were killed or threatened had been active in the Shahbagh protests of 2013 that had brought thousands into the streets seeking justice for those war crimes. They campaigned politically, demanding an end to impunity, and called for the death penalty for those accused at the war crimes tribunals. Most of the defendants are from the Jamaat-i-Islami Party, which had opposed Bangladesh's independence because party members preferred a united Pakistan. And so the three narratives become intertwined—religion, politics, and justice—and it is in that maelstrom that the bloggers have plunged. The tribunal has already sentenced several of the defendants to death, and four have been executed. International human rights groups have supported the principle of the tribunals but criticize its procedures.

The four murdered bloggers mentioned above, who were killed between February and August 2015, were each attacked separately by men wielding machetes. And two years earlier, in February 2013, Rajib Haider, another blogger who was active in the Shahbagh protests, was murdered. While each killing has been reported in greater depth by the international media (but with less intensity), the deaths in Bangladesh have not attracted the kind of instant universal condemnation and solidarity that followed the reprehensible attack on the office of the French magazine *Charlie Hebdo* in January 2015, when two brothers killed eleven members of the magazine's staff in Paris. There are many possible explanations for this, including the fact that the Paris attack occurred in the heart of a western democracy. A less charitable explanation involves the fact that the Paris attacks occurred in a city at the heart of the western world and the victims included people with whom western audiences could empathize, unlike in far-off Bangladesh, where brown people with unpronounceable names were getting killed by unfamiliar religious fundamentalists. Dhaka is indeed far removed from the west, and most of the articles and conversations at *Mukto Mona* are in Bengali, though it is a language spoken by 189 million people, making it the world's sixth most widely spoken language, according to UNESCO (the United Nations Educational, Scientific, and Cultural Organization).

Bangladesh is indeed distant from the capitals of major powers, and it is surrounded by strategically more significant countries (in particular, India) in a region with other, more current conflicts (such as in Afghanistan) or political challenges (such as in Myanmar). Moreover, its history has had to struggle to emerge from under the weight imposed by the narratives of India and Pakistan. More than a million people died during the religious massacres that occurred when India and Pakistan gained independence, and perhaps fourteen million became refugees. Much of the violence was in the Punjab province, which was divided along religious lines, and post-Partition literature about the sub-continent's history has often focused on that narrative. Bengal was also divided at that time, but that division has merited less attention. The Bangladeshi history took a different trajectory by defining its nationalism on more than just religious terms, and the challenges and drama that Bangladesh has faced, and continues to face, are far-reaching and universal. Its story is important for a clearer understanding of our times.

With 158.5 million residents, Bangladesh is the world's eighth most populous country according to World Bank data. More Muslims live here than in any other country after Indonesia, Pakistan, and India. Bangladesh was the eastern half of Pakistan, which was carved out of India when British rule ended in 1947, with Hindu-majority India governed by a secular constitution and Pakistan created as the home for the subcontinent's Muslims, many of whom feared Hindu domination.

But not all Muslims from pre-Partition India left for Pakistan; many chose to make India their home. And not all those who became Pakistanis saw their identity primarily in religious terms. Many Muslims in East Pakistan saw themselves as Bengali *and* Muslim. And at independence, proportionately more Hindus chose to stay back in the eastern half of Pakistan, deciding not to move to India, as many Hindus and Sikhs had done from Pakistan's western half. The political leadership in West Pakistan disregarded the country's multiple identities, particularly the linguistic aspirations in East Pakistan. Pakistan's leaders turned down eastern demands for greater autonomy and equal status for the Bengali language. On 21 February 1952, security forces in Dhaka shot at student demonstrators, killing a few, and the language movement was born. The festival of books that Roy and Ahmed attended before they were attacked is held around the anniversary of those killings. (The United Nations now recognizes 21 February as International Mother Language Day.)

Grievances continued to mount in East Pakistan, including concerns over economic disparities between the two halves. Economists in East Pakistan began compiling data that showed that West Pakistan was treating the eastern wing as its colony. Matters reached a flashpoint in late 1970, when a cyclone caused extensive damage in the eastern half and Bengalis felt that the federal Pakistani government ignored their plight. In the elections that followed, Awami League, the Bengali nationalist party led by the charismatic Mujib, swept East Pakistan, winning an absolute majority in the federal parliament. West Pakistani politicians hadn't anticipated such an outcome, and the military regime of Gen. Yahya Khan dithered over transferring power. Protests continued in East Pakistan, reaching feverish intensity. In March 1971 martial law was declared, and thousands of civilians were killed in the military crackdown that followed. Ten million refugees crossed the Indian border, and India supported the Mukti Bahini, the Bangladeshi guerrilla army that fought for Bangladesh's freedom.

Pakistan felt assured of American backing because Pakistan was providing critical support to the Nixon administration, which wanted to establish diplomatic relations with China, then ruled by Mao Zedong. The United States wanted China on its side to widen the rift within the Communist world and isolate the Soviet Union. Pakistan was willing to be the go-between, and in return, the United States was willing to overlook the atrocities of the Pakistani army in the country's eastern wing.

India started building international opinion against Pakistan, and in December 1971, Pakistan attacked India, which gave India the legitimacy it needed to intervene militarily. In two weeks the war was over. Pakistan surrendered and Bangladesh became free.

Mujib's popularity declined within two years of independence. Poverty worsened and was followed by a famine, and as Bangladesh took a pro-Soviet stance, including trading with Cuba, US assistance was withdrawn. Crime and lawlessness increased and Mujib declared a one-party state to assert his authority. In August 1975, a group of junior officers conspired and staged a coup, killing Mujib and most of his family. In the chaotic years that followed, subsequent governments granted immunity to the assassins and plotters. Bangladesh saw stability briefly under Gen. Ziaur Rahman (Zia), but he was assassinated in 1981. The colonel referred to in the title of this book is Col. Farooq Rahman, one of the masterminds of that coup, whom I interviewed in 1986 in Dhaka. He was executed in 2010.

Politics now revolves around two women: Mujib's daughter Hasina Wajed (the current prime minister) and Zia's widow Khaleda Zia (who has been prime minister twice and leads the Bangladesh Nationalist Party [BNP]). The two had once allied against a dictator but now they can barely talk to one another. Bangladesh holds elections but its divisive politics is deeply fractured. The BNP boycotted the last elections, which means that less than half the parliamentary seats were contested, giving the Awami League a hollow victory. The effect of these political divisions is felt on the streets, with periodic strikes, demonstrations, violence, and, indeed, bloggers and other dissenters under threat or being murdered.

Among the world's largest nations with a Muslim population, Bangladesh is located strategically in an area that has seen political upheavals and instability. Greater volatility is not in anybody's interest, least of all Bangladesh's long-suffering people.

Bangladesh is a poor country—the average annual gross income is $1,080 in current dollars, with nearly three out of every ten Bangladeshis designated as poor, according to the World Bank. Several million Bangladeshis go abroad to find work. Remittances sent by Bangladeshis who work abroad form a large chunk of the country's earnings—Bangladesh ranks eighth worldwide among countries receiving remittances from emigrants.

Many go to work in the Persian Gulf States, where some come under the sway of Wahhabi Islam. Over two million Bangladeshis work in Saudi Arabia. Many of them return with a narrower and more fundamentalist worldview than that embodied in the more relaxed, Sufi-inspired syncretic views prevalent in Bengali Islam and celebrated in Baul music. Remittances and donations from the Gulf States have funded mosques and religious schools in Bangladesh. While fundamentalism in Bangladesh has not reached the levels found in Pakistan, secular-minded Bangladeshis grow increasingly anxious with reports of attacks on atheist or rationalist bloggers or on minorities, or with periodic calls by extremist groups demanding the imposition of Islamic laws.

At a time of religious resurgence in many parts of the world, Bangladesh has a government that professes secularism and is trying to maintain Bangladesh's secular traditions, even though it has a poor human rights record and has cracked down on dissent. As Bangladesh grapples with myriad challenges, it has to deal with profound questions in the rather short span of a few decades: What is the basic building block of a nation—language or religion? Is there a limit to the extent of dissent permissible in a multireligious state? Should a state prosecute people who may have committed mass atrocities, or should it allow the culture of impunity to prevail in order to maintain stability? Is justice served through punishment and retribution, or is it restorative and built on forgiveness? Are certain crimes so heinous that the perpetrators should not be immune from punishment? And is forgiveness possible without the perpetrator expressing remorse? How can a nation reach closure?

◆

I was born in India, in the city then known as Bombay, in a middle-class family of Gujarati origin but with an affectionate obsession with things Bengali. My father chose to learn the music of the Bengali Nobel laureate Rabindranath Tagore, and my mother would tell me Tagore stories. She had chosen Bengali names for me and my younger brothers, Utpal and Pranav. The school I went to was inspired by Tagore's ideals, and two of my teachers introduced me to the cinema of Satyajit Ray. I was hooked. I wanted to see his films without subtitles, so in my teens I chose to study Bengali by attending weekend classes.

I was not yet ten when the Pakistani troops unleashed their reign of terror in what would soon become Bangladesh. Rivers of blood irrigated the land that had inspired the Baul music that the filmmaker Ritwik Ghatak pined for, where Tagore sat by the river and wrote *Gitanjali* (for which he won the Nobel Prize in Literature), and where Jibanananda Das celebrated the beauty of a woman called Bonolota Sen.

Fifteen years after the war, in 1986, I went to Bangladesh for the first time. I spent two weeks in Dhaka and met politicians—most significantly, Farooq Rahman, the colonel who would not repent his role in planning the assassination of Sheikh Mujib. I also met Khaleda Zia (who saw me but declined to be interviewed) and Hasina Wajed (who spoke to me about her father).

From 2010 onwards, I returned to Bangladesh often to travel across the country to interview people and to absorb the stories of the nation as I researched and wrote this book. I went to the market in Chuknagar where a massacre had taken place, the campus in Dhaka where students had been shot, the circuit house in Chittagong where Ziaur Rahman was murdered, the streets of Natore where Bonolota Sen inspired Jibanananda Das, the road that Allen Ginsberg immortalized in his poem, "September on Jessore Road," the ashram in Noakhali from where Mahatma Gandhi campaigned for peace in the violence-torn district, and the estate in Shilaidaha from where Tagore sailed with a boatman in the river, the landscape pale in the golden light, as he captured that ethereal moment, writing the *Gitanjali*.

Bangladesh's independence struggle and its aftermath have remained little known for too long. In terms of the sheer number of deaths, it was a brutal conflict. The systematic targeting of civilians, while not unique, was widespread and exceptionally violent. Sexual violence against women was a central feature of the conflict, not a collateral issue. Perhaps over a quarter million cases of rape occurred—it was used as a weapon of war in Bangladesh long before its use in the Balkan wars of the 1990s. And long before the international community created the International Criminal Court, Bangladesh sought to prosecute genocide, crimes against humanity, and war crimes.

Bangladesh's ordeal symbolizes the central conflict of our time—religious essentialism versus inclusive secularism. Recent violence and the ongoing international crimes tribunals suggest that the divisions that tore the Indian subcontinent apart in 1947, and then again in 1971, remain alive. In spite of it all, Bangladesh continues to amaze its critics with socioeconomic indicators that embarrass its more prosperous neighbors such as India.

For Bangladesh the challenge is to put its blood-soaked past behind without condoning the guilty. It is a young nation taking bold steps to fight impunity. It deserves to succeed so that perpetrators of grave human rights abuses are always made accountable, and to do so it must make the right choices. At independence, Bangladeshis wanted to build a modern nation with space for all Bangladeshi men and women: Muslims, Hindus, Christians, Buddhists, and atheists, whether they speak Bengali or other languages. When the country achieves this, it will be closer to its dream of becoming the golden Bengal that its poets dreamt of. Its people deserve no less.

PROLOGUE: THE HANGING OF
SHEIKH MUJIB'S ASSASSINS

About three decades ago I met a man who calmly told me how he had
organized the massacre of a family. There was no sense of remorse
in his confession. He was bragging about it, even grinning as he spoke to me.

I was a young reporter at that time, on assignment in Dhaka*, trying to
figure out what had gone wrong with Bangladesh. Fifteen years earlier, as a
schoolboy in India, I had followed its blood-splattered struggle for independence.
I remembered the images of ten million people who had crossed the border
seeking refuge in India; I had collected funds for the refugees by staging a
play in Bombay, as the city I grew up in was known at that time; we shouted
'Joy Bangla', the Bangladeshi cry for independence, for no apparent reason
(10-year-old kids do such things); and we eagerly listened to the radio and
read newspapers over two weeks in December, as India defeated the Pakistani
army, assisting Bangladeshi Mukti Bahini forces to gain independence. During
those days, I remember going with my family to the railway station with
home-cooked food for Indian soldiers going to the front.

The man I was interviewing that day in Dhaka lived in a well-appointed
home in Banani, a tony part of Bangladesh's capital. Soldiers protected his
house, checking the bags and identification of all visitors. A week earlier he
had been a presidential candidate, losing by a huge margin to the eventual
winner, President Hussain Muhammad Ershad.

The man I met wore a Pathani outfit that looked out of place in a country
where civilian politicians tended to wear white kurtas with black waistcoats if
they belonged to the Awami League, and safari suits if they were part of the
Bangladesh Nationalist Party, while working class men on the streets went
about in lungis. The Pathani outfit was more in tune with what men from
Pakistan wore, and as I was to learn later, many Bangladeshis who had lost their

---

*Dacca was renamed Dhaka in 1983; it has been spelt accordingly in different chapters of
the book.

loved ones during the war hated that outfit, just as they hated the Urdu slogan 'Bangladesh Zindabad'. They preferred 'Joy Bangla' in Bengali.

The man I had come to interview had a thin moustache and wore gold-rimmed glasses. He stared at me eagerly as we spoke, curious about the notes I was taking, trying to read what I was writing in my notepad. He sat straight on the sofa, his chest thrust forward, as if he was still in uniform. He looked self-assured and confident; not like someone who had overwhelmingly lost the presidential poll. He was part of a high stakes game, and he looked as if he was certain he would win, as if he was assured that someone important held all the cards.

His name was Farooq Rahman, and he had been a major, and later, lieutenant colonel in the Bangladeshi army. He had returned to Bangladesh only recently, after several years in exile in Libya. What he had done in the past was not in dispute.

Before dawn on 15 August 1975, he had led the Bengal Lancers, the army's tank unit under his command, to disarm the *Rokkhi Bahini*,[1] a paramilitary force loyal to Sheikh Mujib. As Farooq left the Dhaka Cantonment, he had instructed other officers and soldiers to go to the upscale residential area of Dhanmondi, where Mujib lived. Soon after 5 a.m., the officers had killed Mujib and most of his family.

I had been rehearsing how to ask Farooq about his role in the assassination. I had no idea how he would react or respond. After a few desultory questions about the country's political situation, I tentatively began, 'It has been widely reported in Bangladesh that you were somehow connected with the plot to remove Mujibur Rahman from power in 1975. Would you...'

'Of course, we killed him,' he interrupted me. 'He had to go,' he added, before I could complete my hesitant, long-winded question.

Farooq Rahman thought he was a patriot. He believed he had saved the nation. The governments that followed Mujib reinforced this self-belief and perception, rewarding him and the other assassins with respectability by giving them political space, and to some, plum diplomatic assignments. Farooq himself stood in presidential elections, which he lost badly. The Oxford-trained lawyer, Kamal Hossain, who was Mujib's law minister and later foreign minister, told me, 'The impunity with which Farooq operated was extraordinary. President Ershad encouraged Farooq to return because he wanted a candidate to stand against him in the rigged elections, so that the process would seem fair.' For Ershad this was important because, as with other dictators, he craved legitimacy, and the opposition boycott of the elections upset his plans. He needed a contest and Farooq obliged.

Farooq was able to operate with impunity for many years because the governments that followed Mujib were not keen to prosecute the killers and in the late 1970s, during the rule of Gen. Zia, the 5th Amendment to the constitution was passed, granting them immunity.

The political landscape in Bangladesh after Mujib's murder was unstable. In its forty-four-year history, there have been several coups, and the form of government has switched from parliamentary to presidential to parliamentary again. The country has had eleven prime ministers and over a dozen heads of state, and there have been times when it has been ruled by generals, or by a caretaker government comprising unelected officials.

Mujibur Rahman's daughter Sheikh Hasina Wajed had first come to power in 1996 but her majority was precarious at that time—her party, the Awami League, had won 146 of 300 seats, and relied on the support of other parties to rule. But when she came to power with an absolute majority in 2009, Hasina was determined to redeem her father's reputation and seek justice. Her quest has larger implications for Bangladesh's citizenry. Hundreds of thousands—and by Bangladesh government estimates perhaps three million—people were killed during the 1971 war. Tens of thousands of Bangladeshis now wait for justice—to see those who harmed them and their loved ones brought to account. But the culture of impunity hasn't disappeared. Even for Sheikh Hasina, it took more than three decades before she received some measure of vindication, and one reason she was elected in 2008 was because she promised to set up tribunals to prosecute individuals accused of having committed international crimes, such as war crimes, crimes against humanity, and genocide.

◆

Sometime in the afternoon of 27 January 2010, Mahfuz Anam received a call from a government official, saying that the end was imminent. Anam was in the newsroom of Bangladesh's leading English newspaper, *The Daily Star*, where he is the editor. He knew what the message meant: perhaps within hours, five men—Lt. Col. Farooq, Lt. Col. Sultan Shahriar Rashid Khan, Lt. Col. Mohiuddin Ahmed, Maj. Bazlul Huda, and army lancer A.K.M. Mohiuddin—would be hanged by the neck until they died at the city's central jail. Anam told his reporters to be prepared, and sent several reporters and photographers to cover the executions.

'We had hints that the end was near, particularly when the relatives of the five men were asked to come and meet them, and given hardly any notice,' Anam told me during a long telephone conversation a week after the executions. 'The authorities had told the immediate families that there were no limits on the number of relatives who could come, and they were allowed to remain with them until well after visiting hours. We knew that the final hours had come,' he said.

Once the families left, the five men were sent to their cells. They were told to take a bath and offer their night prayers. Then the guards asked them if they wanted to eat anything special. An imam came, offering to read from the Quran. Around 10:30 p.m., a reporter called Anam to say that the city's civil surgeon, Mushfiqur Rahman, and district magistrate Zillur Rahman had arrived at the jail. Police vans arrived 50 minutes later, carrying five empty coffins. The paramilitary force known as the Rapid Action Battalion, took positions at various nodal points in the city that were prone to strikes and stoppages at the slightest political pretext, providing support to the regular police force to prevent demonstrations. Other leading officials came within minutes: the home secretary, the inspector general of prisons, and the police commissioner. Rashida Ahmad, who was at that time news editor at the online news agency, bdnews24.com, recalled: 'Many media houses practically decamped en masse to the jail to "experience a historic moment" firsthand.' Anam told me, 'By 11:35 p.m., we knew it would happen that night. We held back our first edition. The second edition had the detailed story.'

Bazlul Huda was the first to be taken to the gallows. He was handcuffed, and a black hood covered his face. Eyewitnesses have said Huda struggled to free himself and screamed loudly as guards led him to the brightly lit room. An official waved and dropped a red handkerchief to the ground, the signal for the executioner to proceed. It was just after midnight when Huda died. Mohiuddin Ahmed was next, followed by Farooq, Shahriar, and A.K.M. Mohiuddin. It was all over soon after 1 a.m.

Earlier that day, the Bangladesh Supreme Court had rejected the final appeal of four of the five convicts. Shahriar was the only one not to seek presidential pardon. His daughter Shehnaz, who spent two hours with her father that evening, later said: 'My father was a freedom fighter; and a man who fights for the independence of his country never begs for his life.'[2]

Sheikh Hasina was at her prime ministerial home that night. She was informed when the executions began, she reportedly asked to be left alone and later offered namaz-e-shukran, a prayer of gratitude. Many people, most of them supporters of the Awami League, had gathered outside her house that night, but she did not come out to meet anybody. A few days later, she told a party convention that it was a moment of joy for all of them, because due process had been served.

Many governments oppose the death penalty on principle and consider it violates human rights, and the European Union had appealed to the Bangladeshi government to commute the sentence of Mujib's assassins. The human rights group Amnesty International had also sought clemency, while agreeing that the men should face justice. These appeals met with no response.

The mood in Dhaka was sober and subdued, although Dhaka residents spoke of celebrations in certain localities. Ahmad, who was at her news desk until late at bdnews24.com, described the mood in the newsroom as sombre. Many in the city could understand Hasina thanking God, and other politicians welcoming the closing of a dark chapter, but some felt it a bit much that parliament itself thanked God and adjourned for the day, she told me.

It had taken thirty-four years for this saga to end. The first politician to grant these men immunity was Khondaker Mostaq Ahmad, who took over as Bangladesh's president after Mujib's assassination. He had even praised the assassins, calling them 'shurjo shontan' or 'sons of the sun'. Gen. Ziaur Rahman, who later became president, confirmed their immunity and later amended the constitution to entrench this. In the years that followed, their political rehabilitation had begun.[3] Lt. Col. Shariful Haq Dalim, a decorated liberation war veteran who had played a major role in the conspiracy, held diplomatic positions in Beijing, Hong Kong, and became high commissioner to Kenya, even though he was implicated in a coup attempt in 1980. Lt. Col. Aziz Pasha served in Rome, Nairobi, and Harare, where he sought asylum when Hasina first came to power in 1996. She removed him from his diplomatic post but he stayed on in Harare, and died there. (A month after the executions, Awami League activists ransacked and set afire the home of his brother in Dhaka.)[4] Maj. Huda was briefly a member of parliament, and also served as diplomat in Islamabad and Jeddah.

Other conspirators at various times served Bangladeshi missions in Beijing, Buenos Aires, Algiers, Islamabad, Teheran, Kuwait, Abu Dhabi, Bangkok, Lagos, Dakar, Ankara, Jakarta, Tokyo, Muscat, Cairo, Kuala Lumpur, Ottawa, and Manila. The government said it would now try to bring the surviving officers back to Bangladesh from the countries where some of the conspirators reportedly continued to live. These were often identified as the United States, Canada, Pakistan, South Africa, Thailand, and Kenya. They have been tried in absentia and some face execution.

Bringing all of them back is not going to be easy for Bangladesh, because some countries where they reportedly live, like Canada and South Africa, have abolished the death penalty, and Kenya has placed a temporary moratorium on the death penalty. They are unlikely to extradite them, unless Bangladesh guarantees that they will not be executed. Bangladesh is unlikely to offer such guarantee.

Bangladesh is among fifty-eight countries (including India) that retain the death penalty. In 2008, five people were executed in Bangladesh. Bangladeshi human rights lawyers have found it hard to challenge the death penalty on a matter of principle because there is public support for the death penalty in Bangladesh. Lawyers do appeal individual cases, but there is no concerted major human rights campaign against the death penalty. There are also political compulsions. One human rights activist told me, 'We are against [the] death penalty but the dilemma is that we are in a country where life imprisonment really means imprisonment guaranteed only until your party comes to power. The death penalty is almost seen as the only way to guarantee justice for such a grisly crime.'

Grisly, it certainly was. This is what happened.

◆

Dhanmondi in 1975 had not changed much from how it looked in the 1950s, soon after Pakistan's independence, when Dacca, as the city was then known, was the provincial capital of East Pakistan. The roads were lined with two-storey houses, the traffic quiet and unhurried. Today, there are multi-storey buildings, English-medium schools, new universities, shopping malls and hookah bars to lure younger crowds. Back in 1975, the area was quieter. In the evening, people strolled along the periphery of the large lake in the middle of the neighbourhood and at night you could hear the tinkling bells of cycle rickshaws.

On 15 August 1975, before dawn, 700 soldiers left their barracks and headed for the three homes where Mujib and his family lived. Everyone was still asleep at Mujib's house, #677 on Road 32. They first attacked the home of Abdur Rab Seraniabat, Mujib's brother-in-law, at 27 Minto Road. Mujib heard about the attack. Seraniabat was a minister in Mujib's government.

Mujib called his personal assistant, Mohitul Islam, who was at his desk, and asked him to call the police immediately.

Mohitul tried calling the police, but was alarmed to find that the phones weren't working. When he used another secure line to call the telephone exchange, the person at the other end said nothing.

Mujib snatched the phone and shouted into the mouthpiece. 'What's going on?' he asked.

At the time soldiers arrived at Mujib's house, the guards outside were hoisting the national flag. They were stunned to find army officers rushing in through the gate, ordering them to drop their weapons and surrender. A few shots were fired.

Maj. Bazlul Huda entered Mujib's house with several soldiers. A frightened servant woke up Mujib's son Kamal, who got dressed and came down. Huda took out his gun and pointed it at Kamal even as Mohitul tried telling Huda that it was Kamal, Mujib's son. But before he could complete the sentence there was a loud burst of gunfire and Kamal fell down, dead. Huda heard Mujib's voice at the top of the staircase and ran to face him.

'What do you want?' Mujib asked Huda, whom he recognized.

The soldiers pulled their triggers, spraying Mujib with dozens of bullets. Mujib's body was thrown back and then forward, gushing blood which splattered the stairs and the wall. He was dead by the time his body stopped tumbling down the stairs. Before his burial the following day at his birthplace, Tungipara, the imam noticed at least ten bullets still lodged inside Mujib's body.

The killers then went inside the house, and one by one, killed everyone they could find: Mujib's wife, Fazilatunnesa; Kamal's wife, Sultana; Mujib's other son, Jamal, and his wife Rosy; and Mujib's brother Naser, who was heard pleading, 'I am not in politics.'

Then they saw Russell, Mujib's 10-year-old son, who was crying, asking for his mother. He, too, was killed.

Around the same time, another group of soldiers had killed Mujib's brother-in-law Seraniabat at his home, and a third group had murdered the family of Fazlul Haque Moni, Mujib's nephew, an influential Awami League politician who lived on Road 13/1, about two kilometres away from Mujib's home.

Mahfuz Anam lived across the Dhanmondi Lake at that time, and had a clear view of Sheikh Moni's house. 'I saw what happened,' he recalled. 'Early that morning I was awakened by the sound of firing. I got up. My room was on the side of the lake. I ventured out to the boundary wall. I saw troops enter Sheikh Moni's house. I heard plenty of firing, followed by screaming. I heard shots—some random, some from sub-machine guns. I saw the troops leave the house. It was all over in four to six minutes. I could hear the people inside groaning; it continued for some time.'

The junior officers' coup had proceeded exactly as planned. There had been no resistance from the moment Huda and his team had reached Mujib's home. After taming the Rakkhi Bahini, Farooq arrived at Mujib's gate, eager to know what had happened there. Huda told him calmly, 'All are finished.'

When we met a decade after those killings, I asked Farooq: 'And the 10-year-old boy: did he have to be killed?'

'It was an act of mercy killing. Mujib was building a dynasty; we had to finish off all of them,' he told me with a degree of finality, his arm slicing ruthlessly in the air, as if he was chopping off the head of someone kneeling in front of him. There was no mercy in his eyes, no remorse, only a hint of pride.

The junior officers who had conspired to assassinate Mujib had tried killing the entire family, but Mujib's two daughters, Hasina and Rehana, were in Germany, where Hasina's husband, M. A. Wazed Miah, a nuclear scientist, was a researcher at a laboratory (he died in May 2009). Kamal Hossain was at that time on an official visit to Belgrade. Kamal Hossain told me: 'I first heard there had been a coup. We received more information from agency reports which were conveyed to me by the officials of the Yugoslav foreign ministry. We heard about Mujib's death, then we heard about the other family members. My immediate concern was Hasina's safety.' He met her in Bonn and decided to sever his relations with the new government. In his autobiography Hossain writes: 'I regarded my relations with the government to have ceased the moment power had been seized through the assassination and coup... I firmly declined to accept any assignment... by the [new] government.'[5] He handed in his official passport to the ambassador, and left for England, because it was easier to get information there. In London he handed in his diplomatic passport and obtained an ordinary passport, informing the High Commission that he was severing relations with the new government. Hasina, too, could not have gone back. She was granted asylum in India and lived in New Delhi with her husband until 1981. Hossain returned to Dhaka in 1980.

In October 1986, I visited Mujib's house, the mute witness to the ghastly events of that dawn. As if to ensure that no one should forget the tragedy, Sheikh Hasina, who showed me around, had made only minimal changes to the house, preserving the crime scene. The bare walls bore dozens of bullet marks. Shattered glass lay on the ground of what was once Mujib's library. On the staircase where Mujib was shot, and on the wall which he had tried to grip for support as he fell, darkened blood stains were still visible. She pointed these out to me.

Mujib was 55 when he was killed. He had been in and out of Pakistani jails, and was widely regarded—and initially revered—as Bangladesh's founding father. At the time of Partition of British India in 1947, what is now known as Bangladesh became the eastern wing of Pakistan. The two parts of Pakistan were separated by thousands of kilometres of Indian territory. Pakistan was supposed to become the home for the Muslims of the subcontinent, even though many Muslims chose to stay on in India. Islam united the two parts, east and west, but culture, language, and the idea of what made a nation would divide them. The eastern half was more populous, and its leaders complained of insufficient attention and inadequate resource allocation. Punjabis dominated the Sindhis, Baluchis, and Pathans in the west, and they had even less regard for their Bengali compatriots in the east. Bingo was the pejorative term West Pakistanis used to describe East Pakistanis.

Things came to a head in 1970, when in nationwide elections the Awami League won enough seats in the eastern wing to form a national government. Mujib should have been invited to become Pakistan's prime minister, but the generals and politicians in the west had other plans. They engaged the Awami League in interminable negotiations even as Pakistan's ruler at the time, Gen. Yahya Khan, quietly sent troops to the east, and later appointed a governor called Gen. Tikka Khan, who had express instructions to crush Bengali nationalism. Many Bangladeshis remember planeloads of young men arriving on flights from the west. They were military men but not in uniform, and they did not carry any weapons. Meanwhile, Pakistan's navy was shipping weapons through the Chittagong port, keeping Bengali officers in the dark, and secretly arming the men who had landed in Dacca.

The military crackdown began on 25 March 1971, as the Pakistani army brutally attempted to trounce Bengali aspirations. Mujib was jailed in West Pakistan. In the east, hundreds of thousands were killed, and millions of refugees made their way to India. A civil war followed, and India aided the Mukti Bahini, as Bangladeshi freedom fighters were called. In early December, Pakistan attacked India on its western front; India retaliated, and its troops defeated Pakistan on both fronts within a fortnight. Indian troops entered the capital, and thousands of Pakistani troops surrendered. A few weeks later

Mujib returned to the Tejgaon airport. A sea of humanity greeted the leader of the new nation, Bangladesh.

Three-and-a-half years later, Farooq and his men annihilated most of Mujib's family. 'Even dogs didn't bark when we killed Mujib,' Farooq told me.

Sheikh Mujibur Rahman had squandered his unprecedented goodwill for two reasons. First, he could not meet the phenomenal expectations Bangladeshis had from his leadership. His closeness to India worried some Bangladeshis who feared a Hindu-majority India would dominate the new nation. Many Bangladeshis had fought for an independent Pakistan during the last years of the Indian freedom struggle and did not see India as a friendly neighbour. At the time of independence, the Muslim League, which was at the forefront for the demand of an independent Pakistan had commanded huge support in the province of Bengal. When Bangladesh became independent in 1971, some within Bangladesh still had residual feelings for a Pakistani identity. Indeed, Lawrence Lifschultz, an American reporter for the magazine *Far Eastern Economic Review* who was based in Dacca in 1974, remembers the day when Pakistan's prime minister, Zulfikar Ali Bhutto, visited Bangladesh for the first time since Bangladesh's independence. As Bhutto's motorcade travelled from the airport into central Dhaka, a section of the crowd lining the street shouted, 'Bhutto Zindabad'.

Lifschultz thought this was rather bizarre, but disenchantment with the new nation and nostalgia for Pakistan wasn't surprising. By mid-1974, Bangladesh was reeling from a widespread famine that experts believe was at least partly due to political incompetence. Citizens were also stunned by the ostentatious weddings of Mujib's sons Kamal and Jamal which took place during an economic crisis. Food distribution had failed nationwide, and people were forced to sell their farm animals to buy rice. Thousands of poor people left their villages looking for work in the cities. Irene Khan, a refugee law and human rights lawyer who heads the International Development Law Organization in Rome and who headed Amnesty International from 2001 to 2009, was a schoolgirl in the early 1970s. She recalls hungry voices clamouring for food outside the gates of her family home every day.

Clearly, there were Bangladeshis disillusioned with freedom, even though their fate under Pakistani rule would have been no better. One reason the Awami League won the December 1970 elections so handsomely was because the federal government had failed miserably in providing relief to its eastern wing after a devastating cyclone had killed many in the previous month. And yet, to Lifschultz, the cheering of Bhutto seemed particularly perverse, given the circumstances of Bangladesh's birth. With public criticism over the mass starvation growing, Mujib had clamped down on dissent. He had abolished political parties and created one national party called Bangladesh Krishak Sramik Awami League (BAKSAL, or the Bangladesh Peasants, Workers and People's League); a few free-thinking experts who did not agree with his policies left advisory and other positions they held with the government; he nationalized newspapers (closing most), and allowed only two each, which toed the party line—in Bangla and in English. He stifled dissent within the party, made huge inroads into the constitution, and declared himself president. A pliant parliament passed these monumental constitutional changes with minimal debate.

Farooq was outraged when we spoke in 1986. He claimed Mujib was threatening politicians who disagreed with him. He alleged that Mujib's son Kamal had raided a bank. Army personnel had to go around carrying personal weapons, afraid that their wives would get kidnapped, he claimed. He sounded livid when he talked of how Mujib had undermined the country's democratic institutions. He said, 'How do you pass an amendment in Parliament which abolishes party membership in just eleven minutes? No discussions, nothing!' Bangladesh, he feared, was becoming a colony of India, and he feared for his South Asian neighbours. 'All other members of SAARC [South Asian Association for Regional Cooperation] are worried that they will end up as part of the Indian Empire,' he said. He called himself a freedom fighter, and said he had to stop that. 'I tried to save the country,' he told me, his tone rising, 'Mujib had changed the constitution so that the court could not do a thing [to stop him]. All power was with the president.'

None of Farooq's explanations justified the terrible manner in which Sheikh Mujib and his family were killed. But the famine and the increasingly authoritarian Awami rule partly explain why there was little outward expression of grief after his assassination. That, and fear. When the new president, Khondaker Mostaq Ahmad, called the assassins shurjo santan, the signal was clear. The king was dead; long live the king. But many Bangladeshis, to this day, feel revolted by the brutality of killing not only Mujib, but most of his family. Many of them felt the death penalty for the assassins was justified.

Mujib's assassins were sentenced to death as early as in 1998. They appealed, but higher courts upheld the sentence in April 2001 and November 2009 respectively. They sought a Supreme Court review, and later, four of the five applied for presidential pardon. While the government meticulously followed the constitutional procedures, many have noted the speed with which the final appeals were dealt with.

Why had Farooq returned to Bangladesh in 1986? Could he have foreseen that one day he would have to reckon with his past acts? When I had asked him, his response was dismissive, 'Go to the people and talk about me. For eleven years I have been gagged nationally and internationally, so I had good reason to want to go to the people. I think my ideas are more popular than those of all the other political leaders.'

I reminded him that he had won only 4.51 per cent of the popular vote.

'If we are given free and fair elections, I can probably win. Ershad has won the elections but lost the politics,' he asserted.

Farooq had spent a decade in Libya. 'Gen. Zia sent us there. We were to be absorbed in their army but I flatly refused. I was not a mercenary. Transfer or secondment is one thing, being a mercenary is another matter altogether. I declined a diplomatic assignment as well. I suppose Gaddafi liked me because of my principled stand,' he told me.

I asked him if he liked Muammar Gaddafi, the Libyan strongman who would himself meet a violent death in 2011.

His response was elliptical: 'What others think of you is irrelevant. What America thinks of you or India thinks of you is irrelevant. What matters to me is what Bangladeshis think of me. Most Bangladeshi leaders are only bothered about what the world thinks of them. That's why I am admired, because I only care about what my people think.'

◆

At 9:25 a.m. on 26 January 2010, a four-member special bench of the Supreme Court's appellate division met to decide on the review petition from the assassins. They rejected it two minutes later. Senior civil servants of the law and home ministry met at noon, and discussed the issue for three hours. Farooq, who had until then resisted writing his mercy petition, did so that afternoon. Officials received it and dispatched his petition to the office of the president within minutes. At 7:30 p.m., President Zillur Rahman rejected the petition.[6] The quick turnaround of the documents was remarkable, although procedurally every step was taken properly. One lawyer remarked, 'What you saw wasn't due process; it was process with undue speed.'

The hangings occurred soon after midnight.

ONE

THE LAND THAT WASN'T EASY TO CARVE

Before there was Bangladesh, there was East Pakistan, and before that, this land was India. But even before that, the people who lived on this emerald land called it Bangaal,[7] and the British, who were to come much later, spelt it Bengal. The Himalaya surrounded the north, its foothills forming the crown, and the rivers—Padma and Meghna and Buriganga and Jamuna—all eight hundred of them, swiftly flowed through the delta, swelling so much during the monsoon season that from one bank of the river you couldn't see the other bank, before slowing down in the world's largest mangrove, the Sundarbans, and then disappearing into the roaring Bay of Bengal. Many times new rivers emerged, creating new tracts of land and depositing the silt so necessary for crops to grow in that soil. New islands known as chars would also emerge, and the people who lived there learned to cope. They were flexible—they had to be, for their lives were intertwined with the fluidity of the rivers. Dense forests became rice fields, and more people began to settle, creating large communities.

Millions of people lived here, in huts with little ponds from which they got their fish—carp and rui, and lately, tilapia, which western experts introduced in 1954 to enrich the Bangladeshi diet with protein. The families grew rice on small farms, the green paddy rising from water and swaying in the wind, reflecting the clouds and the blue sky in the water below. Across the farm, there were fields of mustard. Sonar Bangla or Golden Bengal, they called it. The region's greatest poet, Rabindranath Tagore wrote a song—'Amar Sonar Bangla', and in 1971 it became the national anthem of this land.

In 1931, archaeologists found the oldest inscription in this region—a piece of stone with Prakrit inscriptions in the Brahmi script, dating back to 300 BCE. The text revealed an urban administration distributing food from its granary to victims of a natural disaster.[8] Natural disasters have occurred all too frequently in Bangladesh—either there have been cyclones or floods, destroying homes and killing lives, and swallowing land. And there have been droughts, and on occasion, famine.

Traders from everywhere passed through the region—from Tibet, Persia, China, and Arabia—and Bengal's goods reached as far as Greece, Rome, and central Asia. Xuanzang, the famous Chinese traveller, came here in the seventh century, and in his *Buddhist Records of the Western World* he writes of visits to what is now Comilla and a town called Pundhravardhana (not far from the place where the earliest Prakrit inscriptions were found). Xuanzang discovered a Buddha made of green jade, and enjoyed the taste, sight, and fragrance of jackfruit—'highly esteemed... large as a pumpkin... when it is ripe it is of a yellowish-red colour. When divided, it has in the middle many tens of little fruits of the size of a pigeon's egg: breaking these, there comes forth a juice of a yellowish-red colour and of delicious flavour.'[9]

Arab traders brought Islam to India via the Malabar Coast in the west in the seventh century, but it made its way to Bengal only in the early thirteenth century when a Turkish officer called Muhammad Bakhtiyar, also known as Ikhtiyar al-din Muhammad Bakhtiyar Khalji,[10] rode with his cavalry to Bengal and brought Islam to this region. According to some accounts, his total force was ridiculously small—seventeen or eighteen men, including himself. As historian Richard M. Eaton shows in his monumental work, *The Rise of Islam and the Bengal Frontier: 1204-1760,*[11] Bakhtiyar's men pretended to be horse-traders in the Hindu kingdom when they reached Nudiya and stunned the king by rushing to his palace, brandishing weapons. The surprise attack succeeded, leading to five centuries of Islamic rule in Bengal. They did not advance further because of the sea in the south, the mountains in the north, and the forests and hills further east.

Islamic seers followed. In the fourteenth century, a Turkish religious messenger called Shah Jalal arrived in what is now Sylhet, and settled there, developing a reputation of performing miracles. Hearing of Shah Jalal's miracles, the famed Moroccan traveller Ibn Battuta also came to Sylhet during his travels. He recounts his personal experience of Shah Jalal's ability to foresee events. He had sent no word to Shah Jalal that he would be coming, and yet, he was surprised to meet two of Shah Jalal's followers when he was two days away from Shah Jalal's home. The two men said that they had come to receive him because Shah Jalal had divined that 'a western religious traveller is coming'. Shah Jalal's memorial in Sylhet attracts thousands of visitors every year. Bangladesh takes Shah Jalal seriously, because he was a foreigner who made the region his home. A year after the Awami League returned to power in 2009, Prime Minister Sheikh Hasina Wajed decided to rename Dhaka's international airport after Shah Jalal. (There was political import in that decision: In 1981 the airport had been renamed after the slain former president Ziaur Rahman, whose widow, Begum Khaleda Zia has been Hasina's arch rival. Like her, she has been prime minister for two terms.[12])

By the eighteenth century, the layers of the Bengali society had become clear. There was a Muslim aristocracy, some of whom spoke Urdu, taking pride in being descendants of the Turks and other Muslims who came with Bakhtiyar in the thirteenth century. Below them was an administrative class of upper-caste Hindus who aided the rulers—Mughal or British—to run the state. Below them, there was a large majority of Muslims. They were not converted forcibly. Many in fact were not necessarily Hindus—some followed tribal and animist faiths, and many were Buddhists from the Gupta era. Some academics have therefore argued that Islam was the first formal religion in Bengal.

Eaton contends that the unique feature of Islamic rule in Bengal was that the majority of the local population converted to Islam, unlike elsewhere in India, where force was often used to convert people. Citing figures from 1984, Eaton writes that some 93 million of the 152 million Bengalis in Bangladesh and West Bengal were Muslims; of the 96.5 million people living in Bangladesh then, 81 million, or 83 per cent, were Muslims. The wider significance of so many Muslims who speak Bengali is that it challenges the idea that Arabic is the prime language of Islam. Scholars in Asia have often pointed out that most Muslims don't speak Arabic. A.B. Shamsul, an anthropologist in Malaysia used to remind me: 'Arabic is the language of Islam; Malay is the language of Muslims', referring to the vast population of the Indonesian archipelago, when added to peninsular Malaysia, and Brunei, which made Bahasa and its variants more widely-spoken among Muslims than was presumed. But Bengali too is an important language for Muslims, and spoken by numbers similarly large. Although more Muslims speak Arabic than Bengali, scholars have pointed out that Arabic has many variations, and Arabic spoken in the Maghreb may not be understood easily by Gulf Arabs.

The way Islam grew in Bengal was also different. It coexisted with older traditions because of the strong Bengali culture, which, like the wider Indian culture, was syncretic, even polytheistic, and in many ways distinct from the Judeo-Christian-Islamic, or Abrahamic traditions found in the region between the Oxus and the Nile.

Eaton divides Bengal's frontiers three ways—political, agrarian, and Islamic. The political frontier was defined by the territories that first the sultans, and then the Mughals controlled through their satraps. The agrarian frontier separated the settled communities from the forests. The third was the Islamic frontier, dividing the Muslim from the non-Muslim. But these frontiers were 'superimposed', Eaton argues, 'on a much older one, a frontier defined by the long-term eastward march of Sanskritic civilization in the Bengal delta. Characterized either by an egalitarian agrarian society organized around Buddhist monastic institutions or by a hierarchical ordered agrarian society presided over by Brahman priests, Sanskritic civilization in both its Buddhist and its Brahmanic forms had moved down the Gangetic plain and into the Bengal delta many centuries before Muhammad Bakhtiyar's coup of 1204.'

The persistence and survival of those older traditions helps form the unique identity of people in Bangladesh today, who are proud Bengalis *and* Muslims; the Muslim Bengali often seeing greater kinship with his or her Hindu neighbour than with an Urdu-speaking Muslim from Punjab. Partly because of this sentiment, one of the arguments Pakistan's religious parties made when the two halves were united, was that Bengali was somehow less holy than Urdu. It would have been an academic and possibly hilarious debate except that hundreds of thousands of people died in the tragedy that followed. The roots of the Bangladesh war of 1971 lay in this simple fact, which neither Pakistan, nor India understood fully—that Bangladeshis saw themselves as Bengali and Muslim.

In Bengal, what Eaton calls the Sanskritic frontier survived, regardless of political changes. The political frontier's march was aided by weaponry, enforcing the sultans' authority; the agrarian frontier moved with the shifting rivers, and the Islamic frontier advanced by a slow process of conversions and the indigenous acceptance of Muslim traditions. But the Sanskritic frontier remained. The Turkic advance could establish power in the southwest, all the way down to Khulna and the Sundarbans. But formidable hills prevented an eastward surge, and all that the army could achieve was the gradual conversion of forests into rice fields. According to Eaton, the great theme of Bengal's history is the intertwining of these frontiers.

When I met Mahfuz Anam, who edits *The Daily Star,* Bangladesh's leading English daily, he was fasting, it being the holy month of Ramadan. He offered me tea as he explained the nuances which made the Bengali Muslim identity distinct from the Muslim identity as it was understood in the Indian subcontinent. 'For the secular in this country, the people with beards and caps were seen as Jamaatis (a reference to the Jamaat-e-Islam party, founded originally in Pakistan in 1941, and which opposed the struggle for Bangladesh's liberation, only to be banned in Bangladesh's early years. It was later rehabilitated, and deregistered again in 2013). It took a long time for my secular friends to be comfortable with someone saying their prayers. The cap was seen for a long time as something communal; participating in a Hindu ritual was considered liberal. And religious groups in Bangladesh took advantage of that. For a Bengali Muslim, a Hindu Bengali ritual is *Bengali* first; he does not view it with derision as a conqueror would, nor does he see it as pollution of his faith.'

The intertwining of cultural traditions reinforced a society which was tolerant and the faiths borrowed from each other. I have been invited to Bangladeshi weddings where a Muslim bride is smeared with turmeric in the gaye holud ceremony, common among families across the subcontinent. Many Bangladeshi Muslim women wear saris and bindis, or teeps, the dot on their forehead, usually seen only among Hindu women; they celebrate pujo, a Hindu festival for the goddess Durga, and they have no hesitation ushering in Poyla Baisakh, to celebrate the Bengali new year. To that, add the Sufi and Vaishnavite traditions that combine to form the lilting, haunting music of itinerant Baul singers, addressing God directly, rejecting all other rituals. The tradition is old, dating back to Lalon Fokir and Hasan Raza, who formed important strands in the syncretic Baul tradition, and some reckon that Jayadeva, who wrote the *Geeta Govinda* (Songs of Govinda/Krishna), was the first Baul. Here is Modon Baul, in a song from the eighteenth century, where he sounds almost like Kabir, the fifteenth- and sixteenth-century mystical poet of northern India, who too shunned religious divide.

> *The path that leads to you is cluttered with temples and mosques*
> *O Lord! I have heard your call but cannot proceed:*
> *Hindu and Muslim teachers block my way...*
> *There are many locks to your door: the Puranas, the Koran, and recitations.*
> *Alas Lord! What a terrible torment it is, cries Modon in despair.*[13]

Like vast parts of India, Bengal came under the sway of Mughal rule, which began in India in 1526 when Babur won the first Battle of Panipat, and began to fade in 1707, when Aurangzeb died. Mughal writ didn't run in Bengal until Murshid Quli Khan, a Kannadiga Brahmin who converted to Shia Islam in Iran where he was trading carpets, offered a deal to the emperor: 'Let me rule Bengal, and I will offer you a certain amount of annual revenue'. The Mughals had found Bengal impossible to conquer, and so he agreed. Murshid also set up the new capital of Murshidabad. In the vacuum that followed the end of Aurangzeb's rule, the East India Company spread its tentacles, and its rise coincided with Mughal decline. In 1757, Robert Clive led East India Company's troops and defeated Siraj-ud-Daula in the Battle of Plassey, setting the stage for British rule in India.

While Bengal was the first to fall, its people were among the first to rise against the British rule. One early rebellion was in 1783, when peasants rose against the British, whose policies of punitive agrarian taxation had created the famine of the 1770s. That famine showed the weaknesses of British administration. Lord Cornwallis, who replaced Hastings as Bengal's governor, introduced the Permanent Settlement in 1793, which created a new class of landlords, the zamindars. These men were assured stable taxation, in return for which they were expected to invest in improving the land they controlled. Many zamindars were Hindu; most peasants were Muslim. The British also introduced cash crops like jute and the natural blue dye, indigo. Farmers resented the introduction of cash crops because cash crops earned less than rice did, and they were useless for farmers in a subsistence economy. And yet, by 1800, India became the world's biggest exporter of that natural blue dye.

Bengali peasants would cultivate indigo and take their crop to British factories but they resented the imposition. By 1850, resentment against the cash crops and against British rule grew. Dinabandhu Mitra wrote the play *Nil Darpan* (The Indigo Planting Mirror) in 1859, which documented the revolt against indigo farming that year. (Rebellion came easily to Bengalis: In *Akbarnama*, the chronicle of Emperor Akbar's rule written between 1590 and 1596, the author Abu'l Fazl wrote about this province: 'The country of Bengal is a land where, owing to the climate's favouring the base, the dust of dissension is always rising. From the wickedness of men families have decayed, and dominions have been ruined.')

Bengali society had been undergoing transformation. Appalled by inequitable rituals that clashed with growing rationalism among educated Hindus, Raja Rammohun Roy founded the Brahmo Samaj movement in 1828, and it gained momentum, challenging the Hindu obsession with blind faith, the inequality of women, the ban on widow remarriage, and the prevalence of sati. In 1829, Roy succeeded in getting Lord William Bentick, the East

India Company's governor general, to ban the sati system.

Noting the modernizing trend among Indians and keen to create a durable bureaucracy, Thomas Babington Macaulay wrote his famous 'Minute' in India in 1835, which would make education in English accessible to Indians, in order 'to form a class who may be interpreters between us and the millions whom we govern; a class of persons, Indian in blood and colour, but English in taste, in opinions, in morals, and in intellect. To that class we may leave it to refine the vernacular dialects of the country, to enrich those dialects with terms of science borrowed from the Western nomenclature, and to render them by degrees fit vehicles for conveying knowledge to the great mass of the population.'[14]

There was progressive ferment among Muslims too, at that time. Of the reform movements that emerged, two wanted to keep Islam pure. Faraizi and Tariqah-i-Muhammadiyah saw in the Sanskritized, Hindu-influenced civilization a threat to Islam. For them, Bengal was *dar-ul-harb*, or the place of war, where the unbeliever had to be defeated. Another movement, called Taiyuni, saw the older culture as benign, and considered Bengal to be *dar-ul-aman*, or a place of peace. These seekers of purity presage the Jamaat-e-Islami and Hefazat-e-Islam of today—two organizations seeking to establish Islamic law and practices in Bangladesh.

Regardless, the symbiosis between Hindu and Muslim cultures continued to flourish. In 1868, a Hindu Bengali housewife, Rashsundari Debi, published her memoirs—*Amar Jibon* (My Life), which precedes by three full decades Raden Adjeng Kartini's *The Letters of a Javanese Princess* (written between 1899 and 1904) that many Asian scholars tend to consider to be the first sign of women's emancipation in Asia. Rashsundari Debi reveals how she tried to shape her own life despite social restrictions and intense fear of family disapproval. To understand the context, think of how hard it was for Charulata to publish her writing in late Victorian Bengal in Tagore's novella, *Noshto-neer* (Broken Nest, 1901), of which Satyajit Ray made a memorable film in 1964. Or, the dramatic way Bimala, the aristocratic housewife who has never stepped out of the women's quarters in the large family home, did so to meet her husband Nikhilesh's rebellious friend, Sandip, in another of Tagore's novels, *Ghare Baire* (The Home and the World, 1916, also a Ray film in 1984). Or think of the great heroines in the novels of Saratchandra Chattopadhyaya.

Bengali Muslim women also stepped out. In 1905, Rokeya Shekhawat Hossein, a woman in a prosperous family in Rangpur wrote a speculative futuristic story about a matriarchy, inverting gender norms. The novella was called *Sultana's Dream*,[15] and for its time it was a remarkably progressive, feminist work. Rokeya wrote in English, and her brother and husband had helped her and encouraged her.

To be sure, there was a divide in Bengal, between the east and the west. The east was largely Muslim; the west had more Hindus, but Muslims outnumbered Hindus there as well. The landlords, many of them Hindu, lived in the cities, usually Calcutta, but their rural estates and homes had an emotional hold on their lives and their identity. In *The Autobiography of an Unknown Indian*,[16] Nirad C. Chaudhuri writes: 'The ancestral village always seemed to be present in the mind of grown-ups. Most had acquired extensive properties in Kishoreganj. They had also acquired some sense of citizenship. Yet I hardly remember a single adult who thought of his Kishoreganj life as his whole life. In our perception of duration, Kishoreganj life was the ever-fleeting present, the past and the future belong to the ancestral village.'

The east was predominantly rural, with its paddy fields and rivers, and many Muslims worked as sharecroppers in and around those large estates owned by mostly Hindu, but some Muslim families. The relationship was often exploitative. Saratchandra Chattopadhyaya's short story, 'Mahesh', is emblematic of the harsh conditions in which Muslim sharecroppers lived under Hindu landlords—a relationship which, in the story, forces the sharecropper, Ghafoor, to kill his ox in an act of rage before he leaves for the big city to work in a jute mill.

The relationship between the town and country is not unique to Bengal, but is understood best by the words used to describe the rural home in the village and the urban quarters in the town. The house in the town, no matter what its locality, is always known as *basha*, or temporary lodging; the home in the village is *bari*, a place where you felt you belonged. From Chaudhuri's childhood recollection, nobody referred to the house in the town as bari.

This outwardly idyllic but inwardly simmering landscape was disturbed in 1905. It was the year Lord George Nathaniel Curzon, the Viceroy of India, decided to partition Bengal along religious lines. The famed frontiers Eaton wrote about, which knew how to coexist, were disrupted. Whether the partition was entirely Curzon's idea, or one he implemented upon advice from other colonial bureaucrats is difficult to tell. Describing the cartographical vivisection, Curzon is known to have remarked: '[The planners had been] calmly carving about and rearranging provinces on paper, colouring and recolouring the map of India according to geographical, historical, political and linguistic considerations—in the manner that appealed most to their fancy [...] Round and round, like the diurnal revolution of the Earth went the file, stately, solemn, sure and slow; and now, in our season, it has completed its orbit, and I am invited to register the concluding stage.'[17]

In July 1905, Curzon announced the division, convinced that such a large province could not be governed as one. But the divide was not for administrative reasons alone; there was a clear division of people by their faith. By October that year, the mainly Muslim east was separated from the more evenly divided west. Nobody was happy—the Hindu landowners in the west feared losing control over the land in the east, but they were also concerned about becoming a minority in the new west, where they had become part of a province with Bihar and Orissa, where other languages were spoken. The east also gained Assam.

Mushtaq Khan, a Bangladeshi professor at London's School of Oriental and African Studies, feels one reason Curzon decided to divide Bengal was because the Bengali Hindu elite and the civil service were beginning to get more articulate, and challenged the imperial masters. 'They had to be weakened. Muslims, on the other hand, did not have any self-perception of identity, so Britain wanted to help them create their separate identity. The grand aim of 1905 was to divide the two,' he told me. Indian troops that had rebelled against British officers in 1857, in what Britain describes as 'the mutiny' and Indians call 'the first war of independence', came from all religions. Keeping those religions apart suited British interests. Encouraging groups to assert their narrower identity became a priority. A year after the partition of Bengal, the Muslim League, which would eventually spearhead the movement for an independent homeland for Muslims of the subcontinent—Pakistan—was formed in Bengal.

Curzon maintained that the logic of Bengal's partition was administrative efficiency. Bengal was larger than France and had a bigger population. Curzon argued that the east was neglected and under-administered. By dividing the province, administration could be improved, and development would follow.

The land-owning Hindu aristocrats, also known in the original sense of the word 'bhodrolok' (literally 'gentle folk'), were used to living in two Bengals. Their nationalism radiated outward from Calcutta, but depended on seeking rents from their baris in the east. With the economy changing rapidly, relying on rental income was no longer a lucrative option. As the Cambridge academic Joya Chatterji found when she researched the communal divisions in Bengal, many bhodrolok were turning to Hindu revivalism to seek meaning amidst rapid change brought about by modernity. Aurobindo Ghosh, sent to England as a child to study until his graduation from Cambridge, ended up developing his own spiritual philosophy drawn from his interpretation of Vedanta. He worshipped Kali, the goddess of destruction. Congress leader Bipin Chandra Pal, part of the Lal-Bal-Pal[18] triumvirate, came from a Brahmo family, but introduced among Bengalis the idea of mass celebrations of Kali, just as in western India, in Maharashtra, Bal Gangadhar Tilak would revive the worship of Ganesha, the elephant-headed god. Different, non-ritualistic and modernist ideas of Brahmo thinking often coexisted with Kali-worshipping ritual Hinduism within families—and sometimes within individuals. Extremist organizations also took religious vows. Chittaranjan Das, another leader of the freedom movement popularly known as deshbandhu (friend of the nation), was influenced by Vaishnavism. Later, Subhas Chandra Bose, who dramatically split from Mohandas Gandhi in 1938 and escaped from a British jail to go to Nazi Germany, and then to Singapore where he took over the Indian National Army made up of British Indian army soldiers who had surrendered to the Japanese in Singapore in 1942, was a devotee of Vivekananda and his guru, Ramakrishna Paramhans. Today the word bhodrolok connotes images of a refined cultural class, or people who see the cinema of Satyajit Ray and admire the theatre of Badal Sircar; in 1830, the first bhodrolok organization, Dharma Sabha, demanded the widow's right to commit sati.[19]

The intent of the partition of Bengal may have been to spur growth in both provinces, but the chasm between the two regions was bound to grow, unless investments were made in the east. Factories in the west depended on raw materials in the east, and most trade passed through Calcutta, the major port around which industries were built. It also had the wide avenues of an imperial capital and the leading university of that time. Four decades later, when India and Pakistan would get divided, these economic realities would return to challenge the notion of dividing Bengal.

Protests against the division of Bengal mounted, in Bengal and across India. The protests included terror attacks and an attempt on the life of the governor of Bengal. In 1908, a 19-year-old Indian rebel, Khudiram Bose, was hanged for killing the wife and daughter of a barrister (his intended target was another British official) in Muzaffarpur, Bihar. Bose inspired other young Bengalis to attack British officials. The Bangladeshi poet Nazrul Islam wrote a poem extolling Bose, the 'cheerful and smiling' revolutionary; the story of Bengal's nationalist awakening in Dhaka's Muktijuddho Jadughor (Liberation War Museum) begins with a photograph of Bose.

In 1911, the British gave up the experiment of partitioning Bengal and reunited the province—to the delight of Hindus, but upsetting Muslims who were beginning to see the advantages of the division, sowing the seeds of the more permanent partition thirty-six years later. It was also the year Calcutta ceased being India's capital, which moved to Delhi.

Bose's violent rebellion was not unique. Rebels in Bengal often used violence. Random killing of any British official with authority became popular. In Comilla in December 1931, two Hindu schoolgirls—Santi Ghosh, 15, and Suniti Chowdhury, 14—came to visit Mr Stevens, who was the local district magistrate. They wanted to hand him a petition to start a swimming competition for girls. They were let into his office, where they whipped out pistols and shot him dead. A year later they were brought to trial. It emerged they were members of a secretive group called Jugantar, (a new era). *Time* magazine described them as wearing 'bright coloured saris, with flowers in their hair, they listened unmoved as they were sentenced to transportation for life from Bengal'. They said: 'It is better to die than live in a horse's stable.'[20]

The divisions between Hindus and Muslims across India deepened as the years passed. The spread of the Muslim League elsewhere in India had its impact in Bengal, too. Bengali Hindus frequently used Hindu motifs and slogans (including the song 'Bande Mataram', or Hail to the Motherland, from Bankimchandra Chatterjee's 1882 novel, *Anand Math,* about the rebellion of sannyasins, or Hindu ascetics in the eighteenth century) which accentuated the divide. As Chatterji shows in her study of Bengal's division,[21] 'Many aspects of Indian nationalism were not secular. Nationalist campaigns often used religious imagery and issues to win popular support. Nor did Indian nationalism have truly secular, ideological and philosophical underpinnings. National thought tended to share the colonial view that the basic unit of Indian society was the community, as defined by faith. Secular national ideal was sarvadharma samabhava, that is equality of all communities and spirit of accommodation,' she writes. She points out how most national thinkers tended to describe national identity in religious terms and equated being an Indian with being a Hindu, highlighting the example of Bengal where it was particularly marked, as well in the writing of Bankimchandra Chatterjee,

Aurobindo Ghosh, Swami Vivekananda,[22] 'and in the brand of extremist nationalism they inspired,' she writes.

While Indian nationalism wasn't secular in its western sense, where governance and religion are kept apart, it wasn't communal either. The main thrust was directed against British colonialism. Where it did appeal to religion 'it did so to mobilize religious sentiment against British rule,' Chatterji writes. Communal parties and ideologies saw the universe in binary terms—with religion as the basis of a political unit, and an adversarial relationship with the 'other.' Chatterji contends that communal ideologists owed more to the colonial wisdom about India than the nationalist view. Like colonial civil servants, India's communal leaders too saw India as a land dominated by communities (and not individuals, or Indians). But they also saw, accepted, and propagated the idea that the two main communities could not live together at peace with one another. Chatterji concludes: 'It followed that communal parties were by no means hostile to the Raj, and got its patronage.'

When Britain called Round Table Conferences in London in the 1930s to discuss the future of India, the dominant British narrative was that there were many Indias, not one. Gandhi disagreed with that contention and argued against it forcefully. The British said giving independence to one group would antagonize others; Gandhi challenged such divisive views. Following the inconclusive conference, Britain offered and implemented the provisions first made in the 1918 Montague-Chelmsford Reforms, leading to provincial autonomy for India in 1935. But Gandhi opposed the creation of segregated electoral constituencies, in which people could only vote for candidates of their own religion. Besides, the seat distribution was not proportional. In Bengal, for example, of the 250 seats in the legislature, Europeans, who constituted less than 1 per cent of the province, were granted 25 seats—11 general and 14 representing commercial interests. Of the other communities, Muslims got 119 seats (2 reserved for Muslim women), Hindus had 82 seats, of which 2 were for women and 10 had to be kept for 'depressed classes'; Indian commerce (comprising Hindu traders and landlords) got 5 seats each; university graduates 2, labour 8, and Anglo-Indians (or people of mixed race) 4, of whom one had to be a woman.

Hindus were upset the most by this allocation: there were 22.2 million Hindus in Bengal, representing 44 per cent of the population, but they had got only 32 per cent of the seats. Muslims, who formed 54 per cent of the population at 27.8 million had got 47.8 per cent of the seats. Hindu protests convinced Muslims that the bhodrolok and Congress, which they saw as the party that represented bhodrolok interests, were Hindu first, Indian later. Mutual distrust deepened.

Hindus in Bengal began to feel the need for a secure, safe space for themselves. Some bhodrolok, without a trace of irony, extolled the British period, arguing that the British were better rulers and somehow more fit to rule them than their Muslim compatriots. In one remarkable document from that time, Hindu leaders speak nostalgically of the Battle of Plassey, remembering the conflict not for having led to India's colonization, but for liberating Bengal from Muslim rule. 'From a refusal to countenance being ruled by Muslim inferiors, it was a short step to demand partition and create a separate Hindu homeland. Bhodrolok demanded partition of Bengal; powerful provincial interests rallied behind it,' Chatterji wrote.

Lord Curzon had the last laugh.

With Hindu nationalist leaders and Bengali Congress politicians both seeking to protect what appeared to Muslims to be their own narrow interests, the schism between the two communities began to widen. Bengali Muslim leaders like Fazlul Huq and Huseyn Suhrawardy began organizing the Muslim peasantry, particularly against the largely Hindu zamindars and their monopolization of professions and public jobs. When Fazlul Huq[23] created the Krishok Proja Party (Farmers' and Peasants' Party) and sought an alliance with the Congress, the Congress turned him down, saying it would only represent national, and not sectarian or regional interests. And so Huq turned to the Muslim League for support. And the League, which had no representation in the east, found an opportunity to spread its message of dividing India along religious lines.

The Bengali Hindu elite who had fought for Bengal's unification in 1905 realized in the 1930s that in a united Bengal with voting rights they would become a minority. To preserve their dominance, they began demanding separation. Mushtaq Khan finds it intriguing that just as Muslim nationalism was rising across India in the 1930s, in one of the few parts of India where Muslims formed the majority, there was no great desire to form an independent homeland. 'The debate of 1930s was at a provincial level in Bengal, and quite different from the debate of Nehru, Gandhi and Jinnah. The two strands merged in 1946 for complex reasons. Like it would happen again in the 1970s in Pakistan, in the 1930s in Bengal the established elites didn't want the upstarts who were the majority to take power,' Khan told me one afternoon in his book-lined study in London.

Khan picked up Ayesha Jalal's scholarly study[24] of Muhammad Ali Jinnah, Pakistan's founding father, and said: 'You have to remember that there were two parallel games going on at that time. Across India, Jinnah's power base was among the Muslims who lived in Hindu majority areas, and he was interested in protecting Muslims in these areas. He had no understanding of areas where Muslims were already the majority. But once it became clear that there were important areas where Muslims were a majority, his aim was to seek a balance between Hindu-majority and Muslim-majority areas. He understood that communally divided, separate electorates would disappear in the longer run, and in a first-past-the-post system, Muslims would always be at a disadvantage. This is why he began to support the idea of a federation of areas where Muslim majority and Hindu majority areas could coexist.'

In its statement on 16 May 1946, the Cabinet Mission, comprising three senior British officials who had travelled to India for negotiations with Indian leaders to arrange for a transfer of power, had proposed an interim government of all political parties, giving Congress one more seat than the Muslim League. India would have become a loose federation with a weak centre with central powers limited to areas such as foreign affairs, defence, currency, and communications. But Jawaharlal Nehru would have none of it, and the impact of Nehru's repudiation was explosive in Bengal. Suddenly, Bengal's Muslims began to think that after independence real power would reside not in Dacca, nor in Calcutta, but in Delhi, and they would have no real political power. On 29 July after weeks of negotiations, the Muslim League rejected the 16 May plan and called upon all Muslims in India to observe a 'Direct Action Day' in protest. The date chosen was 16 August.

The speed with which political positions and alignments changed in Bengal in the 1940s has been understood poorly in all three countries— India, Pakistan, and Bangladesh. Khan says it shows Bangladesh's reluctance to own and embrace its own history. 'The dominant discourse in Bangladesh cannot accept that history,' he says. 'It can't accept that Bengal was actually partitioned by Hindus. We keep saying that Punjabis colonized us and we fought for independence on the slogan of Bengali nationalism. But in Bengal, Punjabis didn't come and vote for the Muslim League in 1946. We Bengalis did it, because we were scared. We were scared that Congress would keep all major decisions at the centre where Muslims would always be a minority.' In the 1946 elections, virtually every Muslim vote in Bengal went to the Muslim

League—it was much less successful in Punjab. 'Bengal broke because of the breakdown of trust between the minority Brahminical and upper caste elite of Bengal (who controlled land and capital and were dominant in public jobs and professions) on one hand, and the Muslim jotedar (rich peasant) class who could mobilize the Muslim peasant majority. It was in that context that the minority Hindus voted to partition Bengal and sacrifice Bengali nationalism,' Khan observed. In 1946, Bengal was the only major province where the Muslim League had a majority. In all other provinces, it formed coalition governments.

And there was the famine.

One cold December day in Dhaka in 2012 I went to the National Museum in Shahbagh, weeks before the area would erupt in an uprising over the war crime trials. Men in cycle-rickshaws were dropping off passengers, waiting eagerly to pick up visitors coming out of the museum. A large group of students had just arrived at the museum. They were cheerful and noisy; their teachers tried to keep them in line as they counted them, while one of the older teachers went up to the ticket window, buying tickets. Seeing me, a foreigner, the man selling the tickets abruptly told the teacher to wait while he served me. In my broken Bengali I said I was willing to wait, for the teacher had come before me. At which point, almost miraculously a second window opened. A smiling young man appeared, saying: 'Foreign tourists here.'

The museum had an area blocked off in which there were many exhibits commemorating the Liberation War. My real interest that afternoon was to go to the art section where, in a sparsely-visited, poorly-lit room with fluorescent lights, along whitewashed walls, there were dozens of black-and-white drawings of the great Bangladeshi painter, Zainul Abedin.

Abedin had studied art in Calcutta and London, and later set up an art institute in Dhaka. He painted landscapes and watercolours revealing his enduring relationship with the Brahmaputra River. But he is remembered most for his haunting paintings of the famine of the 1940s. Those sketches have a harrowing beauty—they cry out with agony, tugging at the viewer's humanity and compassion.

That famine was entirely man-made, as the Nobel Laureate Amartya Sen shows in his classic work, *Development as Freedom*.[25] Sen's primary contention is that unlike droughts, a natural phenomenon brought about by the lack of rains, famines are easier to prevent. For the famine in 1943, Sen blames the colonial government in Bengal which made several mistakes in managing rice distribution. It exported rice when it was needed at home, and delayed importing rice until autumn 1943. On the basis of his research into the 1943 famine, and further research on China's so-called Great Leap Forward in the 1960s, and India's drought of 1967, Sen concludes that democracies don't have famines, because democracies have built-in safety valves and mechanisms— newspapers, opposition parties, an independent judiciary—which act as a check on the government's powers. They signal to the government the distress in the country, and the government is compelled to act. In order to get re-elected governments have to keep the voters satisfied, which forces governments to react early when a crisis is imminent.

During World War II, in spite of those provincial legislatures (which the Congress had boycotted), India was anything but a democracy, and the priority of British Prime Minister Winston Churchill was to feed the army and protect Britain's colonial interests abroad. He had an empire to defend. The far more numerous colonial subjects in India were fairly low down in his priorities.

By 1942, Nazi Germany had overrun much of Europe. Britain had survived the Battle of Britain when the Luftwaffe pounded British cities daily during the summer of 1940. With Japan launching an all-out attack in Asia in December 1941 which caught America by surprise in Pearl Harbor, Britain was on the defensive. But by February 1942, it had lost its colonies in the east—Malaya, including the strategically important port of Singapore; and in March, Rangoon, the capital of Burma, the region's rice paddy, also fell.

In October 1942, a cyclone devastated Bengal. The priority of the British administrators was to prevent Japan from blocking the Bay of Bengal. Providing relief to the people of Bengal was not on their mind. Moreover, they wanted to stop the Japanese army from marching into India via Burma. Britain was also concerned about the Indian National Army—a rebel army put together from surrendered British Indian troops led by Mohan Singh (and later, Subhas Chandra Bose)—which was itching to invade India with Japanese help.

Fearing that the Japanese would take over Bengal, some colonial administrators pursued a policy of scorched earth. Called the 'denial policy', and applied in coastal Bengal, it saw the colonial administrators not only seizing or destroying rice stocks, but also seizing and deliberately capsizing boats.

The Bengal Famine began in late 1942 and persisted till 1944. In the first half of 1943, even as people in Bengal were starving, India exported some 70,000 tonnes of rice. Ironically, there was more rice available in 1943 than in 1941. But there was nobody to lead a protest movement, with most of the Congress leadership in jail after Mohandas Gandhi began the Quit India agitation in August 1942. Adding to the agony, ships full of Australian wheat would call on Indian ports on their way to Europe to feed the army and civilians in the West.

The food that was available in India was diverted to meet the military's needs first. Shiploads of food bypassed India for future storage in Europe. The War Cabinet had decided that around 75,000 tonnes of Australian wheat would be transported to Ceylon and the Middle East each month for the rest of 1943, to supply the war effort—and a further 170,000 tonnes would be shipped to a supply centre in the Mediterranean region, stored for future European consumption.

The Governor's palace in Calcutta with its marble busts of Roman emperors had once been the symbolic seat of the British Indian empire. Now it was being surrounded by dead bodies. 'At the height of the famine, unknown protestors laid the dead and dying around the one-kilometre perimeter of the palace, encircling it in a wreath of corpses that marked the passing of British prestige... The pavements of Calcutta were strewn with corpses', the science writer Madhusree Mukerjee notes in her passionately-argued, meticulously-researched book, *Churchill's Secret War*.[26]

Mukerjee bases her account on researching food storage statistics, a trawl through archival documents, and conversations with famine survivors who recounted horrifying stories to her, of parents throwing their starving children into rivers and wells. Many plunged themselves in front of trains. People begged for starch water in which rice had been boiled. Children ate leaves and vines, yam stems and grass. People were too weak even to cremate their loved ones. 'No one had the strength to perform rites', a survivor told Mukerjee. Dogs and jackals feasted on piles of dead bodies in Bengal's villages. 'Mothers had turned into murderers, village belles into whores, fathers into traffickers of daughters', Mukerjee writes.

Meanwhile, at a meeting in August, the Secretary of State for India asked that the colony be sent half-a-million tonnes of wheat by year-end. The grain would feed not civilians, but the army and the war-related industries until the next harvest. His calculation was that news of the imminent arrival of food would bring down prices by forcing hoarders to release stocks. But Churchill sent Iraqi barley to India instead, which had no impact on grain prices. Tens of thousands of people had already died by the time the first shipment of barley and wheat arrived for relief.

Mukerjee concludes that it was not so much racism, 'as the imbalance of power inherent in the social Darwinian pyramid that explains why famine could be tolerated in India while bread rationing was regarded as an intolerable deprivation in wartime Britain.... Churchill regarded wheat as too precious a food to expend on non-whites, let alone on recalcitrant subjects who were demanding independence from the British Empire. He preferred to stockpile the grain to feed Europeans after the war was over.'

The Bengal famine was at its most acute in 1943. Between 2 to 3 million people died not because food hadn't grown, but because it had been taken away from them. An official commission set up soon after the famine recorded 1.5 million deaths. Indian filmmaker Satyajit Ray's 1973 film, *Ashani Sanket* (Distant Thunder) set during the famine (in which the Bangladeshi actress Babita plays a leading role) places the figure at 5 million. The film tells the story of a schoolteacher trying hard to keep his family together in rural Bengal as the war comes closer. His wife is driven to offer herself to an unscrupulous, disfigured trader who gives her rice for the family in return for sexual favours. The teacher prefers not to ask his wife how she has brought the rice.

By late 1943, Churchill had withdrawn almost all merchant ships in the Indian Ocean, which could bring food to India, and redeployed them in Europe to bring civil supplies or support the war effort. By the end of the year, India did get 80,000 tonnes of wheat, which was insufficient even for the army. Bengal harvested its own rice crop in winter; by then, some 3 million had died. Churchill's adamant refusal to provide any relief from the famine had a deep impact on British sense of fair play among some senior bureaucrats. Leo Amery, secretary of India, privately thought that Churchill was 'not quite sane' when any discussion was about India. Churchill made some spectacularly insensitive statements at that time, asking rhetorically: 'If the famine is so bad why hasn't Gandhi died yet?'[27] Mukerjee writes of a war cabinet meeting on 4 August 1943 where Churchill refused to provide relief for famine victims in Bengal. 'Their deaths were of little consequence, he subsequently explained, because Bengalis were "breeding like rabbits" anyway,' she writes. Like a latter-day Malthus, Churchill's logic was that India's population would outstrip available food supply.

In his papers, Amery noted: 'Naturally I lost patience... and couldn't help telling him that I didn't see much difference between his outlook and Hitler's, which annoyed him no little.'[28] Indeed, there are accounts of cabinet meetings where Amery and Sir Archibald Wavell, soon to be India's viceroy, are planning to ship more food to India, but Churchill stops them. An exasperated Wavell writes in his account of the meetings: 'Apparently it is more important to save the Greeks and liberated countries than the Indians and there is reluctance either to provide shipping or to reduce stocks in this country.' Amery is pithier: 'Winston may be right in saying that the starvation of anyhow under-fed Bengalis is less serious than sturdy Greeks, but he makes no sufficient allowance for the sense of Empire responsibility in this country.'[29]

Churchill has an outsized reputation in many countries as the man who defended Britain and defeated Hitler with allied forces. But his attitude towards starving Indians in Bengal in the 1940s was not only callous, it was also profoundly racist and utterly indefensible. While Amery and Wavell should be recognized for trying to influence Churchill's mind, what they did was too little, and too softly, to be effective. For Churchill Bengalis were expendable, ungrateful colonial subjects who didn't know what was good for them—the same Empire that he was defending, but which was deliberately killing them.

Amartya Sen blames the 1943 famine on four factors. First, wartime inflation and the prospect of increased income tempted and enabled traders to acquire and hoard foodgrain. Second, rice prices rose in anticipation of higher demand, and rural wages declined; including farmers' entitlement—bags of rice—making them destitute. Third, the government banned inter-state trade. And fourth, the government wanted to protect urban residents in Calcutta from any discomfort. Prices continued to rise irrationally and destitute farmers began to sell their small plots of land and migrate to cities, looking for better prospects, a tale poignantly told by the Indian filmmaker Bimal Roy in his 1953 film, *Do Bigha Zameen* (Two-thirds of an Acre of Land), which won an honour at Cannes in 1954.

Over the years, at film festivals I had seen Roy's and Ray's films, and I had read Sen's arguments which seemed to arrive at the virtuous logic, that economic and social rights are intertwined with civil and political rights, by linking the right to food with the right of political participation and expression. But in Abedin's sketches I saw what it would have looked like to the artist.

Abedin's art showed the fraying of Bengal's society—how it became dehumanized—and the heroic spirit of its people, who attempted to rise, again and again, from the abyss. I wanted to understand that spirit of the people who knew how to rebuild their lives after suffering repeated destruction from cyclones and floods; how they had survived the famine of 1943, and how they had lived through the communal violence of 1946-47. Crushed by bureaucratic inertia and natural calamity, they knew how to overcome. To understand their resilience in 1971, it was necessary to understand how they had dealt with calamities in the past. In Abedin's sketches I saw how life struggled to survive.

Abedin made his own ink by burning charcoal and used it on cheap ordinary paper, framing the people as if in a photograph. The skeletal figures of men and women, the simple lines revealing the fragility of the children, revealed all the horrors. Another Indian artist was also chronicling the famine at that time. Chittaprosad Bhattacharya, a Communist Party member (who, coincidentally, designed the posters of *Do Bigha Zameen*) travelled from village to village on foot, sketching human misery. His book, *Hungry Bengal,* was considered so incendiary that the colonial administrators seized and burned every copy. But one survived in a bank vault in Calcutta, and was republished in 2012 to coincide with a retrospective of his work in India.

The Communist Party sent Bhattacharya to Midnapore to report on the famine in 1943 for the party's mouthpiece, *People's War. Hungry Bengal* published twenty-two of the most haunting sketches, of boys looking expectantly at food; a woman's bony hands holding a pitcher; a man looking away from food being offered, his pride coming before his starvation. Abedin's sketches have a raw, hard feel; Bhattacharya's drawings have men and women drawn with the fullness of Soviet-style social realism.

Journalists too covered the famine. Tushar Kanti Ghosh, the owner and editor of the nationalist Bengali newspaper *Jugantar* and the English *Amrita Bazar Patrika,* compiled eyewitness accounts of the famine in a book published in Lahore in 1944.[30] In one such account, Sir Jagdish Prashad writes: 'At one of the [gruel] kitchens in Faridpur I noticed a man lapping up food like a dog. I saw abandoned children in the last stages of emaciation; men and women who had been without food for so long that they could now be fed only under medical supervision. Dead bodies were being daily picked up and also those who had fallen by the wayside through sheer exhaustion. A man after vainly wandering for food collapsed on the doorsteps of the Collector's courtroom. As (the) body was being removed, a woman huddled in a corner pushed out a bundle and cried, "Take that also". It was her dead child. At a kitchen, a woman had been walking every day for more than a dozen miles to and from home to take gruel to her sick and famished husband.'

Another case recounts the story of a sick and starving fisherman, all skin and bones, coming to a gruel kitchen. He was too tired to walk back, and decided to rest under a tree. In the morning he was found lying in pain— jackals had devoured parts of his body, but he was still alive. He died later. The Calcutta daily *Amrita Bazaar Patrika* wrote of fuel being so expensive that families opted for mass burials. In some cases, bodies were dumped in rivers.

Bengal's tragedy was not over when the war ended. The Allies had vanquished the Axis powers, but the Empire, which Britain could rule so effortlessly in the past, suddenly became a burden. Churchill's defeat in the 1945 parliamentary elections and Labour's victory presaged decolonization. The new prime minister, Clement Attlee, had no desire to maintain the Empire. Soldiers would begin to return home and he had jobs to create. Shattered cities and homes had to rebuild, and a national health service was to be established. Lord Mountbatten, a naval hero in the Pacific, was sent to replace Wavell as India's viceroy with clear instructions—to give India independence quickly.

In the war years, the division between Hindus and Muslims across India had widened even further. The Act of 1935 had granted India provincial autonomy and Congress had formed governments in many provinces. But when Britain declared war with Germany, it declared that India was also at war with Germany. The Congress ministries resigned in protest. The Muslim League didn't. On 9 August 1942, Gandhi gave a stirring speech in Bombay, calling on the British to 'Quit India'. The entire Congress leadership and thousands of rank and file workers were arrested. The Muslim League remained on good terms with the British.

After the war, Congress leaders were released, but in the intervening years, the League had made the idea of special protection for Muslims acceptable. The only way to ensure that was by creating an independent nation, Pakistan. The negotiations to prevent the division went nowhere; as time passed, Gandhi found himself in a minority, as the majority of Congress leaders pleaded helplessness and argued that Partition was inevitable, given the League's intransigence.

To create a new boundary, Britain sent a judge, Cyril Radcliffe, who had little experience of India, and gave him a deadline of six weeks.

As negotiations between the Congress and the League faltered in 1946 over the Cabinet Mission Plan, in late July the League called for a 'Direct Action Day' on 16 August,[31] and in the violence that followed, perhaps thousands died in what is now known as the Great Calcutta Killings. Those killings lasted four days, from 16 to 19 August. The official toll is not known, but estimates range from 5,000 to 10,000,[32] with at least 15,000 wounded, many bodies brutally mutilated, and there were many rapes. The wealthy were spared as they could hide or buy safety; the poor died. Citing an Indian historian's account of the violence,[33] the French historian Claude Markovits points out: 'Amongst Muslims, Das is able to show that some professional groups were particularly represented: butchers seem to have been prominent and they came with their meat-choppers which, in experienced hands, could be a lethal weapon (this is reminiscent of the original meaning of the old French word "massacre", which refers precisely to the butcher's chopper). Amongst Hindus, dharwans (janitors), who often had links to criminals, also figured prominently, giving the violent crowds a plebeian aspect, which is not really very surprising in the urban milieu of Calcutta.'

The Congress accused Suhrawardy, who was Bengal's chief minister at that time, of inciting violence, in particular singling out a speech he made where he told a large Muslim crowd that he had taken measures to 'restrain' the police, which the criminal gangs took to mean that they could riot, although no official record of such a speech exists. (Contemporary accounts say he spoke in Urdu, and the police did not have an Urdu translator at hand.) Congress also blamed the British administration for trusting Suhrawardy too much and taking too long to take action; charges that the British denied. Two British accounts[34] of that period took a marginally anti-Congress line, although they blamed both communities.

In recreating historical moments like these, there is a major challenge— the absence of a comprehensive archive of oral history. Indian Partition has been no exception: generations of witnesses, victims and survivors have passed on, their stories remaining untold. While the Indian publisher and writer Urvashi Butalia has methodically collected many memories in her monumental work,[35] stories from the east remain under-researched. Collective amnesia has sometimes gripped Bengal, East Pakistan, and Bangladesh with metronomic regularity, allowing embellishment, denials, and rewriting of history. While India sees Suhrawardy as a villainous figure, in Bangladesh he is considered a hero, and Mujibur Rahman acknowledged him as his mentor.

The echo of the Calcutta killings was heard a few months later, in Noakhali, between October and November 1946, where Gandhi was to perform a miracle. Noakhali is the village where the river Meghna meets the Bay of Bengal. It is not an easy place to reach. Phillips Talbot, a reporter with *Chicago Daily News* took five days to reach Noakhali, travelling by 'air, rail, steamer, bicycle, foot'. Describing his journey to a friend in the United States, Talbot (who later became a distinguished diplomat) wrote:[36] 'The journey was worth the effort. It was revealing to watch Gandhi throwing himself during this critical season into the remoteness of East Bengal's Noakhali district for a barefooted village-to-village pilgrimage in search of Hindu-Muslim amity. Here was a 77-year-old ascetic, rising above the physical ordeal, immersed in a peculiarly Indian approach to the cleavage that threatens the country. The region in which Gandhi has secluded himself is deep in the Ganges-Brahmaputra delta; one of the least accessible flat lands of India.' (In Talbot's time, there were no motorable roads; the roads were so bad that, as he wryly notes, even bullock carts were missing. The journey of 200 kilometres remains difficult today. In 2012, it took me over seven hours on a bumpy road from Dhaka to get there.)

The landscape, Talbot writes, is 'amphibious, as fields are always flooded between April and October. In the wet season little remains above water except occasional ribbons of bund and isolated village clumps marked by coconut palms, bamboos, and betel trees. People stay at home or, at best, move about in hand-hewn skiffs. Though some of their crops grow under water, they farm mostly in the winter dry season.' The 2.5 million people of the district lived in a rural area of about forty square miles.

While Noakhali was calm during the Calcutta killings, tension had been building up. Troublesome troubadours travelled from village to village, singing anti-Hindu songs, stoking anger. On 29 August, the day of Id-ul-Fitr, a rumour circulated that Hindus and Sikhs in Noakhali were accumulating weapons. Hindu fishermen were dragged out of their boats in river Feni and one was killed. Elsewhere, other fishermen were attacked. The local Congress office was set afire. Boatmen would not ferry passengers of the other religion and religious leaders issued sermons demonizing the other faith. Suhrawardy visited the area with Frederic Burrows, the governor of Bengal, as did Congress President-elect J.B. Kripalani but his appeals were ignored.

Random acts of violence increased—people returning home were stabbed; homes were looted; students were assaulted; temples were desecrated—in one case, a calf was butchered and thrown inside a temple; at other temples, idols were stolen or broken.

On 10 October, a rumour spread that Sikhs had attacked a Muslim shrine. Muslims marched towards the market, where most shopkeepers were Hindus. They attacked a Hindu zamindar's home. The landowner was tied up and burned alive. More Hindu homes were attacked in the days that followed. Homes of Dalit Hindus were also not spared.

Talbot recounts the violence: 'Roving bands paddled over the flooded fields from village to village, killing Hindus, looting and burning their property, abducting some women, and registering conversions from Hinduism to Islam. Many of those murdered and robbed were the wealthy who had incurred the peasants' ire in 1943.[37] The situation took a communal turn when politicians (subsequently disowned by the Muslim League) led the village crowds with the cry of Pakistan. In some villages mobs burned the huts even of outcastes. The upheaval swept over about half the district. Perhaps a million people were caught up in the turmoil, and refugees eventually were counted in tens of thousands. This was bad enough. But the effect was multiplied a thousandfold across the breadth of Hindu India by exaggerated, inflammatory reports of what had occurred.'

It was in that atmosphere that Gandhi decided to go to Noakhali. Talbot remembers: 'Although he [Gandhi] denied letting emotions affect his judgement, we [Talbot and his wife, Mildred] sensed a feeling of frustration, if not of failure. This had nothing to do with the validity of the creed of non-violence itself. Its truth, he repeated, could never be challenged. But he could not be happy with the way in which his teachings were being flouted. To test the applicability of his faith, therefore, he went to the heart of the trouble. He chose East Bengal, and when people asked why he had not gone to Bihar province where the damage was greater and the culprits were Hindus, he replied that the people of Bihar had repented.' Gandhi understood Bihar and believed that the people had expressed remorse. Noakhali was new; spreading his message here would require patience. Gandhi arrived in November 1946 and stayed till March 1947.

Gandhi walked barefoot from village to village, initially with only four followers, walking 116 miles over seven weeks, covering forty-seven villages. He would spend barely a night or two at the same place. He listened to stories that the villagers told him—of forced conversions, rapes, and massacres throughout the Noakhali district, wiping every tear he could see, and telling them some simple truths—to see the humanity among their rivals, to shun violence, and to forgive. The late Madhu Dandavate, who had been India's railways minister in 1977-79 and finance minister in 1989-90, recounted a story[38] he had heard from Sucheta Kripalani, who had walked with Gandhi in Noakhali: in a village that had witnessed particularly savage violence, Gandhi called out the elders from both communities, Hindu and Muslim, to join him in a prayer. Nobody came out. Gandhi sat; time passed. A curious group of children, some Hindu, some Muslim, watched him. And Gandhi produced a ball and tossed it at them. The children tossed it back. He got them to play with one another. The children enjoyed playing with each other. And Gandhi admonished the elders—your children can play with each other; why can't you?

And slowly, one by one, they came out and prayed with him, and Gandhi got them to promise that they would not fight, nor kill.

Dandavate also recalled[39] Horace Alexander, the Quaker philosopher, who was with Gandhi for a few days in Noakhali, telling him the story of Gandhi going to a village where a Muslim man tried to strangle him. Gandhi was a frail man of 77; he collapsed. While falling, he recited a sura from the Quran to forgive him. The man was stunned. He touched Gandhi's feet and apologized, realizing the sin he was about to commit. He said he was willing to be Gandhi's follower and do whatever he would ask him to do. Gandhi replied: 'Do only one thing. When you go back home, do not tell anyone what you tried to do with me. Otherwise there will be more riots. Forget me and forgive yourself.' In his *Unfinished Memoirs,* Mujibur Rahman writes about being sent by Suhrawardy to accompany Gandhi in Noakhali, and he describes Gandhi as 'a magician' for his ability to calm people down.

The Gandhi Ashram in Noakhali has survived all these years. When I visited the place in December 2012, Naba Kumar Raha, a peace activist who manages the ashram, told me there were many such stories. Gandhi calmed Noakhali, and more than six decades later, it remains a region where violence is abhorred.

Mountbatten called Gandhi his one-man 'boundary force'. On 26 August, 1947, days after independence, Mountbatten wrote to Gandhi:

My dear Gandhiji,

In the Punjab we have 55 thousand soldiers and large scale rioting on our hands. In Bengal our forces consist of one man, and there is no rioting. As a serving officer, as well as an administrator, may I be allowed to pay my tribute to the One-Man Boundary Force, not forgetting his Second in Command, Mr Suhrawardy? You should have heard the enthusiastic applause which greeted the mention of your name in the Constituent Assembly on 15th of August when all of us were thinking so much of you....

Yours very sincerely,
Mountbatten of Burma

Talbot summed it up well: 'I've been a Christian, and in particular a Presbyterian, and yet in Gandhi I saw saintliness. He was a 77-year-old ascetic and the physical ordeal did not worry him. Here, if I ever saw one, is a pilgrimage. Here is the Indian—and the world's—idea of sainthood: a little old man who has renounced personal possessions, walking with bare feet on cold earth in search of a great human ideal.'

That was the miracle of Noakhali, the phenomenon of that one man, walking alone, trying to bring sense, reminding people of the older frontiers of Bengal which had always coexisted peacefully, before the madness of the last decade tore them apart. Gandhi was living out Tagore's poem—*Jodi tor dak shune keu na ashe, tobe ekla chalo re* (If they answer not thy call, walk alone).

In 2011, in the village of Joyag near Noakhali, during the holy month of Ramadan, a local politician called Abdul Wahab, who belonged to the Jamaat-e-Islami went looking for people of his faith who had forgotten their religious obligations and were not observing the fast. At a tea stall, he saw a Muslim man enjoying a cup of tea. Wahab marched to the shop, growling angrily at the man.

People gathered around the tea stall and watched the spectacle of Wahab chiding both the man and the Hindu tea stall owner. Not satisfied with the two of them mumbling apologies that he thought were not contrite enough, he took off his sandals and began hitting them both, sometimes using his walking stick. Fuming and muttering to himself, he left a little later.

But Wahab felt bad about what he did, and the following morning, he went to meet Raha, the peace activist at the Noakhali ashram.

Raha recalled Wahab telling him that he had done something wrong. After he heard the story, Raha said: 'You are right; what happened was wrong. What will you do now?'

'What should I do?' Wahab asked.

'I think you should apologize to the man who owns the tea stall and the man whom you hit,' Raha explained.

Wahab nodded; it made sense. He asked Raha if he could send word to the two men to come to his office the next day, and he would say sorry to them.

Raha shook his head and smiled. 'It is not so simple,' he said. 'You should go to the shop again. You should ask the two men to meet you. And at the town square, in the presence of people, you should say sorry to them. They will forgive you,' he said.

So the next morning, he sent word among the village's Hindu and Muslim communities, saying they should all come to the tea stall. Then, in front of a few dozen people, without prompting from anyone, Wahab apologized to the men he had beaten. The men accepted his apology, and the tension building around an incident, which could have sparked unexpected violence, evaporated.

Today, Joyag looks like a calm village where everyone knows everyone else. The bigger Noakhali district now has a population of about 3.1 million, scattered over hundreds of tiny villages. As Raha and I walked along the periphery of the ashram, he pointed out the school the ashram runs, which some 500 boys and girls from the poorest families attend, irrespective of their faith. Upstairs, I met Jharna Dhara Chaudhori, who was convalescing from an illness. She has kept the Gandhian flame alive. She told me: 'Gandhi had come here to bridge the communal divide, to give moral support to this area. He walked barefoot, went from village to village, spending nights in mud huts. He left us with only one thing—courage.'

I had met her on New Year's Day in 2013. Twenty-five days later, on India's Republic Day, the Indian Government honoured her with a Padma Shri. I didn't know it then, but when I read about it, I felt humbled that I had met her, and that the often-politicized honour had gone to one so deserving. As I prepared to leave Noakhali, she had reminded me: 'Remember, Gandhiji came here in 1946,' and she coughed. She drank some water and continued: 'There has never been a riot here since.'

On a cold winter night, driving through a dark street without lights, we reached a house by the railway tracks of Kushtia to listen to Lalon's songs. Lalon Fokir is regarded as one of the founders of Baul music. He was a nineteenth-century poet who abhorred religious divisions and, without getting pedantic or philosophical, combined the emotions of the Bhakti movement with Sufi traditions. An elderly man with a flowing beard, wearing a khadi kurta and lungi greeted us. Snacks and soft drinks were passed around as various singers, trained in the Lalon tradition, came before us, singing one song after another, their words simple, their music melodious, their bodies swaying gently, their faces thrust skyward, the moon casting its gentle glow in that little square. Occasionally, a train passed by, its mechanical chug-chug trying to override the music, but the singers disregarded it; their devotion was absolute, their voice continued uninterrupted, their eyes now closed, they were one with their music.

Everyone wonders, 'What's Lalon's faith?'
Lalon says: 'I've never "seen" the face
Of Faith with these eyes of mine.'

Circumcision marks a Muslim man,
What then marks a Muslim woman?
A Brahmin I recognise by the holy thread;
How do I recognise a Brahmin woman?

Everyone wonders, 'What's Lalon's faith?'

Some wear a garland and some wear the tasbi (prayer beads)
That's what marks the Faiths apart.
But what marks them apart when
One is born or at the time of death?

Everyone wonders, 'What's Lalon's faith?'

These songs and emotions that had kept Bengalis together were not able to withstand the whirlwind of hatred that was spreading through the countryside. Gandhi had pleaded in his time to keep India united. But by late 1946, his relevance had declined. The Partition was seen as necessary and considered inevitable. Curzon had carved India first, in 1905. Even though Britain had to bring the two Bengals together within six years, a mere thirty-six years later, another partition became reality.

There was another option—Suhrawardy proposed an independent Bengal, affiliated with neither India nor Pakistan. Suhrawardy realized quickly that if Bengal remained partitioned, it would be economically unviable. The coal mines would be in Bihar in India, and industries and other jute mills in Indian Bengal. But 80 per cent of jute was being produced in East Bengal.

Calcutta was going to remain with India—Pakistan coveted it, but as per the 1941 census, Calcutta was 73 per cent Hindu, 23 per cent Muslim.

A hard border would cripple trade and commerce. Railway links were intertwined. East Bengal had remained agrarian, with limited industry. Calcutta was the trade and industrial hub, and now in India. Most government offices too were in Calcutta, and most high-ranking officials in the civil administration were Hindus and expected to leave for India. They were replaced by officers from West Pakistan—a stop-gap arrangement which would have crucial long-term consequences.

In late May 1947, Sarat Chandra Bose and Suharawardy announced a political agreement supporting an independent, united Bengal, but the proposal got little support from the grassroots. The riots of 1946 had scared many Hindus, who preferred safety and security under Congress rule. Besides, Suharawardy wanted to maintain separate electorates for the two religions, a prospect Bose disagreed with. The plan failed, as both the Congress and Hindu Maha Sabha, a Hindu nationalist organization, opposed it.

On 20 June 1947, the Bengal Legislative Assembly had to vote on the proposed partition of Bengal. Of the 216 votes cast, 90 favoured staying within India. Legislators from Muslim areas voted 106-35 in favour of joining Pakistan. Non-Muslims then agreed for the partition. A referendum on 7 July in Sylhet voted in favour of Pakistan.[40]

The mass transfer of refugees between India and Pakistan on the western border has been well documented. There are the photographs Henri Cartier-Bresson and Margaret Bourke-White took, Khushwant Singh 1956 novel *Train to Pakistan*, and Sadaat Hasan Manto's fiction. Stories on the eastern frontier were no less painful. There was bloodshed. In despair, Kazi Nazrul Islam wrote:

Spread your message once more, O Hazrat!
From the heavens, your message of equality
I cannot bear this cruel bloodbath anymore
This strife within humanity[41]

But the violence subsided soon. While in Punjab, the violence was continuous and widespread in the year before the Partition, leading to an immediate transfer of population, in Bengal, cross-border migration was far more gradual, partly because the violence was largely confined to Calcutta and Noakhali. Until the 1965 war between India and Pakistan, the border was permeable.

I have met many Bangladeshis in their fifties and sixties who remember travelling from Dhaka to Calcutta until that war, as though they were travelling within one country.

Once the Partition was announced, many land-owning, upper-caste Hindus and civil servants left for India immediately. Poorer Hindus, many of them sharecroppers whose only property was the piece of land they tilled, stayed back in East Pakistan, as did poorer Muslims in India. The 1951 census of India suggests that some 2.52 million refugees came to India from East Pakistan, of whom nearly 80 per cent remained in West Bengal. The same year, Pakistan's census showed 671,000 refugees as having come to East Pakistan from India.

While India had anticipated a population transfer in Punjab, and allocated land left behind by Muslims who left for Pakistan to Hindus and Sikhs who arrived from Pakistan, such a transfer was not expected in Bengal. Unable to take the burden of continued inflow of refugees on the eastern front, in 1950, India's Prime Minister Jawaharlal Nehru and Pakistan's Prime Minister Liaquat Ali Khan signed a pact to prevent further population exchange in Bengal. Refugees who had already come would be taken back and their property returned. That did not happen.

Many years later, Bangladeshi writer Taslima Nasreen, who would move to India after facing threats to her life in Bangladesh from fundamentalist Muslims who threatened to kill her because she ridiculed them in her fiction, wrote a poem about the Partition:

> Residents of Bikrampur landed on Gariahata crossing
> Some came to Phultali from Burdwan
> Some fled to Howrah from Jessore
> From Netrokona to Ranaghat
> From Murshidabad to Mymensingh
> The outcome was inevitable
> As when you release a wild bull in a flower garden
> Two parts of the land stretch out their thirsty hands
> Towards each other. And in between the hands
> Stands the man-made filth of religion, barbed wire.

From the Indian side, the cinema of Ritwik Ghatak captured the pathos of that era. In his 1961 film, *Komal Gandhar* (Gandhar Sublime, sometimes also translated as the musical note, E Flat) there is a dramatic scene of a train hurtling towards its destination at great speed, and then suddenly coming to a halt, almost rudely. When you first watch it, you can almost feel the jolt, as though someone has suddenly applied emergency brakes. Bhrigu, the protagonist reaches out his hand, as if trying to touch the other side (which is now 'Opar Bangla', 'the Other Bengal'), and says: 'That is my country ... how near is it. Still I can never reach there.' *Komal Gandhar* was the second of a trilogy Ghatak made about Bengal's division, the other films being *Meghey Dhaka Tara* (The Cloud-Capped Star, 1960) and *Subarnarekha* (The Golden Line, 1962). In his essay, 'My Films', Ghatak writes: 'When the camera suddenly comes to a halt at the dead end of a railway track, where the old road to East Bengal has been snapped off, it raises (towards the close of the film) a searing scream in Anasuya's heart.'[42]

Neither India nor Pakistan fully understood that cry of anguish.

TWO

THE GIRL WHO NO LONGER FELT PAKISTANI

Aluxuriant shirishtola tree stands in downtown Dhaka, occupying a spot so central it seems as if life revolves around this very rain tree. Its branches cast a calming shadow in this city blessed by sunlight. There are students sitting in its shade—some are reading, a few are taking naps, a young man starts a hesitant conversation with the shy woman he'd like to go out with for a movie, and she listens, with her eyes cast down, nodding, smiling, while others are gossiping idly between their classes. Nilkhet Road meets Fuller Road here, and all around there are university buildings—students' residence halls and faculty buildings, schools, and institutions. To its east lies Ramna Park; to the north, the National Museum, the court and Shahbagh; and to its south, the Dhakeshwari temple, which may have given the city its name.

Near the tree is a memorial with stone slabs, within which are large terracotta reliefs telling the story of the land in a sequential order. The story begins with an idyllic view of rural Bengal—a hut sits amidst a paddy field. There are trees surrounding the hut, and a woman steps out of the hut, walking on her small plot of land. There is a pond with large fish swimming in it. The scene is pastoral, the kind painted in thousands of watercolours adorning greeting cards. The next panel shows heavy chains symbolizing slavery.

The relief that follows is clearly about the language movement of 1952—it has the Shaheed Minar or the Martyrs' Memorial, showing five rectangular columns, two of the shortest at the extreme, the next two slightly higher, and in the centre, the tallest column, bent at an angle at the top. It symbolizes a mother and her fallen sons.

The image has haunting resonance—you see its replicas in many villages and towns across the country. It commemorates the martyrs who died for the right to think, speak, and express themselves in their mother tongue. A few days after it was built, the government destroyed it; another one was built in 1963, but again destroyed in 1971; it then re-emerged after independence. (The story repeated in 2013. After the Bangladesh International Crimes

Tribunal sentenced the first of the Jamaat-e-Islami party leaders to death and the execution was carried out, irate supporters of the executed leader went on a rampage in many parts of the country, torching public property. Significantly, they also vandalized the Shaheed Minar replicas in some towns. They attacked this icon of Bangla nationalism because to them it represented a narrower identity, that of language, rather than a broad one, their faith; and the language was one shared with Hindus, and therefore not a pure Islamic language, and not holy enough, and not inspired by Arabic. Many Hindu homes were also destroyed.)

The next panel shows guns with bayonets pointing downward. Flames rise, and in the middle, there is the old Bangladesh flag, a red sun on a green rectangle, but within the sun, the golden map of Bangladesh. The next panel has a group of men standing along a wall, blindfolded and tied, with rifles and bayonets pointing at them. They are the activists and martyrs, betrayed by pro-Pakistani Razakars, as East Pakistani collaborators were known. Another relief shows a tank moving slowly along paddy fields. Bandana-wearing rebels now point guns at military targets. There is even a Sikh soldier shown, acknowledging Indian help in realizing Bangladesh's independence. And in the last relief, men and women proudly carry the new flag of freedom, as a dove flies away. Alongside, there is a poem by Nazrul Islam and one by Rabindranath Tagore.

Nazrul's poem reads:

Shoheed bhaider mukh money koro
Aar gobhir bedonay stobdho
Hoiya jawa money koro, tomake
Mukti ditei shey emon koriya
Oshomoye biday loiachhe

(Remember the faces of the martyred brothers
And remember them being silent
With profound pain; To make you free
He left like this, untimely)[43]

Tagore's poem reads:

Moronshagor pare tomra omor
Tomader shori
Nikhiley rochiya geley apnari ghor

Tomader shori

(You, who have crossed over the ocean from life to death, are immortal,
We remember you;
You reside everywhere,
We remember you)[44]

The monument is interesting in what its designer has chosen to commemorate
and what to ignore. To the Bangladeshi born after independence in 1971, the
reliefs tell the story of a nation that shook off its chains, becoming free after
a bitter war and much bloodshed in which patriotic young men and women
sacrificed their lives, facing bullets and bayonets, out of love for their language
and a longing for that pastoral field with banana trees, a pond full of fish; where
the rice paddy swayed gently, the sky was forever blue.

But there is an unspoken history. This country used to be Pakistan once.
The green and white flag with the crescent moon and star flew atop buildings.
The Pakistani rupee, with the photograph of Muhammad Ali Jinnah, was the
currency. Schoolchildren had to sing the half-Persian, half-Urdu Pakistani
national anthem, *Pak Sarzamin*, written by Hafeez Jalandhari. Pakistani
administrators governed this place. There was a time when the people of
Dhaka and Karachi, Chittagong and Islamabad, shared a common dream, but
that history is missing in these reliefs.

It is a pattern that repeats in Bangladesh: while its museums don't tell a
story that begins in 1971—it is not Year Zero—they don't properly tell the
story of 1947 either. They do go further in the past, mourning the loss of
Siraj-ud-Daula at the hands of Robert Clive in the Battle of Plassey in 1757,
celebrating freedom fighters like Khudiram Bose, and later, Suryo Sen, who
raided the Chittagong Armed Constabulary in the 1930s, and honouring
writers from the Indian Bengal. But then the narrative jumps to events that
led to 1971—like a straight linear journey—hopping over the inconvenient
history of the 1930s and 1940s; the Partition itself. In this version, it is as
if the British left and Pakistani occupying forces took over. You don't see
the Pakistani flag in the murals at shirishtola, except in the context of the
war itself.

At Independence, a little more than half[45] of Pakistan's population lived
in East Pakistan. Today's Bangladesh was Pakistan's eastern wing, expected
to be an equal partner in the new nation united by faith, whose main cities

were divided by a distance of over 1,370 miles of Indian territory. From 14 August 1947 to 16 December 1971, for 8,890 days, Bangladesh was part of Pakistan. Of those nearly nine thousand days, the last two-hundred and sixty-six days were the bloodiest, as Pakistani army unleashed a reign of terror to keep its eastern wing united with the western wing. But that violence wasn't sudden; it was the culmination of misunderstandings over nationalist aspirations, combined with western feeling of superiority and arrogance and eastern resentment over humiliation and injustice, which was economic and cultural to begin with, and later became acutely political.

The idea of Bengali nationalism is old. In newly independent Pakistan, the idea can be traced to an inspiring speech made in Pakistan's national assembly on 25 February 1948. [46] The man who spoke was Dhirendranath Datta, a prominent Hindu leader who had chosen to remain in Pakistan.

On that day, Datta introduced an amendment to a discussion about the national language of Pakistan. He wanted the words 'or Bengalee (sic)' inserted after 'English' in Sub-rule 29, which listed the official languages of Pakistan. After getting permission to speak, he reassured the House that he was not being a provincialist. Of the 69 million people who lived in Pakistan at that time, 44 million spoke Bengali. What should be the language of that state, he asked. He then painted a vivid picture of the Bengali peasant who knew no language other than Bengali, going to a rural post office to send a money order to his son studying in Dacca University and finding the forms in Urdu, which he would not understand. He would have to go to another distant town to get the form translated before he could send the money to his son. If he sold a plot of land and went to the stamp vendor, he would never be certain of having received the value of the money in stamps, because the value of the stamp would be written in English and Urdu. Pointing out these practical difficulties, he urged the House:

> The language of the State should be such which can be understood by the common man of the State—(he) finds that the proceedings of this Assembly which is their mother of parliaments is being conducted in a language, Sir, which is unknown to them.... But, Sir, if English can have an honoured place ... (so) that the proceedings of the Assembly should be conducted in Urdu or English, why Bengalee, which is spoken by four crores forty lakhs of people should not have an honoured place, Sir? So, Sir, I know I am voicing the sentiments of the vast millions of

our State and therefore Bengalee should not be treated as a Provincial Language. It should be treated as the language of the State.[47]

Datta's amendment was roundly defeated. Pakistan's Prime Minister Liaquat Ali Khan admonished him and warned the MPs that a vote granting Bengali national status risked reinforcing divisions within the country. He said: 'Pakistan has been created because of a demand of a hundred million Muslims in this subcontinent and the language of a hundred million Muslims is Urdu. It is necessary for a nation to have one language and that language can be only Urdu and no other language.'[48]

When Datta returned to Dacca in March 1948, many young people came to the old Tejgaon Airport to receive him. 'He thought they were going to manhandle him,' recalls Anisuzzaman, now the president of the Bangla Academy, who became a leading student activist in the language movement which started four years later in 1952. 'But they garlanded him and gave him a shawl. Datta understood the feeling was deep.'

Back in the west, Liaquat Ali Khan was furious. He privately told associates that Datta was going to divide the country. But factually Datta was right and Liaquat Ali Khan wrong. The rhetoric of a hundred million Muslims of the subcontinent speaking Urdu was just that, rhetoric; barely 3 per cent of Pakistanis actually spoke Urdu as their first language; a full 56 per cent spoke Bangla.[49] But Liaquat Ali Khan was being astute: while Pakistan was an idea—a nation united by faith—it was, in reality, an amalgam of different cultures, classes, languages, and sects. While it was overwhelmingly Muslim, it was divided by language even in the West, where there were many; people spoke Pashto, Sindhi, Punjabi, Baluchi, Urdu and Gujarati. Urdu, the national language, was an import from India. His hope was that over time Urdu would prevail and other languages would be used less.

In East Pakistan, some Bengali Muslims used Urdu, and they did so because some considered it to be an elite, aristocratic, refined language, since it had been the preferred language of the courts of nawabs, themselves satraps of rulers from Delhi. They also saw Bengali, with its Sanskrit roots, as a language for Hindus. But many more loved Bangla, and West Pakistan's intransigence helped create what the Bangladeshi political scientist Rounaq Jahan calls the 'vernacular elite', which led the struggle for independence.

Liaquat Ali Khan believed that recognizing Bengali as the official language in East Pakistan could lead to demands from other languages for similar status, and Pakistan's founding fathers probably feared that accepting that demand would interfere with their nation-building project. From the narrow perspective of Pakistani nationalism Khan was right, but his reluctance set the tone for the way the relationship between the two halves played out over the next quarter century. Over the years it got more acrimonious, ensuring the inevitable conflict of 1971.

Datta's role in the language politics of East Pakistan is interesting for another reason—he was a Hindu who had chosen to remain in Pakistan after independence. He did not migrate to India, which the Muslim League kept calling the home for Hindus, and indeed, many Hindus had crossed the border to go to India. Datta's granddaughter Aroma Dutta, who grew up with her grandfather in Comilla, is now a sociologist in Dhaka. She has worked for years to restore property to Hindu families which was taken away from them by successive Pakistani—and later Bangladeshi—governments and politicians, built on the assumption that a Hindu was, at heart, an Indian, a foreigner, an alien, and for some time, an enemy. Why, then, did Hindus like Datta choose to make Pakistan their home?

The answer probably lies in a famous speech Pakistan's founding father Muhammad Ali Jinnah made on 11 August 1947, three days before Pakistan's independence. In that speech, Jinnah said that the state had to get out of the business of religion—it had to be blind to religion:

> I know there are people who do not quite agree with the division of India and the partition of the Punjab and Bengal. Much has been said against it, but now that it has been accepted, it is the duty of every one of us to loyally abide by it and honourably act according to the agreement which is now final and binding on all.... A division had to take place... [i]n my judgement there was no other solution, and I am sure future history will record its verdict in favour of it... Any idea of a united India could never have worked, and in my judgment it would have led us to terrific disaster.... Now what shall we do?
>
> If you will work in cooperation, forgetting the past, burying the hatchet, you are bound to succeed. If you change your past and work together in a spirit that every one of you, no matter to what community he belongs, no matter what relations he had with you in the past, no matter what is his colour, caste, or creed, is first, second, and last a citizen of this State with equal rights, privileges, and obligations, there

will be no end to the progress you will make.

I cannot emphasize it too much. We should begin to work in that spirit, and in course of time all these angularities of the majority and minority communities, the Hindu community and the Muslim community … will vanish… You are free; you are free to go to your temples, you are free to go to your mosques or to any other place or worship in this State of Pakistan. You may belong to any religion or caste or creed—that has nothing to do with the business of the State…. We are starting in the days where there is no discrimination, no distinction between one community and another, no discrimination between one caste or creed and another. We are starting with this fundamental principle: that we are all citizens, and equal citizens, of one State.[50]

I met Aroma Dutta at her home, where she sat beneath a swirling sketch of Ritwik Ghatak, who happened to be her mother's twin brother. In a bookshelf nearby I spotted books by her aunt, the illustrious writer Mahasweta Devi. She told me: 'My grandfather never believed in any religion as the basis of a state. He is the first man who formally refuted the existence of a state which was created on the basis of religion. He chose Pakistan after he heard Jinnah's speech.'

Datta, she said, had flown to Bombay after the Calcutta riots of 1946 had started. He wanted to go back to Calcutta where Hindu refugees had begun to arrive. 'I have to go back and work there,' he'd said. Nehru asked him to help manage the influx. 'Nehru told my grandfather, "You alone can do it",' Aroma told me. 'At that time he was still thinking about these issues in his mind when the radio was turned on, broadcasting a speech by Jinnah. And he stopped and said, "Let me listen".'

Dutta says that her grandfather was deeply moved by what he heard. 'That speech said Pakistan is not for Hindus or for Muslims. Pakistan is for Pakistanis. And my grandfather decided he was opting for Pakistan. My uncle and aunt urged him not to do it, but he was insistent. That entire evening he walked back and forth, and in the morning he called Nehru, and said: "Please forgive me, but I am opting for Pakistan. I have to go and stop Hindus from coming to India. I will try. Let me try." And he flew to Karachi,' she recalled.

To understand Datta's thinking one needs to understand the elemental hold of Bengali nationalism, where the love of the language and the culture it represents is larger than spiritual values shared with people of the same faith. Datta felt closer to a Bengali Muslim than, say, to a Tamil Hindu. He could not tear himself apart from the place where he was born. Besides language and culture, for many Hindus there were other considerations too. Many Hindus were zamindars in pre-Partition Bengal, and loathed the idea of having to leave their vast ancestral land by selling it at distress prices, and rebuilding life in Calcutta. The old battle between the basha and the bari manifested again, and the hold of the bari was strong. Besides, while the violence during the Calcutta and Noakhali riots was brutal, overall, Bengal experienced less violence than Punjab did, and what violence it did experience, ended soon after Independence.

Liaquat Ali Khan's response to Datta's amendment revealed another facet of Pakistani nationalism for which Datta was unprepared. Jinnah's vision may have inspired Datta, but it was clear that other leaders of Pakistan saw things differently. Datta was not the only one to feel disillusioned when Liaquat Ali Khan snubbed him. Take the case of Jogendranath Mandal, a Hindu from the Namasudra caste, classified as a 'backward caste'. He was a politician who had supported the Muslim League because he did not trust upper-caste Hindu politicians, and he too had decided to stay with Pakistan.

The Muslim League had approached Mandal in 1943, and he had agreed to support them. He had done so because he had felt that their shared economic backwardness would unite Muslims and Namasudras in Bengal, that their common interests would help them form governments across India. Like his leader, Bhimrao Ambedkar, Mandal believed this could transform Indian politics and society. So Mandal continued to support the League even though he had witnessed the carnage in 1946 in Calcutta and visited the sites of rioting and rapes in Noakhali.

After Independence, the chief minister of East Pakistan was Nurul Amin, a Bengali Muslim League leader. But Amin ignored Mandal's suggestions to make the government more representative.[51] By 1950, Mandal was disillusioned. He was a member of Liaquat Ali Khan's cabinet, but he wrote him a letter[52] 'with a heavy heart' and 'a sense of utter frustration' at his failure to uplift backward Hindu communities in East Bengal, and felt compelled to resign from the cabinet. He then listed a series of grievances, which pointed out betrayal upon betrayal of promises and ideals, which had forced him to leave.

Mandal's pleas for including backward-caste ministers in the cabinet had been ignored; his complaints of ill-treatment of Namasudras by the police were disregarded. A petty fishing dispute would escalate and the police and local Muslims would ravage the Namasudra community; armed police had terrorized Barisal villagers; Hindu women were raped in Habiganj in Sylhet; Santhals were brutalized and forcibly evicted from Nachole in Rajshahi; in Kalshira in Khulna district a few Communist youth had killed a policeman who was assaulting a Hindu woman, and after that Hindus who had nothing to do with that incident were made scapegoats and their property confiscated, and they were forcibly converted to Islam; and then the culmination, the riots against Hindus in Dacca and elsewhere, in which hundreds died. (In his letter Mandal described dogs and vultures feasting on corpses in Muladi village). As per his calculations, 5 million Hindus had left East Pakistan for India in the early years of Pakistan. He was pained to read an editorial in which a prominent Muslim leader quoted approvingly from Islamic history, pointing out how Muhammad had called for Arabia to be free of Jews. The leader was implying that Pakistan, another 'pure' nation, must be free of non-Muslims— which in this instance, meant Hindus.

Mandal found the situation 'absolutely hopeless' and the future 'completely dark and dismal'. He noted the rise of Muslim boycott of Hindu lawyers, doctors, shopkeepers, traders, and merchants, sparking increased Hindu migration to India. Muslim tenants stopped paying rent to Hindu landlords; Muslim buyers refused to pay the market price of jute and other agricultural commodities to Hindu traders. Artisans who made Hindu idols had left, and so did priests, making it harder for Hindus to perform marriage and cremation rituals. Mandal warned Liaquat Ali Khan: 'Islam is being offered as the sovereign remedy for all earthly evils. In the matchless dialectics of capitalism and socialism you present the exhilarating democratic synthesis of Islamic equality and fraternity. In that grand setting of the Shariat, Muslims alone are rulers while Hindus and other minorities are zimmies who are entitled to protection at price, and you know more than anybody else, Mr Prime Minister, what that price is. After anxious and prolonged struggle I have come to the conclusion that Pakistan is no place for Hindus to live in and that their future is darkened by the ominous shadow of conversion or liquidation.... It is really amazing that a man of your education, culture and experience should be an exponent of a doctrine fraught with so great a danger to humanity and subversive of all principles of equality and good sense.'

On 8 October 1950, a little more than a thousand days after Pakistan's birth, Mandal resigned from Liaquat Ali Khan's cabinet.

◆

One evening in 2013 at the Dhaka Club, Anisuzzaman told me the story of the language movement or bhasha andolan, in which he had played such an important part. Dhirendranath Datta's speech in the Pakistani parliament had inspired university students who had begun forming an all-party committee to agitate for official recognition for their language. Booklets began to appear on the language question. On 11 March 1948, students went to the secretariat to protest. Sheikh Mujibur Rahman was a young leader at that time, and he was among those who were arrested.

When Jinnah came to Dacca that month, he said at the university's convocation ceremony: 'Let me make it clear that the state language of Pakistan is going to be Urdu and no other language. Anyone who tries to mislead you is really the enemy of Pakistan. Without one state language no nation can get tied up solidly together and function. Look at the history of other countries. Therefore, so far as the state language is concerned, Pakistan's language shall be Urdu. But as I said, it will come in time.'[53] When Jinnah stressed, 'nowhere in the world are there two state languages', students started protesting, saying feebly, 'no, no,' and Jinnah left Dacca very annoyed.

In October 1950, Liaquat Ali Khan was assassinated in Rawalpindi. His successor Khawaja Nazimuddin came to Dacca in 1952, and in a public meeting reiterated that Urdu would be the state language. Students shouted: 'Rashtrobhasha Bangla Chai' (We want Bengali as a state language). An all-party committee then decided to march to the provincial assembly on the day it was supposed to begin its session—21 February. The bhasha andolan was born.

Anisuzzaman was a first year student in 1952. On the morning of 21 February, his friends had gathered at his home. Reports had spread that the government had imposed Section 144 of the colonial-era code of criminal procedure, which prohibited the assembly of more than five people. (The British had passed that law to prevent nationalist Indians from leading processions and demonstrating against them, and the law was replicated in most British colonies later, and most newly independent nations throughout the former colonies have since kept those laws.) The government decided to ban processions in the city, and the all-party committee had decided to obey the law. But the students had a different idea.

Kamal Hossain, who would later become Bangladesh's minister for law and foreign affairs under Mujib, and in 1981 even ran for president as an Awami League candidate, writes in his autobiography: 'The students were the first to organize themselves in opposition to the activities of the ruling elite. The East Pakistan Muslim Students' League became the platform for an ever growing politicized student community to voice their grievances against the existing order.'[54] There was no doubt in their minds that they would break the ban on public assembly.

Anisuzzaman's friends had met at his home, and his mother and sister fed the young men. His mother took him aside and asked him: what should she do if he were taken away by the police? 'She was accepting that I may get arrested, and she didn't deter me from going,' he remembers.

And so on 21 February, many students and concerned citizens gathered at the Dacca University compound, milling about the area near a large tree. That was a violation of Section 144, a law that bans public assembly, which was in force, and the police beat up the students with their wooden batons and started dispersing the crowds. They burst tear gas shells. Students, men and women, began challenging the authorities by walking in small groups. Many were hurt by the exposed canisters. The injured were rushed to the hospital. At about 3 p.m., the police opened fire and several students died—Anisuzzaman says that besides students, one of the dead was a clerk at the high court, another an office peon, and one a teenage boy. It seemed as if the government had won. Some said eight died, some believe dozens did. But the numbers weren't important. According to Anisuzzaman, 'The impact was so great that immediately after the shooting, the railway workers went on strike, even radio workers were on strike and the news spread by word of mouth.' A martyrs' memorial was built overnight.

Tahmina Saleh was a 13-year-old schoolgirl in Dacca in 1952. Her father was a businessman and her brother studied engineering in Calcutta at the Shivpur Engineering College. She remembers 1952 vividly as the year Pakistan had introduced Urdu as a subject in Bengali schools. One day, student leaders came to her school. They made rousing speeches about protecting their mother tongue. 'People around us said that the West Pakistanis are taking everything from us, depriving us Bengalis of everything. They took away our jute and didn't give us any jobs. And then they said Urdu will be the state language,' Saleh recalled, as she offered me delicious beef kebabs made carefully without cilantro, because her son Asif, whom I have known for some time, had told her of my dislike for that garnish.

On 21 February students were agitating all over the city, and Tahmina too decided to join the procession. Elders around her had told them about the imposition of Section 144, but the young people were determined to march. 'Some of us were worried, but many of us were not,' Tahmina said. There were about fifteen girls in the group—some were Hindu, some Muslim. She remembers she was wearing a salwar-kameez, which was not yet hugely popular in the east, and it was usually associated with what Muslim women wore in the west.

The police saw them but did nothing. Hundreds of students had taken over the roads. Tahmina and her friends went to Chameli House, the ladies' hostel, shouting slogans. But when they returned, the situation had turned grim, the festive mood was missing. There were bullets on the streets, and the police had used tear gas to disperse students. At the medical college, close to Curzon Hall where Jinnah had spoken in 1948, Tahmina saw bloodied students, wounded by bullets and blows from the police. Tahmina was now afraid. She returned home around five in the evening. Her brother, she discovered later, was in jail.

Her parents were beyond relieved that she had come back. Word spread throughout the city that some students had died. Nobody knew how many, some said a handful, others said a dozen; one rumour claimed hundreds had died. Kamal Hossain writes that initially four students were killed, and they were called the first martyrs of the language movement—Barkat, Salam, Jabbar and Rafiq. The days that followed saw hortals and the government retaliated by maintaining the curfew. Abdul Gaffar Chowdhury composed a memorable song—*Amar bhaiyer rokte rangano ekushe February/Ami ki bhulite pari* (How can I forget 21 February, splattered with my brother's blood?).[55]

'I had never felt politically active, but that day changed everything. I still feel political about Ekushe February [21 February], the day Bengali nationalism found its voice in this land. After that, I wanted to learn everything about world politics. I no longer felt Pakistani. My brother used to tell me—the two halves of Pakistan cannot stay together, we will be separated. I now understood why,' she recalled.

Anisuzzaman agreed with the importance of the date: '21 February made people conscious about their language and their rights, and the Pakistan government took several measures which were harmful. They even asked for Bengali to be written in Arabic script. During Ayub Khan's rule (1958-1969), he asked for Bengali to be written in Roman script. This was nothing but a conspiracy against our language.' He remembers Pakistani Radio using a large number of Perso-Arabic words in its broadcasts; the government discouraging observance of the Bengali New Year or Tagore's birth anniversary; the prohibition on celebrating Tagore's birth centenary in 1961 (artists were threatened, functions attacked); the replacement of the word 'bhogoban' (god) with 'rahman' in a poem by Nazrul Islam, because bhogoban was a Sanskrit-based Bengali word, and therefore 'Hindu'. In 1967, the information minister told Parliament that the state media had been directed to decrease the broadcasting of Tagore songs, because those were not in line with the ideology of Pakistan.

These moves backfired; students began celebrating Tagore and the Bengali New Year with greater vigour. Anisuzzaman said: 'There were legitimate concerns about economic and political deprivation of East Pakistan, but the cultural identity became central. Here we are, Bengalis, with nothing in common with Pakistan except our religion, and they treated us this way. We weren't going to tolerate it.'

The feelings were intense. Anisuzzaman's mother went to the Shaheed Minar with her husband, who was a homoeopath. They didn't take their family car—they went in a rickshaw. At the memorial, she put a golden necklace as her contribution for the movement. The necklace had belonged to her daughter, who had died as an infant. 'My mother didn't tell my father that she was going to do it. But she did it,' he said, his eyes glistening. 'Such was the feeling people had for the language.'

Kamal Hossain writes further: 'The Language Movement made a profound impact on politics and society. It led to an active involvement of the youth and students in national politics and in the mass campaigns that were undertaken to mobilize support for this cause. Contacts between the students and the masses provided a vital bridge between urban and rural areas.' Its seminal contribution, he argues, lay in transcending communal barriers. Bangladesh's politics turned more secular from that year on: the students' union and the Awami League party dropped the word 'Muslim' from their names in 1953 and 1955. Hossain continues: 'They also recognized the strong syncretic elements in Bangla folklore and music…. [I]n the sixties…leading TV and radio artists led protests against an Information Ministry order banning Rabindra Sangeet from radio and TV because these symbols were seen as representing Hindu culture. Women TV news readers protested because they were forbidden from wearing a teep (a common practice amongst Bengali women of wearing a vermilion mark on their foreheads.)'

Sultana Kamal is a human rights lawyer who won the John Humphrey Freedom Award for Human Rights in Canada in 1996. She was barely two years old in 1952. She had grown up in a politically active family. Her mother Sufia was a pioneer feminist and renowned Bangladeshi poet, and when she died in 1999, she was given a state funeral. I attended her centenary celebrations in 2011, and heard her granddaughter sing Rabindra Sangeet. Later that month, I met Sultana at her home in Dhanmondi. She told me: 'The seeds of our independence were sown in the language movement of 1952. The fact that Bangladesh would eventually be independent of Pakistan was not at all unusual to us. We Bengalis were always challenged to prove that we were loyal Pakistanis by proving that we were loyal Muslims. The only way to do so was by becoming a Muslim and professing it, by being Muslim in your overt expressions and in your family life, and by knowing the verses of the Quran and the Islamic etiquette. Educational policy was also being changed as though there was no other group in this country.'

◆

While Pakistan's federal government tried to create differences within Bengalis—between Hindus and Muslims—and differences began to brew, life did not change materially on the eastern border with India, which remained porous for a considerable period. People travelled from Calcutta to Dacca and the other way round as though the two cities were still part of the same country. After Partition, many schools and colleges had got separated from their students who had suddenly become nationals of a foreign country. But people continued to study in their old schools, even if they were now in another country. Hasan Azizul Huq was born in Bordhoman in India, and his sister's husband taught at a college in East Pakistan. So he moved there to study, not thinking much about nations and borders. He had an Indian passport, but it didn't matter in East Pakistan, and he studied up to his master's in arts at Rajshahi University. He travelled home to India at least thrice a year, but nobody stopped him or checked him. After getting his degree, he returned to India to teach and he even got a job. But a few months later a school inspector, and India's bureaucracy, caught up with him.

'Where did this young man come from?' the inspector asked the supervisors.

'Rajshahi University, he replied.

'But you can't be an Indian if you studied there,' the inspector said.

Huq showed his Indian passport. Was it a problem that he studied at Rajshahi, he wanted to know. The inspector could not find any rule to say no. But a few months later he got a job at a college in Rajshahi, so he moved back. His parents too went east after that. This was not uncommon. It was all still Bengal. Huq told an interviewer: 'None of my uncles or cousins came. At one time they were keen supporters of Pakistan, and were part of the struggle for Pakistan... But it never entered their heads that they might leave their homes to live in Pakistan.'[56]

The Dutch historian Willem van Schendel recounts a similar and not unusual story of Intaz Ali, who was born in Chor Madhobpur in 1947 as a citizen of British India. At Partition, his village became part of Pakistan, giving him Pakistani nationality. A few years later, an international tribunal awarded the village to India, making him an Indian citizen. By 1959, he was a student at an Indian school. But disturbances broke out in that village, and they fled for safety to East Pakistan. He became a Pakistani citizen again. And in 1971, Bangladesh became free, giving him his fifth citizenship before he was 25.[57]

The permeability of the border began to change after the riots in 1963-64. In December 1963, reports spread that a sacred lock of hair believed to be of Prophet Muhammad's had disappeared from a shrine in Hazratbal, Kashmir. Pakistan protested, and the Pakistan Muslim League called for a 'Kashmir Day' in early January. Indian authorities said the hair had been found, but Pakistani Radio described it as fake. Riots erupted across East Pakistan.

Before the madness of violence gripped Bengal again in 1964, it was as if the two parts had always remained whole. This was partly because the percentage of Hindus remaining in East Pakistan was considerably larger than the percentage of Hindus that remained in the West, and that was because hostility between communities was less than in the west.

The riots of 1964, and the India-Pakistan war a year later, soured relations all across, and the border became firmer. Anisuzzaman, now the president of the Bangla Academy, lamented the loss of access to films and books in his language from the other Bengal. He remembers seeing many Satyajit Ray films and reading the latest Bengali novels from India until 1965, the year Pakistan imposed a cultural boycott on Indian books, films, and products. 'It was the year everything stopped, just like that,' Anisuzzaman told me one late afternoon at the Dhaka Club.

In Amitav Ghosh's 1988 novel, *The Shadow Lines,* the riots in Khulna and elsewhere play a pivotal part. The Khulna riot occurs in retaliation over the riots in faraway Kashmir. In the novel, the narrator looks at an old atlas and tries to understand the meaning of borders and distance.

> I was struck with wonder that there had really been a time, not so long ago, when people, sensible people, of good intention, had thought that all maps were the same, that there was a special enchantment in lines; I had to remind myself that they were not to be blamed for believing that there was something admirable in moving violence to the borders... They had drawn their borders, believing in that pattern, in the enchantment of lines, hoping perhaps that once they had etched their borders upon the map, the two bits of land would sail away from each other like the shifting tectonic plates of the prehistoric Gondwanaland. What had they felt, I wondered, when they discovered that they had created not a separation, but a yet-undiscovered irony ... the simple fact that there had never been a moment in the 4000-year-old history of that map when the places we know as Dhaka and Calcutta were more closely bound to each other than after they had drawn their lines—so closely that I, in Calcutta, had only to look into the mirror to be in Dhaka; a moment when each city was the inverted image of the other, locked into an irreversible symmetry by the line that was to set us free—our looking-glass border.

Ghosh movingly depicted the impact of the tragedy of the division of Bengal on a Bengali Hindu family nostalgic about life in Opar Bangla. They are unable to feel at home in India, finding the basha-bari conflict tearing their hearts apart. When the narrator's father gives his mother a ticket to fly to Dacca, she is unable to conceal her joy, but nor is she able to understand the meaning of that border:

> One evening when we were sitting out in the garden she wanted to know whether she would be able to see the border between India and East Pakistan from the plane. When my father laughed and said, why, did she really think the border was a long black line with green on one side and scarlet on the other, like it was in a school atlas, she was not so much offended as puzzled.
>
> 'No, that wasn't what I meant,' she said. Of course not. But surely

there's something—trenches perhaps, or soldiers, or guns pointing at each other, or even just barren strips of land. Don't they call it no-man's land?... [i]f there aren't any trenches or anything, how are people to know? I mean, where's the difference then? And if there's no difference, both sides will be the same; it'll be just like it used to be before, when we used to catch a train in Dhaka and get off in Calcutta the next day without anybody stopping us. What was it all for then—Partition and all the killing and everything—if there isn't something in between? ... It was not till many years later that I realized it had suddenly occurred to her then that she would have to fill in 'Dhaka' as her place of birth on (the embarkation) form, and that the prospect of this had worried her ... because she liked things to be neat and in place—and at that moment she had not been able quite to understand how her place of birth had come to be so messily at odds with her nationality.

The riots of 1963-64, and the inconclusive India-Pakistan war of 1965, fundamentally changed the relationship between the Pakistani state and the Hindus who continued to stay in Pakistan. After the war General Ayub Khan's administration in Pakistan passed a law called the Enemy Property Act under which, in effect, all minorities were regarded as 'enemies'. Aroma Dutta told me: 'The state identified Hindus with India. Hindus of this part of the soil were branded as Indians, and considered enemies of the state. A large number of minorities had to leave the land because they started confiscating their land and homes. They could not go to the courts at any time, and the government could decide at any time that someone was an enemy, and tell them to leave. And they branded the house as state property. A huge number of Hindus started leaving Pakistan.'

Dhirendranath Datta who later became a minister in Fazlul Huq's short-lived United Front government that defeated the Muslim League in 1954, joined other politicians and fought against the Enemy Property Act in courts. Dutta said: 'How can citizens of the country be branded as enemies? Jinnah's speech had said that the minorities were also citizens. It is true that most of the property in the east and most of the big houses in districts were still owned by Hindus, and Muslims were still emerging. But this was not the way to go about it. It was disastrous. My mother's family lost much of their property in Rajshahi.'[58]

The Hindus who stayed on in Pakistan had taken Jinnah at his word.

Jinnah's view of secularism was different from the Gandhian view. For Gandhi, all religions deserved equal respect and he could knowledgeably quote from many scriptures of different religions. Jinnah was saying something completely different, referring to secularism in its European sense — where the place of worship and governance were apart. According to some accounts[59], Jinnah liked alcohol and ate pork and yet created a nation for Muslims, and his successors banned both. Jinnah died soon after Independence, and the governing ethos of Pakistan began to change. In East Pakistan, Hindu leaders who saw themselves as Bengalis who lived in Bengal which now happened to be in Pakistan, found it hard to reconcile their lives with the direction the nation was taking. What Pakistanis in the west didn't realize was that many Bengali Muslims too were beginning to feel the same way. Not only did they resent the way federal Pakistani leaders treated their language, they were also shocked that during the 1965 India-Pakistan war, the eastern front was left unguarded. The war was entirely fought on the western front, and East Pakistan was spared bombardment only because India chose not to open the eastern front. Had it done so, East Pakistan would have been vulnerable and Indian troops could have reached Dacca within days. Many in East Pakistan were aghast that the federal government hadn't planned for such a contingency, and had left the eastern wing to its own devices. No serious strategic analyst has suggested that India was likely to attack East Pakistan in 1965. Besides, East Pakistanis' view of India was more ambivalent towards India than the view West Pakistanis had. And yet East Pakistanis resented how they had been taken for granted. It reinforced their perception — that they, Bengalis, were second-class citizens.

Besides, what they could not accept was cultural subjugation and linguistic humiliation. Bengalis were hurt by the disrespect shown to their language. Political consciousness had been growing in the East after the peremptory manner in which the Pakistan Assembly had rejected Datta's amendment. They hated being called short, dark, rice-eating peasants. They would find the term anglicized West Pakistanis used to describe them — Bingo — insulting. Irene Khan told me that Bengalis were constantly told that they were supposed to be weak. The civil servants from West Pakistan who came to administer East Pakistan carried with them many prejudices. As the Bengali diet was mainly fish and rice, the men were considered weak and puny, all bones no muscles. The women were resented because they chose to sing and dance and follow many Bengali customs which the West Pakistanis saw as Hindu contamination of pure Islam.

Sultana Kamal remembers Ayub Khan visiting Dacca in 1965 and meeting a group of concerned citizens which included her mother. The Pakistani president was angry because students had roughed up the vice-chancellor. His tone was condescending towards the group. 'Can't you look after yourself,' he asked rhetorically.

Sufia Kamal, her mother, told him that he had just returned from a very serious war with India and signed a truce. 'If you are capable of ending a conflict why don't you do something similar here? Why is there so much conflict all the time, and why not try to end it,' she asked.

Ayub Khan replied in Urdu: 'Wahan ham admi ke sath bolte the; yahan sab janwar hai', (There I was dealing with human beings, but here in East Pakistan there are only animals). Sufia Kamal stood up and calmly said: 'All right; but you are the president of those animals, then. So it is your responsibility to do something.' He glared at her angrily and stopped the meeting.[60]

'The only way we could prove we were Pakistanis was by discarding our Bangla identity,' Sultana Kamal said. This is a view that continued to persist well after Bangladesh's independence. Irene Khan remembers sitting next to a Pakistani general at a dinner in the 1980s. She was at that time a senior executive at the UN High Commissioner for Refugees (UNHCR). The Pakistani general took a lot of interest in her, but when she referred to the 1971 war as a liberation war, he went into a state of denial. He said referring to it as a liberation war was propaganda. 'Among Pakistanis there was total denial about the war. They couldn't understand why we didn't understand them, and why we didn't love them back in return. They'd call me an East Pakistani, and think of it as a compliment,' she told me.

◆

The clash between the Bengali and Muslim identities began to sharpen. Mahfuz Anam told me that the rationale of Pakistan was to create a safe place for Islam in the subcontinent. Bengali Muslims had become convinced that Hindus would dominate India, he added. 'They thought their religious heritage would be under threat. The belief was that the structure of the state of Pakistan will give my religious heritage some security, and so we rushed into it. But very soon we realized that while the structure ensured Islamic heritage, it also threatened Bengali identity. My language and my culture were affected. I couldn't sing or dance; my Tagore was being taken away from me. So the Bengali Muslim wanted to break that structure,' he said.

The tension lay in seeing the Bengali and Islamic heritage as though they were mutually exclusive. Bengali nationalism became necessary to secure the 'schizophrenic existence' of two identities within a nation. 'The questions were existential for the Bengali Muslim: does he want Islamicized Bengali culture, and if so, what does it mean? Could Hindu-influenced Bengali culture coexist with the Islamic identity? That is where 21 February becomes important, because it is a secular celebration—there are no Muslim or Hindu rituals associated with that,' Anam said. Likewise, Poyla Baisakh, or the first day of the Bengali New Year, is observed passionately in this country, he said, regardless of one's faith.

Several decades later, at a seminar in New York, a Bangladeshi diplomat ended his speech quoting from Tagore. A Pakistani diplomat raised his hand and said, good-naturedly: 'Why do you Bangladeshis always keep quoting Tagore when you have such a fine poet in Nazrul Islam?' The political import of the remark was not lost. Tagore was a Brahmo Samaji, but seen by Muslims as a Hindu, and while he spent many years in East Bengal, particularly Kushtia, his home was Jorasankho in Calcutta, and he had died in India. He is revered in India, and indeed, wrote the national anthems of India and Bangladesh. Nazrul on the other hand was Muslim, although he lived a large part of his life in India.

The Bangladeshi diplomat replied, quick-witted: 'Unlike other countries, we are lucky to have both, Tagore and Nazrul, and its significance other countries won't understand.'

It is that feeling—of being both and wanting both—Hindu or Muslim, and yet remain Bengali—that's quintessential to understanding identity in Bangladesh, and which I have seen Indians and Pakistanis struggle so hard to understand about Bangladesh. After one of my visits to Dhaka, I wrote on a social network website: 'Bangladesh was not India, but was it ever Pakistan?' Many Bangladeshi friends loved what I said; several Pakistani friends were shocked by what I said, with a few carrying on a spirited debate with me. One of them asked: if East Punjab and West Bengal could both be 'India', why couldn't West Punjab and East Bengal be 'Pakistan'?

◆

The Partition had also managed to complicate the organic economic links between the two halves of Bengal. The east was overwhelmingly rural; the west was more urban. East Bengal grew food, West Bengal manufactured goods that were then sold in the east. The Partition disrupted this symbiotic rhythm. Industries, communication and transport suffered, with the Assam railway system cut off, affecting trade in tea and timber. Trains from Siliguri to Calcutta were disrupted, as were trains from Chittagong to Assam.

The worst affected industry was jute, which was East Pakistan's main cash crop. In 1947, jute was Bengal's largest industry. But the way the border was drawn during the Partition, almost every jute mill went to India while four-fifths of the jute producing land was in Pakistan. Instead of letting trade flow freely, Pakistan erected trade barriers. It decided to set up its own jute mills, and restricted export of raw jute to India. Jute farmers in the east were naturally upset, because they lost their large market. Jute began to get smuggled into India. Meanwhile India started growing jute, making its mills rely less on Pakistan. By 1961, Pakistan produced 1.31 million tonnes of jute from a cultivated area of 834,000 hectares. India planted jute over a larger area—917,000 hectares, but its production was less efficient at 1.14 million tonnes. Gradually though, India was becoming self-reliant, destroying the symbiosis.

Other industries too were affected, including paper and tanneries. Indian tea was still being exported out of Chittagong, but it now had to pay tariff. By 1950, India connected Assam with the rest of India through a 229-kilometre meter-gauge rail link with Siliguri, and Indian tea began to be exported from Calcutta, avoiding East Pakistan completely. These beggar-thy-neighbour policies, of imposing costs on the neighbour, may have suited Pakistan's strategic goals when seen from Karachi, Rawalpindi or Lahore, but the cities that felt the pain were Dacca and Chittagong. The disruption would, over time, contribute to industrial unrest in West Bengal. There were instances of peasant uprisings and urban strife in the state, and in the longer term it led to capital flight and industrial decline.

One economist who challenged the West Pakistani view was Rehman Sobhan. He proposed a 'two economy policy', which called for completely separate economies with appropriate policies for each wing. It would form the basis of the six-point programme the Awami League unveiled in 1966. Noting that 55 per cent of Pakistan's population was in the east, Sobhan sought greater parity between the regions. Most trade between the two wings was by sea, requiring a journey all the way south and then up north again, covering thousands of additional miles. Air cargo covered barely 1 per cent of trade.

Sobhan noted the geographic differences—the east was riverine, the west was semi-arid. The east was densely populated, with 930 people per square mile, while the west had only 140 people per square mile. Population transfer across regions wasn't an option. For one, the distance was too great, and besides, Bengali-speaking Pakistanis would find themselves in a strange land, if they were moved to Baluch- or Sindhi-speaking parts of West Pakistan. In a paper written in 1962, Sobhan presciently observed: 'Religion is of course a unifying factor and may in some cases exercise a substantial influence on behalf of integration, but it is not certain how far this can counteract economic differences and cultural diversity in other respects.'[61]

What concerned Sobhan was the effect of this disparity on people's incomes. In 1960, he wrote, the per capita income in the east was 213 Pakistani rupees, while in the west it was 305 Pakistani rupees. He conceded that national income accounting in Pakistan still comprised of 'imaginative guesses', but these figures indicated the problem. He pointed out what another economist, S.U. Khan, had shown—that if the two halves started from the same base of 100 in 1951-52 for both the quantity produced and per capita income earned, then by 1958-59, West Pakistan's quantity index had reached 147 while the east was at 110, and West Pakistan's per capita index was at 125, while the east's had shrunk to 96.[62] In other words, over eight years, production in the west had risen by half and income grew by a quarter; the east's production rose by only by a tenth, and income actually declined.

Between 1950 and 1955, the Pakistani government spent 11.29 billion Pakistani rupees in the west, but in the east, only 5.24 billion Pakistani rupees were spent—roughly two out of three rupees were spent in the west even when nearly three out of five Pakistanis lived in the east. By 1965-70, the share of the west rose to 51.95 billion rupees, growing nearly fivefold; the share of the east rose to 21.41 billion rupees, growing fourfold. And in proportionate terms, the west commanded 71 per cent of the resources, while the east had 29 per cent—slower growth, lower share.[63]

Sobhan proposed greater investment in East Pakistan as well as more technical assistance and foreign aid. He was providing an economic rationale in a sober tone compared to what Mandal wrote to Liaquat Ali Khan a decade earlier: 'East Bengal has been transformed into a colony of the western belt of Pakistan... It is a pale ineffective adjunct of Karachi doing the latter's bidding and carrying out its orders. East Bengal Muslims in their enthusiasm wanted bread and they have by the mysterious working of the Islamic State and the Shariat got stone instead from the arid deserts of Sind and the Punjab.'

Perceptions of economic exploitation, if left unaddressed, can rapidly develop into demand for political independence. Many Bengalis in the east felt that their province was being treated as a colony by West Pakistan. In 1901, Dadabhai Naoroji wrote *Poverty and Un-British Rule in India*, which analyzed in great detail India's economic flows and found that the principal cause of its poverty was the enormous drain on India's wealth. Sobhan's economic arguments were making a similar point about Pakistan's exploitation of its eastern wing.

There had been a subtle change by the early 1960s, however. While it is true that in the first fifteen years of Pakistan's existence West Pakistan exploited its eastern wing, by some accounts, by the early 1960s, the east was becoming a drain on the economy. In late 1970, Wolfgang-Peter Zingel was part of a team of economists working under Winfried von Urff to plan German development assistance to Pakistan. Zingel is a development economist at the South Asia Institute at the Heidelberg University in Germany, and he has studied the economic figures of those years closely. I met him in the summer of 2013 in that philosophers' town where Allama Iqbal, the spiritual inspiration of Pakistan had once studied. Zingel told me that in the 1950s West Pakistan used to import almost twice as much as what it exported, and received two-thirds of aid (net capital imports), whereas East Pakistan ran a trade surplus, but received only one-third of aid. There was a substantial transfer of resources from the poorer eastern wing to the richer and more developed western wing. By 1960s, the eastern wing had begun to fall into deficit. The east was now importing more than it exported. While its trade balance was still healthier than the west's, it had gone negative. And the net inflow of resources from the east to the west had begun to decline. Zingel concluded that in the 1950s East Pakistan was the major foreign exchange earner for the country but received little aid. The following decade, East Pakistan's deficit started to mount, and its grievance with the west became different: it was less about unfair distribution of foreign exchange, and more about unfair terms of trade within the two wings. 'The idea that East Pakistan was becoming dispensable, or even a burden has to be understood in strictly economic terms,' Zingel said. 'By late 1960s, East Pakistan's usefulness as a foreign exchange earner for the west was becoming less. If East Pakistan had received a share in aid equivalent to its share of total population, or to the extent of its poverty, there would have been no transfer of resources from east to west. One could therefore say that East Pakistan had outlived its usefulness as a provider of resources and was even becoming a dispensable liability. I have found no reference that any politician has said that openly. But once the civil war began, East Pakistan was no longer treated as a valuable asset that had to be saved, but rather as one that could be disposed of.' Zingel's intriguing and thought-provoking, though tentative conclusion is that by 1970, East Pakistan was becoming a burden for West Pakistan, and possibly dispensable, although it is a point that no nationalist Pakistani concedes and no patriotic Bangladeshi accepts. [64]

Thoughtful economic analysis was far from the minds of Pakistani leaders who saw the east's demands entirely in political terms, threatening their leadership and power. Their response was brutal, but driven primarily by their desire to consolidate their power.

It is in that environment that the Awami League launched a movement whose inevitable consequence would be the war of independence. Few in 1966 could have predicted that outcome, when the Awami League declared its six-point charter of demands. But sustained economic exploitation, restrictions on trade with India, and the lack of federal interest in protecting the eastern frontier during the 1965 war with India convinced the Awami League to take drastic measures. Emboldened by the analysis of economists like Sobhan, stung by the humiliating treatment meted out to the Bengali language, noticing the economic decline that new restrictions in trade with India placed on the east, and resenting the second-class treatment Bengalis faced from the federal government, the Awami League unveiled its six demands. If those demands were met, they said, the east and the west could live with peace and respect. If not, they would agitate for greater autonomy and freedom. The word 'independence' was not used, but looking at the six points it was clear that unless the federal government was able to address the demands with enlightened concern for all citizens and not its own interests, it would see it as a challenge to its authority and react with force. The six points were:

- The Pakistan federation should be based on the spirit of the Lahore Resolution of 1940 with a parliamentary government with a supreme legislature elected based on universal adult franchise.
- The federal government should deal only with defence and foreign affairs.

- There should be two separate, freely-convertible currencies for the two wings of Pakistan. If that was not found to be feasible, there could be one currency for the whole country, but there should be effective constitutional provisions to stop the flight of capital from the east to the west. There should be a separate banking reserve with separate fiscal and monetary policy for the east.
- Each unit—state or province—should have its own taxation and revenue collection regimes, and the federal government would have no power to tax. It would get a share of state revenues to pay for its expenditure.
- Each wing would have its own separate account of foreign exchange, and the federal government would get its share by an agreed formula. Products should move freely between the two wings and each wing could forge independent trading links with foreign countries.
- The east would have a separate militia or paramilitary force.

It is easy to see where the six points came from—perceptions of humiliation, distrust, and resentment. Hard data convinced Bengali economists that their land was being exploited. They wanted control over their finances and a greater share of federal resources. They wanted to pursue economic independence and have autonomous trading relationship even with foreign countries—while not specified, this probably meant India. They wanted to reduce federal power to the bare minimum, and they wanted their own armed forces to defend themselves. It came as close to a charter of demand for independence as possible. Unsurprisingly, the Pakistani government reacted angrily.

As the Awami League began agitating for the acceptance of its six demands, the Pakistani government looked for ways to curb nascent Bengali nationalism. It got its opportunity in the Agartala Shorojontro Mamala or the Agartala Conspiracy Case. The federal government claimed that the Awami League leader Mujibur Rahman was a leader of a conspiracy to start an armed insurrection against Pakistan to liberate Bangladesh. A Pakistani intelligence officer, Lt. Col. Shamsul Alam, got wind of the conspiracy and suspected that one of his officers, Raufur Rahman, who was in the East Bengal Regiment, was involved with the plot. The government claimed that two of Mujib's co-conspirators had met Indian military officials in Agartala in the Indian state of Tripura which borders East Pakistan.

In January 1968 the federal government arrested eight people. On 18 January, more people were charged with sedition, including Sheikh Mujib, who was arrested earlier in May 1966. The government initially wanted to court-martial the defendants. But as national elections were due in late 1970, and as the date got closer, the government decided to have an open civil trial. The trial began on 19 June and the government produced evidence. Of the three judges, two were Bengali. The attorney general led the prosecution. A British lawyer, Thomas Williams, was defending Mujib.

The trial unravelled surprisingly quickly. Some state witnesses recanted their statements, saying that the evidence was gathered from them under coercion. Most Bengalis had long believed that the case was a conspiracy itself, to discredit the Awami League and its leadership, in particular to prove that Mujib was a separatist and 'an Indian agent'. There were processions demanding the release of the accused in East Pakistan. The court announced the date of judgment for 6 February 1969. But unrest had spread by then, forcing the government to delay the judgment.

On 15 February, a Pakistani guard went to the cell of a Bengali man who was accused in the conspiracy and shot him. That incident became the turning point. A violent mob set government buildings afire, destroying many important case papers. In the chaos that followed, the local administration panicked. A week later the case was withdrawn. The accused were released and on 23 February at the Race Course Maidan tens of thousands of people turned up to applaud the accused. Sheikh Mujib was given a hero's welcome as he emerged. People garlanded him and he waved to the crowds. On that day he was given the title Bangabandhu (friend of Bengalis), formally anointing him as the leader of Bengalis. To the international media, Mujib said he was the moral and legal leader of the Bengali nation. Seventy million people were behind him, and they could take on the army, he said confidently.[65]

Within a month, Ayub Khan was forced out of office in Pakistan, replaced by Gen. Yahya Khan as the new president. Elections would be held as planned in 1970, Yahya had announced. And so the stage was set for the confrontation between the Sandhurst-trained general and the pipe-smoking former student leader, now catapulted into national leadership.

THREE

THE MAKING OF A SAINT

All the subliminal fears Bengalis had about being part of Pakistan began to come together towards the end of 1970. All those petty indignities of being called rice-eating Bingos; the cultural undermining of being forced to learn Urdu and being stopped from celebrating Tagore or Poyla Baisakh; the visible disparity the Bengalis saw in development and infrastructure between their province and what they saw when they visited West Pakistan; the composition of the bureaucracy, where only a handful of token Bengalis could be seen at senior levels; the contemptuous disregard of the Six-Point demands; and the persecution and prosecution of Mujib and Bengali army officers and civil servants in the Agartala Conspiracy Case, and its subsequent collapse—all these humiliations came together when Cyclone Bhola struck East Pakistan with overwhelming fury on 12 November 1970.

Bhola is regarded as one of the worst natural disasters in history—the deadliest tropical storm of all time. While at landfall it had lost much of its force, at its peak ferocity, winds blew at 185 km/h. The eastern delta is extremely fertile, with major Himalayan rivers adding silt and nutrients to the soil. It was also vastly populated, with people going farther to grow food, even if it meant their small farms were close to the Bay of Bengal. The farm productivity was low and the farms, almost all at sea level, were susceptible to flooding. The jagged coastline let water in much further and deeper than in other littoral areas. Flooding was usually severe, and when storms struck, which was often, fatalities ran into thousands. Given the populous nature of the delta and the lack of advance warning systems, many people died— estimates have ranged between 300,000 to one million.

When Bhola struck East Pakistan, the federal government was found unprepared. Kamal Hossain recounted to me his experience in the aftermath of the cyclone one evening when we met at his home on Bailey Road in Dhaka: 'The cyclone occurred a month before the elections, and it accentuated the sense of deprivation and the centre's insensitivity to the situation on our side. Yahya flew over while returning from his visit to China and did not even stop over. That certainly gave everyone the objective basis about central insensitivity. We [Awami League leaders] went from Dhaka by river with emergency supplies; we were the only ones, besides the Red Cross. The government itself was doing nothing. It was a martial law government, and they were very slow in responding. That also helped in creating a sense that the central government was treating us in a step-motherly way.'

While Sheikh Mujib and Tajuddin Ahmed, the senior Awami League leader, went to the cyclone-affected areas, Hossain himself went along with party workers from Dhaka to different affected areas. 'One of the things you do when you reach the affected areas is to get information about places where nothing has reached. Water was scarce; tubewells had been destroyed, there were floating carcasses in ponds, and so the water was polluted. Homes had been flattened. People tried to save their lives by climbing on trees, and they were badly injured. Their chests were lacerated and limbs were fractured. And there were so many corpses lying everywhere—we had spades and shovels, and we must have buried 20-30 people ourselves. There were scores of corpses all over the coast and in the interior.'

International aid poured in instantly—from traditional donors like the United States, Japan, France, Canada, and what was then West Germany, but also from India. Yahya Khan's own sluggish response contributed to Bengali anger against West Pakistan. They would take revenge a month later, when the elections were called.

◆

Sheikh Mujibur Rahman was born in Tungipara, a small village in Gopalganj district. His father, Sheikh Lutfur Rahman, was an official in the district's civil court. Mujib had a brother and three sisters. He was physically weak as a child, taking two years to complete one year's study in the third grade. He needed eye surgery and missed four years of schooling during his recovery. He was married at eighteen.

In 1940 he joined the All-India Muslim Students' Federation. He decided to study law at the Islamia College, now known as Maulana Azad College, at the University of Calcutta, but he was quickly drawn into politics. Photographs of him at that time show a handsome, tall man with a thin moustache and hair combed back, revealing a large forehead. His eyes look sharp in those images, and he wears the attire that became his uniform for life—white kurta-pyjamas with a black sleeveless, unbuttoned waistcoat. In 1943, he became close to Suhrawardy, the rising star of Bengal politics. He joined the movement to carve out Pakistan from India. He was with Suhrawardy during the Calcutta riots of 1946. On Direct Action Day, Mujib unfurled the Pakistani flag. In 1986, when I had spoken to Farooq Rahman he told me: 'Mujib was a student leader in Calcutta under Suhrawardy. And Suhrawardy, for all his leadership, basically believed in muscle power. He was perhaps the person most responsible for the Calcutta riots. And who was by his side? Mujib. He was one of the people going around inciting people. He was basically a goonda. He did not even pass his exams—he was a third-class student. He continued the same traditions in the Awami League.' (In his memoir, Mujib writes about being hot-tempered and occasionally beating up student rivals.)

Being one of his assassins, Farooq was hardly an objective source about Mujib, but his chilling remarks about Mujib in the lead-up to India's Partition find some support among other Bangladeshis I spoke to, some among them in prominent positions, who requested anonymity.

In 1947 Mujib moved to Dacca, where he formed the East Pakistan Muslim Students' League at the university. He gained fame and notoriety because of his powerful oratory and access to Suhrawardy. Mujib read about socialism, and began to think that it would offer a solution to mass poverty. But he found his cause in the language movement. When the federal government announced that Urdu would be the sole official language of Pakistan, Mujib was already in jail, but he undertook a hunger strike and goaded other students to protest. He was released but promptly expelled from the university. A year later, he was arrested again for trying to unionize menial and clerical staff at the university.

When Suhrawardy and Maulana Bhashani formed the Awami Muslim League, Mujib joined them, leaving the Muslim League. He set about building the Awami League and was elected to the state legislature in 1954, when the United Front came to power. Under A.K. Fazlul Huq he became a minister, but the federal government soon dismissed Huq's administration. He was later elected to Pakistan's constituent assembly, which called West Pakistan 'One Unit' and renamed East Bengal as East Pakistan; Pakistan was formally declared an Islamic Republic. Mujib challenged[66] these decisions, arguing that ethnic identities should be respected, and the renaming should be decided by a popular vote.

Meanwhile, another coalition government was formed in East Pakistan in 1956, and Mujib became a minister with several portfolios, including industry and labour. But he quit those positions soon to commit himself to developing the party. When Gen. Ayub Khan declared martial law and suspended the Constitution, Mujib was among the first to be arrested, and he stayed in jail till 1961. As soon as he was released, he set about forming the Shadheen Bangla Biplobi Parishad (Free Bengal Revolutionary Council), opposing the military regime. He was back in jail a year later.

Pakistan's experience with short-lived civilian governments had ended in 1958 when Gen. Ayub Khan had seized power. The civilian leader Iskander Mirza had suspended political parties and scrapped the Constitution because of growing unrest and established martial law. He then formed a government which included Gen. Ayub Khan. But Ayub immediately seized power, saying that was the will of the people. From October 1958 to March 1969 Gen. Ayub Khan had ruled Pakistan. Suhrawardy's health weakened after he was removed as Pakistan's prime minister in 1957. He died in Lebanon six years later. But during the early 1960s, one evening in Dacca, Suhrawardy met old friends and allies, and an emotional political discussion followed. One young university student, Sirajul Islam, was also there. Many years later he recalled that evening in a conversation with a friend: 'We were discussing the disparity between the two wings and at one point Mujib said that the secession of the East wing was not a difficult job. He required only a canful of kerosene and a matchbox. When all of us questioned how he would do it, Mujib nonchalantly said he would go to the Kurmitola Airport, splash kerosene on the runway and ignite fire with a matchstick. That would end the bondage between the two wings.'

While Mujib certainly did no such thing, his thinking was clearly influenced by two critical issues—that there was little to unite the two halves of Pakistan; and that tearing apart the link was a simple task, because there were no emotional ties or bonds.

After Suhrawardy's death, Mujib became the head of the Awami League. In the presidential elections that followed, Mujib supported Fatima Jinnah, the dental surgeon and Pakistan's founder Muhammad Ali Jinnah's sister, who was challenging Ayub Khan. She was widely popular, but the electorate wasn't the entire nation; only hand-picked people chosen under Ayub's 'basic democracy' had the right to vote, and an under-resourced Jinnah lost.

After Fatima Jinnah's defeat at the hands of Ayub Khan, some of her former supporters gravitated towards Ayub, and Mujib was forced to rethink his policy of working with other opposition parties. He felt it was diluting his message. A combined opposition does not work because it is too amorphous and divided; the Awami League had to revive itself, he believed. It should work as a party, not as an opposition. Some of his Awami colleagues argued that if all parties decided to revive themselves it would be destructive, but Mujib won the argument.

Mujib was unrepentant after his arrests and release from prison. He said: 'There was a time when all efforts were made to erase the word "Bangla" from this land and its map. The existence of the word "Bangla" was found nowhere except in the term, the Bay of Bengal. I announce today that this land will be called Bangladesh instead of East Pakistan.' For leaders in West Pakistan, that was evidence of Mujib's perfidy and they saw the roots of separatism in his politics.

Student agitations had mounted in West Pakistan with growing frustration over lack of democracy, and by late 1968 Ayub Khan's popularity had all but disappeared. He was forced out of office by next spring and Gen. Yahya Khan had succeeded him. Yahya Khan was not an impressive man. An American diplomat described him as 'short, heavily built and verging on fatness, with black eyebrows and a small, pinched mouth... Yahya was rather proud of his hair. He was known to claim, like Samson, that his strength lay in his hair. His face had begun to reveal the telltale signs of a life of heavy drinking'.[67] Gen. Yahya Khan decided to hold elections in December 1970 and January 1971, the country's first general elections since Independence.

Some 63 per cent of the electorate voted in those elections. The results stunned Pakistan. Mujib had led the Awami League to a resounding victory. In the eastern half of the country, out of the 162 seats at stake, the Awami League had won 160. The western half had 138 seats in Parliament. Awami League did not win any, but with his 159 supporters he had enough numbers to form a government based on simple majority in the house of 300 seats and propel him to prime ministership.

Mujib's main rival was Zulfikar Ali Bhutto, who led the Pakistan People's Party, which had won 81 seats, all in West Pakistan. A barrister who had studied at Berkeley and Oxford, Bhutto had prime ministerial ambitions too. Intelligent and arrogant, he wasn't about to concede defeat to the son of a minor government official from East Pakistan, who had to struggle through his school and college years, missing classes for long periods because of poor health or imprisonment. But it would require more than numerical gymnastics or crafty deal-making to let Bhutto form a government. The PPP had only one elected parliamentarian for every two Mujib's party had. Bhutto found that immensely frustrating. He had run a good campaign. His slogan—roti, kapda aur makaan captured the imagination of the poor throughout the subcontinent. Bhutto thought his slogan would sway the poor masses, which it did in the west. But the people in the east ate rice, not rotis made of wheat; their women preferred saris, not the salwar-kameez; and their homes were made of mud and thatched roofs, not bricks and cement. The food, clothing and shelter that Bhutto had in his mind conjured different images in the east; there, the voters marked their ballot by stamping on the symbol they understood—the Awami League's boat. In a riverine country, the boat connected villages with markets; it offered voters a lifeline.

Nationwide, the Awami League had won two out of every five votes cast—about 13 million out of the 33 million votes at stake. Bhutto's PPP had secured 6 million votes, or about a little less than one in five. Bhutto's irritation with the results was understandable.

Yahya's serious mistake was to ignore these results and somehow try to cobble together a government led by Bhutto, ever the firebrand populist. Bhutto probably blamed Kamal Hossain, the Bengali lawyer who advised Mujib on the Awami League's negotiation strategy. Bhutto had lobbied hard with Yahya Khan to maintain a parity in the national assembly, so that the east and the west would send the same number of elected representatives. But the Awami League had insisted on one-person-one-vote, which ensured that the east would have more seats in the assembly than the west. Bhutto would have to ensure that nobody swept the poll in the east, for only then could he form a government, since the PPP's strength was primarily in the less populous west. But that's just what happened, when the Awami League won all but two seats in the east.

Whichever way Bhutto looked—by the rules of the game, by law, and by right—the Awami League had won the elections. Mujib was expecting a call from Gen. Yahya Khan, the president, inviting him to form the government. Like other political leaders from the east, Mujib had every reason to be wary of the west. There had been three eastern prime ministers in Pakistan's past, but none was elected (they were all appointed), and West Pakistani elite and generals had ensured that each was ousted unceremoniously within a couple of years of their appointment.

Mujib's victory upset many calculations. Pakistani generals had an ally in Bhutto, who was keen to become the first elected prime minister of Pakistan, and he was not alone in trying to prevent Mujib from coming to power. The generals too did not think much of East Pakistanis. Bhutto reportedly told Yahya that his political skills and Yahya's control over the army made them a formidable combination.[68] One by one, political parties dominant in the west too agreed with Bhutto, saying that a party like Awami League which had no presence in the west could not really run the country, even though those western parties had failed to win a single seat in the east. In remarks ascribed to him, Bhutto said: 'Udhar tum, idhar ham', (you are there; we are here), drawing a clear boundary between the two halves. In an interview in 2004, Gen. Amir Abdullah Khan Niazi, who commanded Pakistani forces in East Pakistan (and who surrendered to India in 1971) said: 'Bhutto's fiery speeches were not mere rhetoric, but the actions of a desperate man vying for power at any cost. Had power been transferred to Mujib, Pakistan would have remained united.' His regret was that Bhutto was absolved of all blame, he said.[69] A retired air chief marshal who later turned politician, Asghar Khan, wrote in his memoir that when Yahya asked Bhutto what he intended to do about East Pakistan, Bhutto replied: 'East Pakistan is no problem. We will have to kill some 20,000 people there and all will be well.'[70]

◆

The overwhelming electoral victory of the Awami League had belied the expectations of Gen. Yahya Khan who admitted to US Secretary of State Henry Kissinger that the regime had not expected such an overwhelming majority for the Awami League and had been led to believe that the vote in East Pakistan would be divided amongst several parties. Gen. Yahya visited Dacca in January 1971 to negotiate an understanding on the Six Points with Sheikh Mujib, even to the extent of offering him the prime ministership of Pakistan. Bhutto was opposed to such an understanding and he said that the Six Points formula was unacceptable. Mujib wanted the national assembly to meet on 15 February. On Bhutto's insistence, the date was shifted to 3 March. Bhutto arrived in Dacca in February and met Mujib, but was not prepared to engage in serious discussions on the Six Points. Once back in Karachi, Bhutto told his MPs not to go to Dacca. Members of Parliament elected from some of the political parties in West Pakistan did not agree and came to Dacca. Bhutto now threatened mass agitation if the assembly met on 3 March, and his browbeating worked (privately Bhutto was reported to have said he'd break the legs of anyone who went to Dacca). Gen. Yahya Khan cancelled that session.

The atmosphere was tense. In Dacca, Sheikh Mujib sent Kamal Hossain to meet Vice-Admiral Syed Mohammad Ahsan, who was then the governor of East Pakistan. Hossain told Ahsan that any postponement would be dangerous as it would confirm the worst apprehensions in the east that the west didn't want to give up power. This would have grave implications. 'Can you please inform Yahya?' Hossain asked the governor.

Ahsan rang Yahya's military secretary to speak to the president. But he could not get through. After several delays, he was able to connect with Yahya's secretary, who told him that the president was in a meeting and could not talk. 'What's the point of my being the governor if I can't speak to the president?' was Ahsan's exasperated reaction. When Hossain informed Sheikh Mujib about Ahsan's reaction, Mujib told Hossain to urge Ahsan to stay.

But by the time Hossain returned home, Ahsan was relieved of his governorship. He was replaced several days later by Gen. Tikka Khan. 'That gave us an indication of where things were moving,' Hossain said. Tikka Khan was known to be a ruthless general notorious for having used brute force in Balochistan.

The worst fears were confirmed when around 1 p.m. there was an abrupt radio announcement that the Assembly session that was to commence on 3 March was postponed *sine die*. The Awami leaders called a press conference at Hotel Purbani immediately after the announcement.

A cricket match was going on between the visiting Commonwealth XI against a Pakistani team. While Pakistan had played test cricket since the 1950s, most of its players came from West Pakistan. Cricket was not hugely popular in East Pakistan, and big matches of the kind being played in Dacca in early 1971 were rather rare. The predominantly young and male audience at the match was not in a good mood because of the political developments, and as the match progressed, people had started to leave. The drama at Purbani International Hotel was more interesting and exciting for the people in the stadium. They began to move towards the hotel where Sheikh Mujib was expected to make an important announcement at the press conference. The match was disrupted.

Sheikh Mujib said: 'This shall not go unchallenged. We are calling on the people to join a non-cooperation movement. We are elected, that government has no legitimacy. They have to hand over power to us, and everyone in Bangladesh should withdraw any form of cooperation with the government.' Offices, courts, schools, railways, banks—everything should close, he said. And they did. The chief justice refused to administer the oath of office to Tikka Khan, who wanted to assume the role of governor. Bank workers refused to let West Pakistanis withdraw money from their accounts. Over in Chittagong at the port, workers in the docks refused to load goods unless there were guarantees that the money would be repatriated to East Pakistan, and not deposited in banks in Karachi. An Esso facility in Chittagong refused to allow a Pakistani naval ship bunkering facilities because workers had threatened to destroy the facilities if the ship were allowed to dock. Esso then issued instructions to its staff not to fuel the military, although it would not stop the military from taking fuel supplies.[71] There were no fresh vegetables in the military cantonment. Banks would not honour cantonment cheques.

Thousands now protested on the streets—violence erupted in Dacca, Chittagong, Rangpur, Comilla, Rajshahi, Sylhet, and Khulna. Bengalis began hoisting the flag of an independent Bangladesh. Students—men and women— began marching through the streets carrying rifles. Pakistan tried much to portray the students as anti-national agents supported by external forces, but the reality was more mundane. While some adventurous young men had collected a few arms, the majority of the students had no access to weaponry. Students were worried about a potential attack from the army. The university had an officers' training course, which lasted about four months. As part of that course, the students were given dummy rifles which looked real.

There was a huge stockpile of such rifles at one of the colleges. Mahfuz Anam was the general secretary of the students' union and his brother had a car, so one night the students went to the college, broke the locks, and took hundreds of dummy rifles with them. The students marched with those rifles. 'Some of the most famous pictures show students marching with those dummy rifles that we stole from the campus,' Anam remembers.

People across the country were appealing to Mujib to declare independence. He began collecting his thoughts about what he should tell his people. And so, expectations were high when Mujib called a rally at the Race Course ground on 7 March.

◆

When Sheikh Mujibur Rahman reached the stage at the vast Ramna Race

Course on 7 March 1971, he was aware of the enormous expectations he was carrying. The Race Course was Dacca's biggest ground. He would have to describe to the people how the relations between the two halves of Pakistan had reached a historic low. The elite who ruled in the west were trying their best to avoid handing over power to Mujib's Awami League, which had won an outright victory in parliamentary elections. And the east was still recovering from a devastating cyclone, and stunned by the apathy the west had shown in response. Mujib was the man who led the Awami League; it was to him that the Bengalis had turned. He had to rise to the occasion.

Mujib could see people for miles, whichever way he looked. It seemed as if the entire country had come that afternoon to the grounds to listen to him. Subsequent estimates say there were between one million and two million people there, many of them anticipating that he would declare that they were now free, and their country would be called Bangladesh.

Mujib had a delicate task ahead. Mahfuz Anam vividly remembers Mujib's rally. 'Quite literally, a million people came to the race course,' he recalls. Anam had reached the venue early because he knew it would get packed by the afternoon. By 2, it was filled to the brim and the mood was festive. Many expected that Mujib would declare independence that day.

Mujib was late by twenty-five minutes.[72] He looked thinner; some said he was under so much pressure that he was losing weight. As he spoke, his voice rose, expressing his anger. It reached its crescendo and the audience began to cheer him. He then modulated his voice, bringing it down, slowing the pace to make an emotional point, when describing his helplessness. And then he would gradually raise the volume, shifting the pitch, making the delivery faster as he extended his sentences, making them longer, the crowds awaiting the punch line.

As he began speaking, he recalled the history of Bengali nationalism since Pakistan became independent. He spoke of the language movement of 1952, the United Front government of 1954 of which he was a part, and the military crackdown of 1958 across the country when Ayub Khan took over the country. He built the tempo by reminding the crowd of the Six-Point Movement of 1966, and the deaths that followed. When Yahya Khan took over from Ayub Khan in 1969, Mujib hoped for a new beginning. But even after winning the elections, he was made to wait. New rules were being written and new terms were being imposed to delay the possibility of an elected Bengali prime minister.

Mujib appealed to the emotions of his audience by repeatedly referring to the sacrifices the young had made by shedding their blood and the violence they faced. The streets were 'spattered with blood' of the students. He castigated Yahya Khan because 'he turned his guns on my helpless people, a people with no arms to defend themselves. These were the same arms that had been purchased with our own money to protect us from external enemies. But it is my own people who are being fired upon today.... How can you make your own brothers the target of your bullets?' he asked. The crowd roared in approval.

Instead of agreeing to go to West Pakistan for a round table conference, Mujib asked Yahya: 'Come to Dacca, come and see how our poor Bengali people have been mown down by your bullets, how the laps of our mothers and sisters have been robbed and left empty and bereft, how many helpless people have been slaughtered. Come, I said, come and see for yourself and then be the judge and decide... What round table conference, whose round table conference? You expect me to sit at a round table conference with the very same people who have emptied the laps of my mothers and sisters?... We face their guns, yet it is our fault. We are the ones being hit by their bullets—and it is still our fault!' The applause was now deafening.

Martial law had to be withdrawn, soldiers must return to their barracks, and the killers of students and activists had to be tried. 'Mujibur Rahman refuses to walk to the assembly treading upon the fresh stains of his brothers' blood!' he thundered.

And then he laid out his plans for the non-cooperation movement: everything had to close—courts, offices, and educational institutions. Rickshaws, trains and other means of public transport, on which the poor were dependent, would not be pressurized to close early. Banks could stay open for two hours daily to facilitate business transactions. But no money would move from East Pakistan to West Pakistan; telegraph and telephone communications were to be allowed only within East Pakistan. Raising an alarmist spectre, he said: 'The people of this land are facing elimination, so be on guard.'

Lifting his voice, Mujib said: 'If the salaries are held up, if a single bullet is fired upon us henceforth, if the murder of my people does not cease, I call upon you to turn every home into a fortress against their onslaught. Use whatever you can put your hands on to confront this enemy. Every last road must be blocked. We will deprive them of food, we will deprive them of water. Even if I am not around to give you the orders, and if my associates are also not to be found, I ask you to continue your movement unabated. The Bengali people have learned how to die for a cause and you will not be able to bring them under your yoke of suppression.' He asked government employees to follow his directives, not those of their superiors, and implored them not to attend offices. He told the people not to pay any more taxes. He warned them that enemies had penetrated their ranks. He asked the people not to listen anymore to state-run radio or television, nor read the papers, if they did not report news about 'our movement'. And in the clearest indication of the inclusive, secular nature of his movement, he said: 'Whether Bengali or non-Bengali, Hindu or Muslim, all are our brothers and it is our responsibility to ensure their safety.'

He extended an olive branch. 'Let us settle our differences peacefully and then we can coexist as brothers. But if you choose the other path, we may never come face to face again,' he remarked. 'Give up any thoughts of enslaving this country under military rule again.' He then called upon the people to join committees at the village level and prepare themselves with what little they had for the struggle ahead.

'Since we have given blood, we will give more of it, but inshallah, we will free the people of this land,' he said, his voice getting drowned by the cheers. 'Ebarer shongram amader muktir shongram... Ebarer shongram, shadhinotar shongram (this time, the struggle is for our liberation; this fight is for our freedom),' he said.

'Joy Bangla,' the crowd erupted, the applause reverberated, emotions soared; to many, a new nation was born all but in name.

Khurshid Alam, who is a director at a policy institute in Chittagong, was a student of statistics at Dacca University in 1971. Alam too had gone to the Race Course to listen to Mujib speak. He remembers the mood being peaceful and expectant that day. Mujib looked physically weak, he recalls. 'We were waiting to hear the declaration of independence. Everyone expected that something would be declared—but what, nobody knew. When he said those words—ebarer shongram muktir shongram—my first thought was that this would lead to big trouble for us in Bangladesh.'

His elder sister Lulu's two daughters were also university students, studying pharmacy and biochemistry. He was worried about them. When he got home he warned his sister that there would be severe problems after Mujib's speech. The next day, Lulu decided to leave with her two daughters to Bagerhat, a sub-division close to Khulna. As they left Dacca, they could hear Mujib's words everywhere, broadcast through loudspeakers, on the radio. At mosques, the maulvis too warned young people to stay out of trouble. Even water launches in the rivers were playing Mujib's speech. 'We heard it again and again, and everyone thought there would be big problems,' he remembers.

Mahfuz Anam has written about the rhetorical power of that speech. 'It was extempore, but it is a classic in oratory,' Anam says. 'In terms of speech and its delivery—content, diction, flow, the pitch, and how it went up and down, the way he used symbolism…it was magnificent. He said everything that had to be said without using the word "independence". Some people felt let down, because they wanted him to declare independence. But I thought it was wiser not to declare independence. There were no preparations for it. Pakistan wanted a provocation, and if there were to be a unilateral declaration of independence, we'd be called traitors. If Mujib had declared independence, mass backlash from Pakistan would have followed.'

Mujib was probably wise in not declaring independence. Before reaching the Race Course on 7 March, Mujib had met the United States ambassador that morning, and he was told that if he declared independence, the US would not back him. The Chinese too did not support any separatist idea.[73] Anisuzzaman told me: 'He knew that the time was not right. He had to weigh many factors. His people wanted him to declare independence. He wanted to go as close as he could to that sentiment without using the word "independence". And that's why in his speech he spoke of mukti which can mean liberation, and shadhinota which means freedom.'

Sultana Kamal was also at the Race Course and heard Mujib speak. She recalled: 'We don't know the extent to which he was contemplating declaring freedom. People had chosen him as their leader. Was he keen to take the final step, or was he being pushed by the people? Looking back, he was wise in not declaring independence in the Race Course meeting. Otherwise we would have all been called secessionists, and we would have lost a lot of support, particularly internationally. The integrity of the country and his movement would have been the issue. We didn't know what others would say; we didn't know what India would do. So he did not declare independence.'

The dilemma that Mujib had was a simple one—what would happen after he declared independence? He had won a sensational electoral victory, but would all the people support him in a move to create a new country?

He commanded no troops, and administering and managing a country the size of Bangladesh would have been a complex task. And what if Pakistan rejected the demand flat out, as it had with his demands for more autonomy?

Those who have known Mujib believe he wanted Pakistan to make the first offensive move. What he had not calculated was how brutal that move would be. Mujib was sailing his boat very close to the wind. The waters were buoyant and the territory uncharted.

FOUR

THE NIGHT THE KILLINGS BEGAN

A round midnight on 25 March in Dacca, in a four-room apartment in a university building numbered 34 on Secretariat Road, Jyotirmoy Guhathakurta, a reader in English literature at Dacca University, was quietly correcting examination papers at his desk. Guhathakurta was a scholar who had researched the myths in the plays of A.C. Swinburne, Robert Bridges, Thomas Sturge Moore and T.S. Eliot when he studied at King's College in London, and he was popular with his students.

The campus was closed, as were schools and colleges, in response to the call for non-cooperation that Mujibur Rahman had issued on 7 March. Strikes in Bengal inevitably brought much of public life to a standstill. But students' examination papers could be marked from home, while many of Guhathakurta's students were probably busy demonstrating. Guhathakurta diligently marked their papers so that they wouldn't end up without results, if the strikes went on for too long. The professor's 15-year-old daughter Meghna was worried that her father would get arrested. They had been warned.

On that night they could see the sky being lit up and heard loud sounds of explosions. They could also hear occasional screams. The roads seemed to tremble under the rumble of the army trucks. One convoy stopped at their building.

In a few minutes soldiers began banging the doors. The Guhathakurtas lived on the ground floor. One officer and two soldiers entered their apartment through the back garden. The officer asked in Urdu: 'Where is the professor?' Basanti Guhathakurta, the professor's wife,[74] asked the officer why he wanted to meet her husband. The officer said they had come to take him away.

'Where?' Basanti asked. The officer did not reply.

Basanti called her husband. The officer asked him if he was Professor Guhathakurta. When the professor said yes, the officer said: 'We have come to take you.'

Meghna is now executive director at Research Initiatives Bangladesh, a development think tank. She is an academic who has headed the department of international relations at Dhaka University in the past. She recalled seeing people being brought down: 'One other professor, along with his family members, was being brought down. The families tried to hold them or go with them, but we told them—"let them go, otherwise they will shoot you". We turned around and went back to our homes. But then we heard the firing of guns.'

Meghna and her mother rushed out to see what had happened. Other families had come down too. 'And we saw all of them lying in a pool of blood,' she said in a calm voice, recounting a story she has told often. 'Some were shouting for water. We rushed out to the front of our compound. I saw my father lying on the ground. He was fully conscious. He told me they had asked him his name and his religion. He said he was a Hindu, and they gave orders to shoot him. My father was hit by bullets in his neck, his waist, and he could not move. It left him paralysed. The soldiers had run away. We took my father into the house. We could not take him to the hospital because there was a curfew.'

He remained in pain, and they could only take him to the hospital on 27 March, when the curfew was lifted. He died three days later.

Today, the residential complex is a quiet academic compound with mosquito nets covering the windows of the flats and dahlias growing in the garden. There is little to show the violence that occurred four decades ago at the spot itself—a guava tree stands where Guhathakurta was shot. But he is not forgotten, there is a commemorative sculpture by Hamiduzzaman Khan that shows a red flame rising upwards, below which is a list of names of the professors who lived there and were killed that night. Besides Guhathakurta, the eminent philosopher Gobind Chandra Dev, the statistician Maniruzzaman, and three other family members.

Guhathakurta was among the first victims of Operation Searchlight, as the Pakistani officials called the crackdown in East Pakistan on 25 March. Two days earlier, rumours had been circulating in Dacca that the talks between Mujibur Rahman and Yahya Khan were breaking down. It was a very tense period in the city. Shops, schools, banks, courts, and offices were closed. People had stopped paying taxes. West Pakistanis living in the east found that they could not withdraw any money from their bank accounts. Cheques issued by the cantonment were no longer being honoured.

Students continued to march, without talking of freedom or independence overtly, shouting the nationalist slogans like 'Padma, Meghna, Jamuna, tomar amar thikana' (Padma, Meghna, Jamuna are your home and my home). [75]

While Yahya Khan and Zulfikar Ali Bhutto had visited Dacca and carried on the ritual of talks with Mujib, something more sinister was afoot. Tikka Khan had taken over as the governor of East Pakistan. Many Bangladeshis remember planeloads of young men arriving on flights from the west. Nobody knew who they were or why they were coming. They were military men but they did not carry any weapons. Flights arriving from the west had increased significantly—ten to twenty a day, from one or two a day from Karachi, and each flight was full of these young men in plainclothes. A Japanese diplomat in Karachi also noted that some cargo ships heading for Dacca were carrying soldiers. Meanwhile, Pakistan's navy was shipping weapons through the Chittagong port, keeping Bengali officers in the dark, and secretly arming the men who had landed in Dacca.

Before Martial Law was declared in March 1969, Pakistan had stationed one division, three infantry brigades, and an armoured cavalry with amphibious tanks, amounting to some 14,500 troops in East Pakistan. The air force had one fighter squadron with sixteen aircraft. The navy in Chittagong had two or three patrol boats and a couple of support ships—the air and naval wings adding another 1,000 men. But since March 1969, Pakistan had been slowly increasing its troops in the east. The total strength in March 1971 had risen to about 25,000, according to US Consulate estimates of that time.

Besides the headquarters in Dacca, there was the 14th Infantry Division and 57th Infantry Brigade in Dacca, and 23rd Infantry Brigade in Rangpur, 53rd Infantry Brigade in Comilla, 107th Infantry Brigade in Jessore, and special services in Chittagong and Comilla. There were thirteen wings of East Pakistan Rifles with about 13,000 men, although West Pakistani officers questioned their utility and loyalty to a united Pakistan.

Pakistan's ability to airlift troops had been hampered significantly because India had imposed flight restrictions on Pakistani aircraft, preventing them from flying over India. The Indian decision followed an incident in January 1971 where Kashmiri separatists had hijacked an Indian civilian aircraft to Pakistan and set it afire after all passengers were released. Pakistani flights now had to go south to Ceylon (as Sri Lanka was then called) and then north again, doubling the 2,300 kilometre direct journey. Many planes had to land and refuel in Colombo, the capital of Ceylon, with the flying time averaging between five hours for a civilian Boeing 707 to eleven hours for a military transporter.

Things had turned worse after mid-March. Until then, the Awami League leaders had been negotiating the modality of future governance almost daily with government representatives. But on 21 March, the economists who were negotiating with the Awami League economists had returned to West Pakistan. Students shouted slogans—shashak goshti khotom koro, Bangladesh shadheen karo (End the ruling class, make Bangladesh free). On 23 March, which happened to be Pakistan Day, hundreds of homes in Dacca unfurled the new Bangladesh flag from their rooftops. Many of these flags were home-made, although Bhutto was to claim later that they were made in India and smuggled into East Pakistan. Farhad Ghuznavi, who headed the British multinational company Imperial Chemical Industries' subsidiary, the ICI Pakistan Group Ltd. in Dacca, lived in Banani and had a Bangladesh flag flying from his roof. At 4 p.m. on 27 March five or six soldiers accompanied by an army officer came to his house. They called him out and asked: 'Woh kya hai?' pointing at the flag.

'Nishan,' Ghuznavi said.

'Utaro!,' they commanded.

Realizing that Ghuznavi was a well-off professional, the Pakistanis did not harass him, but the flag was brought down and snatched from his hand. 'If looks could kill I'd be dead,' Ghuznavi recalled. A soldier told him: 'Sector Commander ka meherbani; hum agar hoten, tumhe goli mar dete. Pakistan ka ek hi nishan hai. Marzi ho to woh urao,' saying he should thank the sector commander, otherwise he'd have been shot. Pakistan has only one symbol—if you want, fly that flag.

In a class-conscious society, Ghuznavi was not used to being shouted at or treated shabbily, but he began facing frequent petty humiliations, as soldiers would stop his car to ask if he was 'Bangali or Mussalman?' 'In the end, one was what one was—a Bengali,' Ghuznavi told me when we met at his home in Baridhara, an upscale Dhaka suburb where many diplomats now live.

The new Bangladesh flags were everywhere—all fluttering gaily from mosques, temples, offices, shops, and homes. When the Awami League leaders Syed Nazrul Islam, Tajuddin Ahmed, and Kamal Hossain drove to meet the government negotiators with the Bangladesh flags fluttering on their cars, the government negotiators were upset. Hossain said they had put the flag on their cars to show the intensity of popular emotions. 'Let us resolve this quickly; we should not delay too much,' he told them. The government representatives said they'd meet the next day after some internal discussions. 'We waited. But we also heard tanks were lining up, and the cantonments were being mobilized,' Hossain recalled.

◆

On the morning of 25 March Tajuddin Ahmed told his wife Zohra that he was expecting to leave with Mujibur Rehman because there was an imminent sense that Pakistan was going to use force. They may have to wear disguise and live underground for some time, he told her. He went out and said he would return around 8:30 p.m. They were convinced that the army would act that night. Before the military crackdown around midnight Tajuddin visited Sheikh Mujib in his Dhanmondi house. Hossain along with a colleague Amirul Islam also visited Sheikh Mujib to seek final instructions. When Tajuddin returned home at 10 p.m. he was angry. Mujib had refused to escape; he had told him to leave instead. After some time Kamal Hossain and Amirul Islam came to Tajuddin's house and the three of them left together. On the way, Hossain said he would go to a nearby house of his nephew's, while the other two went off to Lalmatia, near Dhanmondi.

◆

Brigadier Siddiq Salik, who was a senior Pakistani military officer in Dacca, wrote in his book, *Witness to Surrender*, 'The plan for Operation Searchlight visualized the setting up of two headquarters. Major General (Rao) Farman (Ali) with 57 Brigade under Brigadier Arbab, was responsible for operations in Dacca city and its suburbs while Major General Khadim (Hussein) Raja was to look after the rest of the province. In addition Lieutenant General Tikka Khan and his staff were to spend the night at the Martial Law Headquarters in the Second Capital to watch the progress of action in and outside Dacca.'

The first burst of gunfire was heard sometime after 11 p.m. on the night of the 25th, according Mahfuz Anam, who was at that time a 20-year-old honours student of economics at the university. The cannonfire was rapid, followed by other loud sounds. Anam was staying with a friend in Dhanmondi. He was also a member of the central committee of the East Pakistan Students' Union, and general secretary of the students' union hall.

He felt frustrated because he didn't know what was going on. The explosions proved what he had feared—that the Pakistani army had turned on the people it was meant to protect. 'We went to the rooftop and saw that the fire was coming from the university. We saw fires everywhere,' he remembered. It went on the whole night.

Pakistani authorities had long felt that Bengali nationalism was inspired by India. To them, that meant every Hindu was a traitor. Anyone opposing the idea of Pakistan cannot be a true Pakistani, and the one who is not a true Pakistani cannot be a true Muslim either. That made Bengali nationalists who were Muslims also suspect. And, the Pakistani officers believed the Muslim Bengalis behaved the way they did because the wily Hindus encouraged them.

On the night of 25 March, the soldiers had come out with full force—tanks, automatic rifles, rocket launchers, and light machine guns. Among the first targets for the military was Shankhari Bazaar, the Hindu area of old Dacca. Shops were razed, homes burned, and many people killed. Contemporary eyewitness accounts by Americans reported serious shelling and the use of heavy armour and large-scale destruction. Irene Khan, who was a teenager in Dacca during the war, remembers Hindu vegetable sellers who lived near her house in Shantinagar hurrying down the lane and coming to her house and staying with the Khan family until the curfew was over, because the army had arrived and started shooting without warning, killing even the poor who were sleeping on the roads.[76] But the most dramatic assault was on the campus.

The army surrounded the university from all sides. They targeted some of the teachers—Fajilur Rahman and two of his relatives at Nilkhet at Building 23; Anwar Pasha and Rashidul Hassan, who managed to survive as they hid under their beds, but were later found out by the pro-Pakistani Al-Badr militia and killed; geologist Abdul Muktadir at 12 Fuller Road; K.M. Munim at Salimullah Hall; and mathematicians A.R. Khan Khadim and Sharafat Ali at Dacca Hall.

They also went to Jagannath Hall which now has the fading, pale cream-coloured exterior that is all too familiar across the South Asian subcontinent. There is moss on its walls today, and names of random Argentinian and Brazilian footballers, remnants of the rivalries of the last World Cup, are scrawled along the walls. Eyewitnesses who survived have testified that on the day the troops took over the campus, soldiers went from bed to bed beating up students, killing most of them. The next day, Pakistani soldiers asked students to move the bodies of dead students, which many of them did for fear of being killed. Resistance would have been futile, but removing the bodies did not help them either. A grainy video[77] smuggled out of Pakistan shows several students lined up to be shot. One of them, dressed in black, falls to his knees pleading for mercy. The pitiless soldiers shoot all of them.

Soon after the war ended, the Indian film critic Amita Malik was in Bangladesh and came across a twenty-minute film which is very likely the same video, parts of which can be seen on YouTube. That film showed with horrific precision the merciless killing of dozens of students. She wrote:[78] '[The film] first shows small distant figures emerging from the hall carrying the corpses of what must be the students and professors massacred in Jagannath Hall. These are clearly civilian figures in lighter clothes and, at their back, seen strutting arrogantly even at that distance, are darker clad figures, the hoodlums of the Pakistan army. The bodies are laid down in neat, orderly rows by those forced to carry them at gunpoint. Then the same procession troops back to the Hall. All this time, with no other sound, one hears innocent birdsong and a lazy cow is seen grazing on the university lawns. The same civilians come out again and the pile of bodies grows. But after the third grisly trip, the action changes. After the corpses are laid on the ground, the people carrying them are lined up. One of them probably has a pathetic inkling of what is going to happen. He falls on his knees and clings to the legs of the nearest soldier, obviously pleading for mercy. But there is no mercy. One sees guns being pointed, one hears the crackle of gunfire and the lined up figures fall one by one, like the proverbial house of cards or, if you prefer, puppets in a children's film. At this stage, the birdsong suddenly stops. The lazy cow, with calf, careers wildly across the lawn and is joined by a whole herd of cows fleeing in panic. But the last man is still clinging pathetically to the jack-boot of the soldier at the end of the row. The solider then lifts his shoulder at an angle, so that the gun points almost perpendicularly downwards to the man at his feet, and shoots him. The pleading hands unlink from the soldier's legs and another corpse joins the slumped bodies in a row... The soldiers prod each body with their rifles or bayonets to make sure that they are dead. A few who are still wriggling in their death agony are shot twice until they also stop wriggling.'

Malik later tracked down the professor who had filmed the scene, and met him at his home. Professor Nurul Ullah taught engineering at the university. He was looking out of his window from where you could see a street across which were the grounds of Jagannath Hall. He saw soldiers driving towards the entrance to the university. They announced on loudspeakers that people coming out on the streets would be shot. Then Nurul Ullah saw some people carrying out dead bodies from Jagannath Hall. He took out his loaded video tape recorder and began filming through the glass of the window. He saw the people laying down dead bodies on the grass under the supervision of Pakistani soldiers. As soon as firing started, he carefully opened the bedroom window wide enough for him to slip his small microphone just outside the window so that he could record the sound. 'It was very risky,' he told Malik. 'My wife warned me at the time: Are you mad, do you want to get shot too? One flash from your camera and they will kill us too.' But he took no notice and kept filming. 'This macabre procession of students carrying out bodies and laying them down on the ground was repeated until we realized with horror that the same students were themselves being lined up to be shot,' he told her. It continued; a fresh bunch of bodies were brought down; the pile got higher.

Excerpts of Nurul's video showing unarmed students being taken out of hostels and being killed were part of an exceptional 1995 film, *War Crime Files*[79] which was shown on Britain's Channel 4 and won the Best International Current Affairs Award from the Royal Television Society that year. The film exposed how Bengali Islamists who had allegedly collaborated with the Pakistani army during the war had managed to migrate legally to Britain.

◆

Rokeya Hall, the dormitory for women students, was set afire, and students escaping the fire were shot; many died.[80] Archer Blood was the American consul general who was in Dacca during the massacres, and was horrified by what he saw. In one of his despatches he wrote: 'The army plan was to take no prisoners and kill all students in the dorms. We saw traces of two mass graves on the campus, one near Iqbal Hall, one near Rokeya Hall. The rain on the night of 29 March exposed some bodies and the stench was terrible. While some of the students at Iqbal Hall had weapons the army shot in an indiscriminate manner and students were either shot in their rooms or mowed down when they came out of the building in groups. Rokeya Hall, a dormitory for girl students, was set ablaze and the girls were machine-gunned as they fled the building. The attack seemed to be aimed at eliminating the female student leadership since many girl student leaders resided in that hall.'[81]

Kaliranjan Sheel was one of the survivors at Jagannath Hall. He was a student and Communist activist. He vividly recalled that night.[82] He stayed in Jagannath Hall, in Room Number 235. He had returned late on the night of 25 March. He had just fallen off to sleep when he heard loud noises. The rat-tat-tat of machine guns convinced him he was not dreaming. The building was shaking. He crawled behind the low walls of the verandah towards the stairs and climbed up to the third floor. He went looking for his friend Sushil but the room was locked, although there was light inside. 'Who is it,' someone whispered from inside. That voice told him to climb to the roof of the building.

Some students had gathered on the roof to take cover. Kaliranjan discarded his footwear—rubber slippers—and went north instead. He crawled into a toilet whose window was open. From there, he could see the soldiers searching for students and taking them away, towards Shaheed Minar. There, they were shot, their dying screams and the sound of the bullets shattering the silence. Soldiers fired randomly, killing anyone who tried to flee. He could see buildings burning. The army shot flares, illuminating the sky, enabling them to see in the darkness.

Then he saw about fifty soldiers from the direction of Salimullah Hall breaking into the dining hall. They began shooting indiscriminately, and Sheel heard more screams. They forced an attendant to open a locked door and shot more shots; there were more screams, more deaths. Soldiers then entered the building he was in and came to his floor. Sheel remained still, and they left. After a long time, Sheel came out. There was an eerie silence, broken only by some moaning sounds.

At dawn he heard prayers. The soothing sounds felt appropriate. But with sunlight, the military was back, looking for students who had survived, picking them up, and killing them. He could hear announcements of the curfew. He heard voices in a balcony nearby. He thought they were students so he stepped out, but instead he found a soldier pointing a machine gun at him while a few students were carrying a corpse downstairs. They had killed the building's doorkeeper. Sheel carried another corpse and took it down. They brought more bodies down. Then the soldiers asked them to sit down. The military separated the Bengali-speakers from the Urdu-speakers. Some Urdu-speaking sweepers pleaded with the soldiers to let them go.

Sheel and other Bengali speakers were taken to an area where more bodies were lying. They were ordered to move the corpses. There was a huge tree next to the south side of the gate where they started piling up the bodies. They were allowed to rest under the tree after all the bodies were moved. A soldier shared cigarettes with some of the students who had helped move the bodies. The soldiers taunted them and split them into a few groups. Sheel was taken to the building where Dr Guhathakurta stayed. They were taken to the fourth floor, often climbing over dead bodies. The soldiers went through the cupboards and suitcases, looking for valuables. They asked one of the students to climb to the terrace and bring down the black flag and the Bangladeshi flag flying atop the building.

By now Sheel was tired. As he saw a dripping tap, he asked a soldier's permission to drink some water. Instead, he was cursed and told to continue working, or drink the piss the soldier threatened to urinate on his face. Other soldiers were busy helping themselves to anything valuable they could lay their hands on.

Downstairs, the military made a pile of all the black flags and new Bangladesh flags and burned them. The students were told to carry more dead bodies and bring them to another area and form a new pile. Sheel remembers the last body he hauled—it was of Sunil, the gatekeeper. The body was still warm. The military then turned on the sweepers who were summoned from the slums. After they had cleaned the place, they were shot. Sheel realized that they would be shot next. Some of the others were already lined up. One of them was loudly reciting prayers from the Quran, which stopped abruptly when he was shot.

As they walked further, Sheel saw the dead body of Dr Dev, the philosopher. He was wearing a dhoti; his chest mutilated. Sheel dropped Sunil's body there and lay down besides Dr Dev. He was tired and decided to lie down till a bullet ended his misery. He then added: 'At one point I started to wonder maybe they have already killed me and I just don't feel it. I was not in a state to feel anything at the point. I had lost all sense of being. I cannot tell how much time had passed in this stage. I became aware at the sound of women and children crying near my head. Opening my eyes I found the wives and children of the sweepers, gatekeepers and gardeners wailing over the bodies of their husbands, fathers and brothers. I saw Dulal, the youngest son of Goyanath hugging the body of his brother Shankar and crying his heart out. Some of them still had some breath left in their body and they were begging for water. Some were giving them water. I saw one wounded person crawling past the Shaheed Minar dragging himself. I carefully raised my head to look around and found the military trucks were gone. I ducked my head among the grieving women and children and went inside the slum. I first entered the room of the electric worker Chitbali. He was not home. His wife was alone and trembling. When I asked for some water she pointed to a pot, meaning to help myself. I drank some water and thought of hiding behind the pile of dried cow dung piled at the corner of the room. Sensing my intention the woman started screaming in fear, so I had to leave and hid in the latrine at the west end of the slum.'

The sound of firing continued. Fighter planes flew over Dacca. When he left the slum, there were no more military trucks on the road, but he could see the smouldering ruins of slums on either side of the railroad. At the river, a boatman gave him a free ride. On the other side of the river, people badgered him for information about what had happened. Someone he knew spotted him, offered him tea and samosa, and took him to Shimulia. From there he went to Nawabganj, and later to his village in Dhamura in Barisal.

Back in Dacca, another convoy killed the guards protecting the British Council and proceeded towards Shaheed Minar, attacking the monument as well as the Bangla Academy. The army also destroyed two Hindu temples and a Sikh gurdwara.

The Pakistani army later claimed that they were retaliating after they faced a mortar attack from Jagannath Hall. There is little evidence of such an attack from the hall. But even if that were so, the Pakistani response was grossly disproportionate—killing almost all the students, destroying two Hindu colonies, ransacking Shankharipara, and killing, or forcibly removing most of the Hindu population in Narayanganj. Tajuddin Ahmed lived near Shankharipara in old Dacca. His daughter Simeen Hossain Rimi, now a parliamentarian, remembers waking up to the sound of sten guns and the smell of smoke. The sound of gunfire was continuous. She went up to the roof and saw hundreds of homes burning. The next day she heard stories of the army breaking into homes and taking people away. Nearly eighty people had gathered at her aunt's place. They had nowhere to go. There was no food, no power, no water. When the curfew was lifted, her uncle came and picked up Rimi and her sister Sharmeen and took them away. 'We saw dead bodies all along the road,' she told me.

◆

How many died that night? The central problem with the Bangladesh war of liberation is that nobody knows precise numbers. It is possible to know the number of refugees who came to India, because the UN High Commissioner for Refugees kept a detailed record. It is possible to conjecture a range for the number of cases of rape against women, even though women who were raped were unlikely to reveal their identity to social scientists or surveyors and a headcount was impractical. But it is impossible to get a clear idea of the death count. One reason is that in many cases entire families were wiped out. Another is that the country was in a flux, with people leaving cities for villages or for towns near the border, to seek refuge in India. People died in places that were not their hometowns; people changed their identities. There was no administration keeping track of the deaths, and the government itself had no intention of keeping an accurate record. (The Hamoodur Rahman Commission that Pakistan set up after the war claims 26,000 civilians died; Bangladeshis claim 3 million died; other estimates suggest 1.7 million deaths.)[83]

In one of his cables to his superiors in the State Department, the American Consul General Archer Blood wrote: 'From the conversation of military control room and army unit 88, a total of 300 student deaths were estimated.'[84] The dead included students of soil science, physics, mathematics, philosophy, chemistry, and literature. Also dead were members of staff, including gardeners, a pump workman, a gatekeeper, janitors, and spiritual gurus. But it was impossible to estimate the total. Abu Sayeed Chowdhury, who later became Bangladesh's second president, was the vice-chancellor of the university at that time. In March he was in Geneva at a United Nations conference. As soon as he heard about the crackdown on the campus, he resigned and left for London, where he joined the resistance movement.

At the American consulate, Blood had been increasingly dismayed and angry by what he saw. He kept reporting to the State Department: 'Largescale looting, pillaging and murder on part of non-Bengali people against Hindus and Bengalis taking place and Army standing by watching. Last night Hindu village at Dacca Club golf course burned. Twelve bodies seen by American warden.... Local who clears shipments for us told us in tears that Army killed his sister.... Youths (who) went to Mujib's house unarmed "to protect him" were killed by the troops.'[85] Poor Hindu men would get stopped on the footpath and the soldiers would ask them to drop their lungis. If they were not circumcised, they would get killed.

On 18 April, clearly referring to Hindus, Lt. Gen. Tikka Khan, the Military Governor of East Pakistan, said in a radio broadcast: 'The Muslims of East Pakistan, who had played a leading part in the creation of Pakistan, are determined to keep it alive. However, the voice of the vast majority had been suppressed through coercion, threats to life and property by a vocal, violent and aggressive minority, which forced the Awami League to adopt the destructive course.'[86]

Pakistan's intention was that nobody would know what happened that night. But Simon Dring, an enterprising 27-year-old reporter of *The Daily Telegraph* had evaded the round-up of foreign correspondents by hiding on the roof of the InterContinental Hotel and later went around the city to see for himself what the army had done. Two days later he flew out to West Pakistan with his notes hidden in his socks, evading the scrutiny of the security guards who had strip-searched him.

◆

Among the more enduring images from the days before Operation Searchlight is the photograph Rashid Talukder took of young Bengali women marching, carrying rifles. The most prominent face is that of Rokeya Kabir, a young leftist political-science student of Dhaka University who was at the forefront of the movement against martial law. Her father was worried about her conspicuity in the photograph, but also very proud. She told me about her activism when we met at her home in Dhaka, at the end of a quiet street in Banani. She sat on a sofa with a large image of Buddha behind her. There was also a poster of Leonardo da Vinci's *Mona Lisa* and a photograph of Lenin's bust.

Rokeya's father was a well-off farmer in the Netrakona district in the northeast of Bangladesh where she grew up, and the hard lives of sharecroppers had deeply affected her. The family was steeped in revolutionary movements— an uncle of hers had joined Subhas Bose's INA. Of her nine siblings, six were leftist activists.

Rokeya was walking back to the university on 1 March 1971, when Yahya Khan announced that the national assembly would not be summoned. She saw people taking to the streets en masse, agitated. She joined the demonstrators and went to the Palton Stadium area, the only large field where the public was able to gather. Their demand was that Parliament must be convened and power must be transferred to the elected government. 'Otherwise the only alternative left to Bengalis was to fight for liberation,' she said.

Rokeya felt helpless. What were they to do? There was no time to prepare for armed struggle. They had made some preparation and training in arms, but all their marches were with fake rifles. Like other leftists, she did feel confused about the Awami League, which the left saw as a bourgeoise party, and not a revolutionary party, so how would they lead an armed struggle, which needed discipline and dedication?

Classes had stopped and the students were told to leave their halls. She went to her elder brother and stayed with him. Rokeya went to the university daily to attend political meetings that went on from 8 o'clock in the morning till midnight. On 25 March, she heard rumours that there would be a crackdown that night. On her way home, she organized barricades across some streets so that tanks or armoured cars would not be able to go through. 'We had the wishes of the people, but no practical experience, and it was probably childish,' she told me. The students cut trees to make them fall across arterial roads.

By the time she reached her brother's home, she could hear bombardment and saw flashing lights. It went on throughout the night and the next day and night. When the curfew was relaxed on the 27th, she went to the university. The streets were filled with dead bodies. When some of her friends saw her near the medical college, they asked her angrily: 'Are you mad? Roaming around in the city? Go back home; you will be contacted.' She moved to a friend's place, as it was unsafe for her and her brother for her to stay with him. She kept moving from one friend's place to another in those days. On the 29th evening, she got a message that she would be collected the next morning and taken out of the city.

A party activist came to pick her up. They left by a rickshaw for the river and travelled in a ferry. Across, they took more rickshaws and stayed in Gazipur district. Their aim was to reach India. As she travelled through the countryside, she saw many homes burnt to the ground. They did not follow official roads, but went on small roads, forest trails, walking paths, and travelled by small boats. She often hid her face—that photograph of her marching had been seen throughout the country. By mid-April, she reached another river, but heard that the army was on the other side. She contracted smallpox.

A trade union leader came to her with a note from a Communist leader from Dacca saying she should join him. The note said nothing more. There were no names. Rokeya recognized the handwriting, so she trusted the man. They passed different villages and reached Meghna river, and to cross the border, which lay beyond the river, she had to cross the river first, and then get to the road to Agartala.

At the border Indian guards let them in. After days of walking, Rokeya's feet were swollen. She was running a high fever, and had scabs all over her body.

'When I crossed the border into India, I felt very sad. I wondered if I would ever return to my country. I had known how long the Vietnam War went on, how long the struggle against apartheid lasted. I wasn't sure if I would ever see my parents again. Would I be able to complete my education? What if the war went on for another decade? I had left behind everything. I was very weak. I realized the pain refugees experienced at the time of India's partition. I felt acutely the pain of separating from my own country,' she said.

◆

After Kamal Hossain left Tajuddin Ahmed for his nephew's place on the night of 25 March, he moved from house to house, but on 2 April, as he saw the house he was in surrounded by the army, he decided to give up because he did not want bloodshed on his account. The soldiers arrested him but did not assault him. 'We are the military, we have to follow the orders,' they told him. Later, they tried intimidating him by reminding him of the power they had over him. 'If they ask me to kill my mother, I'd do it,' one officer told Hossain. 'They said such things to scare you and impress you,' Hossain said. He was taken to a guesthouse in the cantonment. 'Your leader [Sheikh Mujib] was here; we've taken him to West Pakistan,' they told him.

The next morning, Hossain was taken to the airport. Throughout the ride they kept asking him—where were you and Tajuddin planning to go? The border? Hossain told them he did not know. They had made no plans. They had left for the old town, but beyond that they had no plans, he kept saying. They kept asking him the question again and again. Being a lawyer, Hossain knew one thing—it is always sensible to stick to the same answer. 'If you change your story, they can embarrass you later,' he said.

They flew to Karachi, then to Rawalpindi. Then they were taken in a microbus to a place that he was told was Haripur Central Jail near Abbottabad and Rehana, the birthplace of Ayub Khan, close to the Kashmir border. He was kept in that jail for nine months, in solitary confinement. There were seventeen other cells in one enclosure, but nobody else was there. There was a toilet, a tap with running water. There was a factory outside whose sirens, with their metronomic frequency, indicated to him the passage of time.

Kamal Hossain spent much of the time walking up and down within the enclosure. The guards mainly spoke Pashto, or broken Urdu. They had only a limited way to communicate with Kamal, as did he with them. He asked for a visit from his family, but he was told normal jail rules did not apply to him.

◆

On 26 March, Yahya Khan declared martial law on national radio and said: 'It is the duty of the Pakistani armed forces to ensure the integrity, solidarity and security of Pakistan. I have ordered them to do their duty and fully restore the authority of Government.... I appeal to my countrymen to appreciate the gravity of the situation for which the blame rests entirely on the anti-Pakistan and secessionist elements.'[87]

Dozens of military trucks sped past roads in Dacca, sirens blaring. The soldiers stood in open trucks and looked at the people menacingly, announcing the curfew in Urdu: 'Bahar nahi nikalna; goli mar di jayegi.' Shoot-at-sight orders were imposed. Their announcements were periodically drowned by loud sounds of explosions.

When the curfew was lifted briefly for two hours on the 27th, there was some normalcy, as people tried to repair their lives. As the Guhathakurtas rushed to the hospital so that doctors could treat Jyotirmoy who was fighting for his life, Mahfuz Anam looked desperately for his political contacts, trying to find out who was around and to consider the next steps. Anam went to Shaheed Minar, the meeting ground for politically active students. Along the way he saw the large slum where many people lived beside a railway track. The tracks were blocked, and the slum had been set afire. If people had stayed put in their huts, they had been burned alive; if they came out, the blocks along the tracks prevented them from escaping; and once they were out, they became targets offering shooting practice for the Pakistani troops.

Anam saw bodies everywhere on the street. Some were removed, but plenty remained, still visible, and still bloodied. The dead included young and old, men and women, Muslim and Hindu. Near the slum, there were many dead children, in the area where Kaliranjan Sheel and others had been moving dead bodies.

Anam met a friend who told him to go into hiding. There is no question of getting together and doing anything, he was told. Save yourself, hide. The city was full of wild rumours that the East Pakistan Rifles had already rebelled and their officers had taken control of the barracks. The police had also mutinied. Yahya Khan's martial law, shoot-at-sight orders, curfew: these were real, the idea of an independent Bangladesh? Now that seemed like a distant dream.

That evening, some radio sets were able to hear the faint voice of Major Ziaur Rehman who declared, in the name of Bangabandhu Mujib, that Bangladesh was now a free country. Zia was speaking from a clandestine radio station, called Shadheen Bangla Biplobi Betar Kendra (Free Bengali Revolutionary Radio Station) in Kalurghat, a suburb of Chittagong. Anam said: 'That declaration was a great source of moral support for us and showed great moral courage. It told us that something was happening; that some effort was being made. We didn't know where the declaration came from, but it was important that the declaration was made.'

◆

The radio station at Kalurghat survived for barely a week in its physical form, but it later kept sprouting up from different locations, until it found a permanent home in India. In those early days, it played an extremely important role in keeping the morale high among the bewildered people who had begun to see themselves as Bangladeshis. At a time when they felt leaderless because Mujib had been taken away and Pakistan troops were killing students, academics, children, women, and anyone that got in their way, the radio station stood unbowed, whispering the message to Bengalis that they were not alone; that their language and their songs mattered; that there were warriors out there willing to fight; and that an independent nation was being born.

Kalurghat is a suburb of the southern port city of Chittagong, known for its rebelliousness. In 1930, Surya Sen, a schoolteacher, masterminded a group of young activists to raid the Chittagong armoury, and unfurled the Indian tricolor. He managed to escape, but was betrayed by his host three years later. The British arrested him, and he was tortured and later executed. Nellie Sengupta, an Englishwoman who married an Indian student in Britain and later moved with him to India and joined India's freedom struggle, had lived in Chittagong after India and Pakistan gained independence. The city had its enterprising flair. If Dacca was an establishment city where representatives of the rulers—Calcutta or Delhi—lived, Chittagong had entrepreneurial people who looked beyond the sea for opportunities—being a port, it was more tuned in to interact with the outside world. Chittagong's residents are proud of that heritage.

In late March, *Swat* and *Babur,* two Pakistani naval ships carrying weapons had docked at the port. As they were being emptied, the dockworkers realized what they contained, and refused to unload the weapons. A young man called Haroun along with other students stole some of the weapons. Meanwhile, the workers decided to boycott the ships and surrounded them. Security forces opened fire and several workers died.

Elsewhere in the city, students began to demonstrate. Some activism had turned violent, involving attacks on Urdu-speaking migrants from India, known locally as Biharis. They were suspected of being loyal to Pakistan, and not the emerging nation. Such violence occurred in other parts of the country too. In Chittagong, Bengali-Bihari violence started because there were rumours that the Pakistani forces were arming and training the Biharis to attack Bangladeshi nationalists. Fear gripped the city.

The Chhatra Union, as the Communist students' organization was called, had been busy looting weapons from police stations and the railway station in Chittagong. Together with the weapons from *Swat,* they now had a huge stockpile. They needed a safe place to store the weapons. That night Haroun, the youth leader, brought the weapons to the house of Dr Muhammad Shafi, a prominent local dentist who was married to Mushtari, a 30-year-old feisty woman who wrote for *Bandhabi,* a social affairs magazine, which had taken an increasingly strident anti-government tone particularly after the cyclone. The poet Sufia Kamal also wrote for the magazine. The Shafis agreed to store the weapons, and the weapons were brought in two truckloads at night and kept locked in a large room—'This same room,' Mushtari told me, as we talked in her home. She spread her arms around, indicating where the boxes lay, in a room now full of shields, cups, and awards the dental surgeon had received in his lifetime. In a corner sat the dental chair Dr Shafi used for his practice.

On 26 March, Belal Mohammed from the Chittagong radio station came to see Mushtari. He had sent his family to his village and now wanted to plunge into the liberation movement. He wanted to start a rebel radio station. He had already assembled a fine team of journalists and radio engineers. Would Mushtari join him?

Mushtari immediately agreed. Her role was to compile news from international agencies. They began broadcasting from Kalurghat that evening by first playing the Rabindranath Tagore song, 'Amar Sonar Bangla' (My Golden Bengal) which would become the country's national anthem. The radio station announced itself as Shadheen Bangla Biplobi Betar Kendra. They had a small 10 KW transmitter and operated on short-wave transmission. During its short life, the radio station could be heard not only in Chittagong and parts of Dacca, but also Agartala, and occasionally, in Calcutta. As the Pakistani army had destroyed the radio stations in Dacca and Chittagong, its weak signal was audible from Kalurghat to places far beyond what it would have been capable of otherwise. The station's immediate priority was to declare Bangladesh's independence.

Latifa Siddiqi was married to Mustafizur Rahman Siddiqi, a local Awami League politician better known as M.R. Siddiqi, who was close to Mujib. Latifa was born in Rangoon and her family had moved to Chittagong after the Japanese invasion of Burma during World War II. They were at her father's home on 24 March when their neighbour told them that he had received a message from a trusted source who said that the talks with Yahya Khan had failed and that Mujib had asked people to resist the government and tell the police and the army not to surrender their weapons. M.R. Siddiqi left immediately, realizing that it was time for declaring independence. He asked his wife to be at a safe and secure place. On the morning of the 26th, she got a message from Moinul Alam, a correspondent of the newspaper *Ittefaq*, dictating a message for her husband, which was the call for independence Mujib had sent.[88]

M.A. Hannan, an Awami leader from Chittagong, reported on the radio station that Mujib had announced that Bangladesh was now free, but it went largely unnoticed because Hannan was not widely known. Belal wanted someone with authority to make the announcement. He went with other activists to try to get rebel Bengali officers from the Pakistani army to come to the radio station, but they were busy defending the city. Then they met Major Ziaur Rehman who commanded the 8th East Bengal Regiment, and told him that they had established a rebel radio station and that they needed to protect it.

'I have heard about the station,' Zia said. 'Where is it?"

They invited him to Kalurghat and Zia went there with them. There, Belal asked Zia if he would make the independence declaration—being a major, people would take him more seriously, he said, adding 'aamra minor, apnar major', punning on Zia's position (saying he was a mere minor functionary while Zia was a major in the army). Zia smiled and agreed immediately.

Zia wrote the message declaring Bangladesh's freedom in roman script. Belal suggested—why don't you add Bangabandhu's name? Zia agreed, and so at 7:45 p.m. on 27 March, Zia's voice was heard across the country: Shadheen Bangla Biplobi Betar Kendra theke ami Major Zia bolchhi (This is Major Zia speaking from the Free Bangla Revolutionary Radio Station). He went on to say in Bengali: 'At the direction of Bangabandhu Mujibur Rahman[89], [I] hereby declare that Independent People's Republic of Bangladesh has been established. At his direction, I have taken the command as the temporary Head of the Republic. In the name of Sheikh Mujibur Rahman, I call upon all Bengalis to rise against the attack by the West Pakistani Army. We shall fight to the last to free our motherland. Victory is, by the Grace of Allah, ours. Joy Bangla.'

A Japanese ship in the Bay of Bengal was the first to pick up the message, which was then retransmitted by Radio Australia and the BBC. For five days the message kept being played in a loop from the radio station, interspersed with patriotic Bengali songs and Mujib's 7 March address, and other news that Mushtari and others had compiled. That was the message Mahfuz Anam, along with millions of others, heard.

At 4 in the afternoon on 30 March the Pakistani airforce bombed the radio station. 'We saw two planes come with our binoculars,' Mushtari said. The team at the radio station split into two groups and made their way to India from where they began broadcasting again.

A week later, three Pakistani army trucks stopped in front of the Shafi home. Officers entered the house and asked them if they had any political involvement. They charged Mushtari with seditious writing. They then wanted to open the room with the locked door. Mushtari said it was a rented room. A Bihari gentleman had rented it and he had gone away, she said, and she did not have the key. So the officers called the soldiers who broke open the door.

The weapons were stacked there. The officer calmly asked her when she had rented the room and when the tenant had left. Mushtari said it had happened suddenly, all in early March. But that gave away the story, because some of the weapons were clearly from *Swat,* the ship Bengali dockers had refused to unload, and the *Swat* was raided only a few days earlier, and not in early March.

They immediately took away Dr Shafi. Mushtari never saw him again.

That night, Mushtari collected what little money she had, about 200-300 takas, and left Chittagong, because she knew she would be next. The army had prepared a list of twenty-one 'wanted' people, and her name was on that list. She stayed one night in a cemetery where a man brushing his teeth offered her shelter. The next morning she went in a rickshaw to Bakuliya. Then she had to walk—she saw engineers, doctors, customs officers, and lawyers she had known walking with her through the paddy fields and along the shoreline to reach a village. She stayed there for a few weeks. Roads were dangerous to travel on, so they walked along trails, travelling by riverboats, and reached Noakhali. From there, they turned east towards the Indian border and reached India twelve hours later.

In Agartala she met with Motia Chowdhury, a leftist leader (now a minister in the Awami League government). She began helping refugees, giving rousing speeches about what she had witnessed. Three months later, she moved to Calcutta, and out of Ballygunge, started broadcasting again from the quicksilver radio station, which had emerged there. She spoke on India's state-run radio broadcaster Akashwani as well, using the pseudonym Daliya Mahmud.

◆

The crackdown in Chittagong worsened after the radio station was destroyed. East Pakistan Rifles put up a spirited defence of the city till late March, but they were unable to handle the superior firepower of the Pakistani army. Anupam Sen, who now teaches in Chittagong, was a young man at that time and had seen dead bodies floating in the Karnaphuli river. 'They killed people indiscriminately. They couldn't speak Bengali, and they couldn't tell who was their friend and who was their enemy, so everyone became their enemy.'

On the 30th they took control of the city. All parts of the city came under their control by that time. They had heavy weapons—machine guns, cannons and rifles. East Pakistan Rifles didn't have such sophisticated weapons. They were resisting with old .303 rifles. They were no match for what the Pakistanis had at that time.

On 13 April, a Pakistani army battalion came to a high school where Ramkrishna Pal was a student. The school was located in an area of Chittagong that was considered the personal fief of a local Muslim League politician. The army had been using a students' club building as their camp from where they would go to the city and fight. The next day the army entered a village from the base camp and announced that all the people should gather in one place, and that they would be given food. Some people realized what was to follow and escaped. Nonetheless about 150 people gathered at the designated spot. They were told to raise their hands and were escorted to Mahajanbadi in two lines. Women and the elderly were to form one queue, men the other. They were told to say 'Pakistan Zindabad', raise their hands and kneel. Pal said there were fifty-nine dead bodies.

◆

On 25 March, Fakrul Alam was in Sylhet. The 20-year-old student of Dacca University had gone to the north to visit his sister who had moved there after getting married, and his other sister had come from London to visit. They drove back on 26 March, but he could see that the country was falling apart. Near Brahmanbaria, close to the Indian border, they abandoned their car and took a launch across the river. Then they travelled by a public bus to come to Dacca. As they were coming to Dacca, he saw thousands of people leaving the city. Everyone asked him why he was going to Dacca. There's nothing, everything is ruined. But Fakrul's parents were still in Dacca; he could not abandon them.

Fakrul Alam is now renowned as one of the finest translators of Tagore's writing. His memory of Dacca is of a devastated city, full of fear. Upon arrival, they moved to stay with relatives, and Fakrul kept a low profile, reading a lot, pretending to be working as a desk clerk with an uncle, and anxiously awaiting word from his sisters, from whom he had not had news for three months. It is only when they sent a message from India that the Alams felt relieved.

◆

'There will be a bloodbath after the elections,' Dhirendranath Datta said to nobody in particular, sitting at his home in Comilla in late December 1970. Cyclone Bhola had taken hundreds of thousands of lives and national elections were around the corner. The mood was gloomy. Datta was now in his eighties. He occasionally spoke to Mujib and other Awami League leaders, but otherwise lived a quiet life in his hometown. Few remembered his grand act of rebellion when he had sought an amendment in Pakistan's laws to make Bengali a national language. Datta was now witnessing the last chapter of that saga.

Datta's granddaughter Aroma asked him, 'How can you tell?'

'You don't know the Bhutto family,' Datta replied. 'Shahnawaz [Bhutto's father] was my colleague, they come from a strong, landed gentry culture and they have been seeking power for a long time. They will never compromise, they will not allow anyone else even if he or she is democratically elected. So there will be a bloodbath.'

Datta told his granddaughter that they were moving arms and soldiers. From early January that year Aroma remembers hearing the deep, growling sounds of large aircraft every night. The frequency had increased in February. Unknown to her, and unknown to most, soldiers from Pakistan were being sent to the east.

Aroma was a student in Dacca at that time. On the morning of 7 March, her mother came to her hostel and told her they had to leave immediately for Comilla. They reached Comilla at 4 p.m. Aroma's grandfather was standing in the verandah, but she was still upset that they had been brought back. She wanted to be in Dacca, where all the action was. 'Why did you ask us to come back?' she asked with a frown. And he held her and said, 'Things are going to be worse. If we live, we will live together; if we die, we will die together. After today, there will be a crackdown.'

Datta asked his son to buy more rice because soon there would be no markets. He remembered the akaal (famine) of 1943. They bought what food was available—two large sacks of rice, half a sack of dal, kerosene, salt, potatoes, and matches.

On the night of 25 March, a friend of Aroma's father came running from the Comilla Club and told them, 'Everyone, please wake up and move out of the house, get out of Comilla. Dacca has fallen. There is a crackdown...' but before he could finish they heard the sound of bullets. Soon, they could hear grenades exploding in the cantonment. The Pakistani forces had attacked the police line. Bombs burst and the ground shook. Tanks were moving in the city.

The curfew on the following day was haunting. Not a stray dog in the streets, no crows flying—just an ominous silence. They heard news intermittently—of two local Hindu businessmen having been killed. Another visitor came to ask the Dattas to leave the house.

'No!' he roared like a lion. 'I cannot run away like a coward. I know they will come and get me, but my decision is taken—I am going to die here,' he said.

The visitor said bluntly, 'Then you won't have a natural death.'

He replied firmly, 'I have decided to give my life, and I will die for my country.'

By then the news of the killings at Jagannath Hall and the murders of professors had reached Comilla. Aroma knew that they would come for them.

The curfew was reimposed at 6 p.m. on 28 March. At 7:30 that night, Datta called his granddaughter.

'Come, I have to say a few things. Sit.'

They sat on the floor, and he said: 'Go and get my pocket Gita and red-and-blue pencils. I am going to tell you a few things which you have to understand. I will be picked up tonight. They will come and take me away. They might kill me and leave my dead body. If they do that, leave it as it is. Or they will take me to the cantonment and they will actually try to get me to make some statement and torture me, and I will tell them to stop killing unarmed people; this is not a war,' he added. 'Whoever cries after I'm gone, let them cry, you should not lament, you should not cry.'

Aroma Dutta paused and sighed frequently as she told me the story in her office. She was in tears.

She said she cried when she heard her grandfather say this. He read out a verse from the Gita, and she kept crying, asking him what are you telling me?

'Whoever willingly sacrifices his life for his homeland does not die. Their soul remains omor (immortal),' he replied.

'That's what he told me,' she said, heaving and wiping her eyes with the pallu of her sari, repeating the verse. 'You do what you have to do, he told me. And then he closed the Gita and went to the bed he used to sleep on. And I tucked in the mosquito net. All of a sudden, he got up and he held me and thrice took his hand and caressed my face, "Amar dadur chomotkar meye" (grandfather's miraculous little girl). He then pushed me, and went to sleep.'

She pressed his legs.

At 1:30 that night, there was a lot of banging and it seemed the house was falling apart. The military came. Before they could get to the door, the soldiers had broken it open. Aroma remembered the clop-clop sound of military boots. At one point, four soldiers came to her with open bayonets. They asked her to open the doors of the rooms one by one. She opened the kitchen, and all of a sudden they surrounded her. She was wearing a nightgown. She was 19.

They asked her: 'Where is the person in the university?'

They meant her. She lied: 'There is no one in the university.'

'There is one in the university,' a soldier said in Urdu.

'No,' she said, in Bangla.

'Zaroor hai,' he said—of course there is.

'Ami bolchi na, keu pode na,' she replied in Bengali—I'm telling you, nobody is studying.

One soldier came with a huge torch. His face was big, his eyes popping out. 'What do you study?' he asked her.

'I'm going to give my matric exam,' she said, referring to the school-leaving exams.

He looked at her closely and turned to the four soldiers and said: 'She is not the one.'

The soldiers threw things around. Then an officer signalled and they left. There were six or seven jeeps outside. It was dark. Aroma ran after the jeeps. She was certain they had taken her grandfather. But after a short while, she felt someone pulling her hair. It was her mother. 'Come back inside, are you mad?' she said. Aroma howled, saying she wanted to bring her dadu back. Her mother slapped her and brought her back and locked the door.

The next day a neighbour told them to leave because he had seen jeeps passing by again and stopping, and pointing at their house. He brought two burkhas for them and asked them to take nothing with them. They stayed at a friend's house in Comilla. Each time the curfew was lifted, Aroma would go back to her house, to see if her uncle or grandfather had returned. On 2 April, her hosts said it was now too unsafe for them to stay in Comilla and they must leave. They told her that All India Radio had announced that her grandfather had been killed. The Indian parliament had observed a moment's silence in his honour. If they continued to stay, their hosts' lives would be in danger. 'The army is looking for you,' the host said. 'They will take you in—do you know what can happen to you?'

As a 19-year-old, Aroma didn't have to think what it implied. There were already stories of women being taken away by Pakistani soldiers and raped. 'Your grandfather was our friend, and we have to protect you; but now my life is at risk. Please go with these people across the border,' he said.

Aroma and her mother wore burkhas, put on flip-flops, and left for the river Gomti. The river was dry, and they could cross it by walking. They reached the embankment and crawled over to the other side. Around

5:30 p.m. they reached Sonamura border. Indian Border Security Force guards surrounded them and brought them to safety.

'It was not a war,' Aroma Dutta said. 'The army was doing the killing and there was no resistance. They were systematically killing Hindus. Liaquat Ali Khan had told my grandfather after he made that speech in the Pakistan assembly, 'you will not be spared for breaking Pakistan.' They kept their word. They tortured him in front of his son. They were taken to Mainamati Cantonment that night and brutally tortured and killed. There is testimony of a barber who saw him in cantonment and being dragged, shot, killed, and thrown in a ditch. Their dead bodies were never found, and this country today has a problem recognizing his contribution. Sheikh Mujib certainly was the leader, but many others contributed.'

◆

In the early days of the military crackdown a rumour surfaced that the writers Sufia Kamal and Neelima Ibrahim had been killed. In fact, Neelima had managed to flee to India, but Sufia was very much in Dacca. The Pakistani army was keen to show her on television to tell the world that East Pakistan's cultural icon was indeed alive. They wanted her to say that she was fine and there had been no killing.

Sufia's daughter Sultana, who told me the story, said: 'My mother was frank. She said, "I am alive, but that does not mean that there has been no killing." They tried hard for her to say something else, but they could not get another word out of her mouth.' She also refused to sign a statement that Pakistani officers wanted her to sign.

She wrote several poems about the liberation struggle, invoking Islamic martyrs:

Who are they? Who are they?
They are the plunderers, the followers of a monster
Devoid of rationality, they are like Yazid
Who blocked the bank of the Euphrates
And reddened the desert of Karbala
With the sacred blood of the martyrs
Who had longed for liberty.
On this soil of Bengal
Today killings are going on.

And she wrote of Bengali women joining the fight:

> There is no more time for braiding your hair in patterns
> Or for being concerned with the glamorous border of your saris,
> …
> No more time, no more time—for the battle of life is on!
> …
> No more mere love songs—instead,
> They sing: 'Victory for my motherland,
> My people, the heroic fighters!'
> Dipping their onchol in the martyrs' blood
> Spilled in the street, they repay their debt
> To Mother Earth in blood.[90]

In June, Sultana would leave with her sister Saeeda and other friends, dressed up as if to go to a wedding, and they left by boats for Comilla. From there, they reached Agartala. Once in India, she began working with a doctor who had worked with her mother providing relief to the victims of Cyclone Bhola. Together, they worked with refugees, as well as wounded freedom fighters.

◆

Archer Blood lived through that terrible time. 'March 1971 was the most horrible month of my life,' he wrote in his memoir, *The Cruel Birth of Bangladesh*. Blood was a career foreign service officer who had been posted in East Pakistan early in his career. This was his second tour of duty in the country. He was now the top American diplomat in East Pakistan, and had been widely praised, and later honoured, for his excellent work in providing humanitarian relief after Cyclone Bhola ravaged the countryside. Blood had been observing, with disquiet and then alarm, Pakistan's inexorable slide. He had met the key players and got to know Mujib. He addressed him as Sheikh Saheb, as many others formally did, and had formed an opinion about him—a self-made man, enigmatic, but charming, calm and confident in person. But he had a 'messianic complex... reinforced by the heady experience of mass adulation'.

Blood was stunned when he heard Yahya Khan's speech on 1 March, when he cancelled the convening of the national assembly that was due to meet on the third. 'I knew what they were thinking,' Blood wrote.[91] 'Yahya had broken his promise. The election was not to be honoured. Yahya had yielded to Bhutto's blackmail. Once again, the interests of East Pakistan were to be sacrificed at the altar of West Pakistani concerns.'

He wrote a prescient cable to the State Department, saying: 'I believe I have just witnessed the beginning of the end of a unified Pakistan.' The State Department wrote back, thanking him for his colourful reporting but cautioning him against using the hyperbole. 'But it was not hyperbole. I felt that I had experienced a sudden, clear glimpse of what was to be,' Blood wrote in his memoir.

Indeed, on 29 March, out of frustration and anger, Blood titled his memo 'Selective Genocide' to describe what he had been witnessing. He had been sending increasingly urgent and graphic memos to Washington, but he received 'deafening silence... I was suddenly tired of shouting into the dark and I decided to ratchet the intensity of our reporting up a notch.' In the memo he wrote of the selective killing of student leaders, Awami leaders, supporters, university faculty, elected politicians, and Hindus. The full horror of Pakistani military atrocities will come to light sooner or later, he was certain. He urged Washington to express America's shock, at least in private. But no action followed. Rather, Washington asked Blood to ensure that Americans do not offer shelter to any civilians fleeing violence in American embassy-rented homes.

Blood found an ally in Kenneth Keating, who was the US ambassador to India. Keating supported Blood's reading of the events and appealed to Washington that the US should 'promptly, publicly and prominently deplore this brutality', and should suspend military supplies to Pakistan. 'This is the time when principles make the best politics,' Keating wrote.[92]

On the morning of 6 April, Blood's senior staff met him and presented him with a strongly-worded memo which eloquently dissented from the US policy towards Pakistan. This was unprecedented. Blood would have been expected to talk them out of sending the memo. But Blood agreed with the central message, though he felt he would have phrased the text differently at places. And yet he realized something bigger was at play—his values, morality, and a sense of what was right and what wasn't, what was just and what would amount to acquiescing with tyranny in an act of moral abdication by a superpower.

The memo[93] was sent as 'confidential' and not as 'secret'; there were no instructions on restricting its wider distribution. It was inevitably leaked, and months later when he was back in Washington, State Department colleagues accused him of deliberately putting a lower classification so that it could be leaked. Blood wrote that if he did not classify it higher, it was out of carelessness, not malignance.

What has come to be known as the Blood Telegram read:

> 'Our government has failed to denounce the suppression of democracy. Our government has failed to denounce atrocities. Our government has failed to take forceful measures to protect its citizens while at the same time bending over backwards to placate the West Pak[istan] dominated government and to lessen any deservedly negative international public relations impact against them. Our government has evidenced what many will consider moral bankruptcy, [...] But we have chosen not to intervene, even morally, on the grounds that the Awami conflict, in which unfortunately the overworked term genocide is applicable, is purely an internal matter of a sovereign state. Private Americans have expressed disgust. We, as professional civil servants, express our dissent with current policy and fervently hope that our true and lasting interests here can be defined and our policies redirected.'

Twenty American officials from the Foreign Service, its aid arm USAID and its information service, USIS, signed it. Blood himself wrote in support of the officers' right to voice their dissent. He added that their views were shared by a vast majority of Americans in East Pakistan. He added that he subscribed to their views but did not think it was appropriate for him to sign because he was the principal American officer in the post. And then he added ominously: 'The most likely eventual outcome of the struggle underway in East Pakistan is a Bengali victory and the consequent establishment of an independent Bangla Desh (*sic*). At the moment we possess the goodwill of the Awami League. We would be foolish to forfeit this asset by pursuing a rigid policy of one-sided support to the likely loser.'

◆

What was the White House thinking? Why did it ignore Blood's memos and disregard the mass atrocities in East Pakistan, continuing to support Yahya Khan, whose regime was a textbook example of a dictatorship—annulling elections after the results were not to its liking? Srinath Raghavan, an Indian academic, has written an intriguing book that argues that Bangladesh's independence was not foretold; it came about due to 'conjuncture and contingency, choice and chance'.[94]

Richard Nixon was elected US President in 1968 and inherited the Vietnam War. The nation was divided—the assassinations of the Kennedy brothers (President John in 1963 and Senator Robert in 1968), and Martin Luther King Jr in 1968 had disillusioned many. Young men were dodging the draft and rock stars were singing for peace. The counterculture yelled: Don't trust anyone over 30. Nixon was 55 that year.

He was deeply distrustful of the East Coast elite who looked down on him as a Californian upstart. He had many demons to fight. He found a partner in Henry Kissinger, the émigré from Europe with a grave voice who taught at Harvard and took a bleak view of the world. Kissinger pursued his version of America's strategic interests in which emotions, ideals, and morality had almost no role. Kissinger wanted to defend American interests as he defined them, and if in so doing many had to die, that was incidental, collateral damage. In Yahya Khan they found a friend who spoke with a British accent and talked of his war years (he had fought in World War II) with pride. He was a straight-talking, no-nonsense, direct man, unlike the snooty Indians who were darlings of the East Coast liberal set. Besides, Pakistan was a country that received Nixon with honour during the years he was out of office, and Nixon didn't forget that.

Nixon and Kissinger believed Indians were 'slippery and treacherous' people who would like nothing better than use the Bangladesh tragedy 'to destroy Pakistan'. When Indira Gandhi visited the US in November 1971, the Americans would offer India humanitarian aid for the refugees, besides promising to intervene with Yahya to appoint a civilian governor in East Pakistan in return for amnesty for returning refugees, regardless of whether they had been part of the Mukti Bahini. But Gandhi refused. She spoke to Nixon with the tone, Kissinger recalled, of 'a professor praising a slightly backward student'. (In his memoir Kissinger writes: 'Nixon and Mrs Indira Gandhi, Indian Prime Minister and daughter of Nehru, were not intended by fate to be personally congenial. Her assumption of almost hereditary moral superiority and her moody silences brought out all of Nixon's latent insecurities. Her bearing towards Nixon combined a disdain for a symbol of capitalism quite fashionable in developing countries with a hint that the obnoxious things she had heard about the President from her intellectual friends could not all be untrue. Nixon's comments after meetings with her were not always printable.' He acknowledged though that 'once one cut through the strident, self-righteous rhetoric, Mrs Gandhi had few peers in the cold-blooded calculation of the elements of power'.)

According to Gary Bass, an American academic at Princeton University, the White House objective was to get the Soviet Union to take détente seriously, and to do that, the US wanted to be on the same side as China.[95] And the road to China went through Pakistan. So supporting Pakistan was important because Kissinger wanted to demonstrate to China that the US was willing to 'keep promises, be tough, take risks, get bloodied and hurt the enemy badly'.

Many Indians have wondered why the US and India did not find a common cause, being large democracies. Differing national interests and differing worldviews were two important reasons. American hawks found India's moralistic posture and idealistic exhortations condescending and self-righteous.

The Bangladesh war of liberation interfered with Nixon's and Kissinger's plans. And that plan was to open China, which would help end the Vietnam War and neutralize the Soviets. And to get to China, they needed an ally the Chinese trusted. Yahya Khan was willing to be the go-between. In return, the US would tolerate whatever Pakistan did. In a harrowing account of that period, Bass[96] chillingly lays out the crude language and pithy observations of the Nixon White House about India, Pakistan, and Bangladesh. Analyzing the cables and transcripts of conversations, Bass presents the picture of a White House unhinged, pursuing its own goals with supreme disdain for the effect of the actions contemplated—where the entire world was a chessboard. (In his memoir, Kissinger describes the crisis in more diplomatic terms: 'When the Nixon Administration took office, our policy objective on the subcontinent was, quite simply, to avoid adding another complication to our agenda.')[97]

'The Indians need—what they really need—is a mass famine,' Nixon says at one time in conversations Bass reveals in his book. Kissinger agrees, saying, 'They are such bastards'. At another intriguing moment, Kissinger says: 'If the Soviets move against them [the Chinese] and we don't do anything, we'll be finished.' Nixon asks: 'So what do we do if the Soviets move against them? Start lobbing nuclear weapons in, is that what you mean?' Kissinger replies: 'That will be the final showdown.' After a pause he says: 'At least we're coming out like men.' In his book, Bass accused the two of 'significant complicity in the slaughter of Bengalis' and 'in the dark annals of modern cruelty it [the Bangladesh massacres] ranks bloodier than Bosnia and by some accounts in the same rough league as Rwanda.'

In the end, Nixon would get his prize—he considered the opening of China to be the greatest event since World War II. Kissinger went further back, saying it was bigger than the Civil War. While on a trip to Pakistan in July that year, Kissinger feigned a stomach illness and flew to Beijing to meet Zhou Enlai. The night before he flew, Yahya had hosted a dinner for Kissinger. There, Yahya went around the dinner table asking everyone: 'Everyone calls me a dictator. Am I a dictator?' Everyone chorused, of course not, Yahya was not a dictator.

When Yahya turned to Kissinger, the latter said: 'I don't know, Mr President, except that for a dictator you run a lousy election.'

Yahya took his role as the go-between in the US-China relationship as his personal achievement. Kissinger later told Nixon that Yahya hadn't had such fun 'since the last Hindu massacre'.

◆

Northwest of Jessore towards the Indian border is the village of Chuadanga. From there, as you go towards the border near Meherpur, you reach a village now called Mujibnagar. There is a large monument there, commemorating the 1971 war. It tells the story of the war in a series of tableaux and sculptures, with statues of Mujib addressing crowds, of soldiers burning huts, of Mukti Bahini guerrillas fighting valiantly, and finally, the Pakistani army surrendering. Controversially, but importantly, it also shows a soldier holding the arm of a woman, and with the other, disrobing her sari. Bangladesh has made strenuous efforts to remember the war through sculptures and monuments— memorialising the women who were raped during the war has been infrequent, often as an afterthought, as though the brutality they suffered is a matter of national shame and somehow insults Bangladesh's nationhood or identity. It reveals the patriarchal attitudes prevalent throughout South Asia, that sexual violence against a woman is seen not for what it is—violence—but for an imagined wrong—an insult to a nation's honour.

From the monument you can see India, which is barely 100 yards away. The nearest Indian post is the Chapra police station in Nadia district in India's West Bengal state. The monument stands where it does because it was the easiest entry point from India, and on 17 April 1971, Bangladeshi politicians including Tajuddin Ahmed sneaked into what was still East Pakistan, unfurled the Bangladeshi flag, called the place Mujibnagar, and proclaimed the government of Bangladesh. India would recognize the government seven-and-a-half months later; Bangladesh would be liberated two weeks after that.

Tajuddin and other leaders who had managed to escape to India had formed a government-in-exile in Calcutta. Anisuzzaman, now president of the Bangla Academy, met them in mid-May in Calcutta. He wrote speeches for Tajudin and other leaders—sometimes in English, sometimes in Bengali. 'Tajuddin had a great understanding of the language,' Anisuzzaman said. 'He could find the right word he wanted to say. He showed his guts in the language movement and in exile, and later, even within the party.'

The proclamation at Mujibnagar acted like a signal. Sheikh Mujibur Rahman was named president; Syed Nazrul Islam acting president; Tajuddin Ahmed prime minister; and Gen. M.A. Osmani as the commander-in-chief of the to-be-formed Bangladesh Armed Forces. After that, slowly, Bengali officers of the Pakistani Foreign Service began to defect. Among the first to do so were K.M. Shehabuddin, second secretary, and Amjadul Huq, press attaché, at the Pakistan High Commission in New Delhi, on 6 April 1971. Twelve days later, Hossain Ali, the deputy high commissioner of Pakistan in Calcutta, switched his allegiance to Bangladesh and took sixty-five Bengali colleagues with him. Pakistan appointed another deputy high commissioner, but the Bangladeshis did not vacate the mission. Pakistan then decided to close the mission in Calcutta, and asked India to close its mission in Dacca as a reciprocal measure. On 26 April, Mahmud Ali, Pakistan's vice-consul in New York defected. Of all these stories, Muhammad Zamir's is among the more dramatic.

Zamir was at the Pakistani embassy in Cairo in 1971, studying Arabic and serving under Iqbal Akhund. There were other Bengalis at the embassy. In April, Zamir received a discreet call from the chargé d'affaires at the Indian Embassy. They said that the Mujibnagar Government (which was in Calcutta) had sent him a message. Could he spread 'the truth' about what was happening in East Pakistan to Middle Eastern diplomats in Arabic? He agreed to do so, in a clandestine way.

By the middle of the year, Akhund was replaced and Aslam Malik was appointed as the new ambassador. Malik was harsh on the Bangladesh issue. He transferred one Bengali officer to Islamabad. Wisely, the officer flew to London instead and sought asylum there. Zamir had to travel with visitors from Pakistan and interpret for them in Arabic. When Pakistan sent collaborators from East Pakistan to Arab countries to present the Pakistani version of the events, it fell to Zamir to interpret for them. He began to alter their remarks and pass on the real news. It was a recklessly brave thing to do. One day, a visitor asked him what his game was—since he understood Arabic.

'I am from Bangladesh,' Zamir said.

'Did you use the word Bangladesh?' he asked Zamir.

'I am what I am; that's what they call me,' Zamir said.

'If the government finds out what you are doing, you will be executed,' he warned him.

'But I had to do what I believed in,' Zamir told me at his office in Dhaka, where he now heads the department of information.

'That man told me to make plans to leave. An inkling of what I had been doing was bound to come out. Eventually an order came in November asking me to go to Amman. But I was warned that in Amman they'd put me on another plane and take me to Islamabad. I had to make other arrangements. Taking money out was not possible. The ambassador had told the local bank that we could not withdraw any amount without his counter-signature. So I met an Australian diplomat who said he'd take my car for $500, which was very kind of him, for the car was worth less than that. Another man arranged for two tickets. My wife and I had to pretend we were students from Al-Azhar University.'

'The night we were to leave, we were invited to the ambassador's home for dinner. Our maid-servant was spying on us so we had to be really discreet. I called him, saying I was unwell and could not come,' he said.

They took what they could in a small bag. The Australian diplomat came to their home and drove them to the airport. The next morning they were in London.

'I refuse to call myself a freedom fighter,' Zamir told me. 'The millions who died, the hundreds of thousands of women who were raped, the 10 million who crossed borders and became refugees, the old woman who offered a glass of water to a Mukti Bahini warrior, or cooked a small meal and fed them, or nursed someone by tying up a wound—they are the real heroes. I merely defected; I don't deserve any titles.'

◆

While the proportion of Bengali-speaking Pakistanis in the bureaucracy, administration, and armed forces at the federal level was small, at any given time there were at least a few thousand Bengalis working in West Pakistan.

Their lives now became complicated. They had never felt part of the Pakistani society in West Pakistan. Their colleagues suspected them of being potential traitors. As the crisis deepened and turned violent, their lives were severely disrupted.

Amena Mohsin was nearly 13 in 1971. She lived with her family near Sialkot, where her father was second-in-command of a field ambulance in the army's medical corps. Soon after the crackdown in Dacca, Brig. Maj. Manzur, who was also in Sialkot, defected and became a sector commander for the Bangladeshi forces. (He would later win one of the highest awards for bravery during the war and then ultimately be murdered in the cantonment after the assassination of Ziaur Rahman in 1981.) As a result of Manzur's defection, all Bengali officers, including Amena's father, were grounded. Amena was allowed to continue to go to school in Mandi Bahauddin, near the camp, but she was warned not to talk to any strangers. They could no longer visit the town. Their life was confined to the cantonment. Other girls in the school would stop talking when she passed by, they would stare at her and how. One of her teachers told her that Bengalis could not be trusted. When they were driven to the school, she could see walls smeared with slogans saying, 'Bangalion-ko Maaro'.

When the war ended in 1971, the Bengali officers were asked if they wanted to go to Bangladesh or stay in Pakistan. Those who opted for Bangladesh were put in camps—first in a small one, then in a larger one. They did not realize it, but they had become bargaining chips in the bigger game being played between India and Pakistan over the exchange of prisoners. They could no longer live freely. The camp was surrounded by electrical barbed wires. If you touch the wire, you'll burn to death, they were warned. Amena lived in such camps till 1973, more than a year after the war ended.

Amena missed her school. Her older sister and other army officers' wives taught her and the other children. Her father too taught her. He wrote to the International Red Cross to be recognized as a prisoner of war. He also wanted the Red Cross to intervene so that Amena and her sister could continue to study. Amena didn't understand then why her father persisted with his wish for her to continue to study and appear for exams.

On her journey to the examination centre two soldiers accompanied her each way. 'My father would stand by the wires, waving at me,' Amena recalled. 'Everyone was saying mean things—"what is he [my father] trying to do? Does he think his daughter is Benazir Bhutto?" This was the time when

Bhutto had taken his daughter to Simla, where he had gone to negotiate the transfer of Prisoners of War (POWs) with India. But my father ignored them.' Amena did very well in her exams, and when the results came out, there was a big celebration among the Bengalis, as if it was a victory for Bengalis. 'The way my father cried, it was unbelievable. It was his achievement; he had taught me everything. All those criticisms that people made—he felt vindicated. A friend brought me a bottle of shampoo as a present.'

◆

Meanwhile, the killings in the east continued. On 13 June 1971, *The Sunday Times* of London published a 9,047-word article titled 'Genocide'.[98] If there is one piece of journalism that swayed western opinion about the atrocities in East Pakistan, it was this. Indian Prime Minister Indira Gandhi told the *Times's* editor, Harold Evans that the article had affected her greatly and reoriented her thinking.

The man who wrote the article was Anthony Mascarenhas, a Catholic born in India who had studied in Karachi, and at the time of Partition, stayed on in Pakistan. He rose to be the assistant editor of the *Morning News* in Karachi, and in 1971, he found himself on an embedded assignment in East Pakistan with other Pakistani journalists.

Abdul Bari had run out of luck.

Like thousands of other people in East Bengal, he had made the mistake—the fatal mistake—of running within sight of a Pakistani army patrol. He was 24 years old, a slight man surrounded by soldiers. He was trembling, because he was about to be shot.

'Normally we would have killed him as he ran,' I was informed chattily by Major Rathore, the G-2 Ops. of the 9th Division, as we stood on the outskirts of a tiny village near Mudafarganj, about 20 miles south of Comilla. 'But we are checking him out for your sake. You are new here and I see you have a squeamish stomach.'

'Why kill him?' I asked with mounting concern.

'Because he might be a Hindu or he might be a rebel, perhaps a student or an Awami Leaguer. They know we are sorting them out and they betray themselves by running.'

'But why are you killing them? And why pick on the Hindus?' I persisted.

'Must I remind you,' Rathore said severely, 'how they have tried to destroy Pakistan? Now under the cover of the fighting we have an excellent opportunity of finishing them off.'

'Of course,' he added hastily, 'we are only killing the Hindu men. We are soldiers, not cowards like the rebels. They kill our women and children.'

So began the harrowing account Mascarenhas put together which meticulously showed that the killings were not random, but part of a deliberate policy targeting students, professors, Hindus, Awami League politicians and supporters, and leftists. Mascarenhas also wrote about Bengali fighters killing non-Bengalis—or Biharis—who were being 'mercilessly wiped out'. He estimated that more than 20,000 non-Bengalis were killed in Chittagong, Khulna and Jessore, but the real toll was likely to be much higher. While Pakistan let the world know about that horror, it suppressed 'the second and worse horror which followed when its own army took over the killing'.

In his article, he gave the figure of 250,000 dead on both sides. Senior generals repeatedly told Mascarenhas: 'We are determined to cleanse East Pakistan once and for all of the threat of secession, even if it means killing off two million people and ruling the province as a colony for thirty years.' He wrote: 'The West Pakistan army in East Bengal is doing exactly that with a terrifying thoroughness.'

Mascarenhas travelled for six days with the officers of the 9th Division in Comilla. He saw Hindu men shot once an inspection showed that they were uncircumcised. He heard screams of men being bludgeoned. He saw truckloads of human targets being taken away under the cover of darkness, never to be seen again. He smelt the stench of bodies not removed for days; he saw the heads of students killed on 25 March putrefying on the terrace of Iqbal Hall twenty days after the killings. And he saw the brutality of the kill-and-burn missions.

Other reporters were also writing from East Pakistan at that time. Their reports corroborated what Mascarenhas reported. Sydney Schanberg, the American reporter whose coverage of the Cambodian Holocaust was later the subject of Roland Joffe's film, *The Killing Fields,* was in East Pakistan, and in one of his despatches from Faridpur near Dacca he wrote: 'The Pakistani Army has painted big yellow "H's" on the Hindu shops still standing in this town to identify the property of the minority eighth of the population that it has made special targets.... In April, as a public example, two Hindus were beheaded in a central square in Faridpur and their bodies were soaked in kerosene and burned. Still, there is no sign of a hate-Hindu psychology among the Bengali Muslims. Many have taken grave risks to shelter and defend Hindus; others express shock and horror at what is happening to the Hindus but confess that they are too frightened to help.'

Schanberg also reported the formation of Al-Badr and Al-Shams[99], two pro-Pakistan militia forces which terrorized Bengali nationalists, leftists, and Hindus. He wrote: 'Throughout East Pakistan the Army is training new paramilitary home guards or simply arming "loyal" civilians, some of whom are formed into peace committees. Besides Biharis and other non-Bengali, Urdu-speaking Moslems, the recruits include the small minority of Bengali Moslems who have long supported the army—adherents of the right-wing religious parties such as the Moslem League and Jamaat-e-Islami. Collectively known as the Razakars, the paramilitary units spread terror throughout the Bengali population. With their local knowledge, the Razakars were an invaluable tool in the Pakistani Army's arsenal of genocide.'

On 30 June, Pakistan expelled Schanberg from the country.

Mascarenhas noted that the Pakistani military action was being undertaken to preserve Pakistan's 'unity, integrity and ideology', but he wrote, it was too late for that. 'East Bengal can only be kept in Pakistan by the heavy hand of the army. And the army is dominated by the Punjabis, who traditionally despise and dislike the Bengalis.' He quoted a colonel identified as Naim telling him: 'The Hindus had completely undermined the Muslim masses with their money. They bled the province white. Money, food and produce flowed across the borders to India. In some cases they made up more than half the teaching staff in the colleges and schools, and sent their own children to be educated in Calcutta. It had reached the point where Bengali culture was in fact Hindu culture, and East Pakistan was virtually under the control of the Marwari businessmen in Calcutta. We have to sort them out to restore the land to the people, and the people to their Faith.' Another officer, Maj. Bashir told him: 'This is a war between the pure and the impure. The people here may have Muslim names and call themselves Muslims. But they are Hindus at heart. You won't believe that the maulvi of the Cantonment mosque here issued a fatwa during Friday prayers that the people would attain jannat if they killed West Pakistanis. We sorted the bastard out and we are now sorting out the others. Those who are left will be real Muslims.

We will even teach them Urdu.' Another, Maj. Agha, casually ticked off the names of two Hindus, an Awami politician, and a Christian who was helping Hindus from a list of people who were detained that morning, and asked the police constable to bring them to him that evening. Mascarenhas heard them being beaten up in a cell.

Mascarenhas travelled to deserted villages where the surreal sight of hundreds of Pakistani flags fluttered from rooftops. He saw unsmiling men in khaki with their rifles, and cowering, scared villagers. A Punjabi officer boasted how he killed an old man who had grown a beard to pass off as a Muslim but was a Hindu (after examining him, naturally) and so he had first shot his testicles, stomach, and head, before going to another village looking for another kill.

Mascarenhas was one of eight journalists sent from Pakistan to report on how horrible the Bengalis had been and what a good job the army was doing. But he refused to toe the line. His widow Yvonne said in a BBC interview: 'I'd never seen my husband looking in such a state. He was absolutely shocked, stressed, upset and terribly emotional. He told me that if he couldn't write the story of what he'd seen he'd never be able to write another word again.'

So he pretended he was visiting his sick sister and came to London and went to meet the editor of *The Sunday Times*. The newspaper agreed to publish the story. Mascarenhas sent a coded message to his family to travel to London. He then returned to Pakistan, lest there be any suspicion, and left via Afghanistan by road. Once they were reunited, the story appeared.

◆

The Pakistani troops spared nobody, not even Gandhians.

When Gandhi left Noakhali in 1947, he had asked a disciple, Charu Chowdhury, to look after the ashram until he returned. Gandhi never did, and Chowdhury decided to stay on, looking after the property.

The years that followed weren't easy on Chowdhury: After India's relations with Pakistan worsened in the 1960s when migration accelerated and Pakistan tried to impose Urdu on its Bengali co-religionists, Chowdhury and his charkha-spinning colleagues were arrested by the Pakistani government. It was only after Bangladesh's independence in 1971 that Chowdhury was free again.

The Gandhians at the ashram behaved exactly as you would expect. Jharna Dhara Chowdhury, no relation of the aforementioned Charu, who now heads the ashram and was bedridden when I met her in early 2013, had quietly helped nearly 500 young women escape to India during the 1971 war. Recalling the war's most painful memory, she told me how one day in late monsoon in 1971 Pakistani troops entered the ashram. They singled out four elderly Gandhians—Debendranath Sarkar, Madanmohan Chattopadhyaya, Ajit Kumar Dey, and Jiban Krishna Saha—and, without offering any explanation, killed them in cold blood. The ashram was closed after that till Pakistan's defeat a few months later.

◆

Mushtari Shafi, Sultana Kamal, Latifa Siddiqi, Rokeya Kabir, and Aroma Datta were among the millions of people who were able to seek safety and security in India. These were educated women with good connections, they had survived and were able to rebuild their lives upon return to their country. They could articulate their stories. Many others have only their memories. Many of the poor who were used to floods and cyclones had come to accept forced displacement as an integral part of their lives.

They were able to move to safety because countless boatmen and peasants unhesitatingly helped their compatriots, regardless of their faith. Imtiaz Ahmed, who was to head the international relations department at Dhaka University later in life, was a class nine student who had fled to India to join the Mukti Bahini, but who had been forced to return because he was too young for the Bahini and the latter also had too many able-bodied young men to fight. While in India, he innocently bought two books by Tagore for his mother, thinking it would please her. He did not realize that if he were seen with the books, the Pakistani army would figure out he had been to India and instantly kill him. But the boatman who brought him back to the launch-ghat (river port) from the border area understood that. He saved his books, covering them in a plastic case so that they wouldn't get wet, and handed it to him upon reaching the ghat. He also gave Imtiaz a lungi and a gamchha so that he could pass for a rural child. Over rosgullas at his home during Diwali in 2012, Imtiaz told me: 'Those boatmen were like the underground railway that existed in the United States to free the slaves. They were incredibly generous to the people they helped. They fed us well; they gave us beds; they took us into their homes; they guarded us well. If the military was anywhere near us, they told us where to hide. They created a wall of solidarity around us, and it was astonishing. But unfortunately they never got the recognition of being a mukti-joddha!'

Many had to walk for days to reach the border, avoiding Pakistani jeeps and checkposts. The refugees understood the frailty and humanity of nature. The nature of inhumanity was a different matter—inhumanity not only of the soldiers, but also of the middlemen. There were brokers claiming to help them cross the border but they often changed their terms, demanding more money, changing routes, or passing them on to other, greedier, brokers and agents.

The Indian photographer Raghu Rai had first gone to witness the story of East Pakistani refugees in August. As he wrote,[100] in August 'the monsoon was at its peak. The skies were deep grey and it was raining all the way. The border was not just porous, it was overflowing from all sides. The refugees with their meager belongings were pouring in... they were drenched by the rain, suffering and fatigued. There was a kind of a silence—nobody was talking. There was nothing the others did not know.' Their lives were now lived in public; they were part of a human drama the world was meant to witness. Rai was among those who made sure it did. What the refugees didn't speak about was how their crops were burned (Rai's photographs show scorched land), their homes razed (we see shells of homes), their women raped (in a moving photograph, Rai closed in on a young woman lying on a cot, wearing a sari without a blouse, her eyes still and dry, her belly bigger than her slender frame, indicating the child she was carrying but possibly may not have wanted, perhaps personifying the harrowing saga of rapes during that war). The relentless violence and humiliation the farmers and fisherfolk and boatmen faced are visible in the exhausted faces of the refugees, their wrinkles pronounced, their tears glistening. Hamein mitti chahiye, aadmi nahin (We want your land, not your people), a Pakistani soldier once shouted at East Pakistanis, an insult Simeen Hossain Rimi recalled when I met her.

Rai went close enough to a man's face to let you count the whiskers. His camera stopped near the bloodstains on a sari. The head looked up in another image, making you want to caress the wounded brow. He sharpened the focus on the human being at the centre of the image, separating him from the detritus of what remains of the possessions that he carried with him across the border.

'Future' and 'safety' lay across the river, to cross which the boatman sometimes demanded the last bag of rice the refugee was carrying. They lived on rations, forming orderly queues which went out of focus as Rai fixed the lens on the few in the front of the queue. Children were bathed, old people died, rain lashed the landscape, diseases spread easily and were fought by stubborn nurses and doctors working selflessly, round the clock, in the camps.

When Operation Searchlight began, the international community was unprepared to deal with the humanitarian crisis that followed. On 29 March, the representative of the United Nations High Commissioner for Refugees (UNHCR) in India, F.L. Pijnacker, wrote to his headquarters in Geneva that he foresaw a large influx in India. Within a month, a million refugees had arrived in India.[101] By May, the average daily influx was about 100,000 people, and by the end of the year, the government-estimated figure rose to nearly ten million. Many more were internally displaced. To date, it constitutes the single-largest and most rapid instance of forced displacement in recent history, surpassing the better-known cases of the Great Lakes of Africa, the Balkans and Afghanistan.

The Indian states of West Bengal, Tripura, Assam, Meghalaya, Bihar and Madhya Pradesh hosted most of the 10 million refugees—some 6.8 million lived in camps, while another 3.1 million lived with families, friends, or relatives. By mid-May, 330 camps were established to accommodate 4 million refugees. Of the 825 camps, West Bengal hosted the largest number of camps—492, with 4.8 million refugees in camps and another 2.4 million with host families, followed by Tripura (276 camps with some 834,000 refugees, and another half million with families).

The United Nations Secretary General U Thant decided that UNHCR would be the focal point for all relief efforts. It involved mobilizing funds, procuring and delivering relief supplies, coordinating with the Indian Government, and organizing the distribution of supplies. Several UN agencies—the United Nations Children's Fund (UNICEF), the World Food Programme (WFP), the World Health Organization (WHO), the Food and Agriculture Organization (FAO) among others—worked together with the Indian Government. UN officials wrote of being 'depressed by the situation and the reign of terror which is obvious in the faces of people which are stunned and in some cases expressionless.... Saw many bullet wounded men, women and children. Arson, rape and dispersal is the common topic.' Charles Mace, the Deputy High Commissioner at the UNHCR, said: 'Words fail me to describe the human plight we have just seen.' The UN High Commissioner Sadruddin Aga Khan made several trips to the subcontinent, to familiarize himself with the unfolding crisis so as to seek greater resources from the international community.[102] Peter Kann, who won the Pulitzer Prize for his reporting of the war in the *Wall Street Journal,* recalled: 'My most vivid memory of a refugee was of an old blind man walking down this long road, being led by a cow. I thought of the cow as his seeing eyes, pulling the helpless man forward towards safety. The refugees were truly miserable. Indians did their best for them, and it wasn't enough, but the international community did even less.'

The refugee influx required delicate political handling in India—in some Indian districts, the refugees outnumbered local residents, and local tensions had to be managed. Tripura, which had a population of 1.5 million, hosted 900,000 refugees by May. Such numbers presented a significant logistical challenge for India and the United Nations.

In the days before 24-hour cable news channels and social media, radio and newspapers were the primary sources of information, and access to some of the locations was not always easy. Journalists and photographers from South Asia and beyond took grave risks to witness and document the conflict and its humanitarian consequences. Many of the photographs and stories that were published in newspapers managed to help shape public policy towards the crisis.

The experience of the remarkable photographer Naib Uddin Ahmed is instructive. When a Pakistani officer's camera wasn't functioning properly and he brought it to Naib Uddin to repair it, Naib Uddin figured out the problem, but pretended that he needed to do more work. He used the camera to surreptitiously record images of burnt villages and dead bodies, and smuggled them across to India through the Mukti Bahini. He never saw the negatives again but the photographs managed to reach the international media, which published them prominently, challenging Pakistani claims that the situation was under control, angering the Pakistani military further.

The photographs that many journalists sent out showed grim images of bodies cast at a roundabout; bodies, bloating, rising from a swamp. A man dragged the carcass of another man through the paddy. Some refugees carried their worldly possessions in tin trunks, balanced precariously on their heads; some left with even less, in tiny bundles, with the sole pot they were able to take away. The bundles became their umbrellas, as it began to pour. Many climbed atop buses, some in open top trucks, all headed for the border. Men squatted with tiny aluminum plates turned upside down, waiting for their daily ration of rice and watery dal. Couples huddled under plastic sheets. A man walked carrying an unconscious woman. There, the future Nobel Laureate, Mother Teresa of Calcutta, cradled a child. An old grandmother placed her hands on the head of a child, protecting him, her sad face reminiscent of the elderly aunt Indir in Satyajit Ray's film, *Pather Panchali*.

At the archives of Drik, the photography agency Shahidul Alam runs in Dhaka, I saw haunting images of refugees: a father carrying his son on his shoulders, his wife following behind, wearing a sari but without a blouse, holding the hand of the other child; a woman washing vessels with sand and water, while an elderly man sits in a huge pipe, staring at her, waiting for food; naked, emaciated children playing in the rain; faces sticking out of large pipes, looking hungrily at the camera; the desiderata of a refugee's worldly possessions: a shirt, lungi, a wooden umbrella, a gunny sack, a few vessels; a woman sitting by her dying, emaciated, bony child, sprinkling water, the body a silhouette, with translucent light coming through. There is a tiny hall with dozens of hungry refugees, huddled together, impossible to tell where there are people and where mere bundles. Another haunting image of a young woman, her head uncovered, with a child in her arms, in pain—a woman behind her caresses her hair, holding her mouth with a sari. And some astonishing images of children—a man with a child in his arms, three other children surrounding him. Another man crying with his face looking skyward. A child with arms folded as if in prayer. A girl holding her head, shutting her ears, crying. A boy with a distended belly, staring at the camera. A child, clinging to his mother's dry breast, trying to coax milk out of it. Children filling a bucket with water from a hand-pump; nearby, an old man, naked, lying dead. Another boy, crouching, arms folded, looking at the image of his dead mother, lying flat, thin cloth covering her, on a stretcher.

The refugees walked to Jessore, Comilla, and Rajshahi from where they found their way to India. Itself poor, India opened its doors. Life was hard for the refugees. Monsoon had set in, causing more complications for the operations amidst continuous, heavy rains. With the accumulation of rainwater, the spectre of diseases like malaria and cholera haunted the camps. Children were suffering from malnutrition, even as India was diverting massive food stocks for the refugees. Cases of dysentery increased. A hundred thousand refugees arrived in a single day in Nadia in West Bengal, even as hospitals tried vainly to add more beds. To service that large a population, there were only some 600 doctors and 800 paramedical personnel, according to contemporary accounts.

Cholera spread rapidly, from 9,500 cases in June to 46,000 in September, and there was a shortage of medicines. Vaccines and vast amounts of dehydration fluid were airlifted to the camps. Hospitals had no beds, and many patients lay on metal sheets on the concrete floor. Cases of diarrhoea rose, and flies festered on human waste.

Many people lived in large pipes and in tent cities. They queued for hours for milk or rice. They stood patiently, carrying the sick, old, and infirm among them, hoping for medicines from international aid workers, keen to stay alive and return home. Their eyes vacant, their faces pained, revealed the despair over lost lives, their helplessness over their inability to find out where their loved ones were, or if they were even alive; the bittersweet celebration of new life as a child was born; the desperate attempts to keep the child alive when the baby was sick; the burial of the dead in a foreign land; the compassion of the aid workers, operating round the clock, tirelessly saving lives; the bureaucrats sitting on chairs with rickety tables that had uneven legs; the swarming flies, the oppressive heat, the grime and the sweat; the complex arithmetic of trying to match resources with needs; the shared ramshackle umbrellas, the huddling beneath trees, shivering in a tropical downpour; the yearning to return to a free country, one's home.

Beyond South Asia, Edward Kennedy, then a young senator from Massachusetts, came to the camps and cradled babies in his arms and vowed support. George Harrison, the former Beatle, raised global consciousness that August, putting together the Concert for Bangladesh at the Madison Square Garden, with the sitarist Ravi Shankar, poet-singer Bob Dylan, guitarist Eric Clapton and former Beatles drummer Ringo Starr among many other great performers. And there was Joan Baez's haunting melody: 'Bangladesh Bangladesh; When the sun sinks in the west die million people of Bangladesh; The story of Bangladesh is an ancient one again made fresh.'[103] Gita Mehta, author of *Karma Cola* and the daughter of Biju Patnaik, an Indian politician, made a film which was shown widely internationally on television, which also built worldwide opinion in support of Bangladesh.[104] According to Lt. Gen. J.F.R. Jacob, who was in charge of India's Eastern Command, India supported Mehta by granting her access to refugee camps.[105] And the Beat poet Allen Ginsberg heard the plaintive cries and wrote the lyrical anthem, *September on Jessore Road*.

Millions of fathers in rain
Millions of mothers in pain
Millions of brothers in woe
Millions of sisters nowhere to go

One Million aunts are dying for bread
One Million uncles lamenting the dead
Grandfather millions homeless and sad
Grandmother millions silently mad

Millions of daughters walk in the mud
Millions of children wash in the flood
A Million girls vomit & groan
Millions of families hopeless alone

Millions of souls nineteen seventy one
homeless on Jessore road under grey sun
A million are dead, the million who can
Walk toward Calcutta from East Pakistan

◆

Jessore Road was one of the lifelines that connected the refugees with India. When I drove along the road in the winter of 2012, it was a weatherbeaten two-lane road with waterlogged fields on either side, the landscape occasionally interrupted by a few shops with mechanics, a petrol pump, or a tea stall. From Jessore the road took the refugees to the south to a town called Chuknagar which lies 30 kilometres to the west of Khulna, the gateway to the world's largest mangrove forest, Sundarbans.

This was Bengal's jute territory. Jute was grown in Khulna and before Partition, jute would be taken to Calcutta where it would be processed in its mills. After Partition, West Pakistan decided to reduce dependence on India and set up mills in East Pakistan, and some of those were in Khulna. Manzur Alam was the manager at one such factory. At his home on the night of 25 March 1971, he and his wife Sarwari were celebrating their wedding anniversary with friends when they heard gunshots. The army had come and taken over his factory in Khulna and the soldiers had started shooting the Bengali workers. Dozens died. Manzur and Sarwari sensed danger and immediately left their home, leaving everything behind. Sarwari, whom I met in Dhaka in 2011, remembers that even their presents lay unopened. The guests also left hurriedly. The Alams got into a boat and crossed the river and walked from the other shore all the way to Dacca. It took them several days to reach Dacca. Sarwari Alam remembers seeing many dead bodies lying by the road, possibly running into hundreds. They had slept in the open under trees and eaten only puffed rice along the way. Their feet were bleeding when they reached the city, to the home of their relatives.

There was a reason why dead bodies lying by the road were not being cleared. Azm Abdul Ali, who worked with the railways in Chittagong told me that the Pakistani troops did not clear the bodies as a warning to others. Their tactic changed after June, near the onset of the monsoon season. They began herding the people in trucks, taking them to riverbeds and then shooting them, dumping the bodies into the rivers, where the bodies would float downstream.

◆

To the north of Khulna is a town called Chuknagar, which is an important junction on the way to India. It is a dusty town with a derelict centre that had a large market. The town had proportionately more Hindus than other parts of East Pakistan. By local estimates, in the 1970s some villages were as much as 40 per cent Hindu. Razakars and other pro-Pakistani militia were active here, both to spy on the villages and to intimidate the people. Achintya Biswas, who teaches French revolutionary history at a college in Batiaghata near Chuknagar told me that Hindus and Awami supporters in the area decided to move to India after April, after the Pakistani army shot villagers near Chuknagar and a few people died, including some of Biswas's family.

Word had reached rapidly in these remote villages that contrary to what the official radio stations were telling them, the Pakistani troops hadn't come to protect them; they were busy killing Bengali men and boys, and no Bengali woman or girl was safe near them. Violent incidents continued and the people constantly lived under the fear of Khan Sena, as they called the soldiers sent from West Pakistan. The smart Bengalis with a keen survival instinct spread the word: go to Chuknagar, walk to Satkhira, and sneak into India. Once across the border, they were told, Sikh soldiers would lift their children, embrace them, carry them to safety, and Indira Gandhi would give them tents, saris, medicinal tablets, and injections. For thousands of villagers living in inaccessible parts of the delta like Rampal, Sarankola, Morrelganj,

Fakirhat, Bagerhat, and Gopalganj, Chuknagar was the transit point to reach.

But each village had its Razakars whose job was to spy on Bengali separatists, and some of them soon found out that people were gathering in Chuknagar, and they mobilized other Razakars to rush to the area to collect intelligence on villages like Badamtola, where many villagers had gathered. On 19 May the Muslim League followers came to Badamtola and killed more than a hundred people, but only twenty-three were identified because the rest were from other villages.

On the morning of 20 May, Chuknagar was teeming with thousands of people—it was the day of a local festival. Some families had come by boats. Some were bargaining with agents who could get them across to India. Many were buying food or selling their possessions, to raise money for the journey to India. The mood was not festive, but looked like a country fair.

Around 10 a.m. on that unusually bright day, two trucks[106] carrying Pakistani troops arrived in Chuknagar. Ershad Ali Morel, who was 23 then, was working with his brothers and father on his family's jute farm. He heard the rumbling of trucks—faint at first, but then gradually getting louder. The trucks were heading towards the large open field where thousands of people had gathered, forming small circles, squatting or lying down, waiting to hear from men who had made it their business to smuggle them across to India. The Pakistani army's job was to prevent them from leaving. Ershad's 65-year-old father told him to go back to the hut, which was about a hundred yards away. Ershad wanted to stay and see what the noise was all about, but he obeyed his father and ran towards home. He looked out of the small, misshapen hole that passed for a window, and saw Pakistani army trucks driving at an even pace, emitting dust.

Ershad heard one of the soldiers shout at his father. He remembers his father standing tall in the field, gesturing angrily, waving his sickle, as if telling them not to drive over their field. The soldiers needed only one shot to kill him. Ershad heard the shot, and he gasped. He saw the truck move; his father had fallen. Ershad rushed out through the back door, taking his family with him to a safer place in the bushes. He thought they would come and attack his siblings. He heard more gunshots, from all sides. He heard cries of help. After leaving his family in a secure place near a tree, his heart pounding, he rushed back to see his mother.

She was wailing. She told him his father had died, and he should get the white cloth from the shops for the burial. 'I had no time to think,' he said, recalling the incident four decades later.

Meanwhile the trucks reached the town centre and the soldiers saw the open field where thousands of people were sitting in small groups. The soldiers stepped out of the trucks, and without any provocation or warning, started shooting. Achintya Biswas was hiding in a school with his family. They could hear the sounds, but did not know what was going on.

As Ershad Ali ran through the town, he saw that most homes were empty—many people had already left for India. He saw a girl, about 11 years old, bleeding profusely as her leg was shot, asking for water. Ershad went into a house nearby and filled a glass of water from the clay pot to give the girl some water, but while drinking the water, she died in his arms. 'I felt a lot of pain, looking at the dead bodies,' he said.

And then he saw Sundari. She was a child, barely six months old, clinging to her mother's breast. Her mother lay beside her, and there was blood all over her body. The mother was beautiful, and she had sindoor in her hair, indicating she was married, and a Hindu. Her eyes were wide open; she was dead. She had been feeding her daughter when the bullet got her.

'I carried the girl in my arms,' Ershad said, 'but I was very confused. The baby was unhurt, but she had blood all over her body, her mother's blood.'

Oh God, what am I doing, Ershad asked himself, as he ran with the child. He ran through the market, seeing many more dead bodies, including Hindus he had grown up with—Kalachand, who played the drum at Hindu weddings, Bhogirath, who worked as a butcher, Digambar, who was a farmer, and Babunath Biswas, the grocer—all the while he kept hearing more and more gunshots. There were many Muslims too among the dead—Saifuddin, the butcher, Murshid Ali, the shopkeeper who sold coal, his five children, and Inayat, the mentally disabled man with the mind of a toddler. They were all dead.

Ershad crouched low and passed the maidan and went to the home of Mandar Das, a Hindu man he knew. 'My father has just been killed,' he told Mandar. 'I am going to get the cloth to bury him. On my way I saw this girl, whose mother has just died. I don't know who she is. I don't know her mother's name. But her mother is a Hindu. Can you look after her? I will come back tomorrow after the funeral and take her back,' he said.

Mandar Das took her. Ershad found the cloth he needed and returned home to bury his father. The following morning Ershad went to Mandar's house to take the girl back. But Mandar's wife told him that they wanted to keep her. They had been married twenty years and did not have a child. They would now bring up the girl as their own daughter; she was God's gift, they said; and they would name her Sundari. She was beautiful. 'I knew she was a Hindu, that's why I had taken her to a Hindu family. I did not want her stolen from her people,' Ershad told me.

Nitai Chandra Gayen was a 24-year-old Communist volunteer. He was to meet his family in Chuknagar. He ran to warn the people gathered in the grounds when he saw the soldiers moving towards them. He shouted to tell his cousin Ranjit and nephews Binoy and Dhiren to flee. Nitai hid in a mosque, where many people were loudly reciting the namaz, as if to show the soldiers that they were devout Muslims, and not Hindus. A woman put a mat around him, in which he hid. Nitai had thought the soldiers would spare the elders in his family. But from the mosque, to his horror, he saw a soldier place a gun at the head of one of his uncles, then another uncle, and then his brother, and shot all of them, one by one. Binoy and Ranjit came back and tried to fight with the soldiers. An aunt tried to pacify the soldier, by pleading he should not shoot anymore. One of the soldiers shot all three of them.

Gayen said that the shooting went on for about four hours. After the soldiers had gone, he slowly went to the large tree where his family lay dead— Abinash Gayen, 65; Badal Gayen, 60; Malati Gayen, 67; Adhar Mandal, 60; Ranjit, 17; Binoy, 27; Ishwar, 58; Dhiren, 35.

'There were dead bodies everywhere,' Gayen told me in Batiaghata at the college where Biswas taught. 'In brush fire it is easy to kill so many people. I can't say with any certainty how many died, but at least a thousand, and maybe many more were killed. Wherever there were people, the Pakistanis shot at them. They even shot the people who jumped in the river to escape. The army then shot the boats so that the boats would drown. All I remember seeing are dead bodies,' he said, moving his face to the right and left, his voice dropping to a whisper, his eyes glistening.

Along with twenty-odd survivors they started looking through the pockets of the dead and collected whatever they could find, so that they would have some money to pay for their journey to India. Then he saw an infant suckling its mother; she was dead. Nitai carried the child with him to a boat. A woman in the boat asked him if the child had a scar on its forehead. Seeing the scar, she took the child—she was the sister of the dead mother.

Once in India, Gayen began training young men to use weapons, and those among them who showed promise were then sent to the Mukti Bahini.

Abul Bashar Mohammed Shafiqul Islam was a student in the tenth standard at that time. He estimates that the shooting went on for several hours. I walked with him through the fields as he described the violence. He pointed out the spot where Chikan Morel, Ershad Ali's father, was shot. When we reached the riverbed, I saw a boat with fresh, delicious-looking cauliflower being unloaded to be sold in the market. But Abul Bashar seemed to be in another world. He was momentarily speechless, as he spread his arm, showing me the riverbed. That day, four decades ago, the riverbed was full of dead bodies. 'There was a huge amount of blood,' he said, regaining composure. 'I saw blood flowing into the river; I saw the river water turning red. I have never seen anything quite like it,' he said, wiping away tears. Some hid in shallow ponds. When a few raised their heads to breathe, the army shot them, turning the pond dark vermillion.

The next morning he heard voices from the trees. He thought he was losing his mind. When he looked up, he could not see anything. But then slowly, he saw someone starting to come down from the tree. He was an old man. He was whimpering. He was not sure if Abul Bashar was a Pakistani sympathizer or a Bengali partisan. It is only after Abul Bashar put his arms around him that he howled. He had stayed in the tree throughout the day, worried that if he made a single move he would get shot. He had seen the soldiers aim randomly at the trees and shoot, and people would drop dead, like fallen birds.

◆

It is impossible to say with any certainty how many people were killed in Chuknagar. Abul Bashar says he had found forty-four manual labourers who had disposed of the dead bodies at the behest of the Pakistani army. The army had paid them two annas per body. Each labourer claimed to have disposed of at least 100 bodies. That gives a figure of 4,400 people killed. Abul Bashar nonetheless claims the figure is closer to 10,000, since many bodies were also washed away. Dragging an adult body, however, takes time, and it is improbable that each labourer could have disposed of so many bodies in such a short time. Regardless of the number of deaths, a massacre had indeed occurred.

The Chuknagar massacre remained forgotten for a long time. Noted Bangladeshi filmmaker Tanvir Mokammel has researched the massacre for years, and recently completed a feature-length film, *Jibondhuli* (The Drummer)[107], based on the life of a low-caste Hindu drummer, whose family was killed in Chuknagar. Muntassir Mamoon, a historian at Dhaka University, who has written several volumes on the war, edited a compilation of testimonies of more than eighty survivors in Chuknagar, and he accepts the figure of 10,000 deaths.[108] Some activists in Bangladesh would like the government to declare 20 May as Genocide Day. It is nearly impossible to gather the names of victims, because the incident occurred more than forty years ago, and Chuknagar was a transit point; not all those who died lived in Chuknagar and nobody carried identification papers. In many cases entire families were killed, leaving no survivors who would later come looking for them.

Many villagers emotionally say that 'thousands' died in their villages, but when social scientists have attempted to add up the numbers, they can rarely get more than thirty to fifty names. Reporters have been frustrated by the lack of precision. Martin Woollacott, who was the correspondent for *The Guardian* during the war, wrote: 'The eyes would widen and the head move from side to side in the striking Bengali gesture of affirmation. "How many were killed?" we would ask refugees who had fled from areas where the Pakistani army and its auxiliaries were attempting to suppress the Bangladesh independence movement. "Lakhs and lakhs!" came the answer. Journalists who covered the Bangladesh war in 1971 remember the phrase with a mixture of amusement and frustration. Lakh is the Indian word for 100,000, and it sometimes seemed as if the majority of Bengalis knew no other number, or, if they did, it was "crore"—1 million (*sic*)[109]—at least when describing the atrocities and depredations of their West Pakistani oppressors. Reporters had no doubt that there were such atrocities. Some of them witnessed bloody incidents or their aftermath, but for the most part correspondents had to rely on the accounts of others. Between the protestations of the Pakistani military, for whom all Bengali deaths were those of "miscreants" or criminals, and the manifest exaggerations of inflamed and sometimes bereaved East Bengalis, it was difficult to steer a measured course.'

Sarmila Bose has written a controversial book[110] about the war where she meticulously goes through Pakistani records and attempts a forensic dissection of Bangladeshi claims about the number of deaths and the scale of atrocities. Her account is broadly sympathetic to the Pakistani Army. She is the granddaughter of Saratchandra Bose, the older brother of Subhas Chandra Bose, the Indian nationalist who allied with Hitler in World War II and took over the Indian National Army in Singapore. Bengalis on both sides of the border revere the Bose brothers,[111] and Sarmila Bose received warm cooperation from Bangladeshis when she began her research into the war. Many now feel betrayed by her writing. Bose interviewed several witnesses, Hindu and Muslim, men and women, and drew from internal reports of the Pakistani army to conclude that the Pakistani army has been 'demonised' by Bangladeshis and accused of 'monstrous actions regardless of evidence'. Her writing is transparent about her frustration with what she sees as lack of precision. She challenges two central beliefs in Bangladesh—that all Bangladeshis were victims, and that they always fought bravely.

Bose examined the Chuknagar massacre in some detail. She found it hard to believe that fewer than 30 soldiers, who arrived in two or three trucks, carrying limited ammunition, could have killed 10,000 people in a few hours. She wrote: 'What is interesting about the number is that while estimates of the dead range widely in various accounts, the number of the killers is consistent—they were very few, according to all accounts, some say twenty to twenty-five, or even fewer. They arrived in Chuknagar in about three vehicles. Also consistent is the evidence that the attackers were lightly armed, carrying only their personal weapons. Given the type of weapon and extra ammunition carried by a soldier at that time, a band of thirty soldiers would not have more than 1,200 bullets to use in total. Not all of the bullets would hit their targets and not each hit would kill.'[112]

When I asked the witnesses I met in Chuknagar—teachers, a school principal, shopkeepers, and a priest at the Hindu temple—I got a range of responses about the number of deaths. Some said ten thousand; twenty thousand, said others. There are no records of the dead, no graves to visit, no memorial stones from where one can humanize the statistics, by giving names to the victims.

To be sure, applying rigour to understand the scale of the massacre is a sound academic principle. In the context of Chuknagar, Bose writes: 'The attempt by some Bangladeshis.... to establish the "largest mass killing" of 1971, with the attendant claims that 25-30 soldiers armed only with their personal weapons killed 10,000 people in a morning's expedition, are unhelpful obstacles to chronicling what was clearly a major massacre.' But she overstates her case when she goes on to blame the massacre entirely on 'a band of twenty-five to thirty men'[113] who 'brought lasting disgrace to an entire army and a whole nation'.[114] In so doing, she takes at face value that

Pakistani armed forces were exemplary and professional, fighting an armed insurgency supported by a belligerent neighbour, and trying to play fair in a hostile terrain with which they were unfamiliar, and only a few units had rogue elements. That analysis is far too generous to the Pakistani army, completely unwarranted by the hundreds of stories of atrocities people in East Pakistan suffered for no fault other than wanting to live peacefully in their own country. Her credulity in taking at face value the defence that Pakistani generals put up, and her deep skepticism over any claim Bangladeshis make both suggest that she has pre-determined her finding: that Bangladeshis were exaggerating their suffering, and Pakistani generals deserved better. For example, while writing about the Khulna jute mill massacre, she writes about 'several thousand' Bihari victims. No doubt Bengalis killed many Biharis during, and particularly, after the war was over. But she does not examine the claimed Bihari deaths with the same rigour she applies while scrutinising Bengali claims. Many Bangladeshis insist what they experienced was genocide. Legal scholars wedded to internationally-agreed definitions are reluctant to use the word 'genocide'. It is not merely a semantic battle.

Missing in her analysis is the simpler, grand narrative: that a nation with two halves separated by 1,000 miles with little in common except faith, was probably a bad idea to begin with. And when the part, which felt discriminated against, protested and demanded respect, cultural autonomy, and greater resources, and even won majority in nationwide elections, the dominant half ignored the verdict, cancelled the election outcome, sent in troops, and killed at least tens of thousands of people, before surrendering to a superior army working with a local guerrilla force, but not before destroying the new nation's physical infrastructure and killing intellectuals who could have helped lead the country.

Call it what you will, argue over whether to call it genocide. The fact is, it was terrible, and it remains a crime against humanity.

FIVE

THE FREEDOM FIGHTERS

The brutality and ferocity of Operation Searchlight had stunned the people in East Pakistan. Well-trained Pakistani troops established superiority over rebellious Bengalis with ease. While it is true that the Pakistani troops killed many innocent civilians, Bangladeshi nationalists weren't Gandhian pacifists. Unprepared they certainly were, and under-resourced too. They simply did not have the weapons or command and control structures which could help mount a successful rebellion. There were several cases of Bengalis attacking Biharis, suspecting them of being potential fifth columnists. But on the whole, their protests were peaceful. Students had marched on the streets carrying mock rifles as if the coming revolution was a college play, even though some of them had received genuine weapons training and knew how to sabotage civic life. But they were incapable of taking on an army. The revolutionary academics were professors and intellectuals who knew the theories of revolutions but were unlikely to take a practical step, preferring to make their arguments through words, pamphlets and poems. The Awami League itself was in a shambles— Mujib had been arrested on the night of 25 March, leaving the party rudderless. Tajuddin and Syed Nazrul Islam and several other senior leaders had crossed over to India, and Kamal Hossain had been arrested and taken to Pakistan; many of the elected representatives were in jail and some were killed. The Left, which talked of revolution, was simply not powerful enough to mount a nationwide response. Among the security forces, the East Pakistan Rifles did mutiny in some parts of the country, but they were disarmed quickly. And Bengali officers who decided to defect and join the liberation movement had no central figure who could offer command and control leadership. The Bengali nation was in a state of shock.

On 21 April, Peter Kann wrote in the *Wall Street Journal*: 'It was a storybook sort of revolution, with thousands of Patrick Henrys issuing courageous calls to arms and thousands of Betsy Rosses sewing little red, green and yellow

Bangla Desh (*sic*) flags. The civil service, police and East Pakistan Rifles…
joined the liberation, as indeed did Bengalis of every social class and political
persuasion. The Bangla Desh flag flew from primitive mud huts as well as
from city offices, from oxcarts as well as from Jeeps. The revolutionary slogan
Joy Bangla was shouted by peasant children as well as portly politicians.…
But there were things the Bengalis didn't have and didn't do. Except for the
militiamen of the East Pakistan Rifles, the liberation army was almost entirely
lacking in arms and training. Even the Rifles had only light, old-fashioned
weapons. In many areas the Bengalis did little to supplement these arms with
homemade weapons like Molotov cocktails or primitive mines. The Bengalis
were surprisingly unprepared for a war that many of them had deemed possible,
even likely, for years.'[115]

The Pakistani army was extremely well-prepared for Operation Searchlight.
In the weeks leading up to 25 March, Pakistan had sent two divisions to the
east—the 9th and the 16th, amounting to some 25,000 men. They had travelled
from Karachi to Multan carrying light bedrolls and battle packs and flown to
Dacca by the national carrier, Pakistan International Airlines. Over fourteen
days, the divisions had moved to Dacca via Ceylon, and so unprepared were
the East Pakistanis that hardly anyone noticed anything unusual, even though
many young men kept arriving from West Pakistan. When the crackdown
took place, the troops used the equipment of the 14th Division, which was
the Eastern Command. The 9th Division operating from Comilla, was meant
to seal the eastern border, and the 16th was sent to Jessore, and meant to
seal off the western border. All together, Pakistan had 80,000 regular army
troops, some 24,000 rangers, and close to an estimated 50,000 collaborators,
comprising Razakars, Al-Badr and Al-Shams militia. Lt. Gen. Tikka Khan was
the chief martial law administrator till August 1971. Lt. Gen. Amir Abdullah
Khan Niazi took over from him after that, and their advisor was Maj. Gen.
Rao Farman Ali.

The general who set Operation Searchlight into motion was Tikka Khan.
Born in Jochha Mamdot village in Kahuta tehsil near Rawalpindi, he graduated
from the Indian Military Academy in Dehradun and was commissioned in
1939; one of the freshly-minted officers who would soon see action with the
British Indian Army, because many senior British officers from India were
called up for duty to defend Britain during World War II. Tikka Khan would
see action in Italy and on the Burmese front. After Pakistan's independence,
he commanded an artillery regiment and rose to be a lieutenant general in

1969, earning a reputation of being a tough disciplinarian.

Tikka Khan took over the Eastern Command on 7 March. A few months after Operation Searchlight was launched, Tikka Khan was recalled to Multan in West Pakistan, from where he supervised troops till the end of the war in December 1971. After the war he became Bhutto's defence minister. He remained loyal to Bhutto, and when Gen. Zia-ul-Haq overthrew Bhutto in 1977, Tikka Khan went to jail; he became governor of Punjab in 1988, and left politics after Benazir Bhutto's removal in 1990. When he died, Benazir Bhutto recalled that Tikka Khan 'rose to the highest offices of this country due to his hard work and respect for the rule of law'. While Benazir Bhutto certainly fought for democratic rights in Pakistan, she was no champion of freedoms beyond Pakistan's borders, and arguably, not even of the freedoms of her own opponents. Neither in her book, *Daughter of the East*,[116] nor in her remarks in her political life did she condemn any of the actions the Pakistani state undertook in 1971—in fact, unsurprisingly, she was uncritical of her father's actions, which had such a major role in creating the crisis.

Pakistani forces were commanded by Amir Abdullah Khan Niazi, who took over as commanding officer in April, after Operation Searchlight was already underway. He was born in 1915 in Balo-Khel, a village near Mianwali in the Punjab. During his military career he received twenty-four medals. He was part of the British Indian Army that fought the Indian National Army on the Burma front in 1943-45 under the command of Gen. William Slim. This army halted the INA and the Japanese in Imphal, a battle that changed the course of the war. Niazi was honoured with the Military Cross for his action on the Assam-Burma front in June 1944. His British superiors warmly praised his valour and agile mind, commending him for 'personal leadership, bravery and complete disregard for his own personal safety'.

Directly under Niazi and in charge of Dhaka was Maj. Gen. Rao Farman Ali. Commissioned as an artillery officer in 1942, he had some experience operating in East Pakistan, where he was promoted to major general and became an adviser to the governor of East Pakistan in 1970. He understood the region well and would later be named by several victims' accounts as the mastermind behind some of the targeted massacres.

Bengali resistance began soon after Operation Searchlight. In April 1971 Dan Coggins reported in *Time* magazine that a Bangladesh Mukti Fauj (Liberation Army) was already operating in the country, controlling about a third of the territory, which was clearly an exaggerated claim on the part of the Bengali rebels whom Coggins interviewed. Coggins had managed to sneak into Kushtia, about 70 kilometers from the Indian border, and he spoke to peasants who had fought back and taken Pakistani troops hostage.

Kushtia is a quiet town steeped in Bengali culture. In the nineteenth century, Lalon Fokir, the Baul mystic, set up his institution dedicated to Sufi music in Kushtia. Nearby is Shilaidaha kutibari, the family estate of Rabindranath Tagore where in the early twentieth century he wrote the poems that became *Gitanjali,* for which he would win the Nobel Prize in 1913.

According to the report in *Time,* on the night of 25 March, twelve jeeps from the 27th Baluch Regiment from Jessore Cantonment came to Kushtia, and its 147 soldiers quickly disarmed the 500 policemen at the police headquarters. They also took over the government house, the radio transmitter, and the boys' school. The villagers realized what had happened only at dawn the next day, when the soldiers drove around in jeeps, making loud announcements that a curfew was in operation. Seven unfortunate farmers who hadn't heard the announcement, had gone to the town centre on some business and were shot down. People's anger was simmering.

On 28 March, after the curfew was relaxed, fifty-three East Pakistani policemen easily overpowered the soldiers guarding them and began the attempt to liberate Kushtia. Pakistani soldiers were afraid of the thousands of Bengali farmers who congregated, shouting slogans, including Joy Bangla. The soldiers spoke the Baluchi language and understood Urdu, but they found Bangla incomprehensible; it was as if they were in a foreign country. By noon, the rebels had retaken the government house and the district headquarters. Panic-stricken Pakistani troops fled in jeeps, but the rebels managed to stop two jeeps and the soldiers were pulled out and killed. While other jeeps tried to flee, they found the roads blocked with trees deliberately felled. A fierce battle ensued. The soldiers killed several Bengali peasants before the peasants overpowered them and hacked them to death. The body of the assistant deputy commissioner of Kushtia, a 29-year-old Punjabi deputed to the east, called Nassim Waquer, was dragged through Kushtia's streets.

The next day Pakistan sent another infantry company to take over Kushtia again. But the peasants had lain booby traps, and two of the Pakistani vehicles fell into those. Seventy-three soldiers died instantly; the rest were chased down and slain. 'All last week, the green, red and golden flags of Bangladesh fluttered from rooftops, trucks, and even rickshaws in Kushtia',[117] wrote Coggins.

◆

Niloufer Huda was born in Calcutta and had come to Dacca in 1965, where
she met Najmul Huda, a young army officer who was recovering from a
horse riding accident. When the war between India and Pakistan broke out
that year, the India-Pakistan border was closed, leaving Niloufer stranded in
Dacca. She got to know Najmul better and they got married in 1966. Najmul
was a commissioned Pakistani officer but he took greater pride in his Bengali
identity. In 1968, he was accused in the Agartala Conspiracy Case along with
Mujib. After the case collapsed Huda was released but along with other army
officers accused in the case, he was dismissed from the army. As Huda was
accused in a politically sensitive case, few people were willing to meet him or
offer him another job. Life was hard for them after that, and Niloufer once
had to sell her jewellery to make ends meet. Huda began working with his
brother Nurul, who was a government contractor, at a construction project
in Kushtia district.

Huda had heard Sheikh Mujib's historic speech on 7 March, and began
preparations to leave Dacca with his wife. While he was in Dacca, his close
friend Khaled Mosharraf, who was an army officer, came to inform him
confidentially to go into hiding because they expected a military crackdown
anytime. They left for Mujib's house at 32 Dhanmondi and informed him
about the imminent crackdown. Mujib's home in those days was teeming with
Awami leaders, political supporters, neighbours, family members, and foreign
correspondents. Mujib heard them but gave no indication of what he thought
or would do next.

On 21 March Niloufer moved to Kushtia. On the 25th Huda took
Niloufer and their children Ehtesham and Naheed on a drive to look around
the town, when they noticed Pakistani Army in full battle gear and weapons on
main roads and on some rooftops. Ominously he told Niloufer, 'The situation
is worse. Something will happen tonight,' as they drove back carefully. The
next morning, they came to know from an All India Radio broadcast about
the massacres in Dacca. They quietly left the rest house and took shelter with
a relative.

After the curfew was lifted two days later, they went to the ferry point
and took two boats with their relatives to Faridpur and reached Pangsha
village. They went to their family home on a bullock cart. The next morning,
Najmul Huda gave Niloufer 200 Pakistani rupees, kept the last 50 rupees

he had for himself, and decided to go to Rajbari to find out what had happened. A few days later he sent her a letter telling her about the massacres and said he was joining the Bengali resistance against the Pakistani Army. He requested an uncle to look after his family, saying: If you survive, she will survive; if you eat, she will eat; if anything happens to me, please send Niloufer to her father in Calcutta.

And he left, without looking back at her and joined the war.

A few days later she received a letter from Najmul saying he had reached Faridpur. He had met many people leaving Dacca and come to know of the horrors the people had gone through. Fighting for freedom was now the only option.

On 9 April, she received a telegram from an official in Kushtia, addressed to Nurul Huda, but not in Najmul's name. She was staying with Najmul's uncle, who told her not to accept the telegram, nor to trust it, since there was no way of knowing if it was really from Najmul. If she accepted it, word would go out and people would find out that she was Najmul's wife. But Niloufer knew it was from him because 'Nurul Huda' was the secret code name he had used during the Agartala Conspiracy Case, and was determined to follow up on the cable. The cable instructed her to go back to her father's home in Calcutta. She asked the uncle to arrange for a bullock cart; Yusuf, a young man who worked for her husband, would take care of us, she said.

Early next morning, they left for Pangsha railway station on a mule cart where she met an Awami League leader who told her to go back because no train was expected from Rajbari to Pangsha. It was not safe for her to travel, he said. 'Take out your jewellery; if anyone does any mischief, just give them the jewellery,' he advised. 'But please go back.' Niloufer though, was determined to go on, and two medical students, who had joined the resistance, helped her.

At 4 p.m., a packed train of World War II vintage came and she squeezed in. She carried her six-month-old daughter Naheed in her arm and held her three-and-a-half-year-old son Ehtesham's hand, while Yusuf carried their bag. Before they reached Hardinge Bridge they had learned that the Mukti Bahini had already attacked the bridge and taken off the rails. They had to cross the river Gorai and reached Kushtia. They walked along the sandy riverbed, changed two rickshaws, and entered the deserted town. A few people who saw them told them to go back. But she sent Yusuf to the official who had sent the cable, letting him know she had arrived. He said he would provide her transportation to cross the border.

She was heartbroken as she went to sleep—would she see Najmul again? She prayed to Allah that he would remain safe.

At 1:30 a.m. she heard someone knocking the door. And then she heard Najmul's voice: 'Yusuf, Yusuf, Yusuf...' She rose immediately, rushed to the door and opened it. He was with about a dozen East Pakistan Rifles troops. He told her to get inside quickly and lie low.

'He looked so miserable,' Niloufer said. 'He hadn't showered for ten days. His beard had grown. His clothes were torn. He had not taken out his shoes for several days and he had walked many miles. He asked Yusuf to boil some water. He said he didn't want to eat. He wanted paracetamol painkillers. There were blisters on his feet.'

The next day Huda, appointed sub-sector commander for Sector 8 (Jessore) was instructed to leave for India and reach Fort William in Calcutta. The road journey to India had become too dangerous because Pakistani troops had increased patrolling the border, so they took smaller roads and forest trails to cross the border via Dorshona and reach Gede, the border town in India's Nadia district. There were hundreds of people and India's border checkposts were open. They called Niloufer's father Dr M. Abdullah in Calcutta to come to Gede and waited. They had no Indian money with them and they were hungry. At 4 o'clock that afternoon Ehtesham suddenly shouted: 'See, nana, nana!' And Niloufer started crying as she saw her father. He had brought some rosgulla and cucumber for them which they shared with other refugees who had managed to cross the border. That night in Calcutta many friends and relatives came to meet them. One of them was her father's old friend Subrata Mitra, who was Satyajit Ray's cinematographer.

But Pakistani troops had meanwhile made rapid advances, and Huda was summoned back to the battlefield of Jessore. Kushtia had fallen back under Pakistani control and the freedom fighters needed Najmul because there was dearth of trained commanders. Najmul started to pack. Mitra gave him a pair of Leadler binoculars from Germany, a radio transistor, a Salvation Army compass, and a first-aid box to take with him. Niloufer's brother Hasan gave him some clothes. Many years later Mitra would tell Ehtesham that Huda had used the compass to determine the locations of enemy positions, and his troops would then fire mortar shells. In the months that followed Niloufer remained in Calcutta while Huda fought in the battlefields, making occasional trips to Calcutta to meet his family.

◆

The story of the Kushtia rebellion spread across the country, inspiring other villages. But while in several cases East Pakistanis managed to push back the Pakistani troops, they lacked military and logistic support, and they were not able to hold on to their gains for long, crumbling once Pakistan deployed more troops and responded with greater force.

India was caught in a bind. On one hand, the unrest in Pakistan was in India's interests because it would mean Pakistani commanders would no longer be busy plotting attacks on India. But on the other hand, India was unsure of the end game. While India saw the advantage of inflicting a blow on Pakistan by supporting the Bengali nationalists, it had two crucial worries: would the Indian state of West Bengal join the struggle and seek unification with Bangladesh? What if it wanted independence? It wasn't an absurd thought: separated halves of Bengal had fought the province's division that the British viceroy Lord Curzon had announced in 1905, and they had succeeded in overturning the division a mere six years later. Besides, until 1963, the Indian Constitution granted political parties the right to advocate or preach secession.[118] Southern states, in particular the Dravid-dominated parties in Tamil Nadu, came close to preaching secession. What if Bengal followed suit, demanding a united Bengal?

This hypothesis may sound absurd today to many Indians, but in 1971, India was still a young nation and the wounds of the Partition were still fresh. This was the time when insurgencies were growing in the northeast, and India was still absorbing Goa, which it had taken over from the Portuguese just a decade ago. Some western newspapers at the time speculated whether India was worried that a united Bengal might emerge as a threat to Indian unity.

India's second worry was the Naxalite movement which had begun in Naxalbari, a tea estate in West Bengal, but was now spreading throughout the state and parts of the northeast. Bengali intelligentsia romanticized the movement. Inspired by Mao Zedong and Communist China, the Naxalites organized peasants to attack their landlords and government officials. Besides, West Bengal was at that time run by a shaky coalition—the United Front—and dominated by various Communist parties with uncertain ideologies and the Congress Party had limited influence over the state. Calcutta was under curfew for nearly three years, as students took over university campuses, occasionally killing senior administrators and denouncing others in the establishment as 'CIA agents'. What would be the impact of supporting the Bangladesh movement on India's domestic Naxalite insurgency? There were too many imponderables in that equation. India's initial political response was therefore cautious.

For Awami leaders, their quest for independence was now no longer an intra-Pakistan debate with coreligionist brothers. This was war now, a war to liberate their country. They would need international diplomatic backing, financial assistance to travel to international capitals to present their case, and critically, military support for the young men now in India, who were anxiously awaiting orders to return to their country and start fighting the Pakistani troops. They would need to be led properly and trained, and for that, Bengali officers from the Pakistani army would have to provide leadership.

That leadership came from Gen. Muhammad Ataul Gani Osmani, the tall man with a bushy moustache who was appointed in April as commander-in-chief of the 'Bangladesh Armed Forces'. At that time that armed force was less of a reality and more of a bold aspiration. Osmani led the sector commanders who overcame enormous logistical odds and kept the morale of their troops high, at a time when India was in no position to join the battle openly. India was not at war with Pakistan and it would break international laws if it intervened militarily in Pakistan's internal affairs. Besides, India had its own views on conducting the war, which were more conventional.

Osmani had joined the British Indian Army in 1939 and seen action in Burma during World War II. After India's partition, he joined the Pakistani Army as a lieutenant colonel. After retiring from the army in 1967, he joined the Awami League and was elected from Sylhet in the 1970 elections. Osmani liked good food. The Indian lieutenant general, Jack Jacob—a Baghdadi Jew from Calcutta who spoke decent Bengali and was known as Jakes or Rafa—who was in charge of India's Eastern Command during the war, remembers: 'In matters of food, his tastes were Epicurean and he liked to dine as in peace time. On the occasions he dined with me I would serve him a *pucca* sahib's dinner which he appreciated: soup, a fish course, a roast with vegetables, dessert, and a savoury followed by coffee.'[119] Osmani had to create a cohesive army drawn from defecting soldiers from the East Pakistan Rifles, police and other paramilitary forces, and the many civilians keen to join the army. In a way, the task was not unlike what Subhas Chandra Bose faced in creating an Indian National Army. Osmani had to meld the diverse elements into a force which could fight. That was the beginning of the Mukti Bahini, which resounded with slogans like 'Bir Bangali ostro dhoro, Bangladesh shadheen koro' (Brave Bengalis, pick up your weapons; help liberate Bangladesh).

Giving the Mukti Bahini formal shape and structure was not easy—in particular, integrating the enthusiastic civilians who were keen to get back into what was still officially East Pakistan and start fighting. The commanders had to organize logistics, including creating safe houses in East Pakistan and assess which villages would have hospitable homes where the guerrillas could hide, recuperate, get food and shelter. And this had to be done without inviting the attention of the Razakars who were also found in nearly every village, spying on the villagers and collaborating with the Pakistani Army.

The strength of the Mukti Bahini rose at a sustained level because of the work of women like Raunaq Mahal Dilruba Begum. She is a war heroine not known widely even within Bangladesh. I had come to know about her through the work of Elizabeth Herman, a young American photographer whose Fulbright project was about photographing the impact of war on women. Raunaq Mahal dressed in a conservative way, wearing a long dress that covered her hair in an outfit closer to a Persian chador than an Arab abaya. Her eyes twinkled and her warm face was always smiling. I met her at her home in Bogura during Ramadan. Her orthodox Muslim attire was misleading; I had expected a serious woman speaking gravely about the war, but Raunaq Mahal was a feisty, talkative and cheerful woman. Being Ramadan, she was fasting and would not eat, but she had laid out a feast for me and the two activists from Nari Pokkho, an NGO that works on women's rights, who were travelling with me. She neither asked our religions nor minded it when she found that the two activists (who were Muslim) were not fasting.

Raunaq Mahal was 24 in 1971, and her job was to organize the boys (as she referred to the Mukti Bahini fighters) in her area. She was inspired by Sheikh Mujib's speech at the Race Course, and she told the local boys to start collecting weapons—whatever they could collect—knives, swords, machetes, and be ready. She organized them into village units and distributed weapons. As the army got closer to Bogura and ordered that all weapons be surrendered, she decided to take the boys to India for training. She took more than 250 boys to India, sometimes covering 40 to 50 kilometres over two days to get to the border. She also fed them rice, milk and biscuits. The boys called her mausi, or maternal aunt.

Friends had warned Raunaq Mahal to leave the village, as she was visible and taking grave risks, which made her vulnerable. She accepted and moved to a small village where she stayed with relatives in a two-floor mud house. It had a tin roof and she hid on the top floor. It was May and it got very hot. Her relatives gave her food but forbade her from coming down except at night to sleep. Soldiers often came and asked where the 'young woman' was. But her hosts said they didn't know.

One day she decided to cross the border herself. The head of the village told her she could not go alone because her life was in danger. But when she insisted, several older men agreed to accompany her. She sent a message to the boys in the village to pack their bags and join her. Eight boys joined her. It was a long journey and she felt very tired. Her legs felt heavy. She asked her 14-year-old nephew if she could hold on to him. He looked at her and said, 'If you do, I will fall,' for he was frail too. At Mangalbarer Hat (Tuesday Market), the village where they had to cross the border, the line of refugees was so long, she could not see the other end. There were little children, some carrying baskets on poles slung across their shoulders, others who had children in the baskets.

From the market they could see the Pakistani army camp. So they decided to turn off their clay lamps and lanterns. If the Pakistanis saw a line of lights moving towards India, they would know refugees were leaving. With even a bit of light, or one child's cry, the army would find out and come looking for them. If the army started firing, they would all die. Each glint of light was a potential hint of death.

They walked alongside the camp for nearly half an hour, but not even a child cried. They waded through the knee-length water of the river and crossed into India. When they reached India, she had no energy left. The two men who accompanied them said they would return home and convey the news that she had crossed the border safely.

Back in her village, her large ancestral home was used to train the Mukti Bahini. A retired police officer would train thirty to forty young men at a time. But one day Pakistani troops found out what was going on in the house and surrounded it. Raunaq's mother was at home with Raunaq's sister, sister-in-law, and three children. Sensing trouble, Raunaq's mother took them to the back door. Her sister Jaulush Mahal Akhtari Begum jumped over the wall and unlocked the back door.

The army was about to blow up the house when they saw a middle-aged man running towards them. 'Why are you blowing up the house?' he asked. The soldiers said they had heard there was military training going on in the house. The man said there was no such camp, and produced a card which showed that his son was a Razakar. The soldiers believed him because of the card and spared the house. It is one of the peculiarities of the Bangladesh war that close kinship trumped political ideologies. The man who protected the house was indeed a Razakar sympathizer, but he was related to Raunaq's family, and for him, those family ties came first.

There were others like him too, confused about who they were meant to hate and who to protect. Ramakrishna Pal of Chittagong remembers a classmate of his who became a Razakar. Ironically, his name was Sheikh Mujib and he had joined the pro-Pakistan movement in Chittagong because he liked their khaki uniform and because he was scared he would get killed otherwise. He remained friendly with Pal till the end of the war. His job was to help other Razakars. One day Pal saw him on the road where he was with other Razakars, and Pal was terrified that the other Razakars would attack him. But Mujib told him not to worry. 'We were good friends at school; nothing will happen to you,' he told him. Pal survived, but Mujib wasn't so lucky. In September, the Mukti Bahini got to him, and he was killed.

◆

Many refugees who had crossed over to India wanted to join the guerrillas. In Agartala, Rokeya Kabir tried to volunteer herself. But the Mukti Bahini did not want her because her face was too well known, thanks to that Rashid Talukder photograph. Rokeya accepted that, though she felt frustrated that she could do nothing each time she heard the news of another massacre.

And the news from the countryside was relentlessly gloomy. M.A. Hasan, a physician who was a Mukti Bahini fighter during the war, has compiled copious amounts of data on Pakistani atrocities during the war. His studies make deeply disturbing reading. In Baraitala, hundreds of men were tied to each other with their hands. Then they were lined up and machine-gunned. In Dacca, 150 Hindu men were called for a meeting in the cantonment and locked in three rooms. Then their homes were looted, and they were taken to the railway station and put in a train, ostensibly headed for India. But the train stopped two kilometres later. The passengers were brought down and then killed with swords. Women were brought to an army camp in Rajarbag where they were raped and brutally assaulted, their breasts bitten, their vaginas and anuses penetrated with bayonets. Hasan's research graphically describes the kind of pain and suffering inflicted upon the victims: cutting parts of a victim's body while the victim is alive; hanging a naked victim upside down and peeling off the victim's skin; putting victims in sacks, closing and tying them, and throwing the sacks in rivers; ripping off people's toenails; pressing parts of the victims' bodies in pairs of bamboos or rollers; piercing the stomach and bringing out the intestines; and throwing victims in boilers. Many Bangladeshis tell variations of these stories. It is impossible to verify them individually, but collectively, the sheer range of people from different walks of life, unconnected with one another, sharing such stories suggests that at its core, there is a broader truth to these stories. And that truth is simple: many civilians were brutalized in unconscionable ways by the Pakistani army, often aided and abetted by the Razakars.

Such stories strengthened the resolve of young men and women in refugee camps to fight for their country. Indian officers had begun providing military training in the camps, but Rokeya felt it was important for someone to educate the refugees politically as well. A revolution without an ideology was meaningless. So she introduced the young men to political theories and orientation. 'At that time India was our hero. We knew we were not alone. All the world's communists were with us, the Soviet Union was with us, and our whole nation was mobilized. We were not afraid of getting killed. The only thing was that we didn't want to lose our lives for nothing,' she told me. 'It was an emotionally charged time!'

Bangladeshi freedom fighters didn't enter East Pakistan only to fight. Spying for the Mukti Bahini was an important part too, to learn about the location of Pakistani camps, where the nearest bridges were, what roads could be taken to undertake missions, where the Pakistanis were getting their electricity from, how many informants they had in different villages, and so on. The border was not well-guarded, and it was easy for people to slip in and out in twos and threes. There were hundreds of such couriers all along the border who regularly provided accounts of villages and troop movements. Some even went as deep as Dacca and came back with fresh information. There was also a clandestine postal network, and to manage the flow of communications, there was also a censorship office which looked at outgoing letters to ensure that they did not contain any sensitive material, in case they fell into wrong hands and revealed the existence of military training camps or the locations of the fighters based in India.

◆

With the number of refugees arriving in India crossing the million mark, India had a logistical nightmare and an economic burden. As more stories about the atrocities began to emerge, often from photographs smuggled from East Pakistan, the government felt political pressure from within the country—from states neighbouring East Pakistan (West Bengal, Tripura and Assam), which wanted more resources, to chest-thumping, revenge-seeking politicians across Indian political parties, demanding that India intervene militarily immediately.

It was tempting to do so. India had established its external intelligence network, Research and Analysis Wing (RAW) only two years earlier, and the immediate priorities for RAW were to strengthen intelligence gathering from Pakistan and China, and covert action in East Pakistan to stop Pakistani supported insurgencies in India's northeast. India had two major insurgencies to contend with in its northeast—Nagaland and Mizoram. Pakistan's Inter-Service Intelligence had been providing sanctuary in the Chittagong Hill Tracts (CHT) to Phizo's Naga rebels since 1956. (They had received Burmese support as well.) Likewise, Laldenga's Mizo National Front (MNF) was offered sanctuary and weapons in the CHT since the 1960s. India wanted to end that not only to protect its territorial integrity, but also because the Northeast is rich with natural resources, and those internal conflicts hampered any meaningful extraction of resources there.[120]

And yet the decision to send the troops into East Pakistan was particularly difficult for India, since its foreign policy was officially based on peaceful coexistence and non-interference in the internal affairs of other countries, in particular its neighbours. The policy was based on hard, cynical and practical reasons—India didn't want the world to intervene in Kashmir, and it already had Tibetan refugees, it did not want to appear to be interfering in internal affairs of others.

But with the growing refugee crisis, India faced a real question: to what extent was the Bangladesh crisis Pakistan's internal affair? Pakistan was engaged in a full-scale assault on civilians in East Pakistan, and the sheer number of refugees in some states was overwhelming those states' resources. Particularly hard hit was Tripura.

Gen. Sam Manekshaw who commanded Indian forces at that time, narrated an incident in a lecture he gave in October 1995[121] in India, which is indicative of the various pressures at play within the Indian government at that time. Indira Gandhi had received telegrams from the chief ministers of

West Bengal, Assam, and Tripura, demanding that Delhi take immediate action. Manekshaw was summoned to a meeting the prime minister had called, with senior cabinet ministers Swaran Singh (external affairs), Fakhruddin Ali Ahmed (agriculture), Jagjivan Ram (defence), and Yashwantrao Chavan (finance).

'What are you going to do about it?' Mrs Gandhi asked, referring to the East Pakistan crisis.

'Nothing,' the General said. He pointed out that he wasn't consulted when India's Border Security Force, Central Reserve Police Force, and the Research and Analysis Wing had encouraged the East Pakistanis to rise. 'Now that you are in trouble you are coming to me. What do you want me to do?'

'I want you to enter Pakistan,' Mrs Gandhi said.

'And that means war,' the General replied.

'I don't mind if it is war,' she said.

Manekshaw asked if she had read the Bible. God said 'Let there be light,' and there was light. 'Now you say,' he told the assembled leaders, 'let there be war, and there will be war, but are you prepared? I am certainly not. This is the end of April. The Himalayan passes are opening and there can be an attack from China if China gives us an ultimatum.'

'Will China give an ultimatum?' Swaran Singh asked.

'You are the Foreign Minister, you tell me,' the General said.

He then told them that his two armoured infantry divisions were away— one in the Jhansi/Babina area, the other in Samba and the third in Andhra Pradesh and Tamil Nadu. He would need all the available roads, all the railway wagons, and the entire railway system to move these formations to the operational areas. Harvesting was in progress in Punjab and Uttar Pradesh and the farmers would not be able to move their harvest, which would then rot. He also pointed out to the agriculture minister that it wouldn't be his ministry's responsibility if there were food shortages. Besides, of the 189 tanks he needed for his striking force, only 11 were fit to fight, he added.

'Sam, why only eleven?' the Finance Minister asked.

'Because you are the finance minister. I have been asking you for money for over a year and you say you haven't got it!' the no-nonsense General said.

And then he turned to the prime minister and said that the rains were about to start in East Pakistan and when it rains there, it pours, and when it pours, the whole countryside is flooded. 'The snows are melting, the rivers will become oceans. If you stand on one bank, you can't see the other. All my movement will be confined to roads,' he said. The air force, because of climatic conditions, would not be able to support the army.

'Now, Prime Minister, give me your orders,' he said.

Indira Gandhi looked grim. She clenched her teeth and said: 'The Cabinet will meet again at four o'clock.'

The members of the Cabinet started walking out. Manekshaw being the junior-most waited for the others to leave. As he rose, she said: 'Chief, could you stay back?"

He turned around and said: 'Prime Minister, before you open your mouth, may I send you my resignation on the grounds of health, mental or physical?'

But she said: 'Everything you told me is true.'

'Yes! It is my job to tell you the truth,' he said. 'And it is my job to fight, it is my job to fight to win and I have to tell you the truth.'

She smiled at Manekshaw and said: 'All right Sam, you know what I want?'

'Yes,' he said, 'I know what you want.'

It became clear to Manekshaw that war was inevitable. Manekshaw was a tough-talking Parsi who had seen action in Burma during World War II and later commanded the Gorkhas. He rose to command the Indian Army in 1969 and steered the Indian armed forces during the war that would follow.

India postponed any plan it had to invade Pakistan. It decided to sit through the monsoon, continued to support the Mukti Bahini, and waited for the rains to ease: the air would cool, the leaves would fall, the sun would set earlier, the daylight would turn paler. The strategists in Delhi would wait for the snow to fall again in the Himalaya, and wait more—wait for Pakistan to make a grave mistake that would legitimize India's entry into the war.

India was prepared for hostilities. In 1968 it had conducted war games where the 'Blue Army' simultaneously fought the 'Green Army' and 'Red Army'. This war game helped Indian defence forces figure out optimal ways to transfer troops between the two fronts. One of the critical decisions was to set up a major operational base in Meghalaya which created the base for a thrust by the army corps (under Lt. Gen. Sagat Singh) which would play a crucial role in helping India ultimately win the war.

◆

India's strategy was constrained and restrained. It supported the Mukti Bahini, training its officers and men in tactics and boosting their morale; it provided relief to refugees; and it actively worked to create international opinion against

Pakistan. The Mukti Bahini saw itself as a guerrilla force, and its strategy of destroying bridges was making life difficult for Pakistani troops. But the freedom fighters were not able to hold on to many of the gains they made. They had some successes, such as when they dug in at Feni, an important town on the way to Chittagong from Dacca or Comilla. They destroyed all bridges and culverts in the area, making the Pakistani 9th Division immobile and susceptible to lightning raids and attacks at night.

The 9th Division could no longer use most roads, and its military supplies were piling up at the Chittagong port. The Pakistani army needed those in the north, but there was no way to transport them. While Pakistani troops managed to regain Feni in May, the Mukti Bahini fighters succeeded in escaping to India with their weapons. Pakistani commanders were livid. One Pakistani officer, Lt. Col. Aslam Baig, told Anthony Mascarenhas: 'The Indians obviously will not allow them [Mukti Bahini] to settle there. It would be too dangerous. So they will be allowed in on sufferance as long as they keep making sorties across the border. Unless we can kill them off, we are going to have serious trouble for a long time.'[122]

Pakistani troops saw Bengalis as unreliable Muslims who had to be re-educated and Islamicized properly. They also thought that by evicting Hindus from Bangladesh, the troops would be able to lure poor Muslims towards their fold, by offering them the land and property the Hindus had vacated. The remarkable part about these assumptions is the breathtaking certitude. Pakistani commanders kept getting frustrated because the Bengalis did not succumb to their plans. And Mukti Bahini continued to irritate Pakistani troops by sabotaging their attempts to secure major cities and transport routes through their flash attacks, and in many areas Bengali Muslims continued to protect Hindu neighbours, hiding them from predatory Razakars. When Pakistani officers tried to figure out a pattern in the Mukti Bahini's actions, they found none, nor could they understand their motives. Why would Bengali Muslims protect Bengali Hindus? Rather than try to understand the Bengali identity, they concluded that Bengali Muslims were not really Muslim.

The rebels seemed uncoordinated, even isolated, and there was much truth in that. But the continued havoc they caused—destroying roads and bridges—kept delaying Pakistani plans. As the Indians understood, and as the Pakistanis were learning, once the rains came, no action was possible for three months—artillery and air power would be ineffective.

But the imminence of rain and collapsing transport links posed a different challenge for Pakistan—how to transport food from the ports to the troops. When the roads and bridges were operational, some 15 per cent of food movement was by boats. Now many arterial roads and bridges were destroyed. Relying on boats was not possible because boats were slower. And destroyed roads made it harder to ship the food easily. If food delivery got delayed, it would spark fears, and even the slightest rumour of food shortages would lead to the traders and the people hoarding food. The elderly still remembered the aakaal of 1943. If the crisis became acute, international donors would step in to provide aid, and Pakistan would find it hard to say no to western generosity. However, if aid came, so would aid workers, and those aid workers would go swarming through the countryside. And once those altruistic do-gooders spoke to the villagers, it would be impossible to keep the stories of Pakistani atrocities and massacres suppressed.

Anthony Mascarenhas asked the chairman of Pakistan's Agricultural Development Bank in Karachi what the government would do in case of a famine. The banker's callous reply stunned him: 'The famine is the result of their acts of sabotage. So let them die. Perhaps then the Bengalis will come to their senses.'[123]

◆

Peter Kann made several trips from Hong Kong to cover the war for the *Wall Street Journal*. In the early days Kann was able to travel to many villages, away from the main cities. We spoke one warm afternoon in 2013 at his home in Princeton, where he lives in retirement after having risen to publish the *Journal* and later, as Chairman and CEO of its parent, Dow Jones & Company.[124] Kann had travelled in the countryside with Lee Lescaze of the *Washington Post*. Few villagers sought them out to talk to them because all the villages had Razakars who kept an eye on any unusual activity and reported it to the Pakistani troops. Kann also saw people being stopped at buses and taken away. He saw men's lungis being pulled up to see if they were circumcised or not. 'If it was genocide, it was quite selective,' Kann said. 'But it was certainly what we would call ethnic cleansing, with Hindus being the main targets.' The Pakistani military officers he spoke to were arrogant. 'You tended to get the Punjabi swagger from them—"We are in control; these little people can't bother us",' he said.

Once in India, Kann could speak to refugees who talked to him openly, and he could write about Babar Ali Khan painfully recounting how seven of his ten family members were mowed down by Pakistani forces, and how Minu Bibi, a 26-year-old woman saw her parents being killed and her sister raped and killed, because she managed to escape and saw the tragedy from behind trees.[125] Kann noted that many Mukti Bahini fighters were 'kids who had never held guns in their lives. Some had a few days' training and came from India. Some, not even that.'

Everyone, he noticed, exaggerated. There were the unreliable narrators, the refugees, who shared stories of their personal pain, but were not trained to note down the sort of facts a reporter needs to present an accurate picture. Aid workers wanted to exaggerate the crisis to generate sympathy and get the international community to commit more resources; Indians wanted to exaggerate because they wanted to show the world how cruel Pakistan was. And Pakistan wanted to deflate the numbers because only 'a few miscreants' were causing the trouble. The embassies and consulates knew even less; they had to be circumspect about the degree to which they could travel around freely. It was a war. The closer you were to the ground, the better your information. It was war; truth was the inevitable casualty.

◆

Terror works in different ways—sometimes people are frightened not by the act itself, but by what is possible. Tahmina Saleh, who as a teenager had marched with other students in 1952 at the dawn of the language movement, was a married woman in 1971. She lived in Chittagong, where her husband was working on a government project. Pakistani officers had visited their colony and assured them that being government officers they had nothing to worry about.

But an hour later, more soldiers came. They first took away their valuables— wristwatches, wallets, jewellery. Then they asked Tahmina's husband, Abul Khair Saleh, to raise his hands. Tahmina told the manager's wife: 'They are going to take away our husbands now.' They had an American neighbour who told the soldiers not to take away these men, surely there was a mistake? The soldier pointed his gun towards the American, who said he was willing to go with the men and the soldiers. At this, the soldier placed his finger on the trigger and the American stepped aside.

The men were taken away. Tahmina was anxious, with no information about where her husband had been taken. An hour later he returned.

In a shock, Tahmina asked him: 'Where is Mr Samsudin?' referring to his colleague who had also been taken away.

'They shot him,' he told her.

Then, slowly, he recounted what happened.

First they told them to stand against a wall, and they did. Then they shot Samsudin in the front and the back. He fell down in front of Abul Khair. Then they asked Abul Khair to stand where Samsudin had stood a moment ago. Abul Khair stood there with his hands up.

'Are you a Muslim?'

'Yes,' Abul Khair said.

'Say the kalima!'

And Abul Khair recited: 'La ilaha illallah, Muhammadun rusulullah (There is no God but Allah, [and] Muhammad is the messenger of Allah).'

The major had his finger on the trigger. He put the revolver down and told Abul Khair to leave.

'The prayer meant something to the major. My husband came back alive,' Tahmina said quietly.

◆

The Mukti Bahini guerrillas began penetrating the countryside, but their activities were often uncoordinated, and their successes were limited. By pushing them back, Pakistan felt they had managed to ward off the threat of the monsoon offensive. Civilian morale was weakening and Pakistani officials in Dacca even began saying that the situation was returning to normal. Indeed, in their authoritative history of the war, Richard Sisson and Leo Rose wrote that despite Indian assistance, the Mukti Bahini's performance was far from spectacular in the early days. They said that since April 'the Mukti Bahini had not been able to prevent the Pakistani army from regaining control over all the major urban centres on the East Pakistan-India border and even establishing a tenuous authority in most of the rural areas'. From mid-October to 20 November 'Indian artillery was used much more extensively in support... and Indian military forces, including tanks and air power on a few occasions, were also used... Indian units were withdrawn to Indian territory once their objectives had been brought under the control of the Mukti Bahini—though at times this was only for short periods, as, to the irritation of the Indians, the Mukti Bahini forces rarely held their ground when the Pakistani army launched a counterattack'.[126]

During the early monsoon months, the Mukti Bahini carried out many attacks inside Bangladesh, but the impact was negligible. Pakistani forces were able to hold their own and fight back, even inflicting heavy damages on the attackers, and later they would destroy villages they suspected of harbouring the Mukti Bahini fighters. To counter the Bangladeshi irregulars, Pakistan also created its own militias of pro-Pakistan East Pakistanis. These included Razakars, Al-Badr and Al-Shams—comprising Urdu-speaking Muslims from Bihar, or Bengali-speaking Muslims.

In July, senior officers of the Mukti Bahini met in Calcutta for a week and divided the country into eleven sectors. The aim of the week long meeting was to give the fighters some strategic direction, coherence and structure. The eleven sectors were under the command of specific officers. Maj. Ziaur Rahman commanded Chittagong. Maj. Khaled Mosharraf took charge of Dhaka and Comilla. Others included Maj. K.M. Shafiullah (near Sylhet), Maj. Chittaranjan Datta (Habiganj and the border with India), Maj. Mir Shawkat Ali (Durgapur), Wg. Cdr. Khademul Bashar (Rangpur and Dinajpur), Maj. Nazmul Haq (Rajshahi), Maj. Abu Osman Chowdhury (Kushtia and Jessore through August. After August Maj. Abul Manzoor took charge of the sector), Maj. M.A. Jalil (Barisal), and Maj. Abu Taher (Mymensingh and Tangail). Each commander was in charge of training the forces and preparing for guerrilla warfare. Each guerrilla unit sent into East Pakistan would have between five and ten trained fighters. Each group would have a base that would provide them with food, medicines, and accommodation. An action group would carry out attacks, and they would be armed appropriately. Another group would be trained to observe and pick up intelligence—only some of them would be armed. The regular force would be organized in battalions.

Typical attacks would include destroying bridges, damaging critical infrastructure, disrupting power supply, destroying warehouses and boats carrying military equipment. Pakistan had over 90,000 personnel in the east; the plan was to disrupt their rhythm by forcing them to disperse into smaller units and then attacking them. There was a strong guerrilla force in Barisal and three brigades named after three officers—Z-Force (Ziaur Rahman), K-Force (Khaled Mosharraf), and S-Force (K.M. Shafiullah). Besides, there was an independent Mujib Bahini which included student leaders, and the Kaderia Bahini, under the command of Kader Siddiqui who would acquire legendary reputation by the time the war ended.

◆

Of all the freedom fighters of Bangladesh, the one who acquired Che Guevera-like mystique is Kader Siddiqui. Called Bagha Kader (Bagha meaning tiger), Siddiqui was 23 at the time of the war. Siddiqui, a tall, fit man now in his sixties, preferred to speak only in Bengali with me even though he understands English well. He was not a language chauvinist. He told me that the issues I wanted to discuss were serious and complicated, and he did not want to use any wrong word in English, which was not his first language, because that might convey his thoughts inaccurately. Photographs of Siddiqui with Indira Gandhi were displayed proudly on the wall—he pointed out one such picture and told me how much he admired her.

In those old photographs Siddiqui looks sharp, dashing and handsome. He was a true guerrilla who showed no mercy towards his Pakistani opponents and developed the reputation of being as elusive as the Scarlet Pimpernel, as admired as Robin Hood, and as feared as Che. He created a guerrilla force in Tangail, the town famous for its handloom saris. His fighters were fiercely independent to the point of being insubordinate to all except Siddiqui. He was so popular himself that several Bangladeshi women I interviewed, who are now in their fifties or sixties, admitted having had a crush on him when they were teenagers.

Siddiqui was a student of political science at Saadat College in Karatia village near Tangail. He was an activist in the student wing of the Awami League. He had taken part in demonstrations against the government. From 25 March to 3 April, local leaders had seized power from the local administration and ran Tangail. On 3 April, the Pakistani Army came to Tangail, blocking its only road link to Dacca. But the people in Tangail rebelled, and the Pakistani troops were stunned by the scale of devastation—nearly thirty cars were destroyed and some 100 people were killed.

'We resisted them though we were untrained,' Siddiqui remembered. But the Pakistani Army hit back and the Tangail fighters had to retreat—nearly 150 people died. The army reached Tangail in the evening and burned down the homes of three prominent local leaders. Siddiqui fled to Shafipur hill with a few boxes of bullets, and rifles that he had stolen from the police, taking with him about fourteen followers—they included students, rickshaw pullers, and farmers.

By May, his support dwindled—he was down to about half a dozen compatriots. He circled around Tangail, looking for opportunities to attack the Pakistanis, but he felt frustrated without any guidance from anyone. And yet, people in the villages nearby knew him as a student leader and asked him how they could join the Mukti Bahini.

By then, Siddiqui had run out of ammunition so he quietly went home with Faruk Ahmed, who had stayed with him all along. There was no one at his home. Siddiqui felt depressed, he saw no way forward. As he lay down to sleep, he heard a song on Akashwani (All India Radio)—Tagore's famous poem: 'Jodi tor dak shune keu na ashe tobe ekla chalo re'. It was about 10:30 p.m. 'The song stuck with me. My sister Rahima used to sing it. It revived my spirit and I rose. I felt the song was being sung for me. After that, whoever I saw, I thought he was waiting for my call, although earlier I was suspicious of other people,' he told me.

He wrote a letter to his friend, Saidur: 'There is no one here. But I cannot sit around idly. Come to me with some trustworthy people.' And Saidur came with ten people and they went to Maricha, to Kalihati, and later to Mymensingh, Dacca, Pabna, and Manikganj. Of the ten people he had, only two could handle rifles; others had never seen a rifle before.

Siddiqui heard that the cigarette factory at Sangrampur had some long-range rifles, so he decided to raid the factory and steal the weapons. He divided his people in three groups with three rifles each. When they arrived, word went out in the factory that 'Bagha Siddiqui' had come with his fighters. There was panic in the area, and the police who were meant to guard the area fled, leaving their weapons behind. People in the village collected the weapons and brought them to Siddiqui.

He then went to Safipur and people who wanted to join his army surrounded him. 'We wanted only twenty-thirty people, but there were over one thousand, perhaps two thousand people waiting to see us and join us,' he said. Siddiqui selected twenty-seven men that day. A young boy stubbornly insisted on being chosen. Siddiqui tested him by threatening to pull the trigger, but the boy did not flinch. He was clearly brave and he was chosen, but he died near Bahadurabad Ghat in August in a battle.

Pakistani troops were greatly helped by the Razakars, so Siddiqui decided to target the homes of Muslim League members and other Razakar supporters. 'People criticized and mocked us, saying we did not have the guts to fight the Pakistani army. They didn't realize that Pakistani army depended hugely on the Razakars, and we wanted to cut that link,' he said. As the word went around of the surgical attacks on Razakars, people's perception began to change. More people joined Siddiqui.

In August, the Kaderia Bahini had one of its most stunning successes—they captured two ships laden with weapons. They helped themselves to the weapons that significantly enhanced the group's combat capability. Reports of Siddiqui's exploits reached Gen. Niazi. Formerly of the Rajput regiment, Niazi was the cousin of Pakistan's cricketer, and now politician, Imran Khan. Niazi was furious and demanded his army fight Siddiqui's fighters. Siddiqui claims that the Bahini fought nearly 300 battles, of which they lost only about a dozen. He laughed as he recalled how legends about him grew, of how the Pakistani army began to fear them and escaped if they heard the Kaderia Bahini was headed towards them.

In August that year, the Kaderia Bahini captured twenty-two police stations. From that month, he was in regular touch with the Indian Army, which was not yet formally engaged in the war. During Ramadan in October, they blocked the road linking Dacca to the north and blew up forty-two bridges. They also captured three Pakistani ships, after which Akashwani, Shadheen Bangla Betar Kendra, Voice of America, and the BBC began broadcasting news of their exploits. But the fame brought unwanted attention as well—Pakistani intelligence began focusing on the Bahini's activities, including bombarding one unit aerially.

Siddiqui's success as a guerrilla commander is remarkable, even if it is not easy to verify all the claims he or his admirers make about his exploits. His troops gained fame for their bravery but also notoriety for their brutality against their enemies. I asked him if he had read books on military strategy. He laughed and shook his head, and with his index finger gently tapped his head. 'It is all here. I read nothing of the sort,' he said. 'I have read some books after the war. But I learned everything on the battlefield. People had started calling me the Fidel Castro of Bangladesh.' In *Surrender at Dacca: The Birth of a Nation,* his wartime memoir, Lt. Gen. Jacob was less kind to Siddiqui, describing him as a man of bluster and bravado who could not be relied upon and often created problems instead of solving them. Siddiqui certainly had a mind of his own, and not trained in an organized army, he was less respectful of hierarchy and authority, compared to officers who had been part of military academies. But just as his spectacular, unexpected attacks surprised Pakistan and made the job easy for Indian troops to advance, his impetuousness complicated careful plans Indian commanders may have wanted to implement.

◆

Bangladesh's riverine landscape posed significant strategic challenges for both the Pakistani forces and the Mukti Bahini. The monsoon compounded matters and made transport and communication across the country particularly difficult, forcing Pakistan to learn quickly how to control major inland waterways. The Mukti Bahini knew the geography of the waterways, but they weren't skilled at fighting in rivers. Their attempts to use civilian boats for naval operations had not been effective; the more superior Pakistani boats sank them easily.

Pakistan had made a significant breakthrough after gaining control of Dacca, when its forces destroyed rebel capability to control their operations from Barisal. At the end of the operations in Barisal, many Mukti Bahini fighters had been driven to India, where they began to reorganize in June and July. Indian support was largely logistical and moral. They advised that Mukti Bahini should send up to 5,000 trained guerrillas each month into East Pakistan and seize territory step by step.

Mukti Bahini then decided on a naval commando operation, whose aim was to dismantle the capability of Pakistan's eastern naval command. India supported the operation, which was called Operation Jackpot. The operation's origins lay in France, where a Pakistani submarine was on a goodwill visit. The East Pakistani crewmen there received training from a commissioned officer, and eight crewmen decided to take control of the submarine. Their plans got leaked but they managed to escape. The crewmen eluded Pakistani Intelligence and reached the Indian mission in Geneva, from where they were taken to Delhi and provided training.

On 23 May, in Plassey in West Bengal, Indian officers began training the Mukti Bahini volunteers—ultimately near 500 commandos were trained. They were taught swimming, survival training, how to use limpet mines, hand-to-hand combat, and navigation skills. The actual operation was to take place in late July. Commandos were sent from Plassey to forward bases in Tripura and West Bengal. The groups slipped into East Pakistan between 3 and 9 August and reached Chittagong, Chandpur, Mongla, and Narayanganj on 12 August. Each commando had a pair of fins, a knife, a limpet mine, and swimming gear. A few carried sten guns and hand grenades, and each group's leader had a transistor radio.

On 13 August at a pre-determined time, Akashwani played a song, 'Amar putul ajke prothom jabe shoshur bari' (My doll will go for the first time to the in-laws' home). It was a coded signal to prepare for the operations. The next day another song was played—'Ami tomay joto shuniye chilem gaan tar bodoley chaini kono daan' (When I sang all my songs for you I wanted nothing in return).

Sixty commandos left for Chittagong, of whom 31 took part in sabotage operations on 16 August. Between 1:45 a.m. and 2:15 a.m., they succeeded in sinking three ships—*Al-Abbas*, *Hormuz* and *Orient*, sinking 19,000 tonnes of weapons. In Chandpur, 18 out of 40 commandos took part and damaged three ships. In Narayanganj, 20 commandos took part in operations that sank four ships. And in Mongla, 20 commandos damaged six foreign-owned ships.

Mahfuzur Rahman supported Operation Jackpot by destroying electrical pylons in Chittagong. He is now a pathologist with a busy practice in Chittagong. The night I went to meet him, there were over a dozen patients in the waiting room. After he had finished seeing them, we sat in his cabin and he told me his story.

Rahman had left for India after the crackdown and enlisted with the Mukti Bahini. He was sent for military training first to Assam and then Dehradun. He slipped into India with other fighters in August with the specific target of demolishing electric pylons, as part of Operation Jackpot. Their targets were in Chittagong. Rahman recalled wistfully going from one electric transformer to the next in Chittagong, blowing them up. For good measure, they also destroyed petrol pumps. They then attacked a fire brigade station and later carried out other acts of sabotage, including tossing a grenade into a car carrying Pakistani officers, killing them. There were plans to attack Salahuddin Quader Chowdhury, who, with his father Fazlul Quader Chowdhury would later be accused of war crimes, and Salahuddin would be tried and found guilty by the Bangladesh International Crimes Tribunal. 'The people knew we were freedom fighters and they supported us. They took care of us. Even children learned to keep secrets,' he said.

Operation Jackpot represented a quantum shift in Mukti Bahini's ability to fight. Kann had told me: 'In the beginning the Mukti Bahini was so unprepared for anything like a war, and in some ways so incompetent as well as naïve, that it wasn't surprising that many looked down on them. But once the guerrilla war expanded, they did really well, even though they had only limited arms. They did destroy a lot of Pakistani communications lines, blew up bridges, and forced the Pakistanis back into the cantonment.'

There were some incidents of valiant but futile bravery. In August, Flight Lieutenant Matiur Rahman attempted to hijack a trainer aircraft from Karachi to India, to defect from the Pakistan air force and join the Mukti Bahini. But he crashed in Thatta, 40 kilometres from the Indian border, because Rashid Minhas, his co-pilot, struggled with him to regain control of the plane. Then there was Nur Mohammad, who was chosen to lead a patrol of four Mukti Bahini soldiers to monitor Pakistani troop movements in Goalhati in early September. Pakistani soldiers found out where they were, and surrounded them from three sides. Nur Mohammad wanted to retreat to his base and fire towards them. But one of his soldiers got shot. Nur Mohammad carried him and tried to reach a safe place. But then he got hit. He was badly injured and bleeding, but he continued to provide cover fire to protect his team. He kept a self-loading rifle and continued to shoot till he died. In another battle, Mukti Bahini fighters who wanted to control the Dhalai border outpost at Srimangal in Sylhet were being repulsed because of stronger firepower coming from Pakistan's Frontier Force Regiment. Hamidur Rahman, who had enlisted with the East Pakistan Regiment only in February, crawled through the canals and started lobbing grenades. He threw two grenades but then he got shot. He jumped on the gun post and fought hand-to-hand with the two Pakistani soldiers who were guarding the gun and managed to neutralize it. Other fighters moved quickly and took over the post, realizing only later that inside lay Rahman's dead body.

After the initial shock of Operation Jackpot, Pakistan boosted security around its assets. Mukti Bahini's attempts to damage the Hardinge Bridge near Kushtia failed. Some commando teams were apprehended and caught. The commandos could not attack oil depots at Narayanganj, Bogura, Faridpur and Chittagong. Of the 515 commandos India trained, 8 died in action, 34 were wounded, and 15 were captured. Those caught were treated mercilessly. A commando called Hussain Farid was killed in the second Chittagong operation of Operation Jackpot. He had reached Chittagong pretending to be a devotee of the saint Mohsen Aulia and crossed the river. He had fastened a limpet mine to his body but it was attacked by a troupe of shrimps. He struggled to fight them off, but soon lost consciousness. The Pakistani army found him, possibly already dead, and put him in a manhole and bent his body till his vertebral column was broken.

The Mukti commandos managed to sink or damage some fifteen Pakistani ships, eleven coasters, seven gunboats, eleven barges, two tankers, and nineteen rivercraft.[127] About 100,000 tonnes of shipping, including weapons was sunk, jetties and wharves were disabled and channels blocked. The remarkable thing was that the commandos accomplished all this without having a single vessel of their own.

Recognizing their success, the Indian navy gave the Mukti Bahini four gunboats and the Calcutta Port Trust donated two patrol craft, *Ajay* and *Akshay*, to the Mukti Bahini, creating the nucleus of the Bangladesh Navy. These patrol craft were refurbished with guns and renamed *Padma* and *Palash*. Escorted by an Indian frigate, the two ships sailed in November and mined the entrance of Mongla port.

The exploits of the commandos gave enormous support to the ground forces, which had now grown to 30,000 soldiers comprising eight infantry battalions, and 100,000 guerrillas. As the attacks mounted, the toll of destruction in East Pakistan rose. By November the havoc reached 231 bridges, 122 railway lines, 90 power stations.[128] Many soldiers were killed. Nothing that seemed normal to Pakistan soldiers could be normal. The Mukti Bahini was able to use an informal network of supporters from among civilians—Pakistani troops could never be sure whether schoolboys carrying their bags had books in those bags or something more sinister. One day two soldiers guarding an area casually asked an old man, carrying two bags of vegetables, what was inside the bags. The man trembled with fear. Beneath the vegetables were fuses. Another day, a boat filled with fruits was stopped. Below the fruits lay mines and grenades. Such was the reputation of the Mukti Bahini, that Siddiq Salik, who was an aide to Gen. Niazi, wrote that by November some Pakistani soldiers left their bases only when and if the need arose.[129]

◆

Just as Operation Jackpot was underway, Pakistan began to make final arrangements to try Mujibur Rahman at a secret military court in West Pakistan. People in Dacca didn't take the news well. The same afternoon a bomb exploded in the lobby of Dacca's InterContinental Hotel. David Greenway, who was a correspondent for *Time* magazine, was in the hotel lobby and suffered a concussion in the blast. Later, he wrote: 'I was standing in front of the cigar store in the lobby when, with a flash and a roar, the wall a few feet in front of me seemed to buckle and dissolve. I was flung to the floor. That was fortunate, because great chunks of bricks and concrete flew over me, crashing through the lobby and blowing men and furniture through the plate-glass windows onto the sidewalk. Part of an air duct came down on my head and I could not move. There was thick, choking smoke and water spewing from broken pipes. Soon the smoke began to clear. People milled about the crumpled, crying victims lying bleeding on the lawn. None, luckily, was dead. One girl, an employee of the hotel, had been completely buried under three feet of rubble. When they dug her out, all she could say was, "I knew I should not have come to work today".[130]

Nobody in East Pakistan doubted that the secret military court would convict Mujib under charges of 'waging war against Pakistan and other offences'. A western diplomat told Greenway: 'You know how hot the Punjabi plains are this time of year. You might say Mujib has a snowball's chance of acquittal.'

The trial was to be held in a one-storey, red-brick jail in Lyallpur (now known as Faisalabad), a textile city south of Rawalpindi. Pakistan claimed it wanted to keep the trial secret to prevent rebels from attempting to rescue Mujib, but Yahya's real fear lay in giving Mujib a platform. He remembered well the 1968 attempt to try Mujib in the Agartala Conspiracy Case, which collapsed because of widespread protests. As *Time* pointed out, no Pakistani leader had managed to draw million-strong crowds at his public meetings, and few subcontinental politicians since Mohandas Gandhi's days had spent as much time in jails for political beliefs as Mujib had. 'Prison is my other home,' Mujib once said.

Time reported that in August Mujib's brother Sheikh Abu Nasser arrived in Delhi wearing tattered clothes. He said Mujib's aged parents (his father was 95, mother, 80) were driven from their home by Pakistani troops. Their house was burnt, servants shot, and they hadn't been heard from since. Nasser didn't know the whereabouts of his own family. He requested Senator Edward Kennedy, who was visiting refugee camps in India at that time as chairman of the US Senate Sub-Committee on Refugees, to get some information. But Pakistan refused to grant Kennedy permission to visit either of Pakistan's halves.

The legal case against Mujib was never going to be easy. He did not formally declare independence or call for secession—he used words like 'freedom', 'autonomy', 'liberation', but never formal independence. (Pointing out that Bengalis formed the majority in Pakistan, he once asked: 'Why should the majority secede from minority?') *Time* concluded that if Yahya tried Mujib and executed him to please Pakistani generals and politicians, he would have to face an unprecedented backlash in the east. But if he were kept alive, Yahya would finally have to negotiate some amicable separation, since keeping Pakistan united seemed increasingly impossible.

◆

Throughout this period, the Indian prime minister Indira Gandhi played her cards with great skill. Shrewd and articulate, she mobilized international public opinion skillfully, by meeting heads of government and diplomats, permitting foreign dignitaries to visit refugee camps, and giving interviews to the western media in which she inevitably came out on top.

When a television interviewer asked her if India should refrain from supporting the Mukti Bahini, whose guerrilla warfare was escalating the conflict, she responded firmly: 'Does that mean we allow the massacre to continue? What happened first? Look at newspapers. The massacre began long before there was a single guerrilla... Being quiet means we have to support genocide. Do you think people are going to allow and watch their women be raped?'

She then gave the interviewer a history lesson: 'May I take you back? When Hitler was on rampage, why didn't you say—let's keep quiet, let there be peace in Germany, let the Jews die, let Belgium die, let France die—would you stay quiet? (This) would not have happened if (the) world community had woken up to the facts when we first drew their attention.'

The journalist asked her if India would join the war. She replied: 'I hope not (but) we can't endanger our security... Pakistan has moved its troops forward a considerable time before we did. While they were there, nobody said it would endanger our country. When we sent them the intention of our defence, the whole world seems to have woken up. We have never attacked anyone but we have been attacked thrice. (So) it is not a question of supporting (the guerrillas) or not. We can't shut our eyes to a situation in a neighbouring state... Pakistan as it existed cannot be the same again. I understand (the situation) perfectly well. Our troops are there because we were threatened by the military regime in Pakistan. And I don't think you can point out any head of government would be so restrained. (And yet) what we get is (to) equate us with a government which has killed a million people which has created conditions of barbarity which the world has very seldom seen, perhaps (only) against the Jews in Hitler's time.'

The journalist asked if she would meet Yahya Khan. She said: 'Have you read some of Yahya Khan's speeches? Do you think it would serve a useful purpose if we meet?'

On 9 August, India sent shockwaves around the diplomatic world by signing a 20-year treaty of peace, friendship and cooperation with the Soviet Union. It was as close to a military alliance as India would sign, and therefore remarkable, given India's long-standing commitment to non-alignment. It wasn't a formal defence treaty, but the implication of the strategic relationship was clear. Diplomatically it was a masterstroke, for it significantly enhanced India's ability to manoeuvre world opinion, since it now had the backing of one of the five countries that had a veto at the UN General Assembly. This would be hugely beneficial to India, and by implication Bangladesh, when the crisis inevitably reached the UN Security Council.

By mid-October, Indian involvement in the war was getting more obvious. Its spies and soldiers made frequent forays into East Pakistan, gathering intelligence or laying the groundwork of a future invasion. Nixon took the Indo-Soviet Treaty almost as a personal affront. Bass quotes him as saying: 'It makes your heart sick to be done so by the Indians and after we have warned the bitch.'[131]

The Indo-Soviet Treaty neutralized any threat China may have posed to India. The Soviets more or less said they would step into military action if China applied any pressure on India militarily, as Nixon and Kissinger might have hoped. And the Chinese would remember that only a year earlier, in 1970, China had fought an undeclared border war with the USSR and the Soviets had won several brutal large-scale battles. In fact, there are still derelict Chinese tanks visible at the bottom of the Ussuri River.

◆

Meanwhile, the killings continued throughout the country. Abdul Gofran owned a shop near the Akbarshah Mosque in Pahartali in Chittagong.[132] On 10 November at 6 a.m. about fifty Biharis came to his shop and took him away to Foy's Lake, a beautiful man-made lake created in 1924 to provide water for the residents of a large railway colony situated there. And as they passed through the gates Gofran saw many Bengalis who had been brought in and tied up. Many Biharis were carrying knives, swords and other sharp instruments. The Biharis were kicking and beating up the Bengalis brutally and pushing them towards those carrying weapons, who then jabbed the victims in the stomach and then severed their heads with swords. 'I witnessed several groups of Bengalis being killed in such a manner,' Gofran wrote. 'When the Biharis came for me one of them took away my sweater. I then punched him and jumped into the lake. ...I swam to the other side and hid among the bushes. The Biharis came to look for me but I was fortunate and barely escaped their notice. From my hiding place I witnessed the mass murder that was taking place.'

According to Gofran, the massacre went on till 2 p.m. After they had disposed of the last Bengali victim, they brought a group of about a dozen Bengali men who were asked to dig a grave for the bodies lying about. Once those bodies were buried, the Biharis killed the gravediggers too.

The massacre at Foy's Lake is etched in the memories of Chittagong residents, like the 25 March killings among Dacca residents, and the May pogrom at Chuknagar in the minds of those who lived between Khulna and Jessore. As with those massacres, it is impossible to get an accurate account of the number of people who died though eyewitness accounts survive. Besides Gofran, whose memoir has been cited in several publications, there are others who have taken to recording the massacre. I spoke to several people who randomly said '10,000', or '20,000', when I asked how many people were killed. One man assertively said 3,000 women were killed, their stomachs slit open. There is no way to verify these numbers, and killing so many over a few hours with swords and knives seems difficult to believe. But Pradeep Dewanji, a theatre activist, told me that cumulatively the number could be large. Foy's Lake had become the dumping ground for dead bodies throughout the war, and the incident on 20 November was only the worst. Could as many as 20,000 people have been killed at Foy's Lake over the months? Possibly, but there is no way to establish it one way or another, unless a major excavation exercise is undertaken, and there is no governmental or private interest at the moment to account for the numbers.

What's known is that the lake was in an isolated place and not easily accessible from the city. Leaving dead bodies there suited everyone's convenience, particularly the killers'.

I met Ghazi Salehuddin, whose brother, Kamaluddin; uncle, Ali Husain; and two relatives, Mohammed Gofran and Abdul Mannan were picked up from home and taken to Foy's Lake. Salehuddin was in Noakhali that day. His younger brother had managed to escape, and met him the next night in

Noakhali. On 12 November, Salehuddin returned to Chittagong to collect his father's dead body, but he was not allowed to go to the lake. He heard stories of scores of heads chopped off, of stomachs cut, of holes made in people's bodies. Salehuddin could go to the lake only after the war ended. He saw some bodies in an advanced state of decomposition. There were dogs and vultures. He saw a big stone, some knives that had been sharpened on a stone, two drums full of congealed blood, and darkened leaves with congealed blood.

◆

While India was not formally at war with Pakistan, its troops first saw action on 20-21 November, when they fought a pitched battle with Pakistani troops in Garibpur in India. The Boyra salient juts into Bangladeshi territory, about 40 kilometres from Jessore, and is a critical threshold on the highway to Jessore from India. There was a battalion of Mukti Bahini fighters in Garibpur. Indian cavalry and tanks supported the Bahini, whose fighters had planned an incursion into East Pakistan. But on the 20th the Pakistanis found out about the attack and sent an infantry brigade and an armoured squadron with tanks to protect the territory. Pakistani troops were numerically superior to the combined Indian-Bangladeshi manoeuvre, but the Indians dug in. They maintained a defensive position and sent their tanks forward. Indian tanks pounded Pakistani charge, and the Pakistanis were not able to identify exactly where they were being hit from because of fog-like conditions. Pakistani tanks persisted, but Indians rolled them back. By noon, eleven Pakistani tanks were destroyed and three captured. Pakistan then sought air cover, and the Pakistani Air Force began hitting Indian positions. But Indians were prepared for that, and they were able to neutralize the attack from the sky. Indian Gnats shot down three Pakistani Sabres in dog fights. Two pilots[133] managed to evacuate, but were arrested by the Mukti Bahini. From that day, India was effectively at war with Pakistan, although it was never declared formally by either side.

This victory was strategically very important for the Mukti Bahini, for it meant that the Bahini now had many strategic advantages in the north. While such successes had military significance, civilians in Dacca and beyond were getting impatient. Fakrul Alam, who was in Dacca during the war, told me: 'We eagerly listened to Shadheen Bangla Betar Kendra and the BBC, which were our main sources of inspiration, as well as AIR, Calcutta. Initially, we thought by April or May there would be an armed intervention, but the Mukti Bahini kept retreating and Pakistan boasted of flushing out Mukti Bahini. And we wondered why India wasn't intervening. Why this silence, why not say enough is enough, and send troops? That was our initial feeling. At first we were thrilled by the Mukti Bahini's initial successes. We had growing awareness that India was supplying arms and trained the fighters in camps, so we thought it would work on its own, and we thought we wouldn't need intervention. But then there was despair, and we wondered why India had not interfered. This went on, and by November it was clear that Indians and Mukti Bahini were combined, and an attack had to be imminent. But when and how? Each day seemed long. We were dying to break the shackles.'

As Pakistan began losing control of its border areas, it started withdrawing its troops to Dacca, to defend the capital. Pakistan had expected an attack on Eid (19 November that year), but that did not happen, so Niazi became confident. Buses and trains were running; no Indian jets were seen in East Pakistani skies. Niazi followed his schedule of daily visits to the border areas in his helicopter 'and continued to thrive on bawdy jokes and plentiful chicken tikkas', Salik wrote in his memoir.

He insisted that all-out war had started for him on 21 November and that he was fighting back successfully. At a press interview he defended his border deployment as 'a forward posture in defence... My troops in the border outposts are like the extended fingers of an open hand. They will fight there as long as possible before they fold back to the fortresses to form a fist to bash the enemy's head'.

'I was fascinated by the simile', Salik wrote. 'But I recalled his latest decision prohibiting any withdrawal unless 75 per cent casualties had been sustained. When three out of four fingers are broken, or wounded, is it possible to form a fist? I can't form one if I have so much of a damaged nail. That was a novice's way of analyzing Gen. Niazi's operational strategy, the professionals considered it as "undue confidence in his capabilities". The fact remains that he refused to admit that he was deployed for defeat.'[134]

By late November, Pakistan was indiscriminately attacking camps along the Indian border. Indian civilians were not spared and Indian politicians grew impatient and demanded action. Rokeya Kabir was among the more than 700,000 refugees in Agartala, and she understood Indian frustration and dissatisfaction. On top of demands on public services and food that the refugees placed, the regular supply lines to India's Northeast now had to make way for military trucks, which took precedence. Indians now feared getting sucked into a war they hadn't wanted. The mood towards the refugees was no longer as welcoming and pleasant. Rokeya was told not to travel alone in the city.

Back in East Pakistan, Pakistani troops continued to attacks villages. While Christians were usually spared, their faith was no guarantee for safety. Jerome D'Costa's father Peter was a homoeopath trained in Calcutta who later taught at a school and retired in 1968, as he had suffered a stroke. On 26 November Pakistani troops waded through thigh-deep water in the marsh to attack Rangmatia village, where he lived. Jerome had already sent his mother and sister away, to protect them from Pakistani forces. On that Friday, Jerome and his father watched the fires across the village and heard bullets whizz by. Jerome tried to coax his father to leave with him, but Peter could walk only with a cane, and he told his son that if they were to kill him anyway, he'd rather die at his home than in the fields. He then asked Jerome to leave.

Jerome touched his hand for the last time and ran towards another village. As he neared the canal, a bullet flew past and Jerome cried out, 'Jesus, save me!' He fell into the canal and waded through the water and reached the other side. On the other side, about 300 people had huddled together. His fiancee and her family were also there. He saw two Mukti Bahini fighters running towards them. He asked them if they had fired at the Pakistanis. When they said yes, Jerome realized that the soldiers would soon chase them to this spot. He told his fiancee's father Joachim Costa that they'd better leave. They walked to the villages Deolia and Bakhtarpur, before reaching Kapashia. 'It was a Muslim village where we had never set foot in our life but they received us with such care and empathy that we immediately felt at home', D'Costa wrote in a tribute for his father.[135] They offered them water and muri and gave them rooms to stay in.

Pakistani troops killed Peter D'Costa in Rangmatia village that night.

◆

The Mukti Bahini's successes—in particular an attack on Jessore—showed that for Pakistan, an open conflict with India was now inevitable. Pakistan had to act, and Yahya Khan followed his predecessor Ayub Khan's strategy: the defence of the east lies in the west.[136] This policy was based on the assumption that Pakistan could not sustain a prolonged conflict with India because of India's numerical superiority and the likely international diplomatic pressure. And since India surrounded East Pakistan on all sides except for a small part that bordered Burma, Pakistan's strategy should focus on occupying chunks of Indian territory quickly, so that it could negotiate a good deal at the ceasefire.

With that in mind, Pakistan decided to take the fateful step, to attack India from the west, hoping that it would draw Indian troops westward. Tikka Khan recommended attacking India with a solid air cover. On 30 November, the top Pakistani commanders decided on a pre-emptive air strike on Indian air bases. This, they thought, would surprise India's forward airfields, neutralize them, and help Pakistan establish initial superiority. Called Operation Chengiz Khan, Pakistan aimed to paralyse and disable the Indian Air Force.

Friday, 3 December was chosen for the attack, around 5:45 in the evening, when Indian air force control centres changed shift. There would be two waves of strikes, followed by attacks throughout the night. Planes were to be hit, but also to be attacked were runways, air defence radars, and fuel tanks. The stage was set for another full-scale war with India, within six years of the last one.

SIX

A FRIEND IN NEED:
IN WHICH INDIA JOINS THE WAR

There is an old military adage that says that generals like to fight the last war. It became famous during World War II, when France's famed Maginot Line, built to prevent German aggression from the east, proved useless, because Germany invaded France through Belgium instead, avoiding the newly-built fortification along the Franco-German border. During the Six Day War in Operation Focus[137] in 1967, Israel launched spectacular simultaneous attacks on Egyptian, Syrian and Jordanian air bases making runways and hundreds of aircraft of the three countries inoperable. Pakistan decided to do the same and launch a pre-emptive strike on India.

But the Pakistani commanders apparently forgot that many Indian commanders had gone to the same British military academies, and some had also served together in the British army. They too had followed battles elsewhere and knew what lessons to draw. The Pakistani raids failed badly because India had anticipated Pakistan's plans and had already moved its aircraft elsewhere, keeping them protected in bunkers. In fact, on the same night the Indian air force was able to retaliate with massive air strikes.

As planned, Pakistani aircraft took off at 5:30 p.m. Pakistan's official explanation was that the attack was a response to Indian attacks on Pakistani border outposts on the western front, a charge Indians denied. Indian radars however failed to pick up the approaching formations, and Indian airfields first learned about the attack when they heard the roar over their skies. Two Pakistani Mirage IIIs attacked Pathankot unopposed and damaged the runway. Four Mirages attacked the air base in Amritsar, hitting the runway, but the Indians repaired it in a few hours and planes took off to attack Pakistan the same night. Two Pakistani B-57s bombed Ambala, but the damage to the runway was minor. Uttarlai and Halwara were attacked more effectively, but the damage to the Agra base was minor. Some bombs dropped over Agra didn't explode. The Sirsa runway was heavily damaged. In Jaisalmer, Pakistan cut off the power supply and phone connections by hitting the cable units, though the damage was temporary. Jodhpur and Jamnagar were also attacked. What Pakistani planes wanted most was to inflict damage on parked aircraft, but there were no sitting ducks for them to shoot. India's aerial combat strength was not affected. Pakistan had targeted twelve Indian airfields and dropped 183 bombs and reported 120 hits, but damage to Indian aircraft was minimal. Pakistan had managed to surprise India, but the raids failed to disable Indian air power.

Later that night, Indira Gandhi addressed Indians on radio even as the Indian air force was striking back. She said: 'I speak to you at a moment of great peril to our country and our people. Some hours ago, soon after 5.30 pm on the 3rd December, Pakistan had launched a full scale war against us... Today a war in Bangladesh has become a war on India... I have no doubt that by the united will of the people, the wanton and unprovoked aggression of Pakistan should be decisively and finally repelled... Aggression must be met and the people of India will meet it with fortitude, determination, discipline and utmost unity... We must be prepared for a long period of hardship and sacrifice.' What was at stake was not merely India's territorial integrity but the basic ideals which had given strength to the nation.[138]

Squadrons of Indian Canberras flew against airfields in Murid, Mianwali, Sargodha, Chander, Risalewala, Rafiqui, and Masroor, and caused severe damage in Sargodha and Masroor. The IAF also hit the east—Tejgaon and Kurmitola airports in Dacca. Within two days, India had complete air superiority in East Pakistan.

Rokeya Kabir heard Indira Gandhi on the radio that night. 'We now knew that the end would come soon. We saw Indian fighter planes in the sky. We saw the Indian army going into Bangladesh—we were filled with joy,' she said.

◆

James Sterba was a reporter at the *New York Times* based in Jakarta. He was on a temporary assignment in Tokyo covering disputes in the textile industry when his editors asked him to go to Dacca that November. Reports from Sydney Schanberg in New Delhi and Charlie Mohr from the western front indicated an inevitable escalation of tensions, and the *Times* wanted a reporter in East Pakistan. Pakistan had already expelled Schanberg.

There was no way to reach Dacca from Tokyo except through Karachi.

(The correspondent in Delhi had to go from India to Pakistan via Frankfurt, since there were no direct flights between the two countries). Sterba went in November and then again on 2 December, and stayed till the end of the war. When he reached Dinajpur, he met supremely confident Pakistani officers who showed him how the Pakistani troops were prepared for any Indian aggression. There were also veteran reporters who had covered the Korean War (1950-53). They asked where the frontline was. The officer said, 'Out there,' pointing in one direction. The reporters decided to go take a look. They saw some artillery positions. One of the reporters looked down and saw wires. The Pakistani army had communication equipment from World War II, and Sterba and his colleagues immediately realized that they were at the frontline because that's where the wire stopped. There was no shelling, but there it was, the line beyond which lay what was, in effect, enemy territory for the Pakistani troops.

The conflict had begun by the time Sterba returned to Dacca from Dinajpur, and along with Kann and many other reporters, he was confined to Dacca. They played poker during the curfew in candlelight. The Red Cross had managed to get the InterContinental Hotel declared a 'neutral zone', which meant a thorough search had to be undertaken to rid all weapons from the premises. Donald Wise, a former British paratrooper who was now a reporter was informally selected to lead journalists on a search of all guest rooms, some occupied by Pakistanis, and even disarmed a bomb. One day there was bombing near the hotel and shrapnel was found in the swimming pool. It was fished out with a magnet on a pole. The guests were relieved when the pool was later reopened. Food was in plentiful supply despite growing shortages in the city, and when a Danish dairy closed down, the hotel manager bought the entire supply of butter. But a man can't live on butter alone, Kann wryly observed.

Whenever the curfew was relaxed, the reporters could get around the city, and at night, India's MiG aircraft came in. 'We were at the roof of the InterContinental. It was the best vantage point to watch Pakistan's F-86s fight India's MiG-21s. The F-86 would outturn the MiG; the MiG would get on its tail, and the F-86 would turn and get behind the MiG, because it had a bigger turning radius. And we were watching this from the roof. All the TV cameras could see it. It was probably the greatest aerial combat photography since World War II. They got pictures of an Indian MiG being shot down and the pilot bailing out—all on camera. In between the raids we'd call room service and order fruit cups. We had to jump behind the air-conditioning unit because the Indian jets would come after bombing the north and flare up before going above the hotel. The Pakistani jets fought, but they lasted a day or so before they went out of action,' Sterba told me when we met at his apartment in New York. Sometimes these aerial dogfights were during the day. Kann described one such battle: 'From an upper storey window in the Hotel InterContinental here, one could look out and see the Indian MIGs making almost hourly rocket runs on Dacca Airport a mile or so away. The blue sky sporadically was sprinkled with tiny white clouds of Pakistani antiaircraft fire. Several pillars of black smoke rose from the direction of the airport—Indian rockets that found a flammable target or the burning wreckage of Indian planes that were shot down in the first morning of the war. It was like watching an old World War II movie in three-dimensional colour and Cinemascope, with the sky as the wide screen.'[139]

The challenge for the correspondents was how to get the film out of Dacca. Pakistani officers agreed to let the film be taken out as documentation of Indian aggression. It went out at night in a single engine aircraft but the Burmese customs confiscated it when the flight reached Rangoon.

◆

The land battles began in the west before spreading to the east. Indian land forces were ably commanded by Lt. Gen. Jagjit Singh Aurora, who headed India's Eastern Command. Maj. Gen. K.P. Candeth who had helped India take over Goa in 1961 commanded the Western Command. And Lt. Gen. J.F.R. Jacob of the Eastern Command made detailed plans to take over Dacca. On 4 December, Pakistani troops attempted to reach Jaisalmer but India pushed them back at the desert border post of Longewala in Rajasthan. When the mechanized Pakistani infantry moved in, the Indian infantry was able to hold out because it was confident of receiving air cover. Pakistan's failure to destabilize the IAF was now hurting its advance. It had not anticipated that the IAF would be combat-ready, because it had thought that Operation Changez Khan would have demolished many Indian aircraft. But the Indian ability to bomb from the air made Pakistani ground troops vulnerable. Obstacles India had placed along the border confused Pakistani troops in darkness. The following day, India took over Pakistani territory in Basantar in the Punjab-Jammu sector.

On 8 December, the Indian navy attacked Karachi in West Pakistan. That battle, known as Operation Python, was the code name for the Indian attack on Pakistan's main port, Karachi. India had made an earlier attack, called Operation Trident, after which Pakistan had stepped up its aerial surveillance. India had mobilized a large number of navy ships on the west coast, which made Pakistan think that a new attack was imminent. Pakistan gathered aircraft to make air strikes and Pakistani ships mingled with merchant ships to confuse the Indians. On the night of 8 December, an Indian missile boat, *Vinash,* and two frigates—*Talwar* and *Trishul*—approached Karachi. They fired missiles which struck fuel tanks in Karachi and a Panamanian fuel tanker in the Karachi harbour. Other missiles hit a Pakistani naval fleet tanker and a British ship. Indian ships also attacked Karachi's ammunition depots, and reportedly, half the fuel needed in Karachi was blown up; most of the country's oil and ammunition reserves, warehouses, and workshops were also hit. Merchant shipping traffic with Pakistan stopped immediately, which would have significant impact on Pakistan's import-dependent economy. Pakistan's naval ships could no longer leave the port. The flames in Karachi harbour could be seen for miles. In early December Pakistan lost its submarine, *Ghazi,* on the east coast, where it was looking for the Indian aircraft carrier *Vikrant.* A few days later, Pakistan had its revenge, when it torpedoed INS *Khukri,* an Indian frigate, in the Arabian Sea.

Once the battle shifted east, Pakistani vulnerability was exposed. India's Eastern Command was backing three Mukti Bahini brigades and thousands of irregular troops (such as the Kaderia Bahini), against Pakistan's three divisions. Planes took off from the Indian aircraft carrier *Vikrant* and struck Chittagong, Barisal and Cox's Bazar, making Pakistan's navy in the east inoperative and blockading the ports, cutting off escape routes for Pakistani troops. Indian ground attack quickly overran the country. Pakistan could not mount an effective defence, because its soldiers were scattered along the border to deal with small incursions from the Mukti Bahini.

East Pakistani towns along the border fell quickly to the Indian forces. An Oxford scholar, Frank Jackson, wrote a paper on the war soon after it ended, in which he explained that Indian border advances were successful because 'Pakistani forces had largely withdrawn from scattered border-protection duties into cleverly fortified defensive positions at the major centres inside the frontiers, where they held all the major "place names" against Mukti Bahini attacks, and blocked the routes of entry from India'. But the defensive move was not effective in keeping Indians at bay.

Kaderia Bahini was supporting the Indian army. Siddiqui said he had sent field-eye sketches of possible targets to bomb in Dacca, and the IAF bombed those spots on the first few days. When the Indian forces found it difficult to cross the Brahmaputra in Jamalpur, Siddiqui's fighters attacked Pakistani defenders so that Indian troops could advance. Siddiqui's moment of vindication was on 11 December, when Tangail fell.

◆

The work of two Indian photographers—Raghu Rai and the late Kishor Parekh—exposed the world to the agony and inhumanity of the conflict with outstanding understanding and sympathy. Rai had joined the first column of Indian troops crossing the eastern border from the Khulna border in early December. Pakistani forces had retreated to defend the capital, Dacca.

After they had travelled about 50 kilometres, Pakistanis attacked with artillery fire. Rai got busy and began shooting photographs of wounded soldiers being taken away. After the situation subsided, Rai saw a tea shop and felt relieved. He decided to have a moment's respite, although the Indian army major told him to be extremely careful. Just as Rai ordered tea and biscuits, a bullet whizzed past him. 'The major shouted for me to lie down', Rai wrote in his book, *Bangladesh: The Price of Freedom*. 'I did, and another bullet went past me. I crawled back to the shop and was told by the shopkeeper that the Pakistani army was on the other side of the railtrack, just half a kilometre away.'

However close to reality a photographer gets, essentially he has to stay aloof, detached, and distinct. Susan Sontag writes that while real people are out there killing other real people, the photographer must remain firmly behind the camera. Non-intervention is critical. She writes: 'Part of the horrors of such memorable coups of contemporary photojournalism as the pictures of the Vietnamese bonze reaching for the gasoline can, of a Bengali guerrilla in the act of bayonetting a trussed-up collaborator, comes from the awareness of how plausible it has become, in situations where a photographer has the choice between a life and a photograph, to choose the photograph. The person who intervenes cannot record; the person who records cannot intervene.'[140]

To the Pakistani sniper that day, Rai was a participant, entering enemy territory, accompanied by a foreign army. He was a target, fair game. He may have come to record, but he was intervening. To intervene or not is a moral choice; the veteran *Newsweek* correspondent Edward Behr had a point when he titled his memoir of reporting from the war in what was then Belgian Congo, *Anyone Here Been Raped And Speaks English?*[141] For the photographer, as it is for the reporter, the story is more important than finding relief for the victim.

Parekh, who died tragically early in the Himalaya in 1982, also covered the same war, and was often shooting pictures at the same locations as Rai. His book[142] has several images similar to Rai's. If Rai showed hungry children crying out for food, Parekh showed a dead boy lying on the road, the bottom half of his body soaking in blood. Parekh's Pakistani soldiers knocked down doors, beat up people, look inside the lungis of men to see if they were concealing any weapons—or if they were indeed Muslims. Rai's Mukti Bahini guerrillas rode a cycle-rickshaw with their guns, smiling at the photographer. In Parekh's universe, death was real: a crow picking at the open wounds of a dead body. His soldiers were loading weapons, ready to battle. Rai showed the cloud of dust that the army trucks emitted as the convoy left for the battlefront.

At the Drik archives I saw more images of horror: of five men dragging a dead body through a paddy field as Pakistani soldiers watched; blindfolded prisoners of Mukti Bahini being taken to a firing squad, their hands tied behind their backs; a soldier walking through a field, passing by a maggot-infested dead body; an Indian military truck driving by, emitting dust, leaving a shattered Pakistani truck behind, its wheels destroyed; the destroyed carcass of a Pakistani jet, revealing its twisted innards; two men tied with a single rope with a row of free men pointing guns at them; a child soldier, wearing shorts, shirt, a helmet and a sweater, carrying a rifle too big for him, and looking with considerable fear at some sight; a woman praying in a brick house, with some bricks destroyed, creating a window through which a soldier keeps a watch on her; another man, in his thirties, pleading for his life, as Mukti Bahini fighters taunt him; a tied prisoner, kicked repeatedly in the stomach; a Mukti Bahini soldier holds a Pakistani sympathizer by his hair, and his victim holds the tormentor's legs, seeking forgiveness, as another man places the muzzle of the gun on the man's head. There were more primitive images, of a soldier using a bow and arrows; more gory images, of young boys standing with guns next to a trophy—a ditch with seven dead, bloodied soldiers. And some joyous ones—a tailor stitches the new Bangladesh map, which a child applauds; a short Mukti Bahini fighter shaking hands with the Indian Gen. Manekshaw who is wearing a gorkha hat at its rakish angle. And the final shot, like a Zainul Abedin drawing photographed, of a dead man lying on the road, a dog eating his flesh.

If the war had a noble purpose, it was to end the inhumanity those photographs showed. While India rarely spoke about its imperative morally, and few people steeped in realpolitik can shed their cynicism when a politician speaks of morals and the intervention certainly suited India's strategic interests, the fact remains that in the annals of humanitarian interventions, few were as swift, successful, purpose-driven and consistent with humanitarian goals as the Indian intervention to liberate Bangladesh. India went in when it was attacked, and left before its troops became unpopular.

◆

India's numerical strength was overwhelming. It had two army corps from West Bengal, one from Meghalaya, and one detached formation that included paratroopers who would land in Tangail. The air force provided air cover. Pakistan had more than four divisions. But Pakistan was unable to add new troops from West Pakistan because Indira Gandhi had forced Ceylon not to offer its airport to refuel Pakistani military aircraft anymore.

If Indian armed forces were successful, it was not only because of their preparedness, but also because of the masterly diplomacy Indira Gandhi showed in the months leading up to the war. She travelled around the world, charming some governments, annoying others, and gradually changed public perception and diplomatic opinion while effectively cutting off all supplies to East Pakistan. She agreed to wait for the torrential monsoon to subside, and then forced Pakistan to make the error which justified the massive Indian retaliation. On 6 December, she declared in the Lok Sabha that India recognized Bangladesh. Bhutan followed in a few hours, and later that week, Poland joined. The radio station Shadheen Bangla Betar Kendra changed its name to Bangla Betar (Bangladesh Radio), dropping the assertive 'Shadheen', independent, because it now believed it was independent. Once you are independent, you don't need to proclaim it. On 7 December, Mukti Bahini troops took command of Jessore, Sylhet, and Moulobi Bazar.

◆

India's success also owed much to the brilliant planning of Lt. Gen. Jacob. Manekshaw's early thinking was to invade East Pakistan by capturing the

border provinces of Khulna and Chittagong. But that would leave the prize—
Dacca—beyond reach, because other Indian officials thought the UN would
intervene and demand a ceasefire. Marching through Bangladeshi wetland
wasn't an easy prospect either. Jacob however felt advances were possible
by ensuring that the army would keep moving throughout the country. A
successful campaign had to end with the surrender of Dacca. As the Pakistani
army was staying close to towns and defending them, the smart strategy lay in
bypassing the towns and following trails that the Mukti Bahini would identify,
and thus neutralize Pakistani strength in towns by using alternative routes to
reach Dacca.

The strategy would eventually succeed. India sidestepped facing Pakistani
troops, their communication was disabled and they were left encircled. Jacob
thought Dacca would fall within three weeks; in the end it would crumble in
two weeks.

In order to cut off Pakistani forces in the north from the rest of the
country it was important for India to secure Bogura, an important junction.
India wanted to break through Pakistani resistance there and force them to
withdraw. Pakistan had placed screens along the railway line and the defensive
positions covered the entire route. Indians decided to bypass Hilli and blocked
it from its rear. Pakistan withdrew forces to fortify Bogura. But Bogura was
surrounded on all sides by vast numbers of Indian troops. Pakistani troops
kept resisting till the bitter end. The Pakistani brigadier, Tajammal Hussain
Malik, refused to surrender even after 16 December when the Pakistani army
eventually surrendered in Dacca. As he kept fighting, the victorious forces
had no choice but to continue to attack his forces. Malik divided his brigade
into smaller units, to keep fighting unto the last. But on 17 December, his
jeep was ambushed and he was severely injured. Mukti Bahini treated him
harshly and brought him semi-conscious to an Indian army hospital. Pakistan
sent a major general to Natore in Malik's place to surrender Malik's rogue
formation on 18 December.

On 7 December Niazi had an extremely uncomfortable meeting with
East Pakistan's civilian governor, A.M. Malik. While official military reports
suggested that the Pakistan army was fighting gallantly, the civilian reports
were very gloomy. Malik wanted to know the truth. In his memoir, Brigadier
Salik later wondered: 'Officially and publicly Niazi had maintained a posture
which was not supported by the facts. Should he admit his setbacks to a
civilian governor as early as the fourth day of the all-out war? Or should he

keep up a façade of defiance and fortitude? If he chose the latter course, how long would he be able to fool the governor, the government and the public?'

Salik continued: 'Governor Malik, Gen Niazi and two other senior officers sat in a comfortable room at Government House. They did not talk much. Every few minutes, silence overtook the conversation. The Governor did most of the talking and that too in general terms. The crux of his discourse was: things never remain the same. Good situations give way to bad situations and vice versa. Similarly, there are fluctuations in the career of a general. At one time glory magnifies him while at another defeat demolishes his dignity. As Dr Malik uttered the last part of his statement, the burly figure of Gen Niazi quaked and started sobbing like a child. The Governor stretched out his elderly arm to Niazi and consoling him, said: "I know, General sahib, there are hard days in a commander's life. But don't lose heart. God is great".

'While Gen Niazi was sobbing, a Bengali waiter entered the room with a tray of coffee and snacks. He was immediately howled out as if he had desecrated the room. He came out and announced to his fellow Bengalis: "The Sahibs are crying inside." The remark was overheard by the West Pakistani military secretary to the governor who told the Bengalis to shut up,' Salik concluded.

Malik quietly told Niazi that he would now write to Yahya to arrange a ceasefire. Niazi kept his head down, and said weakly, 'I will obey.'[143]

◆

On 9 December, the Indian army entered Kushtia, where they met some serious resistance. But elsewhere Indians were making critical inroads. In the north, Gorkha troops beat back Pakistani resistance in Sylhet. To its south, India gained control of Brahmanbaria and crossed the Meghna River, heading towards Dacca. India also took over Comilla. Pakistani troops abandoned Chandpur. By 11 December, Mymensingh, Kushtia, and Noakhali fell to the Indian troops. As Sisson and Rose note: 'The outcome of the conflict on the eastern front after 6 December was not in doubt, as the Indian military had all the advantages.' What turned the tables firmly for India was the thrust out of Meghalaya into Sylhet and the paradrop into Tangail, for which the Pakistanis were unprepared. They were not able to hold Sylhet and the river crossings, and they hadn't expected the Tangail airdrop. The river crossings involved very innovative use of helicopters, given that Meghna is 30 kilometres wide. While Pakistan could hold the Indian attacks out of

West Bengal, the Sylhet thrust broke through.

Indian advances were far quicker and bolder than Pakistan had anticipated, and Americans too were surprised. India's strategy involved a variation on the German blitzkrieg theme. The Indian army avoided pitched battles at strong points and just bypassed them, leaving Pakistani garrisons surrounded. It worked because of precise local intelligence from the Mukti Bahini and also because Indian soldiers, who were trained to know what to look for, had been embedded in those formations. Brigadier Shahbeg Singh was among several dozen Indian officers who had spent weeks in Bangladesh before the war had formally started. He was a brilliant tactician and his contribution to the victory in Bangladesh was significant. But years later he was cashiered from the army for financial impropriety. He would later command Sant Jarnail Singh Bhindranwale's Khalistan Liberation Force in the Golden Temple in Amritsar, where he died in June 1984 during the Indian military's Operation Bluestar, fighting the army of which he was once part.

Americans were not only surprised, they were also getting frustrated over the turn of events. Bass writes of an exasperated Nixon privately hoping for a Chinese intervention to scare 'those goddamn Indians to death'. Since that wasn't likely, the US decided to show its hand at last. On 11 December, it instructed its fleet commanders in the Pacific Theatre to send USS *Enterprise*, an aircraft carrier, to the Bay of Bengal.

What the American intentions were, nobody knew. It was clearly not about to join the war. But its bias towards Pakistan was known, and Indian opinion was livid. As Raghavan points out in his book,[144] it convinced Indians to race towards Dacca and secure a decisive Pakistani surrender quickly, instead of fighting a long drawn out battle of attrition. Help came India's way on the 13th, when the Soviet Navy decided to deploy a group of warships in the area, to counter USS *Enterprise*. That would escalate the conflict to a new level not known since the Cuban missile crisis of the early Kennedy years.

On 14 December Yahya Khan wrote to Gen. Niazi: 'You have fought a heroic battle against overwhelming odds. The nation is proud of you... You have now reached a stage where further resistance is no longer humanly possible nor will it serve any useful purpose... You should now take all necessary measures to stop the fighting and preserve the lives of armed forces personnel, all those from West Pakistan and all loyal elements...' This letter has raised one of those unanswerable debates at dinner tables in Pakistani cantonments ever since. What did the letter mean? Was Yahya instructing

Niazi to surrender? Or was he letting him decide the next steps? Was it an opinion or an instruction? An interpretation or a command? Towards the end of the war, Yahya had become elusive, with senior generals unable to talk to him about decisions that needed to be taken. Niazi too became absent-minded and moody, not indicating what his game plan was. Sisson and Rose, who cite Yahya's message in their book, describe it as 'implying that the armed forces in East Pakistan should surrender'. A few hundred, if not a few thousand, lives were lost amidst this indecisiveness.

◆

Meanwhile Dacca was a picture of chaos. John R. Kelly was an Irish official with the UN High Commissioner for Refugees in Dacca who had been an infantry officer in North Africa and Europe during World War II. He maintained a diary of the crucial last three days of the war. When hostilities broke out, Paul-Marc Henri, who was assistant secretary-general at the UN, was coincidentally in Dacca, and assumed charge of all UN operations. He appointed Kelly as his liaison with military and government authorities. On 14 December, Governor Malik called Kelly and asked if he and Peter Wheeler, also of the UN, could visit him at the governor's house. 'By this time the course of the war was obvious', Kelly wrote. 'The front was crumbling and from within Dacca the situation seemed very similar to Berlin in early 1945.'

Malik wanted personal advice for his own situation. Kelly told him that he was in grave and imminent danger of being killed, and unless he came to the neutral zone—the InterContinental Hotel—he might not survive that night. But before entering the neutral zone, he would have to resign all official positions. Malik said his cabinet was discussing just that but was unable to decide. He felt if he resigned, history would judge him harshly, as having deserted his post. He asked if he could send his wife and daughter. Kelly said he could, but the hotel was also full of journalists, and the moment they saw Malik's wife and daughter, they would write that Malik had lost confidence and was sending his family into safety; they would conclude it was a matter of time before Malik too joined them.

At that moment, the governor's house shook violently under heavy explosions. The building had been hit by an IAF bomb and Kelly and Wheeler left immediately, jumping over the balustrade and taking shelter under a jeep. Six Indian planes made two strikes at the building, followed by cannon fire. Kelly saw Muzaffar Hussain, who was the chief secretary, emerge from the building, looking very pale, and they greeted each other half-heartedly. As the strikes continued, Kelly ran to a ditch which was full of soldiers and jumped in, lying on top of them. All this while, he had his walkie-talkie handset radio on, with which he was informing Henri of what was going on. Rao Farman Ali, the Pakistani general who had been in charge of operations in Dacca from early March, emerged from the building and joined Kelly, asking: 'Why are the Indians doing this to us?' The answer was obvious, but Kelly wrote: 'Under the circumstances as the Indian aircraft were continuing to attack the building some 20 yards away with rockets and cannon fire, it did not seem a suitable occasion to engage in a discussion, and I let the general find his own shelter.' When the attacks ended, Kelly got out, found Wheeler, and the two left in his car.

At the UN office, Kelly briefed Henri and ran into Gavin Young, the correspondent for the *Observer*. Young told him confidently it would be another hour before the Indians attacked again, since they'd have to go back to India, refuel and reload, and then return. Young and Kelly left for the governor's house, where an aide told them that Malik and his cabinet were meeting in a bunker. Kelly found them. They still looked shaken but they were unable to decide whether or not to resign. Kelly told them that they were at risk not only from the Mukti Bahini, but possibly their own guards, and certainly the IAF.

At that moment, the IAF struck again. Young was clearly misinformed about Indian ability to reload and refuel. The bunker was not underground, and they did not know if the IAF knew its location. One of the ministers took the matter in his hands and wrote out the resignation addressed to Pakistan's president, which Malik and all other ministers signed promptly. Malik went to another room to meet his wife and daughter and prayed. Now no longer government officials, Malik and his former ministers moved later that day to the InterContinental Hotel.

The following day at the hotel Malik told Kelly that after he resigned and before he left the governor's house, he had received a message from Yahya Khan recommending ceasefire negotiations. He had been unable to contact Niazi. The letter clearly said, 'You should now take all necessary measures to stop the fighting'. What should he now do?

Kelly contacted Col. Gaffur who was the Pakistani liaison officer in the neutral zone and they went with Malik to Kelly's room to phone Niazi. Malik asked Niazi what action he was planning to take, based on Yahya's instructions. Niazi asked Malik to come to the cantonment so that the matter could be discussed. Kelly said that if Malik left, he would no longer be under protection, and given that he was the governor and a known face, his life would be in danger. Instead, he should ask Niazi to come to the neutral zone. Niazi said he would send Farman Ali.

Once Farman Ali came, Kelly withdrew—he had no official position in the conversation, nor was he a Pakistani. They invited him back and showed him a draft note of their understanding, with the message that Niazi would send Yahya.

'To stop further bloodshed it is agreed:

a) To ceasefire and stop all hostilities immediately in East Pakistan;
b) To hand over peacefully the administration of East Pakistan as arranged by UN;
c) UN should ensure:
    i.   Safety and security of all armed forces pending their repatriation to West Pakistan;
    ii. Safety and security of all civil servants of Pakistan pending their repatriation to West Pakistan;
    iii. Protection of all non-locals settled here since 1947;
    iv. Guarantee of no reprisals of persons who helped and served the Government and cause of Pakistan since March 1971.'

Farman Ali went back to the cantonment and returned that night, saying that the message had indeed been sent to the president's office, and while Yahya's officials had approved the proposals, they rejected (b), which would have paved the way for handing over the administration of East Pakistan.

On the morning of the 16th India sent an ultimatum to Niazi, to surrender by 9:30 a.m. that day. Col. Gaffur, Malik, Sven Lampell of the Red Cross, and Kelly tried to contact Niazi, but they could not. As a former infantry officer, Kelly was aware of the destruction an all-out attack would cause. The Pakistani communication centre was destroyed, so it was difficult to know if Niazi had accepted the ultimatum, or if he had been able to convey his response to the Indians. IAF planes were circling over Dacca with impunity, and the Indian army had been gathering in the suburbs, so that they could launch a concerted artillery and infantry assault. It was urgent to save the city and the civilian population, so at 8:30 a.m. Col. Gaffur, Lampell and

Kelly left for the cantonment. Kelly informed Henri, who placed all UN radio signalers on alert for 'an extremely important announcement'.

They reached the command bunker, but Niazi was not there. Kelly saw Farman Ali there, 'ashen faced and completely broken… staring into space, he gave the impression of having given up everything'. He said he was authorized to speak for the whole army and that they had accepted the Indian ultimatum. But the communication centre was destroyed, so they had not been able to inform the Indians that they accepted the ultimatum. Kelly offered the UN radio communication network, purely for this communication. Farman agreed, so they stepped out so that the handset would work. Kelly called Henri and gave the message in Farman's presence to Henri and Farman added two further points: to request Indians for a six-hour extension to the truce because of the breakdown in the Pakistan army's communications, and to invite the Indian army to send a party of staff officers to discuss further arrangements by helicopter to Dacca airport where they would have safe conduct and proper courtesies. Kelly passed the message to Henri, who passed it on to New Delhi.

Kelly left for the InterContinental with Col. Gaffur and Lampell. IAF aircrafts were circling overhead. The message had reached the Indians. It was 9:20 a.m.

◆

Siddiqui wanted to be in Dacca and witness the Pakistani surrender. He went to see the Indian general, Gandharv Nagra, who had been his ally in Tangail, to ask when he could march towards the capital. Nagra said there were no immediate plans, and Siddiqui didn't like that idea. 'We had fought for independence, but without grabbing Dacca, real independence was not possible,' he said. Nagra said it was not mandatory for Siddiqui to be in Dacca. He was asked if the Kaderia Bahini would block the Aricha Road, which connects the capital to Manikganj and then to the west. Siddiqui was distinctly unhappy about it because it relegated his role. He wanted to fight and go all the way to the capital.

There was one fundamental difference between the Kaderia Bahini and Mukti Bahini. While the Mukti Bahini included civilians recruited from villages, it was essentially under the command and control of officers who had been part of a formal army and understood, respected, and complied with the laws of war. Kaderia Bahini, on the other hand, was made up of people extremely hostile towards Pakistani forces, who only listened to one man, Kader Siddiqui. Kaderia Bahini had been amazingly resourceful and brilliant in some of the tactical battles. But it created its own rules and lived by its own laws. Would the Bahini's thousands of fighters listen to other commanders and play by the rules, or would they take the law in their hands and seek revenge? Nobody could tell; it depended on whether Siddiqui himself could control his men.

But India saw the virtue of having Kaderia Bahini as a backup. India had sent a feeler to the Pakistani troops to surrender on 14 December, but Pakistan had derisively rejected the offer. Tens of thousands of Pakistani soldiers had retreated to Dacca; in contrast, the advancing Indian troops numbered only a few thousand. In a man-to-man combat, demoralized Pakistanis significantly outnumbered resurgent Indians. But a mention of the Kaderia Bahini as backup, and the Pakistani mood changed. They knew of the Bahini's bravery as well as brutality. The Pakistanis knew that if they had to choose between surrendering to Indian troops or to Kaderia Bahini, the choice was clear— Indian troops, who would follow the Geneva Conventions and the laws of war. 'It was a total victory over a formidable, well-trained army. Had Pakistan fought on, it would have been difficult for us. We expected higher casualties', Jacob would write in his memoir.

By the 15th, Indian troops were 40 miles from Dacca. That afternoon, Gen. Nagra sent a letter to Gen. Niazi, addressing his old acquaintance as 'My Dear Abdullah', suggesting the terms of a Pakistani surrender. The Pakistanis promised them safe conduct; the road was clear and they drove. Siddiqui and an Indian officer went to the quarters of a Pakistani general called Jamshed. He gave Siddiqui his cap and revolver, as part of the surrender. They tried to call Gen. Niazi, but the phones were dead.

Later, they met Niazi at the cantonment. Nagra knew Niazi from their days in Burma and they spoke to each other comfortably, although Niazi looked grim. Then Nagra introduced Siddiqui to Niazi. Niazi saluted him. Siddiqui stared back. Niazi extended his hand to shake hands. Nagra told Siddiqui, 'Hath milao, it is a good thing when you shake hands.'

'But I could not,' Siddiqui said. 'Niazi had killed so many of my people. I couldn't do it. I refused. I was embarrassed; they were also embarrassed. I abhorred the idea of shaking hands with him.'

India wanted a public surrender ceremony at the Race Course—where, on 7 March, Mujib had made his famous speech. Niazi did not wish to surrender there, fearing for his security. But the Indians insisted. Niazi had no choice.

The next day at 4 p.m., Gen. Jagjit Singh Aurora arrived and at 5 p.m. the surrender document was signed. Sterba remembers seeing Niazi take off his gun and hand it to Aurora. Raghu Rai was at hand, and took photographs that showed the public surrender ceremony[145] where Aurora strode confidently towards the desk alongside Niazi, who kept his eyes low, unable to look at Rai's camera, trying hard not to betray any emotion. The two witnesses were Air Commodore A.K. Khandker, who was also deputy commander-in-chief of the Bangladesh armed forces, and Lt. Gen. Jacob of the Indian Eastern Command. Sterba recalled: 'It became emotional at the Ramna Racecourse. Niazi was in tears. He stood up, took off his belt and gave it to Aurora. The war was over.' In his diary, Sterba wrote: 'Today I saw the birth of a nation.'

◆

In New Delhi that afternoon, Indira Gandhi rose to speak in the Lok Sabha and said: 'I have an announcement to make... Dacca is now the free capital of a free country.' The House interrupted her with thunderous applause and the banging of desks. Opposition leader Atal Behari Vajpayee of Jana Sangh looked exultant as he called her Durga. She continued, raising her voice: 'This House and the entire nation rejoice in this historic event. We hail the people of Bangladesh in their hour of triumph. We hail the brave young men and boys of the Mukti Bahini for their valour and dedication. We are proud of our own Army, Navy, Air Force and the Border Security Force, who have so magnificently demonstrated their quality and capacity... India will remember with gratitude the sacrifices of those who have laid down their lives, and our thoughts are with their families.' She then confirmed that the Indian Armed Forces would comply with the provisions of the Geneva Conventions and treat the Pakistani prisoners of war with dignity and 'in a humane manner.' She noted that the commanders of the Mukti Bahini have issued similar orders to their forces and pointed out that the Government of Bangladesh, which had not yet had the opportunity to sign the Geneva Convention, would abide by it. There must be no reprisals, she emphasized.

She reminded Indians—and the world—that India's objectives were limited: 'assist the gallant people of Bangladesh and their Mukti Bahini to liberate their country from a reign of terror and to resist aggression on our own land.' Indian armed forces will not remain in Bangladesh any longer than is necessary, she added—and indeed, by mid-March 1972, the last Indian troops had left. She also pointed out that 'the millions who were driven out of their homes across our borders have already begun trekking back…The time has come when they can together look forward to a meaningful future in their Sonar Bangla. They have our good wishes. The triumph is not theirs alone. All nations who value the human spirit will recognize it as a significant milestone in man's quest for liberty.'

◆

For Niazi, signing the surrender instrument was the lowest point in his life. Decorated by the British, he was a respected Pakistani commander, but all his achievements would now be forgotten and turn meaningless, and he would become an object of national ridicule for having brought humiliation to Pakistan, losing half the country. And in India, he was seen as the poster-child of a defeated army. He was removed from the army in 1975 and denied pension. While the Hamoodur Rahman Inquiry Commission recommended that Niazi face court martial, no such trial took place. Niazi was the man who knew too much.

Kader Siddiqui too surrendered his men and weapons. He claimed there were 18,000 soldiers and 72,000 volunteers under his command, and he said he had over 104,000 rifles, which he surrendered to the Bangladesh authorities. Of these, he told me, India had given him only 4,000 rifles. 'Where did I get the rest from?' he asked me with a chuckle. 'Stolen from Pakistani army.'

'I had begun with one soldier, Faruk Ahmed. At the end of the battle I had 18,000 men and 72,000 volunteers,' Siddiqui recalled wistfully.

◆

When the war ended, in many parts of the country Biharis became targets of reprisal killings. In many villages they were singled out and killed. Kann was at the InterContinental Hotel in the last days of the war with other foreign correspondents and diplomats. He was on guard duty one night, and he was uncomfortable having to play 'the strange role of manning the guardhouse to keep people out, many of them Biharis, when they were arguably at greater risk. It is the closest I came to playing God. I was very uncomfortable. But if you opened the gate, thousands would have come in, and then the hotel would have become a war zone. There were petrified people who had sympathized with the Pakistani army. But it is to the credit of the Indian army and its discipline that there was no terrible mass bloodbath after the victory.'

Elsewhere, reprisal killings continued. When the war ended, some international newspapers published photographs of Kaderia Bahini fighters rounding up prisoners that they claimed were Razakars, and beating them up, bayoneting, and later shooting them. Kishor Parekh's book shows a photograph taken in the streets of old Dhaka, where the Mukti Bahini guerrillas have some unfinished business to deal with. Parekh is right behind them as they crouch and move stealthily towards abandoned homes from where snipers have fired, as they remain unwilling to surrender. A single shoe lies abandoned in the lower right corner of the photograph, suggesting someone escaped in a hurry.

Settling of scores and mob justice may seem inevitable after a bloody conflict, but it is a clear violation of Geneva Conventions and the laws of war. Common Article III of the Geneva Convention,[146] which applies to all conflicts, even those that are not international, describes the minimal protection that must be offered to all captives. It seeks to ensure that civilians and other non-combatants, surrendered fighters, and injured prisoners must be treated 'humanely', and 'outrages upon personal dignity, in particular humiliating and degrading treatment', are prohibited. When prosecuted and sentenced, the authority judging the individuals must be a properly constituted court and the proceedings must follow due process. The Article applies even to those who are not classified as prisoners of war.

The way Siddiqui's guerrillas treated some detainees on 19 December at the Dacca Stadium was a violation of the Geneva Convention. Siddiqui had given an hour-long speech. The prisoners were killed after they prayed with their captors.[147] Shortly before their murder, they were promised 'a fair trial'. There are photographs of Siddiqui about to bayonet three prisoners, and foreign film crews were invited to witness the event and they filmed it.[148]

The Indian army arrested Siddiqui. In his defence, Siddiqui argued that the photograph was staged, and that he was trying to show what the Bahini could do to the prisoners, so that other collaborators would surrender voluntarily. There is a crowd of people watching the spectacle—they are not in a frenzy and baying for blood, some are even smiling. All the observers are men, some are taking photographs.

Mob justice was not the norm, but it was not exceptional either. Kann remembered seeing mobs on the street shouting 'Joy Bangla' and waving the new flag. If they found a Pakistani military man, beating him up became their priority. When a jeep of Indian soldiers saw a mob attacking Pakistani soldiers, the Indians jumped out and beat the Bengalis saying, 'Leave him alone!'

In recent years, Siddiqui has spoken about these incidents. Yasmin Saikia, who is a professor at the Arizona State University, refers to the Dacca Stadium incident in her book, *Women, War and Making Bangladesh: Remembering 1971*, and describes an incident where Siddiqui shot a Mukti Bahini soldier who stole a shawl from a Bengali civilian, and writes: 'At the time he did not think of his act as a crime against humanity, being swayed by Bengali public sentiment for revenge. Today he knows that both the acts—killing a younger soldier for a petty theft and killing the Biharis for being different from the Bengalis—were public acts of violence disguised under the label of national morale to establish the power of the Bengalis and claim victory, but they were violent acts nonetheless, and he is pained by his past.'[149]

Siddiqui was not tried for any of those incidents. The recent war crimes trials too do not feature him as an accused. Siddiqui would not say why, and Bangladeshi authorities have not disclosed any reasons why specific people have been charged and others not.

◆

For what remains of Pakistan, the loss of Bangladesh has raised critical existential questions. The British-Pakistani writer Tariq Ali titled the book he wrote a few years after Bangladesh became free, *Can Pakistan Survive?* (1983). In that book Ali questioned the country's long-term survival. In an essay in the *London Review of Books* in 2007 when Pakistan turned sixty, Ali wrote: 'I had argued that if the state carried on in the same old way, some of the minority provinces left behind might also defect, leaving the Punjab alone, strutting like a cock on a dunghill. Many of those who denounced me as a traitor and a renegade are now asking the same question.'[150]

That question continues to haunt Pakistan. The elite in Pakistan have seen Bangladesh's independence as part of an Indian conspiracy in which they were largely innocent. For Bangladesh, the idea that their country—their golden Bengal—was somehow a burden for Pakistan undermines their sense of national pride and reminds them of the insulting way Kissinger referred to the new nation, calling it 'an international basket case'. More than four decades later, Pakistan's fragility has only worsened, with many coups and natural disasters. In the same period, Bangladesh has managed to improve its social development indicators.

On his last day in Dacca, Sterba saw dead Pakistani soldiers on the streets. The city seemed anarchic. He heard reports of civilians suspected of being Razakars getting executed. The Indian army tried hard to keep order, but there was a sense of chaos. However, there were also celebrations.

Sterba was ready to leave but he wanted a Bangladesh flag as a souvenir. That night at the hotel, he saw the hotel boy who had a nice, hand-stitched flag. Sterba asked if he could buy it. The hotel boy didn't want money for it, but he was willing to trade his flag. What he wanted was Sterba's short-wave radio, which he gave the boy happily in exchange for the flag. 'Someone had stitched it incognito during the war, when it was dangerous to do so,' he said, as he took me to the study in his Upper East Side apartment in Manhattan, where he had framed and hung that old Bangladesh flag: a red circle on a green rectangle, an embossed golden map of Bangladesh in between. 'Joy Bangla,' he said softly, smiling.

Sterba went to the airport on 21 December, but the airport was closed for commercial traffic. So he and other reporters, including Kann, decided to hitch a ride on an Indian military transport aircraft. 'We wanted to get home for Christmas,' he told me. The Indian military agreed to fly the reporters to Dum Dum Airport in Calcutta.

They landed on the military side of the Calcutta airport. The pilot pointed out where the terminal was, and told them to take their stuff and walk. 'So we walked across,' Sterba said. 'We got underneath the civilian side and we were looking for a way up to the ticketing area. And suddenly, someone saw us and came to us and told us to stop. "What do you think you are doing," he asked us. We said we had just come from Dacca and we wanted to go abroad. He asked us to wait.'

He went and brought an immigration officer. That wasn't a good sign, Sterba thought. Indeed, the great Indian bureaucratic machinery took over. 'Do you have visas?' he asked them.

Of course they didn't.

'Why not?' the officer asked.

Sterba explained patiently that Bangladesh is a very new country, born only a few days ago, and they could not have obtained a visa. The country hadn't set up a foreign ministry and the Indian mission wasn't issuing visas yet.

So the official demanded to see their passports. Sterba and others didn't want to give up their passports and they began arguing. Sterba said they had to leave for Bangkok. The officer started shouting, and then, Sterba said, 'He uttered the classic Indian bureaucratic line: "Whatever you are wanting, I am not giving".'

They somehow managed to get into the terminal building. They joined the ticketing queue—there were hippies who were also waiting to leave. The planes were full, Sterba and his colleagues were told to buy first-class tickets and pay another $100 to get on the plane, which they did. 'And we got out.'

Sterba met Gen. Aurora one more time, in 1984, after Indira Gandhi had been assassinated. He had gone to Delhi to cover the funeral. Delhi was a devastated city—rioters had rampaged through Sikh neighbourhoods. Sterba went to see Aurora. They talked. He was fine, living as a retired general, but deeply troubled by the violence in his city. Entire neighbourhoods looked ruined in the rioting.

'And there was a guard protecting him,' Sterba said, noting the irony of a war hero needing protection in his own country.

◆

Two days before surrender, Pakistani troops made one final attack to cripple the emerging nation.

Asif Munier was 4 years old that year. He lived in his grandparents' house in Dacca. Asif's father Munier Chowdhury was a sensitive linguist who taught at the Dacca University. They used to live in a part of the campus near the British Council and after the crackdown on 25 March and the killing of academics they did not feel safe and left their home.

Munier Chowdhury taught English and Bengali and was a well-known playwright. Some of his writing was political—in the 1960s he wrote a play, *Kobor*, about the resurrection from death of the martyrs of the 1952 language movement. He was jailed, and his health suffered, so upon release he focused on writing and teaching and stayed away from overt politics, although he stayed engaged with ideas—he was part of the Pragatisheel Lekhok Songho (Progressive Writers' Union). Munier was involved with the development of the Bengali keyboard for typewriters, and with the German company, Optima that developed a keyboard, Munier-Optima, which later became a standard in the industry. He was a strong proponent of Bangla.

The house in which they lived was old. It had two storeys and plenty of rooms. Munier had eight brothers and six sisters, and while some had gone to live in villages during the war, and a few had gone to India, only two siblings had stayed. Asif's oldest brother (who is now a UN official) was 20 and joined the Mukti Bahini. He secretly left home with cousins and friends, leaving behind a letter for his parents. His father Munier was devastated with the uncertainty of the war and about his eldest son. Asif was too young to understand everything, but he sensed that things were not all right. His mother, the actress Lily Chowdhury who had grown up in Calcutta and Delhi, told him later that she noticed him observing everything, and he was not behaving like other children.

On 14 December, Munier sat at home, listening diligently to the BBC and VOA. He said aloud, 'It is reaching the end. The good day will come very soon, I can feel it'. Lily had had a surgery so she was resting. Asif's grandmother was cooking lunch. His younger brother was in the shower. Asif had just had his bath and his father had wiped him dry.

The house had an iron gate. The main entrance had a courtyard. Somebody knocked and shook the grill. Asif's uncle went over to see who it was. When the gate was opened, Munier's wife and mother could see that there were two or three boys whom they did not recognize, and they were wearing grey kurta pyjamas. The boys asked Asif's uncle if he was Munier Chowdhury. Asif's older brother who was 12 was standing nearby, so the uncle sent him away and spoke to the boys. 'Can you call him? We need to talk to him,' the boys said.

Lily saw a camouflaged van. She could not see the full car, but she could see its roof and its window. It had branches and leaves, and there was mud on the window.

Munier was about to have lunch—chapatis, vegetables, and fish which his mother had prepared. It was around 1:30 p.m. He got up, put on his white kurta and started going down. 'They want to talk, let me find out', he said.

Al-Badr took away many people like Munier that day and brought them to Rayer Bazaar in the Beribadh area of Dacca where potters had lived since Mughal times because the red earth of that area was excellent for making clay pots. The men and women brought here had been tortured and their hands were tied; they were killed near Turag River, where their bodies were dumped—Shahidullah Kaiser, an award-winning novelist from Mazupur; Santosh Chandra Bhattacharyya, a Sanskrit scholar; journalist Syed Nazmul Haque who was arrested during the war and taken to West Pakistan to testify against Sheikh Mujib in his secret trial and then returned to Dacca;

linguist Mofazzal Haider Chaudhury whom Tagore's university in India, Vishwabharati, had honoured; journalist Nizamuddin Ahmed, who frequently acted as a go-between for foreign correspondents, taking them to Mukti Bahini; Dr M.A.M. Faizul Mahi, who quietly helped Mukti Bahini; Sirajul Haque Khan, a US-trained educationist; historian Ghyasuddin Ahmed; physician Mohammad Fazle Rabbi; and poet and journalist Selina Parvin. Between 14–16 December Al-Badr and Al-Shams tried to enfeeble Bangladesh at its birth. The men and women became part of the clay of this land two days before it became free, their blood joining the water that flowed through the land.

Munier's son Asif is one of the founders of Projonmo Ekattor, an organisation of people orphaned by the war. One night at my home in London he recounted the story of his father being taken away. 'His body was never found; to us, he just disappeared,' he said quietly.

Farhad Ghuznavi, who was a senior manager at ICI Pakistan, the British chemicals company's subsidiary, had gone for a board meeting in Karachi on 3 December. The war had broken out so he decided to leave for London, because he had sent his family there. His departure was quite dramatic, as Bengalis leaving the country needed government permission to do so. He was able to leave because ICI had bought his ticket. He returned to Dacca in March. When he went to his home, his neighbour told him he was so glad Ghuznavi was not in Dacca during the final phase of the war. 'They came for you three times between 3-14 December', he told Ghuznavi. Ghuznavi's mother and sister had already moved to her sister's place, the home was empty. 'Had I been in Dacca those days, I'd have been taken to Rayer Bazaar,' he thinks.

Niloufer Huda heard about the fall of Jessore in a radio broadcast and decided to go to Jessore. They saw thousands of people walking to the border. 'You know that poem, *Jessore Road*? I had the same image in my mind,' she told me. 'But this time they were going home.'

When she reached Jessore she heard that while most Pakistani forces had surrendered, a few platoons had not surrendered and Huda was fighting them, trying to secure a microwave station in Bhatiyapara under the control of a Pakistani unit. He came on the 17th night, but when he saw her there was no smile on his face, nor any greeting. He held his head in his hands and fell on the bed. Niloufer asked him why he was looking so down and depressed despite the end of the war. He said, 'You don't know what they have done. They have killed all the intellectuals in Dacca. They didn't spare doctors, lecturers, women, not even our family friend Dr Fazle Rabbi.'

While people in Bangladesh were quick to learn about the Rayer Bazaar killings, the international media, caught in the frenzy of Pakistani surrender, wasn't there to witness the killings. Kann of the *Wall Street Journal* had heard that there had been an atrocity, but he never saw any bodies. 'But I am prepared to believe it,' he said. 'It would have been consistent with Pakistani actions—towards the end of the war they were crazy as they were close to defeat. Killing a thousand or two thousand people at such a time would not have bothered the army at that time.'

Who had organized those killings? The Bangladesh International Crimes Tribunal has sentenced in absentia one British Bangladeshi for playing a role in those killings, but it has been widely assumed that Maj. Gen. Rao Farman Ali bore some responsibility. After the war was over, a list of Bengali intellectuals (most of whom were killed on 14 December) was found in a page of Farman Ali's diary that he had left behind at the Governor's House. Ali confirmed the list as genuine but denied that the aim was to kill the people. Altaf Gauhar, a former Pakistani journalist and bureaucrat, also confirmed the list. He said he had seen the name of a friend of his on the list and requested Farman Ali to cancel it, and Farman Ali had obliged.[151]

Gen. Farman Ali continued to deny that he had any role in those killings. But he understood the city well, knew the elite, and since Operation Searchlight, had a very good idea of what the troops were doing. A woman whose husband had been taken away went with a friend who knew the general to find out where he might be. He asked her about her husband's name and details. She wrote down the information anxiously, hoping that Farman Ali would be able to find out the information. Farman Ali looked at the name for some time, folded it, and put it on the table, saying nothing. The woman bowed in gratitude and left. Her friend, who told me the story, had taken her to see Farman Ali and is convinced that Farman Ali knew exactly what had happened but didn't want to tell her that her husband would never return.

Farman Ali's defence over the Rayer Bazaar killings is that the bodies were found only on 17 December, by which time the Pakistani army had surrendered. He claimed that a week earlier Maj. Gen. Jamshed had called him to the army headquarters and asked him to join him on a car ride.

During the journey he told him that they were thinking of making some arrests of civilians. Farman Ali claimed he advised against it and did not know what happened after that.

But in his book, *The Betrayal of East Pakistan,* Gen. Niazi described Farman Ali as an opportunist and a conspirator. Niazi also said that Farman Ali insisted on being sent back to Pakistan because 'Mukti Bahini would kill him of his alleged massacre of the Bangalees and intellectuals on the night of 15-16 December. It was a pathetic sight to see him pale and almost on the verge of breakdown'. Brigadier Salik, whose memoir does not spare Niazi from criticism, wrote: 'He [Farman] was the major general in charge of civil administration. As such nothing would happen which he would not know.'

◆

Mujibur Rahman was in jail in Pakistan until early January, but his family was in Dacca during the war. The day after the war ended, an Indian officer, Maj. Ashok Kumar Tara went to visit the Mujib family. He found one platoon of Pakistani soldiers near the house. They were indiscriminately firing on civilians who had gathered to greet Mujib's wife, Fazilatunnesa. Maj. Tara approached the enemy troops unarmed and used his tact to persuade them to lay down their arms since the war was over and Niazi had already surrendered. They had earlier threatened him, saying they would shoot him. Instead, they laid down their arms.[152]

◆

In Khulna, Abul Bashar came from Chuknagar to the Circuit House to see the surrender ceremony. He could hear sporadic gunfire along the road, as some Pakistani soldiers had refused to surrender. But after the ceremony people went from house to house, dancing and singing. 'We felt free as we had never felt in our lives,' he told me. 'We were free from the jail, free from being occupied. There was a feeling of freedom in the air. There was so much hope that time. That our country would be peaceful, that it would grow. I cannot explain the joy of the time. All restaurants gave free biryani to everyone. Everything was open. All shops open. We gave fruit to the Indian soldiers. We celebrated with them, with Mukti Bahini and all of us local people. We danced together. We lifted the Indian jawans and carried them on our shoulders.'

◆

Bangladeshi anger against Pakistani soldiers was simmering. Simeen Hossain Rimi, daughter of Tajuddin Ahmed remembers seeing Indian army trucks taking unarmed Pakistani soldiers, now prisoners, and one woman chasing after the trucks, crying, screaming—please give me one Pakistani soldier; I want to kill him. They killed my only son.

A few Pakistani soldiers, unable to understand Bengali and unwilling to understand her trauma, were laughing.

But all Pakistani soldiers were not cruel. Kann said: 'There were some who acted like butchers, but not all of them did. Quite a few were bothered by what the army was doing. Many who had grown up in the North-West Frontier had no idea why they were in this Bengali swamp. Like every army, they wanted to go home.' Rokeya Kabir remembers treating a wounded Balochi soldier captured by Indians at a hospital where she asked him why he had come to fight this war. And the young soldier said he was told East Pakistan was full of Hindus and he was sent to kill them because those Hindus were destroying Pakistan. Some, like that soldier, were misinformed; others tried to act reasonably, and a few brave ones even dissented.

Indeed, there is the story of M. Zafar Masud, who was a flight lieutenant with the Pakistani air force. He was known for his infectious enthusiasm, and his nickname, Mitty, was drawn from James Thurber's famous short story, 'The Secret Life of Walter Mitty'. He flew with great courage in the 1965 war against India and he was given a gallantry award. In April 1970, he was assigned to Dacca as the top Pakistani air force commander in the Eastern Wing.

When Yahya Khan visited Dacca in March, Masud was among the senior officers who met Yahya where the political situation was being discussed. Tikka Khan's staff spoke first, presenting the assessment on the civilian and military situation. Masud sought permission to speak next and then for over an hour he gave a frank overview of what was going on. He argued that military force wouldn't solve the problem, which was essentially political in nature. He pleaded not to opt for a military solution, because the mismatch between Indian and Pakistani forces was so vast that a war would be suicidal. A semi-autonomous East Pakistan was preferable to the certainty of a military defeat if India intervened.

Yahya interrupted him a few times, agreeing with Masud's arguments, and at the end said: 'You must surely know that I too do not want a war and am doing my best to persuade Mujib and Bhutto to find a way out of the crisis.'

Masud felt he had made the breakthrough. But he was shocked when a week later Yahya ordered the military crackdown. As the president boarded his Karachi-bound Boeing on 25 March, Masud tried once more to change his view. But Yahya's close advisers had convinced him that East Pakistani aspirations could be crushed easily and things would get to normal soon.

Once Operation Searchlight was launched, Masud knew he had only one honourable course left, even if it meant his career would end quickly. He would not allow the combat aircraft under his command in East Pakistan to be used in a policing role where it would have to kill any civilians. Using such disproportionate force against civilians violated his sense of ethics and, indeed, the laws of war. He wanted to save his firepower against India.

In the official history of the Pakistan Air Force there is a story about Masud: 'At the end of March, when Operation Blitzkrieg was in full swing, Masud was asked, as he had feared, to mount an air strike against a mob of armed civilians on the outskirts of Dacca. For Masud it was the worst imaginable moment of truth: should he allow the PAF to participate in what he believed to be a wholly dishonourable operation? On the one hand was his revulsion at the brutality of the proposed strikes when viewed against his concept of the justifiable use of military force. On the other hand was the oath he had taken years before which now demanded his unquestioned obedience...'

Masud refused the order. He refused to send combat aircraft to kill the people who were Pakistani citizens armed only with spears and sticks, because doing so would be unlawful and violated his sense of honour.

Masud was not the only conscientious objector. There is the story of Col. Nadir Ali, who briefly lost his sanity because of the brutality he saw his soldiers being forced to commit. He was discharged from the army and later wrote poetry in Punjabi. Nadir Ali first saw action in mid-April 1971 near Tungipara, in Mujib's home district. His officers told him that it was a hard area, with violent insurgents, and he should 'kill as many bastards as you can and make sure that no Hindu is left alive'.

'Sir, I do not kill unarmed civilians who do not fire at me. That is against the laws of war, even if it is martial law', Nadir Ali replied.

'Kill the Hindus. It is an order for everyone. Don't show me your commando finesse', he was ordered.

Nadir Ali was dropped behind Faridpur. He made a fire-base and his troops started firing all around. But there was nobody to shoot at. Suddenly he saw some civilians running towards him. They appeared unarmed so Nadir Ali ordered his troops to stop firing. He shouted at the villagers and asked them what they wanted.

'Sir we have brought you some water to drink!' they replied.

He told his troops to put the weapons away and ordered a tea break. They stayed there for a few hours. Somebody even brought and hoisted a Pakistani flag. A day earlier, the village was flying the new Bangladesh flag. Later that day the main army column caught up with them. They arrived firing their machine guns all around and Nadir Ali saw smoke columns rising in the villages behind them.

'What's the score?' the Colonel asked.

'There was no resistance so we didn't kill anyone', Nadir Ali told him.

And the officer fired from his machine gun and some of the villagers who had brought them water fell dead.

'That is the way, my boy', the Colonel told Nadir Ali.

Nadir Ali was livid. He had been posted in East Pakistan from 1962 to 1964, and then again in 1965-66, and counted many Bengali officers, including Ziaur Rahman, among his friends. He had saved the lives of Hindu families during the 1965 riots and his superiors had admonished him even then, saying 'You are not the Red Cross, my boy!'

At a lecture he gave at the BRAC University,[153] Nadir Ali recounted many other incidents of purposeless violence: 'I unfortunately, was a witness and participant in those events, though I never killed anyone or ordered anyone to be killed. Still, I knew and heard about a lot of killing and other atrocities.' Killing Bengalis, regardless of the threat they posed, seemed to have been the plan. Nadir Ali recounted Col. Zaheer Alam, who had gone to arrest Mujib at 1 a.m. on 26 March, wrote in his memoir that he saluted Mujib and told him: 'Sir, we have been ordered to take you into custody.' He was shocked when three generals—Hamid, Tikka Khan, and Mitha—asked him later: 'But why did you not kill him?'

When Nadir Ali returned to West Pakistan, he suffered a mental breakdown and was diagnosed with paranoid schizophrenia. He lost touch with reality, even losing his memory. He was a patient in a psychiatric hospital for six months and remained a patient under care for two years. In a brief memoir he wrote, 'I remained in the [insane asylum] for six months in 1973. What drove me mad? Well, I felt the collective guilt of the army action'. He was retired in 1973 as a disabled person. But gradually he recovered, and over the years rebuilt his life as a Punjabi poet. 'I acquired a literary and artistic consciousness from Bangladesh and I hope I can now validly represent the literary conscience of Punjab', he told his audience in Dhaka.

Then with his voice breaking, he told the audience: 'Now, as a Punjabi poet and writer I offer apologies and ask forgiveness from those who suffered so terribly in 1971. And I want to say that there are many more in Punjab who feel the same shame and regret and who are also discovering a connection between the military mindset that led to those tragic events and our own loss of culture,' and he quoted the great Pakistani poet Faiz Ahmed Faiz's lines on Bangladesh:

After how many Sraban[154] rains shall be washed the blood stains
After friendly intimacy we became strangers again[155]

While the cultural cohesion between the two halves was never strong, it was affected. Pakistan's film industry would suffer, because as with the Indian film industry, the influence of Bengalis on the industry was significant. The actor Rahman, the actress Shabnam, her husband Robin Ghosh, all contributed to Pakistani cinema, and the singer Runa Laila—popular across Pakistan, India, and Bangladesh, returned to Bangladesh only in 1974.

Muslehuddin was a famous Bengali composer who had married Nahid Niazi, who was a singer from West Pakistan. Niazi sang many Bengali songs and was popular in both halves of Pakistan. At the time of the war, they were in Britain, performing concerts among Pakistani communities. As the situation on the ground worsened, they heard reports of Bengali husbands abandoning their wives and children. She told an interviewer[156] that they decided not to return to Pakistan and her regret was that she could no longer visit Bangladesh because, as she revealed, her mother's uncle was Gen. Niazi. Nahid and Muslehuddin remained married even though in the mid-70s it was rumoured that he had left her to become Bangladesh's ambassador to the Soviet Union. He died in 2003 and Bangladeshis with long memories remember fondly her singing Bengali songs.

◆

Nixon got the prize he wanted. A little over nine weeks after the fall of Dacca,

Nixon was in Beijing, raising a toast with Mao Zedong and Zhou Enlai.

When the war ended, the man most relieved was probably the one Kann met in Dacca on Bangladesh's first night as a free country. A Bengali man had not been able to take his 3-year-old son Aupoo out of the house for months. Kann wrote: 'Last March, during the brief period before the Pakistani Army cracked down and imposed a reign of terror in the east, the child learned to shout "Joy Bangla". But for the past nine months the parents feared that the child might shout "Joy Bangla" in public and thus get the family killed.'

'Today both father and son are on the streets, yelling "Joy Bangla".'[157]

SEVEN

THE BRAVE ONES

There is a sense of finality about death. Someone dies; those who loved the person grieve. The person who has died is now beyond pain, feeling nothing, as the body is lowered in a grave or a fire is lit on the funeral pyre, the ashes becoming part of the ether.

With rape, as with any other violent crime, it is different. In one sense the woman's life changes fundamentally, and not because she has chosen it that way. As a rape victim testified in the Foca trial following the Bosnian conflict, 'They have taken my life without killing me.' The woman has not done anything; horrific violence has been committed against her. And yet, in many societies, she has to bear the blame and the shame for what happened. In many places, those who loved her once may not love her anymore. They worry about the shame she has brought to the family, about what society will think, who will bring up the child if she ends up getting pregnant, and sometimes wonder why the rapist didn't kill her as well.

Rape is a heinous crime, and the victim relives the nightmare, the trauma, again and again. It is an invasion of another person's bodily integrity. It is violent, it is intrusive. It is meant to subjugate and humiliate. It is about power, not sex. Soldiers in armed conflict have often thought of rape as one of the 'spoils of war'. Raping women in a conquered land is not only about sexual gratification. Nor is it about fulfilling a physical need or instinct. It is about reminding the powerless of the power the invader has; that the invasion is not only of the country, city, village, and home, but also an invasion of the person's body, and the person subjected to it is the woman whose defeated family, home, village, or indeed the country, is too weak to protect. It is part of a patriarchal discourse where the woman is seen as a man's property, and by humiliating her, the invader humiliates the man who was meant to protect her. If her family—the father, the brother, or her husband—regarded her as one under their protection, the invader is saying, she is no longer theirs; she is his. And he can, and will discard her later. A physical act that's meant to be mutual, expressing love between two people who consent to be intimate with one another, is drained of those tender feelings, and instead becomes the manifestation of brute strength and raw cruelty.

Many Pakistani soldiers raped many women in Bangladesh during the nine months of the war. Numbers, again, are impossible to ascertain. Some women were raped only once; many were raped repeatedly. Some were taken away to cantonments as sexual slaves. At the end of the war, there were 93,000 Pakistani POWs. The crackdown lasted from 25 March to 16 December—that is, 266 days. That much we know. How many of the affected women would report such rapes, knowing that in a conservative society they would have to carry the stigma and the backlash?

◆

Tajuddin Ahmed's daughter Simeen Hossain Rimi had returned to Dhaka on 31 December. She saw a convoy of Indian jeeps on the roads, and people were so happy, greeting them with flowers. She had seen flattened homes in Jessore and been to a bunker where Pakistani soldiers had hoped to stay put for the long haul, assuming the war would go on. In the bunker she saw the head of a woman with long hair, and four or five dead bodies of women. She was still very young and the elders with her didn't let her enter the bunker. But she wondered—why were there women in a military bunker? 'I was still very small and yet to know what a war did and what they were doing to my country. I couldn't imagine,' she said, tears welling up in her eyes.

Tahmima Anam's second novel, *The Good Muslim,*[158] begins with Sohail, the protagonist returning home after the war in which he has been a freedom fighter. He comes across military barracks where he discovers a young woman kept as a sexual slave in an abandoned camp, and he realizes how the abstract notion of war does not only involve the bravery of valiant young men like him but also the suffering of young women of the kind he meets. In a society that looked at raped women with pity, and not sympathy, each day these women showed courage in their determination to go on living their lives, often without family support, without jobs, and sometimes, after being abandoned by their loved ones.

There are accounts of Pakistani officers telling their soldiers to go forth and multiply—to rape Bengali women again and again so that they produce children who would no longer be only Bengali. They wanted those children to be more like them, fitting their self-image—brave and proud, like the

Punjabi and Baluchi men that the soldiers were—and not the cowardly lungi-wearing peasant Bengalis that they thought the local men to be.

What does one call the women whose suffering is individual as well as collective? The word 'victim' suggests passive helplessness. The word 'survivor' is more positive, but implies that the woman is just about getting by. Six days after the war ended, the interim Bangladesh Government announced that the women and girls who were sexually violated during the war would be given full respect with the honorific title birangona or 'the brave one'.[159]

Meeting the birangonas wasn't easy. Like in its neighbouring countries India and Pakistan, Bangladeshi society is conservative and there is a huge stigma attached to rape in most parts of the country. (The one exception is the Chittagong Hill Tracts, where the society does not think that women who have suffered sexual violence have anything to be guilty of, and sexual violence within the community is relatively rare). Why would women want to open up their lives to me, a foreigner, an outsider, a man who came to visit them and asked questions, asking them to go over some of the most painful moments in their lives, to recount what happened, how they felt, how they dealt with the aftermath, how others treated them, and how they coped subsequently? And what would they get out of that exercise? What was I offering them? Did they really want the world to know their story?

In the six trips I made to Bangladesh to research this book, I met twenty-eight rape survivors, in Sirajganj, Bogura, Kushtia and Dhaka. In Chuknagar, Khulna, Chittagong and Comilla I heard more stories of sexual violence from men and women who personally knew such cases. I also heard more stories from researchers, of cases in Barisal, Rajshahi, Dinajpur and Natore. All the stories involved rape against women—but it does not mean there was no sexual violence against men. There have been claims that Hindu women were more likely to be raped than Muslim women, but almost all the women I interviewed were either practicing or nominally Muslim, and I hadn't specifically sought to interview rape survivors based on their faith. I felt as if there were stories waiting to be told throughout the country, stories that had remained suppressed for long. I sensed a nation deeply ashamed by what had happened to its women and by the helplessness of its men and women who often felt guilty, having failed to prevent rape or to do anything for the women who survived rape in the decades after the war. I saw elderly men committed to a pact of silence, unwilling to come to terms with what had happened, unable to figure out what to do with the women among them who had suffered. I met lawyers and activists uncertain about how to secure justice for those women. There was no forensic evidence left, no records with most cases never even having been filed, and the perpetrators in many cases had gone back to Pakistan, and others lived quiet lives in Bangladesh; many may have died.

There is a macho aspect to journalism. A reporter goes with a writing pad and a pen in the pocket amidst hostile forces, gunfire and explosions. He or she talks to soldiers, commanders, diplomats, civilian leaders, and then for authenticity, speaks to a taxi driver, a hotel concierge, or other civilians who are not too afraid to talk. When he meets victims, he may show some empathy, but it can be feigned, as Janet Malcolm reveals in her 1990 study on the ethics of journalism:

> He is a kind of confidence man, preying on people's vanity, ignorance or loneliness, gaining their trust and betraying them without remorse. Like the credulous widow who wakes up one day to find the charming young man and all her savings gone, so the consenting subject of a piece of nonfiction learns—when the article or book appears—his hard lesson. Journalists justify their treachery in various ways according to their temperaments. The more pompous talk about freedom of speech and 'the public's right to know'; the least talented talk about Art; the seemliest murmur about earning a living.[160]

I was aware of that warning. Amena Mohsin who has researched violence in Chittagong Hill Tracts had told me that speaking to the women who had experienced violence required a lot of empathy. The women often referred to what was done to them as otyachar or atrocity. 'You can't ask what kind,' she told me. 'Their body language is such that you can't look at them into their eyes. You violate their private space when you talk to them. You need to be acutely sensitive.' I would have to put aside that cynicism, that arrogance, and that illusion of self-importance that Malcolm warned about.

To meet the birangonas, I left Dhaka for Sirajganj with Shamuna Mizan and Farhana Begum, two women who helped in the rehabilitation of birangonas with the NGO Nari Pokkho. Shamuna is a wedding planner and Farhana is a teacher.

We drove through Kader Siddiqui's hometown Tangail. The landscape now turned prosaic, where smokestack chimneys of brick kilns churn out thousands of bricks daily. The town of Natore passed by, the Natore of Banalata

Sen, whose beauty the poet Jibanananda Das celebrates in his great, lyrical eponymous poem. We crossed the Jamuna river, navigating narrow, bumpy roads with ponds on either side, ponds in which ducks swim and peasants cast their fishing nets. Dozens of children started running alongside our car, patting its exterior gently, because as visitors, we were unusual, unexpected, and unknown. The children were happy seeing us—when Bibhutibhushan Bandopadhyaya wrote the chapter in *Pather Panchali* to describe the joy Apu and Durga feel when they see a train for the first time, he titled it 'Achenar Anand', the delight of the unknown.

Bangladesh had turned full circle, where a car full of foreigners turning up in a small village was a matter of delight, not fear. Forty years ago, such vehicles would have brought Pakistani soldiers, escorted to the village by obliging Razakars, and the children would have had to run away from the road to hide in the thick foliage.

Safina Lohani runs the Sirajganj Uttaran Mohila Sangstha (SUMS), a nonprofit that provides healthcare and financial assistance to the birangonas in the area. Lohani is a muktijoddha too, a war heroine in her own right. She was eighteen then, and she had a small baby. Her husband Aminul Islam Chowdhury was an area commander for the Mukti Bahini during the war.

When the crackdown began, she found that many people she knew had left for India, but she felt a sense of responsibility and chose to remain behind. She became a messenger for the Mukti Bahini. They trusted her and kept their weapons in storage at her home. She would keep the weapons hidden at different places. She even travelled with the freedom fighters. She never stayed at one place for long. She would hide and redistribute weapons and cook for the troops. She would slip unobtrusively past Pakistani soldiers and pass messages from one unit to another. Sometimes mukti joddhas would carry her in a palanquin from one place to another, as if she were a bride being taken to her marital home.

One night in the summer, Razakars came to her house because a group of Mukti Bahini fighters were inside. She was serving them dinner, and the Razakars had found out about their presence. The area had many Biharis, some of whom helped the Pakistanis by identifying pro-liberation Bengalis, who were then tortured.

The Mukti Bahini fighters had already left when the Pakistani troops arrived around midnight. They shook the door, saying: 'Dorja kholo! (Open the door)'. She had hidden Chinese rifles in that room. She didn't consider shooting at them, for then they would have found all the weapons.

She went behind her house but fell into the pond. She lost her baby in the darkness, but the girl who worked in her house came running and picked up the child. She could see bullets on the ground around her. Her husband Aminul was not at home. He was hiding near the Indian border when he was shot in a battle around Bogura and was hurt badly. Safina found out about his injury two months later. 'They told me when he was almost dead,' she said. 'He could not move and had lost a lot of blood. He was carried on a stretcher from one place to another by other Muktis. There were compounders to help him, but there was no proper surgeon who had treated him. The Muktis did not want to leave him behind, because sooner or later the Pakistanis would have got him.'

Other Muktis took her in a palanquin to meet him. When Safina saw him she could not recognize him. He had become skinny, his skin had turned yellow, he had a scraggly beard. The stitches were so bad that she could see his flesh rotting. She brought him home and nursed him. He finds it difficult to walk even now.

Lohani generously let me use her office in Sirajgonj to meet the birangonas. There were three images on the wall, a portrait of Tagore, a poster of Sufia Kamal, and one of Selim Al-Deen, a writer and muktijoddha. When the war ended and the rumoured stories of rapes turned out to be real, Lohani set up SUMS and sought out women who were raped, and provided them with care. Mujib's government encouraged her and provided financial backing. But after his assassination in 1975, the new government cut support for such projects and forced the organization to disband. Many of their families had already shunned the women, who were now left without any guarantee of support. But Lohani would not give up. She sought out the women they used to support, and with her husband began raising funds to bring them back together and rebuilt SUMS, this time not depending on government support. It now runs on private donations and provides financial support to the women.

Thirteen women sat outside, waiting to meet me. The women were older than me—the youngest was in her mid-fifties, the oldest in her late sixties. In 1971, they were between fifteen and thirty. One wore the burkha; the rest were in saris, covering their head with their pallus. Some wore the teep on their forehead. They looked at me with great curiosity. Later, I was told they had rarely been interviewed by a man. They stared at my laptop, listened to me intently as I explained, clearly and honestly in my elementary Bengali what my purpose was.

Most women I interviewed had no problem talking about the day itself—who was at home, how many soldiers came, how they behaved, who they beat up, how they were pushed and knocked down. But after that, without fail, the women paused. And virtually every woman said: 'And then I fainted,' a euphemism many rape survivors use, regardless of the context in which they had suffered violence. The rape itself had become part of the subconscious; she had become unconscious. Their faces were still at that time, staring back at me, revealing no emotions. It is only later that some of the women broke down, reflecting on the miserable conditions in which they lived.

I felt like a voyeur, an intruder, indeed, a violator. I explained my purpose. I told them I wanted to hear what happened to their village in 1971, and what had happened to them. I wanted to know what they felt then, and how they feel now. I wanted to hear their stories; I wanted to learn from their experiences—most of all, I wanted to understand how they coped, what gave them their strength. And I wanted them to know that I could not promise any help. Non-government organizations had made visits in the past. Some had promised jobs, a few had said income support would be possible. But this did not always happen. I was in no position to make any grand promises. I said I would listen to their stories, and tell my readers what had happened to them. My aim was to convey their pain to my readers so that they could understand what happened, and they could take steps to make sure that nobody has to go through such pain again. I share those stories—a few are here, the rest can be found in Appendix II.

◆

'I want the soldiers caught; I want them tried.'

SB heard gunshots one night at 3 a.m. The army had come to the railway station. She did not know that, and she left her home to catch the train, but she could not get in. She realized that the Pakistani army had come on that train and they were killing the people who were trying to come onboard. She kept low and walked away. The army was busy burning houses and killing people.

Her older sister was pregnant, so she took her to a pineapple plantation where they could hide. SB herself wasn't married and she was menstruating. They managed to avoid the army that night. Her father had decided that she should marry her cousin, because they were told the army was taking away all the women who did not have husbands. Her cousin was suffering from tuberculosis.

In May, the army came again. They went into hiding again—her sister along with her child, her parents and herself. The child cried, and the Pakistani army followed the sound and came to where they were. When they saw them they pointed their gun as if they were going to shoot the child. Her neighbour was a Razakar named B. He told the soldiers that their family was a bunch of cowards and they should let them be. The troops left.

SB's family had a false sense of security because B. had intervened. But the next day the soldiers came in the afternoon. They were burning houses. They hid in a shed. They decided not to run because they thought they'd get shot. Her father sat at the door, smoking a hookah. Her brothers were keen to fight but they did not have any weapons. Her sister carried her child out of the cot when the soldiers entered the house and pulled her hair. They raped her and beat her up. She bled—she had just had a child—and collapsed and died. They poked their gun at her mother. They collected all the young women of her family. One sister was so scared she urinated and the soldiers laughed.

And then they came for her. She had been hiding behind a door but they saw her and took her. They were all raped, one after another. Some were raped several times by different soldiers. One of her sisters-in-law also died.

SB got a few jobs after the war was over. Her husband initially did not want to take her back, but eventually he did. One day Mujib came to their village. The women who were raped carried a banner, calling themselves birangonas. Mujib turned towards them and said: 'I am your father; I will accept you.'

After the war, the freedom fighters looked for B, but he was hiding in the neighbouring village. He died a natural death many years later. All these years later, she is determined to get justice.

'I want the soldiers caught. I want them tried,' she said.

◆

'During that war, men fought with their guns; I fought with my honour.'
SH was a 15-year-old orphan who lived with her uncle and had been married recently. She lived in fear after she heard Razakars and Pakistani soldiers taking eighty people to the river, lining them up in two rows of forty each, and then shooting them. Her husband had seen the army coming and he fled. One day there was a knock at her door

and the man on the other side said he wanted water. She refused to come out of the house. The soldiers knocked down the door. There were thirteen of them. All of them raped SH, one after the other.

She never saw her husband again after that. After the war she tried to work as a domestic help, but only those who did not know of her rapes let her work in their homes. Some years later she married an older man. He was already married, and he had heard her story. But he wanted a younger wife. He is now dead. She lives with her younger son who is a construction worker. Her older son left for Dhaka eight years ago and has not kept in touch with her after he found out what had happened to her.

'I gave my honour for this country but there is no recognition,' she told me. 'Sheikh Mujib hugged me, but he is now killed. He did to me what a father would do for his daughter. People like you have come and interviewed me many times, but still I have received no justice. It always ends with just an interview. I want those men from Al-Badr and the Razakars to be tried. During that war, men fought with their guns; I fought with my honour.'

◆

'My daughter's husband left her because she is the daughter of a birangona.'

R's father told her to go to a Hindu home when he saw a car coming. The men driving the car looked scary. They had broad shoulders and big eyes.

R went to the Hindu house. There were several women in that house— they were all very pretty and wore teeps. They were hiding under the bed. There was no space there, so they told R to hide behind a door.

The soldiers came in and saw two young girls playing and pulled them by their hair. While she was trembling and watching, someone grabbed her by her hair. She turned around and saw a man who had taken off his trousers. 'I don't remember anything after that,' she said.

When she regained her senses she found that she had been dumped near the river. The Hindu women were nowhere to be seen. There was an old lady next to her. She wasn't wearing any clothes.

R's husband abandoned her. She said: 'When Bangabandhu died, we lost all hope. We got respect from nobody—not from our village, nor from our husbands. My daughter's husband left her because he found out that she is the daughter of a birangona.'

R is now a weaver and can make two saris daily. 'People listen to our stories and do nothing about us,' she continued. 'I am history, I will die. I have to live my life like this till I die. Every year on 16 December people talk about us but nobody does anything about us. We won't even die in peace.'

◆

What would you like to do to the men who harmed you, I asked all of them when our conversations ended. At once, the women became animated and started speaking together. Trial, we want a trial, some said. We want those men punished, a couple of women said. They humiliated us. And one of them said quietly: 'We want justice. We want trials of Razakars. They killed us like helpless birds.'

As I sat with Safina Lohani after my interviews were over, she told me how villagers tried treating the women as untouchables to grab their assets. She managed to stop that, but she could not get the state to provide any further benefits.

In December 2012, on another visit to Bangladesh I went to Kumarkhali, a small town near Kushtia, where Sikha Saha runs the local branch of Nijera Kori (We Do It Ourselves), a women's rights awareness group. Saha set up her centre in 1980 where she provides women training and education, particularly raising awareness, including dealing with violence and how to claim their rights. Some human rights lawyers represent them for free. I met more birangonas there.

◆

'We made this country free—and how do we live now?'

MK was nineteen and a mother of three children in 1971. She and her husband helped the freedom fighters by carrying their weapons. Her husband would take refugees or the freedom fighters to India in his boat; MK would cook for them.

From her window, MK could see what was happening in the street. One day in October, the army came to her village. She took her sons and escaped. When she heard that the army had left, she made her way back to her home. But she saw the military coming.

MK was sitting with her three-month-old son in her lap. The soldiers snatched away the child. They threatened to throw him away and MK pleaded with them for his life. Then two Razakars and the soldiers took her with them. Her mother fell at their feet, but they loaded their guns. They saw that they had a farm with goats and chickens, so they asked for eggs. Her mother was shaking with fear. The officers took MK away and set her home on fire.

At that time, her husband was looking after some Hindu families. The river behind his home was a busy route for freedom fighters, so the military always kept an eye on the riverfront. Her husband frequently helped freedom fighters—to flee, to hide, or to help take them across wherever they wished to go. He wanted to join them, but he thought it would not be right for him to leave his wife alone.

His business was trading ilish, the traditional Bengali river fish. He would buy the fish from fishermen and sell it in the market. He was aware that a Shanti Committee, as pro-Pakistani local committees were known, was active in his village. He was quietly helping refugees who wanted to cross the river from the village to the other side and go to C'pur, across the river. 'I would take 8-10 refugees at a time in my boat,' he said.

Biharis had been burning homes in H'pur, and a friend told him to escape. He heard that Biharis were tying fishermen in their fishing nets and then burning them. 'I was too scared to go back at such a time,' he said.

On the day the army reached his home, her husband was at the river, buying fish. He heard sounds of shooting. A man whose son was a freedom fighter rushed to him, saying he must take him across the river so that he could hide. He took them across and helped them set up a camp.

When he returned to his shore, a cousin told him the news about the attack on his house. He rushed home and found MK lying unconscious. He comforted her. 'I could understand what happened to her and accept it,' he told me. 'If I were in the house at that time, I know I would have been killed, so I have nothing more to say about what happened,' he added. A school teacher in his village explained to him that whatever had happened was not MK's fault. 'Eventually he accepted everything,' MK said.

In December, MK's husband remembers seeing the sky filled with Indian planes, and then bombing at the Pakistani camp. 'I felt very happy,' he said. 'We made this country free—and how do we live now? Nobody values us, no one honours us. We are made fun of,' MK said.

◆

'They then attacked me, but I fought back. I punched them, I kicked them. I was bleeding but I fought them. I was to give my life away, but not my respect.'

DN remembers well the night about a dozen freedom fighters came to her father's home. They were hungry, but they did not have rice at home. She was twenty and pregnant. The freedom fighters had planned to attack the Pakistani army the next morning.

Her husband left with the young men to hide their weapons by wrapping them in plastic and keeping them besides the river in the mud. DN was with her mother-in-law and her sister-in-law. Several Pakistani soldiers came and raped the sister-in-law first (she later committed suicide). 'They then attacked me, but I fought back. I punched them, I kicked them. I was bleeding but I fought them. I was to give my life away, but not my respect. By that time my husband also came, and he too fought,' she said.

'The incident (as she refers to her rape) had already happened but I kept fighting them. Then I ran away to save my life. They were more powerful,' she said. They left her husband nearly dead. He was in a coma, and after the war he died.

Her voice softened when I asked her the name of her sister-in-law. She no longer remembered her name; she had been married only recently. One of her sons works as a rickshaw driver. One daughter is a homemaker. Of all the women, she received some direct benefit from the government. Hasina Wajed gave her 50,000 takas and 4 kathas land, which she has distributed among her children. She is on a list of freedom fighters and guards her photographs with Hasina carefully. She showed me fragile sheets with evidence of her suffering. 'Bangladesh is free, but what about us? We did so much for Bangladesh. What did Bangladesh do for us?'

◆

I asked simple questions to start with, asking the women about their lives, how old they were in 1971, leading up to the day. I could then only ask 'and then what happened?' Many of the women were animated and friendly when they began speaking, but as our conversation entered the room, or the field, or the riverbed where they were attacked, their voices would get softer. There were often long pauses. Some looked down. Some stared back at me. Some said, matter-of-factly, that they did not remember anything. And many used the euphemism that they had chosen to describe the rape—they had fainted. I did not probe further. It is only after I let them complete the sentences, the thoughts, after they had let the memory of those soldiers and Razakars leave their minds, as they once left their rooms, that their faces became animated again. Some sobbed; some turned angrier in their tone.

In all this, they were generous to me. They willingly told me intimate, painful details of their lives, expecting nothing in return. I had promised to cover the costs of their journey from their villages and back, and the lunch that was provided. But I was not going to offer them any money to hear their stories. It would violate a specific journalistic ethic; it would also demean the value of what they told me—it was incalculable; it was impossible to assign a monetary value to their time, their trust, and their honesty.

And I decided to tell the story of each woman I met, because each experience taught me something new. It is easy to talk of 'a quarter million rapes' and think that each violent encounter was the same. It never is. Each story has a different background; each woman finds herself in the complex situation because of unique circumstances; and most important, the response of each woman is different. I owed them the decency, the courtesy, of recognising that and not to see them as an undifferentiated mass. The dilemma I had was whether to name them. Not naming them would perpetuate the idea that somehow there was some shame associated with what had happened, as though their name needed to be hidden. Naming them would respect their agency, their right—they hadn't told me to anonymize them; by deciding for them, I would deny them their agency. I asked women's rights activists and feminists—lawyers and academics advised me not to name them; journalists and writers, including a few feminists, suggested I should. Eventually I decided not to name them because as per the laws of the land where I was born—India—and the laws of the land where I live now—England—it is illegal to name a rape victim in a legal case. Indeed, some have gone on camera and given interviews, and I respect that. But they hadn't told me if I could name them, and I didn't think I had the right to decide that on their behalf—too many men have taken decisions on their behalf over the past forty years. I didn't want to add another number to that.

The interviews were uncomfortable. Once the stories multiplied, and the scale of the horror became more vivid, I felt subdued and numb. By the time the interviews ended, I felt powerless and angry. Later that evening in Bogura, Shamuna and Farhana, who had travelled with me from Dhaka, decided to go for a walk along the river before meeting me for dinner. I was too distraught to go with them; too disturbed to enjoy the dinner later. I made my excuses and left early for bed.

◆

Rape has been part of armed conflict since time immemorial. Women of a conquered country have been abducted, sold as slaves, taken as trophy wives or concubines, and traded away as war booty. International law recognizes crimes against women during an armed conflict to be an international crime—meaning, there is no room for cultural relativism, and that the gravity of the crime is so serious and severe that regardless of when the crime took place, and irrespective of where the perpetrator now lives, prosecutorial and regulatory authorities are obliged to continue to investigate and pursue every possible lead, to bring the accused to trial. Our awareness of such crimes has risen in the past few decades, particularly after stories of rapes during the Rwandan and Bosnian conflicts came out. But the stories are older, going back to World War II and the Japanese 'Comfort Women', and even further back, to the rape of Nanking.

Margot Wallström was the first Special Representative to the UN Secretary-General on sexual violence in conflict between 2010 and 2012. She is a Swedish politician with a deep commitment to human rights. When I asked her what we had learned about rape as a weapon of war, she told me: 'There are three misconceptions about rape as a weapon of war. First, that it is *inevitable* since it has been used and recorded since time eternal. Second, that it is *unspeakable* since it is believed to have to do with sexuality with a violent expression, and not the other way around. And third, that it is somehow a *lesser crime* than murder. During the Foca trial the Serbian soldiers who were accused of rape defended themselves by saying "but we could have killed them". What I've found is that conflict-related sexual violence can be commanded, condoned or condemned. But it can only be understood in the bigger picture and context of the role of women and men in society, women's subordination, and the way we look at honour and shame.'

Rape during the 1971 war was not only widespread; it was also systematic. Gita Sahgal, the human rights expert who produced the award-winning documentary on the Bangladesh War, *War Crime Files,* told me: 'The attack on women was so systematic and intended to create a nation of Pakistanis, that it should clearly be recognized as an element of genocide, as sexual violence is under the Rome Statute. Sexual violence played a central role in the Pakistani attack on Bangladesh's liberation movement. Bangladeshi women were among the leading activists who worked towards a recognition of rape as part of crimes against humanity and genocide because of their experiences in 1971. The world has forgotten what they suffered, but also what they achieved.'

Geoffrey Davis, an Australian doctor who came to Bangladesh at the invitation of international agencies to help perform late-term abortions on Bangladeshi women who had been raped systematically during the war, explained in a 2002 interview with Bangladeshi academic Bina D'Costa, researcher at Australian National University, how the Pakistani army operated in its war on women: 'They had orders of a kind or instruction from Tikka Khan to the effect that a good Muslim will fight anybody except his father. So what they had to do was to impregnate as many Bengali women as they could. That was the theory behind it… There would be a whole generation of children in East Pakistan that would be born with the blood from the West. That's what they said… They'd keep the infantry back and put artillery ahead and they would shell the hospitals and schools. And that caused absolute chaos in the town. And then the infantry would go in and begin to segregate the women. Apart from little children, all those were sexually matured [sic] would be segregated … And then the women would be put in the compound under guard and made available to the troops.' 'The West Pakistani officials didn't get why there was so much fuss about that. I interviewed a lot of them. And they were saying, "What are they going on about? What were we supposed to have done? It was a war!".'

Another reason—perhaps subconscious—why the women were targeted was because many Pakistani officers assumed that Bengali women were less conservative and more flirtatious. They sang and danced, and they wore saris (a garment that reveals the waist) and went about without blouses in rural areas, Pakistani soldiers who were used to seeing women dressed more conservatively in West Pakistan felt Bengali women were easy prey. In Sarmila Bose's book she writes about a general who asks her with some annoyance why Bengali Muslim women danced. Bose makes light of it, saying they were not only Muslim, they were also Bengali; but it is a point the officer is unable to understand.

Meghna Guhathakurta, whose father was among the first intellectuals the Pakistanis killed on 25 March, says Bengali Muslim women sing and dance because being Bengali is an essential part of their culture. To them, culture is broader than religion and held close to the heart. Many Pakistanis could not understand how Bengali women from middle-class families could perform on stage as dancers or actors. 'They see it as a baiji's culture (meaning a dancing girl's culture); for us it was Tagore's culture,' she said. 'A Bengali Muslim may teach his daughter to pray, but he also wants her to be able to recite poetry, dance and sing. The two are never mutually exclusive.'

I asked Nayanika Mookherjee, an Indian Bengali social anthropologist in Britain who has studied the cases of Sirajganj and Kumarkhali as well as other women in different parts of Bangladesh, why this was so. Mookherjee is writing a book[161] which is an ethnographic study of public memories of sexual violence during the Bangladesh war of liberation. She was born in Calcutta (now Kolkata) and now teaches at Durham University in Britain's northeast. Mookherjee told me that she became interested in sexual violence in conflict after the destruction of the Babri Masjid in India. The backlash against the demolition in Ayodhya spread across the subcontinent; Hindu temples were attacked in Pakistan and Bangladesh, and communal riots spread across India, and many women were raped across communities.

Mookherjee said: 'I became interested in the whole issue of why women are raped, and not killed. Within that feminist debate was the war in Bangladesh. And within it was the very public nature of the birangona issue. Only in Bangladesh had the raped women been given a public name by the government. This is globally unprecedented.'

There is a dominant stereotype around discussions on wartime rape, which closes down discussions, which sees women as vulnerable, passive victims. And yet, Bangladesh is seen to be 'Islamic', which seems to be a self-evident explanation of how the women are supposed to have been treated in post-conflict Bangladesh, and all conversation ends, Mookherjee said. 'This kind of limited perspective cuts all nuances and complexities. It does not highlight how people lived with such violence. Focusing only on wartime violence does not capture it,' she added.

Mookherjee went to Bangladesh in 1997 on a month-long work trip during which she met key women's rights and human rights activists. Six months later she travelled back to Bangladesh for her year-long field work. 'If you look closely at the lives of these women, they are all complicated and different,' Mookherjee told me. 'I am not saying that just because some families have taken their daughters, daughters-in-law, wives, or sisters back, everything is fine. The poison of violence faced everyday in all kinds of ways is subtle. Even the human rights narrative, which places a premium on the victim's narrative, can be problematic. The idea of financial compensation is also complicated.'

This is because, Mookherjee says, in many cases the women don't want money. There are various codes of needs—health, jobs, even a tubewell without arsenic in the water. Money is not the only solution. Money placed in a bank has no meaning. They want to reclaim their dignity and respect. Those codes of needs have to be addressed. The right to remain silent also has to be respected. 'Voice isn't always a redemptive thing—that mistake has been made often,' Mookherjee told me. 'There is no one umbrella of solutions. Bangladesh needs to address these concerns, which are otherwise lost in feminist and human rights accounts, because of their search for testimonies.'

Just as it is useful and important to know that a large number of deaths occurred during the war, that total number isn't critical in concluding that crimes against humanity were committed in Bangladesh. And it is the same with rape. Mookherjee says, 'Numbers don't matter. Even if there were "only" two thousand cases of rape, and not 200,000, it matters. You don't have to go down to the root to know the monstrosity of the events. Victims may inflate numbers to attract greater attention. But does the narrative remain shocking even after the numbers have been discounted deeply'?

The incidents were certainly shocking. In Rashid Haider's collection of experiences of 1971, M. Akhtaruzzaman Mondol[162] recalls an incident in Bhurungamari. The fight to liberate the village began on 11 November. The Mukti Bahini had been attacking from the west, north, and east, and the Indian forces had begun bombing the Pakistani bases. On 14 November, the Pakistani guns fell silent and the Mukti Bahini entered the village, shouting 'Joy Bangla'. The town was quiet. They captured about 60 Pakistani soldiers. They found the body of the Pakistani officer, Ataullah Khan, in a bunker. He had his arms around a dead woman whose body bore marks of torture and injuries. Bose challenges Mondol's testimony in her book, citing Pakistani officers.

Later, Mondol headed east towards Bhurungamari, when he was told to go to the circle officer's office. There they saw several young women through the windows. The doors were locked. They found four young women, naked, who had been abused for months. They immediately offered the women lungis and bedsheets to cover themselves. They were in a state of shock and could not speak. One of them was pregnant. Another was a college student from Mymensingh. In the bushes they found other dead bodies and skeletons. Some skeletons had long hair and torn saris or bangles on their hands. In another room they saw sixteen more women. Later, the women said they were repeatedly tied to windowbars and raped several times a night.

In 2011 in Dhaka, a woman told me the story of a relative whose daughter had been taken away by the Pakistani forces for several months. When they were reunited after the war, she had lost her mind. At home, she refused to wear a sari; instead she went about wearing a blouse and a petticoat. And whenever any man she did not know came to the house, she would let her petticoat slip and spread her legs. They had to keep her in a locked room. She died in the mid-1990s, taking her life by hanging herself from a ceiling fan.

Yasmin Saikia is another academic to have worked on the war and its impact on women.[163] She critiques women's invisibility and draws insights from the narratives she captures to open new lines of inquiry. The main thrust of her book collects personal memories and gender narratives, focusing on women's private trauma and public shame. Saikia is troubled by the lack of attention paid to Bihari voices, which have been excluded for decades in most accounts of Bangladeshi independence.[164] Bangladesh-based human rights organizations, such as Ain-O-Salish Kendra, Odhikar, and Bangladesh Legal Aid and Services Trust (BLAST), have often pointed out the abuses suffered contemporaneously by diverse war-affected communities.[165] Saikia lays great hope in the notion of humanity to heal the wounds (as against a confrontational justice system that may not lead to conviction and which may force the victim to relive traumatic experiences). She suggests 'Islamic spiritual meanings of humanity…as exploration of certain fundamental principles that resonate within the Muslim communities in Pakistan and Bangladesh may serve as a starting point for new possibilities.' However, that leaves out non-Islamic communities which form a sizeable proportion of victims. D'Costa points out[166] that unlike other conflicts, the politicisation of religious identities and the warfare discourse of Pakistan featured a systematic targeting of Hindus. In response to Saikia's work, D'Costa writes: 'Approaching reconciliation through a religious lens may evoke anxiety, given the rise of the religious right and the nationalist forces that seek to undermine the rights of non-Bengali communities, including the indigenous population.' However, there are traditional modes of non-adversarial dispute resolution, such as the work of Ain-O-Salish which has been written about in the developmental discourse on justice. Such an approach could provide an alternative dispute resolution mechanism for crimes that are not egregious, nor war crimes, but relatively minor disputes and conflicts arising from the war. Rape, it must be understood, is a war crime.

◆

For several decades after 1975, the year Mujib was assassinated, it became impossible in Bangladesh to talk about the issue of accountability of any war crimes including rape. Partly it had to do with the rise of Jamaat-e-Islami as a political force, and the Jamaat had opposed the movement to create Bangladesh. The Islamist political party became an alliance partner of the Bangladesh Nationalist Party, and later also of the Awami League when the BNP was in opposition. It was also because of the collective sense of shame which overwhelmed many in the country. As more time passed, more people began to think that raking up that past was somehow wrong. Of the many sculptures you find near the Dhaka University campus which commemorate the war of liberation, only one shows a soldier attacking a woman, and even that is part of a larger sculpture with many characters, and unless you are specifically looking for it, or unless someone points it out to you (as indeed happened in my case) you are likely to miss it. Likewise, among the statues at Meherpur, where the Awami League declared independence, there is the tableau where you see a soldier disrobing a woman by pulling off her sari. Shame continues to overpower the state.

The enforced silence around the issue of rape was broken when Ferdousi Priyobhasini came out and spoke about her experiences. The academic Sonia Amin took me to meet her at her home in a quiet part of Dhaka. Ferdousi had a smiling face and was warm and hospitable, willing to talk about what was done to her without any diffidence. 'I was at the Crescent Jute Mill in Khalishpur. I was there as a kept woman,' she told me plainly, without any emotion—neither shame, nor guilt.

In December 1970, Ferdousi was twenty-three. She had been married nearly seven years. There was friction between her mother and father, and she had left home to get married and start work at sixteen. She regretted her choice: 'The marriage was a wrong choice—at that age, it is always the wrong choice,' she told me. By early March 1971, she had legally separated from her husband, but unofficially, they had already been living apart. She had three sons. 'There was no happiness in my life,' she said.

She was working as a sub-divisional clerk at the mill. Then the disturbances started—first the strikes, then the burning of vehicles on the road, and then the divisions among Bengalis and Biharis. Once the crackdown began, she remembers Biharis and other non-Bengalis in East Pakistan cheering the massacre of Bengalis. There were many Bihari labourers in the area who fought frequently with the Bengalis.

She lived in Khalishpur, about four miles outside Khulna in a house from where she could see the Jessore Road. She saw hundreds of trucks full of soldiers going towards Khulna. It is an industrial area with jute mills, near the river Bhairav.

When she came home one day she found that her sons had gone—she could only see some of their clothes all over the ground, and some wet towels on the bed. She figured that her husband had come and taken away their children. She was distraught and lived alone. She had a male friend, but there were too many societal pressures, and he could not come and visit her. 'I wanted him to come, but he could not come to see me,' she said. The East Pakistan Rifles had already surrendered and the Biharis were angry and on a rampage. Ahsanullah Ahmed, who was her boyfriend could no longer help her; he had to leave as his name was top on the list of people the Biharis wanted killed.

She shivered alone at night, missing her children. The fan moved listlessly, papers swirled on the floor. The sound felt like someone was walking in the room. She struggled to pass the night. She woke up to the smell of burning petrol, of ashes, of fire everywhere.

Ferdousi sent her mother back to Jessore, as there was no home that could shelter so many of them. She was alone—a single woman and a divorcee whose children were taken away from her. Other families were not hospitable to her; they thought of her as a 'loose woman' who'd entice their husbands.

Ahsan met her periodically, suggesting they run away. But she reminded him she had no place to go. One day, a businessman she knew gave her a lift in his car and said he would take her to an office where he said she could work. Instead, he brought her to a large house. She asked where the office was. She was told she'd have to go to the house first.

Once inside, he attacked her. 'He was like a hound. I tried to break his fingers, but he slapped me hard and pulled my hair and beat me,' she said. 'Stupid Bengali coward, you are a woman of the streets. You have no prestige,' he told her. 'Stay here until I come back,' he said.

One of the gate-keepers who was not older than twenty told her: 'Didi, if you want to go back, I will open the door and you can slip away. Otherwise they will rape you.'

She escaped and went straight to another businessman whom she knew.

She told him her story and spoke of how she was all alone. When he heard her story he laughed and said she would be well looked after; he had thought she had gone over to the Mukti Bahini. He asked her if she wanted to return to work.

I want a job, any job, she said.

He said he would hire her as a secretary, and asked her to change and come back. But she had neither any clothes nor any money. She had been wearing the same clothes for fifteen days. So he gave her some money to buy some clothes and hired her. She then told him she did not have a home either, and he offered her accommodation.

She started to live in the mill area from then—the last week of April. Her ordeal began soon, when army officers pulled her out from a three-storeyed building, dragging her down because there was no lift, and taking her to an apartment. 'It wasn't only on the first night. After that it became night after night. Every night I had to accept two or three army officers—every night,' she said. 'Sometimes it was a gang rape. It became so bad and so routine that I felt—this is my life now; I cannot change it. I should try to stay positive. Make something positive out of my life. I stopped weeping. I could no longer cry.'[167]

Later, the rapes became a routine, and she stopped thinking. A car would pick her up from work and take her to an apartment where the officers could come. Sometimes she had to walk through mud and the edges of her sari got dirty. They gave her a new sari to wear the next day so that she could go to work. There would be several cars at the gate each evening, and she would not know which car would take her home each night, because each belonged to a different officer. Her manager would come to her and simply say, 'Mohtarma, General X has invited you for tea; please go in the black car', and she would.

She pleaded with the manager—why are you putting me through this? You have saved my life; I'm like your sister, your daughter.

And the manager would only say—please go to the car and stay with the officer tonight.

'But you are from a good family, why do you do this to me,' she asked her manager.

'You must not have a negative attitude,' he told her.

'And it kept happening, night after night,' she said. She can name some of the officers responsible for her continued humiliation and the violence inflicted upon her — Capt. Abdullah, Col. Khatak, Maj. Banuri, Cdr. Gulzarin. That commander, Gulzarin, was known to be a 'lady-killer', she said. He would tell her that some women who hadn't pleased him never went back. 'But I have seen something in your eyes so I won't kill you,' he told her. 'If you make me happy, I will look after you. I will give you money.'

She fell at his feet, wept, and said: 'I am like your daughter, please don't do this to me.'

When she looked up, she could only see his golden teeth. He was smiling. 'Come inside my arms. Don't hold my legs; your place is here,' he said, lifting her, bringing her closer.

Then she fell silent. 'My English is very poor. I cannot tell you more. It was irritating; I cannot explain it to you,' she said. And for the first time that afternoon, I saw her eyes glistening.

During those months she also saw other atrocities — the slaughter of people, headless bodies being dumped in rivers, men in black masks arriving at night in trucks, bringing blindfolded young men. And then there were screams, loud screams that penetrated the curtains of her room and kept her awake at night. She once saw a man being killed—he was a professor, whom she used to call 'uncle', because he was her father's friend. She stopped counting the number of dead bodies she saw after some time.

'These days women are unable to protest for their rights, but men haven't changed. They haven't changed,' she said. 'You have to remember that what happened to me was in a small part of the city. You have to multiply this across 65 districts. I wasn't alone; there were many more women like me. This was a very normal sequence of behaviour for Pakistani officers.'

Things changed after India joined the war. On 3 December, she went to her office, but it was deserted. A driver who used to take her to the officers' quarters saw her. He asked her why she had come—the officers had all gone away, some to Pakistan. Go away while you can, he said. The driver was on duty and he offered to give her a lift up to her house.

But Ferdousi was worried about her job. He gave her a snack of fried chickpeas and told her to join him in his car and he would drive her to some place safe. But she didn't want to join him. He said the American seventh fleet was coming and would support Pakistan, and after that India would lose the war.

They left in an Austin Mini. At the main road he turned off to an alley and said—let us go and have a good drive. We can drink some whisky.

'You are only a driver; how dare you talk to me like this,' she said.

He was already drunk. He took out his revolver. But she held his collar and pulled him hard. With her other hand she opened the car door. Her hands were shivering. She kicked the door open.

He angrily told her to walk wherever she wanted to; he was not going to help her anymore. She was already on the road. Bihari men were watching them.

She hailed a rickshaw, not knowing where she would go next. She didn't think she could go to her family. 'They would think I was a woman of loose morals, of a bad character,' she said. So she went to the home of an officer she knew. He said he was going to his guesthouse and she could come with him. 'I knew what would happen afterwards,' she said, 'but I had no choice.' At the guesthouse he raped her repeatedly.

'I got raped so many times, but what was the consequence?' she reflected. 'I know the questions—people ask me why I didn't leave; why I didn't go to India... I am ready to answer questions. I know why I couldn't go, but I don't owe anyone an explanation. Sometimes mistakes are bound to happen. And you are bound to your mistakes. You cannot leave your fate. I had nowhere to go. I had no money. Ahsan could not offer me shelter. He was more worried about what would happen to his dog. My family had disowned me. My ex-husband had gone away with my sons. I had nobody I could trust. I have never looked back and asked what society would say.'

In the end she married Ahsan. He took care of her and that, she said, made a big difference. 'I am not blaming him, although he could have been braver. But then they would have killed him. His name was on a list and I didn't want him to die.'

Over the years, Ferdousi has been an outstanding advocate for rape survivors. She spoke at the Tokyo Tribunal on the case of comfort women[168] where she said: 'I saw that the history of the Muktijuddho was being altered and the torture of women was being forgotten, and then I saw rural women coming from the villages to be witnesses at the public court (a people's tribunal which was attacked by the then government). I decided from the civil society I will speak up. If I speak of my experiences, a space will open up, women will learn how to fight.' And yet, in a recent list of state honours for many birangonas, she was not included.

◆

Between the time when Bangladesh was liberated and the assassination of Mujibur Rahman on 15 August 1975, the government took some remarkably progressive steps to acknowledge the abuses raped women had suffered and compensated for them. The government had established a rehabilitation centre that started preparing a list of women who had suffered at the hands of Razakars or Pakistani troops. They were offered skills training and loans to start small businesses. Those who were traumatized and unable to work, or were abandoned, were offered financial support.

Sahgal told me: 'It is a grave mistake to think that all countries deal with rape in the same way. It is a truism that women suffer stigma within their families and communities as a result of rape. But Bangladesh is the only example that I know of where women's suffering was recognized as a contribution to the war of liberation.'

Bangladesh even amended its laws, making abortion more easily accessible. Many women who had become pregnant as a result of rape were able to terminate their pregnancy. Aid agencies worked with the government to find foster homes for the children who were born, and whose mothers were neither willing, nor able to bring them up for emotional or financial reasons. Those children were adopted and often sent abroad. It wasn't simple: at independence Bangladesh did not have a law enabling adoptions, and even local Muslims could only be named foster parents, and not declared parents of a child they took under their care. Some children being sent to countries like Canada were less than two weeks old. Bangladesh then changed the law to enable adoption, which was truly remarkable for a Muslim country. It was repealed later when fundamentalists raised panic about Muslim children being sent abroad and converted to other faiths.

Foreign NGOs helped Bangladeshi NGOs set up abortion clinics, whereas Mother Teresa's Baby Home Project enabled adoptions. Her Missionaries of Charity set up a 250-bed hospital in Natore to take care of rape survivors. Abortion clinics were opened in Dhanmondi in Dacca. Sweden's International Planned Parenthood Federation set up a clinic in the city.

Bina D'Costa is a Bangladeshi research fellow at the Centre for International Governance and Justice at the Australian National University in Canberra. She has researched violence in South Asia and written extensively about Bangladesh's war babies and the early dilemmas of adoption versus abortion. 'There is still complete silence in Bangladesh when it comes to talking about the babies of the war,' she told me one cold evening at her home in Geneva where she lived when we met. She showed me an account of Yahya Khan telling a group of journalists by pointing out a crowd of Bengalis who had gathered on the fringes of the Jessore airport: 'Pehle unko Mussalman karo (first make them Muslims)'.[169] D'Costa said that the remark was significant for it showed that the Pakistani leader didn't think that Bengalis were loyal Muslims. Pakistani officers 'always considered Bengalis to be not only weak and powerless, but Hinduani—too close to Hindu religious and cultural practices. For Pakistan, Bengalis/East Pakistanis needed to be purged of this Hinduness', she wrote in an essay. She cites the work of Ain-O-Salish Kendra, where activists and scholars Salma Sobhan, Hameeda Hossain, Shaheen Akhtar, and Sultana Kamal worked with others to document the horrors. D'Costa refers to accounts that suggest how the Pakistani army saw the military crackdown in 1971 as an opportunity to convert East Pakistan through engendering true Muslims, which she takes to mean forced impregnation.

Giving credence to the orders many officers gave to their soldiers to rape—and impregnate—Bangladeshi women, Maj. Gen. (Retd) Khadim Hussain Raja, who was among the commanders in the build-up leading to Operation Searchlight has written[170] a devastating revelation, where Niazi is addressing his officers: 'General Niazi, wearing a pistol holster on his web belt became abusive and started raving. Breaking into Urdu, he said: "Main iss haramzadi qaum ki nasal badal doonga. Yeh mujhe kya samajhtey hain (I will change the race of this bastard community. Who do they think I am?)". He threatened that he would let his soldiers loose on their womenfolk. There was pin-drop silence at these remarks. The next morning, we were given the sad news. A Bengali officer Major Mushtaq went into a bathroom at the Command Headquarters and shot himself in the head. He died instantaneously... he was dignified and self-respecting.... It is a pity that he should have been the first casualty of Niazi's words and deeds.' When Raja left his command in April to return to duty in West Pakistan, Niazi put his hand on his shoulder and said: 'Yaar, ladai ki fikar nahi karo, wo to ham kar lenge. Abhi to mujhe Bangali girlfriends ke phone numbers de do (Man, don't worry about the war; that we will deal with. Right now give me the phone numbers of some Bengali girlfriends)'. Raja left, saying, 'General, you should have known me better.' Raja was aghast by the systematic occurrence of rape that followed. He was unique because he was among the very few Pakistani officers or men who saw how wrong their conduct was and to actually write about it. Others were unrepentant. In his book, *How Pakistan Got Divided*, Maj. Gen.

Rao Farman Ali, Adviser to the Governor of East Pakistan defended himself and other seniors by saying: 'Harrowing tales of rape, loot, arson, harassment, and of insulting and degrading behaviour were narrated in general terms.... I wrote out an instruction to act as a guide for decent behaviour and recommended action required to be taken to win over the hearts of the people. This instruction under General Tikka Khan's signature was sent to Eastern Command. I found that General Tikka's position was also deliberately undermined and his instructions ignored...excesses were explained away by false and concocted stories and figures.'[171]

Regardless of this avoidance of responsibility, the fact was that women were raped in homes, offices, cantonments, local areas, riverbeds, forests, in paddy fields, and in sheds. Rape was also seen as a weapon of war—to terrorize the population, to extract information, to boost soldier morale, and to crush the burgeoning Bangladeshi national identity, D'Costa wrote. After the war was over, Bihari activists have alleged that Bangladeshi men too raped many Bihari women and girls, as a way to extract revenge.

There were also rape camps. By one estimate, there were at least 200 military camps in cantonments, and each of them may have held up to 300 women captive at a given time, suggesting at least 60,000 women kept in sexual slavery. D'Costa says lists were created with names and numbers. But in 1972, the Mujib government burned many of those records, probably out of a desire to preserve the women's anonymity but thereby making future prosecutors' task difficult. And between 1978-80 and again in 1985-86 successor governments allegedly destroyed what remained of the records.

It was inevitable that war babies would face stigma and prejudice. Bangladeshis rarely talk about war babies the way Amerasian kids are spoken about in Vietnam (where, to be sure, the children were not necessarily born out of rape, but often because of romantic relationships between American soldiers and Vietnamese women). Rubaiyat Hossain is a Bangladeshi film-maker, whose 2011 film *Meherjaan,* attempted to portray one such relationship. It became hugely controversial and was withdrawn from general release after widespread protests.

Some documents refer to at least 25,000 cases of forced pregnancy. The government handed over the responsibility of dealing with the raped women to doctors and social workers. Inevitably, the responsibility fell on the Catholic Church to promote adoptions, the International Planned Parenthood Federation to enable abortions, and the Red Cross to provide relief. Some decisions were forced on the women; in some cases social workers decided for the prospective mothers, believing that the women were too young and traumatized to take such important decisions. Ruby Ghuznavi, who worked at one of the rehabilitation centres for a few months in 1972 was aware that it was dangerous to abort a foetus if the woman had been pregnant for six months. She said: 'The thought of killing a baby is not an easy one, and very young women were forced to make such choices. Their guardians were always men who said they had to guard the women and an abortion was essential otherwise they might not be able to take them back.' A large majority of them were from rural Bangladesh. But she said it was entirely possible that urban women, being better off, may have travelled to Calcutta to arrange their own abortions without letting anyone know. 'For all of them the important thing was that nobody should know,' she told me.

While Mujib extended verbal support by referring to the birangonas as his daughters and asking the nation to welcome the women back, he also said that 'none of the babies who carry the blood of the Pakistanis will be allowed to remain in Bangladesh'. In *Ami Birangona Bolchi,* a composite account[172] based on real-life experiences of several women, the feminist author Neelima Ibrahim asks Mujib about the war babies, and he says: 'Please send away the children who do not have their fathers' identity. They should be raised as human beings with honour. Besides, I do not want to keep those [with] polluted blood in this country.'(Other accounts say he was pithier, he told Ibrahim: 'Apa, I don't want these bastard children in this country.')

Adoptions and abortions proliferated. The Bangladesh Central Organisation for Women's Rehabilitation in Dacca and seventeen outlying areas helped women cope with unwanted pregnancies. Geoffrey Davis, an Australian doctor who worked in Bangladesh for six months in 1972 administered the state-sponsored abortion programme. Davis, who died in 2008, told D'Costa how women considered pretty were kept for the officers, while the rest were distributed among the ranks. These women never received sufficient nutrition, and when they fell ill, they were ignored, and many died in the camps. Many women were treated so harshly that they would not be able to bear children due to psychological and physical abuse. Some 5,000 women had undergone abortions with the assistance of local dais (midwives) or untrained local doctors, often with unsafe medical methods.

Mother Teresa, in keeping with her faith, urged women not to have abortions. Her sisters went to nursing homes and asked them not to discard the babies in the dustbin when they were born (indicating that some newborn children were thrown in the dustbin). 'Bring them to us if they are alive,' they would tell them. But the nursing homes weren't interested; their sole concern was the mother, not the child. Mother Teresa visited a camp with a social worker and found only women's hair, petticoats and a few items there. There were no women. Pakistani officers often cut the hair of the women because they feared they would hang themselves by tying their long hair to ceiling fans, as some had done.

In 1972, Bangladesh passed the Bangladesh Abandoned Children (Special Provision) Order, encouraging foreign adoption agencies to take war babies from Bangladesh. This was pathbreaking, because as a predominantly Muslim country, Bangladesh—or East Pakistan earlier—did not allow adoption. People could take care of orphans as foster parents. Several agencies, including Missionaries of Charity, International Social Service, Families for Children and the Kuan-Yin Foundation (both in Canada), the Holt Adoption Program (US) and Terre des Hommes (Switzerland) assisted in getting the children adopted and sent to countries in North America and Europe.

Some Muslim clerics initially opposed the adoptions, because of their fears that ostensibly Muslim children would now be brought up in Christian countries. Some young mothers didn't want to give away their babies.[173] Ibrahim told D'Costa that '[they] even had to use sedatives to make the women sleep and then take the babies'. Clearly, the women had little choice in the matter. The social workers intended to help the women, but the eventual trauma the woman faced multiplied when her child was taken away from her without her consent.

Consent, in fact, was ignored at almost all levels. In order to 'protect' the women, some were forcibly married off, regardless of what the women wanted. If pregnant, some women were forced to abort. If it was too late to abort, some were compelled to give up their children for adoption. In each instance, others took decisions on the woman's behalf, disregarding her choice, assuming she was not in a position to decide. Those who took the decisions often meant well, but the decisions were made to fix a problem, and not necessarily to identify what the women wanted. The assumption was that a marriage was preferable to being an abandoned wife or a daughter nobody would marry, or that bringing up a fatherless child was worse than undergoing abortion. Well-meaning though such decisions may have been, there were no provisions to help the woman to deal with the trauma of giving up her newborn child to adoption, or indeed to terminate her pregnancy, as, indeed, to marry a man, often older, whom she had scarcely known. Indeed, some who decided for the women did so to protect their own sense of honour and their status in the village, and not caring for the well-being of their sisters, daughters, daughters-in-law, or wives.

One of the enduring mysteries is what happened to the children who were given away for adoption. D'Costa said: 'Today almost nothing is known about the destiny of those war babies. By now, they have largely disappeared from the official history of Bangladesh. There is very little information about these children—about how they have developed, about how they often lived without social recognition within their societies, about what happened to those who were adopted by people from other countries.' In recent years, the humanitarian community has shown interest in integrating children born out of sexual violence during conflict through post-conflict humanitarian efforts, migration policies and refugee-settlement programmes. D'Costa sent appeals to several adoption agencies, Bengali websites and newspapers to talk about the war babies, but only a few wanted their stories to be public or learn more about what happened. One website owner wrote to D'Costa: 'I had a lousy dad, who just insulted me ... I tried to commit suicide four years ago ... I often wonder why I am here in Canada, adopted by parents who divorced three months after I was adopted ... I hated being a kid, and I am angry at Bangladesh for not taking care of me when I needed it most. I don't have any roots and that makes me cry. So that is why I am trying to learn more about where I was born.'

The stories of the missing war babies will probably never be known, unless there is a coordinated effort on the part of adoption agencies to share data with researchers compiling the information. It isn't an easy process. Many individuals may not wish to be found at all. Retracing their footsteps may enable Bangladesh to regain some of its past intertwined history, where the state, families, and communities constructed a haphazard process of giving new identities to the children, uprooting them from their homeland.

◆

Who was Geoffrey Davis and what motivated him to do what he did? In the 1960s when medical termination of pregnancy was not yet legal in Australia, Davis used to discreetly carry out abortions, from two clinics in the suburbs of Sydney. He became famous for performing late-term abortions in Bangladesh following the war. The World Health Organization and the International Planned Parenthood Federation were among the organizations that wanted him in Bangladesh, but due to the sensitive nature of his work, no organization claimed credit for bringing him over. He worked in Bangladesh for about six months, often performing late-term abortions which were sometimes medically complicated, ethically sensitive, and legally questionable in many parts of the world at that time. In subsequent interviews he said that he had heard of many cases of women committing suicide and of infanticides, and estimated that some 5,000 rape victims had performed self-induced abortions. He was a vocal critic of the mass rapes, and told D'Costa: 'I felt that Tikka Khan's programme (ordering his soldiers to violate Bengali women indiscriminately) was an obscenity, comparable to Heinrich Himmler's Lebensborn Ministry in Nazi Germany. It gave me some satisfaction to know that I was contributing to the destruction of the policies of West Pakistan.'[174]

The abortion clinic Davis set up with another physician, Leonard Laufe, was described as an 'industrial scale' enterprise. Between them they probably carried out 95 per cent of the abortions in Bangladesh at that time. Davis would travel to remote areas of the country to carry out abortions. Davis also helped international adoption agencies find families for the children who were already born.[175]

◆

Critics who doubt the scale of rapes in Bangladesh have often pointed out the small number of women who have come forward to talk about their experience. While the arithmetic of rape suggests that there may indeed have been at least a quarter million instances of rape committed during the war (and maybe half a million), the skeptics ask that if that were so, why is it that academics, journalists, and writers who have tried to investigate the issue, have been able to produce fewer than forty direct testimonies? Of course that's partly because Bangladesh is a conservative society where it is not easy for a rape survivor to step forward, as the cases[176] show. Irene Khan said: 'A conservative Muslim society has preferred to throw a veil of negligence and denial on the issue, allowed those who committed or colluded with gender violence to thrive, and left the women victims to struggle in anonymity and shame and without much state or community support.' Indeed, this is a society where women fear being ostracized by their families if they acknowledge and report what had been done to them. Besides, forty years have passed.

It is hard enough in a rape case that has occurred recently for a woman to argue her case successfully. To try to prove abuse that occurred so long ago is nearly impossible, and women are aware of the futility, considering that it is impossible for the type of forensic evidence that rape trials require, including items of clothing, to have survived so long. Besides, many of the perpetrators may have died, or are in Pakistan, and any extradition request is unlikely to be successful. That would still leave local perpetrators, and Bangladesh, as a state, failed its women in not pursuing those cases.

The list that was prepared in the early years after the war would have been extremely useful in at least building legal cases. But Khushi Kabir, a human rights activist who runs Nijera Kori told me: 'It is believed that at some point it was decided to remove those records in order to protect the identity of women and their privacy, and to rehabilitate them without any finger-pointing, so that there is no linkage between the women and what had happened to them.' While the intent was practical and pragmatic, the effect was that evidence was lost. Nobody can satisfactorily explain why that happened.

When human rights groups approached the present Bangladesh government for some action on the issue, Prime Minister Hasina Wajed's response was that if they established a pension scheme the government would get inundated with requests. What if a lot of women claim they were raped? The NGOs replied that that was unlikely, given society's proclivity in assigning blame to the victim. But if such a scheme is institutionalized, some of Bangladesh's poorest, most vulnerable, and marginalized women will have some steady support from the state, particularly when their families have shunned them.

◆

What hundreds of thousands of women went through during those nine months is painful in itself. An overpowering sense of shame prevails as a matter of cultural orthodoxy. Could art capture the emotions and celebrate the women's courage? In recent years, some women have responded to the sisterhood's experience through fiction, poetry, drama, and art.

Shaheen Akhtar is a fiction writer and a researcher in Dhaka who had interviewed many women affected by the war. One of her interviews has been included in a book called *Narir Ekattor* (Rising from the Ashes: Women's Narratives of 1971). One afternoon at her office in Dhaka, Akhtar told me: 'When I talked to Ferdousi Priyobhasini I was in confusion about her. Although she was abused many times, she remained composed. Ferdousi was able to use the contacts she had in the Pakistani military to get others who were harassing her punished. In 1972, some people thought she was a collaborator, because she was seen in cars with army officers. But understanding her survival strategy is not easy. She was a rape victim. She was brutally assaulted. There were times she had been gangraped. She was very vulnerable. But she has a very unique persona which is difficult to figure out.'

Akhtar then looked at the transcripts and instinctively felt there was a novel waiting to be written out of that material. Drawing on those interviews, she wrote a novel in Bangla called *Talaash* or The Search, which dealt with rape and received wide acclaim. Tarfia Faizullah is a Bangladeshi-American poet who has recently published a collection of poems, *Seam,* which is based on interviews she conducted with birangonas. Her poems are about young women, ignorant of the harm about to come to them, and how their lives get shattered with the arrival of the army. A grandfather calls her granddaughter mishti maya or 'a girl of sweetness'; a Pakistani soldier calls her kutta, 'dog'. 'I didn't know my body's worth until they came for it,' she writes in another poem. And in yet another poem, she encapsulates the central question about identity in this country:

Are you
Muslim or Bengali, they
Asked again & again.
Both, I said, both—then
Rocks were broken along
My spine, my hair a black
Fist in their hands, pulled
Down into the river again
And again. Each day, each
Night: river, rock, fist.

It is a theme that recurs in the play, *Birangona: Women of War,* which the British-Bangladeshi actor/writer Leesa Gazi staged in Britain in the summer of 2014. The story is about a newly-wed Moryom who is blissfully happy in her village, married to a local boy and experiencing the joy of life stirring within her when she is seized by the army and taken away to a rape camp. Gazi heard about cases of rape first from her father in Bangladesh, who told her how he saw many women standing back to back in a convoy of trucks after they were rescued from Army barracks and rape camps and brought to Dhaka. She then read Ibrahim's *Ami Birangona Bolchi* which left a deep impact on her. She went to Sirajganj and interviewed the women on camera, and some of those interviews feature in her play.

◆

Rebuilding life from such experiences is not easy. But the most remarkable transformation, in fact, is what Ferdousi's life has undergone. In recent years she has discovered a gift—art. And it is not ordinary art—Ferdousi picks up the city's refuse—twigs, branches, waste, and other material she comes across on the city's teeming streets. In those objects, which are cast away and of no use to anyone, she sees beauty. Showing me around her garden, she said: 'I collect rejected material. I pick up waste. And I turn it into art. I have looked into my own life, and I have discovered how much I love nature. I like rain, I like the seasons, and I love the forms of art. Tagore's songs are always playing in my heart. I am absorbed in them; poetry makes me happy.'

Ferdousi picks up what the city does not want and brings it home. She twists those twigs and branches, turns them, gives them a different shape, and transforms them, unleashing the beauty within, giving those wounded parts of a city's debris a new identity, a new birth. The branch crushed beneath the tyres of rickshaws and kicked around by schoolboys returning home now becomes the outline of a bird taking wings. The stump of the tree becomes a stool. And the messy leaves are reborn in a collage where they tremble gently, like waves in a lake. Like Ferdousi's own life, their renaissance is complete.

EIGHT

THE ASSASSINATION OF A FAILED
REVOLUTIONARY

Sheikh Mujibur Rahman returned to the charred landscape of a scarred country. Everything was devastated—all six airfields had gaping holes; hundreds of bridges were destroyed; the Chittagong harbour was mined; electricity supply generators had been blown up; roads, which were never in pristine conditions, now felt like rocky terrain; and families were still trying to figure out where their loved ones were. Nobody had an idea how many people had been killed, were missing, or been raped, and nobody knew what had to be done with the Biharis who lived in fear in refugee camps run by the Red Cross. Junior civil servants, some of whom were under-qualified, had executive responsibilities thrust upon them, as they were suddenly asked to supervise departments of a size and scale that they simply didn't have the experience or expertise for.

The refugees had in fact begun returning to their new country on their own, without waiting for orders or instructions from authorities. By the end of January 1972, some six million refugees (of the total of ten million) had returned home. A UNHCR report stated: 'Visitors to the camp areas marvelled at the unending streams of people on the trek, walking, riding bicycles and rickshaws, standing on truck platforms, with the single purpose—of reaching as soon as possible their native places in East Bengal. In January, a daily average of 210,000 persons crossed the Bangladesh border.'

Each refugee was given food for the journey, medical assistance, and two weeks of basic rations. There were 271 transit camps in Bangladesh, where they received medical aid, food rations, and free transport. On 25 March 1972, a year after the military crackdown, India estimated that only 60,000 refugees still remained in India. However, it is likely that a lot more had quietly integrated in neighbouring villages and towns in India and decided not to return.

In August 1973, the governments of Bangladesh, India, and Pakistan signed an agreement that facilitated simultaneous repatriation of three groups of people: Pakistani prisoners of war and civil internees in India; Bengalis in Pakistan; and non-Bengalis in Bangladesh who wanted to be repatriated to Pakistan. Airplanes ferried tens of thousands of people across the three countries in late 1973, in a project overseen by the UNHCR. In the end, some 116,000 Bengalis returned to Bangladesh from Pakistan, 104,000 non-Bengalis left for Pakistan from Bangladesh, and 11,000 Pakistanis left for Pakistan from Nepal.

Amena Mohsin was among the Bangladeshis who returned with her family to her own country where she had not spent much time. Her father, a Bengali, was a doctor with the Pakistani army, and he was stationed in West Pakistan when the war broke out. His loyalty to Pakistan had suddenly become suspect (as was the case with many other Bengali officers), and their family had to live in an internment camp in Pakistan.

When she saw Bangladesh from the airplane, Amena was thrilled. 'It was an imagined land for us, a land of freedom. Those three years in the camp had changed my mind. I knew what freedom meant, even though I wasn't in the country where the battle was fought. I would try to put my feet outside the barbed wire, to let my toes touch the land which was beyond the barbed wire, to feel what the land outside felt like, and to understand what freedom meant. Unless you are caged, in a camp, you don't know what freedom means. We were caged, and felt connected with our language listening to overseas Bengali programmes which we had to listen to very quietly. Now I was in a land where the language was spoken with pride.'

An imagined land—what did that mean? The academic Benedict Anderson has called nation states 'imagined communities',[177] suggesting that national boundaries are drawn by the powerful based on history and politics, and the project of a nation state is imagined by a community of people who think of themselves as one. Anderson was writing about Indonesia, a vastly heterogeneous nation of 17,000 islands and thousands of languages and ethnicities. Bangladesh was imagined as a nation of one language, one ethnicity and one faith, although there were indeed many other languages spoken in Bangladesh. Besides, there were other nationalities and ethnicities with different narratives, and Islam was not the only faith in the nation.

◆

Sheikh Mujib had had plenty of time to think about what his imagined

Bangladesh would look like while he was in jail and facing death sentence. When he returned from Pakistan on 10 January and as the plane descended, from his window he could only see human heads. There were thousands upon thousands of them. The city was devastated after the war and many trees had been cut. The Race Course, where he spoke, was teeming with people. He said that terrible things had happened and much could have been avoided. He appealed to them that there should be no further bloodshed and that nobody should take the law in their own hands. And he promised that there would be trials to do justice for the terrible crimes that had been committed during the war.

Kamal Hossain was appointed the law minister, and besides drafting the country's constitution, one of his first responsibilities was to set in motion a process for the investigation of the international crimes that had taken place during the Liberation War. He told me: 'We appointed two senior lawyers— Serajul Huq and Sabita Ranjan Pal—as prosecutors, to be assisted by advocate Aminul Huq. They began gathering and examining available evidence. By 1973, Bangladesh passed the law allowing prosecutions, and the team was told to move ahead in early 1974. A specific law was passed to try collaborators for complicity with the Pakistani army, which would primarily affect Bengalis or Biharis who were in Bangladesh.' Kamal remembers detailed discussions about conditions in the prison including the size of cells and ventilation, all as per the rules adhering to the Geneva Conventions. They had identified 195 Pakistani military officers and men against whom substantial evidence had been compiled. They were to be tried in Bangladesh. At that time, these officers and men were in India, part of the 93,000 POWs. Pakistan objected to the planned trials and called for talks. Bangladesh assured the Pakistanis that the trial would be conducted strictly as per the law. Following the Tripartite talks held in Delhi between Bangladesh, India and Pakistan in 1974 an agreement was reached that Pakistan would seek clemency for the 195 who would be repatriated. There was an undertaking by Pakistan, however, to try not only the 195 but also others against whom evidence would be available.

In the meantime a large number of trials of those who had collaborated were started and some had been convicted but thousands of other cases were pending while investigations were going on. In this context a decision was taken to grant amnesty except for those against whom there were grave charges of murder and rape.

There were other immediate priorities—dealing with the destruction and rebuilding of infrastructure; reuniting families and rehabilitating the women who were raped; disarming militias. Food distribution was critical—there were new citizens with old memories of the famine of the 1940s. Food distribution was going to be difficult. Many bureaucrats were inexperienced, most bridges were destroyed, the economy was collapsing and incomes were low, and river transport was too slow to distribute food efficiently.

To complete the picture of misery, in 1974 floods and torrential rains had ravaged parts of Bangladesh. There were increasing reports of Awami officials offering aid only to those who could offer bribes. Mujib asked Monwarul Islam, who was his political secretary from 1974, to look into the allegations. He returned with many stories of corruption. He was livid as he told Mujib what he saw. He said Mujib's party was full of robbers and dacoits. Mujib heard him calmly and said: 'Listen, when I started my party, I could not get brilliant students like you to come to join my party. You were too busy pursuing your career in civil service. And I had with me only ma tarano baap khedano chheley[178] (homeless urchins). Isn't it natural that they should engage in such activities once they are in power?'[179] He said this not in a tone of levity, but of resignation, implying it had to be tolerated.

All over the country there was a breakdown of law and order. Many Mukti Bahini fighters joined the regular army and were allowed to hold on to their weapons. Many more of Kader Siddiqui's fighters laid down their weapons dramatically at a rally in front of Mujib. Siddiqui then tried to make up for his lost education but his personal popularity got in the way. 'Other students called me Fidel Castro,' he told me, 'and thousands would drop classes to come and see me. Teachers addressed me as sir and at Jahangir Nagar University the vice chancellor came to see me on my first day at the university. I could not continue because of my popularity.' He returned to Tangail, and received Awami League patronage.[180]

Many other fighters ignored Mujib's call and preferred to hold on to their weapons, and for a while, used them to secure advantages over others, including taking over property belonging to refugees who had not yet returned. Guerrillas still roamed around the countryside and the central government in Dacca was powerless to do anything.

Mujib felt deeply committed to support those who participated in the Liberation War. He made official appointments out of turn, and got called upon to intervene in cases at district and village level, where he would not have access to all the information but would be expected to decide between candidates for specific positions. Some new appointees saw these jobs as a way to get rich and began demanding bribes, assuming, not without reason, that their status as freedom fighters made them immune from criticism or any future prosecution. Mujib's preference of people with sound liberation credentials meant he had to bypass several officials who had continued to work with the Pakistan Civil Service. Not all of them were supporters of Pakistan, and many of them performed the important work of keeping the water supply running and food being distributed during the war. Their contributions seemed in vain when compared with a guerrilla who claimed to have destroyed a few bridges.

Such policies infected appointments in the army too, which eventually had fatal consequences. Some Bengali officers who had been taken off duty by the Pakistani army during the war and detained or interned in West Pakistan found that when they returned to their chosen country they had to report to officers who had been their juniors, because the junior officers had superior liberation credentials. The freedom fighters looked at the repatriated officers with suspicion. They could not be sure if they would be loyal to Mujib. But the repatriated officers were military professionals, and as the cult around Mujib grew, some among them found it harder to reconcile their professionalism with the new ideological demands. While Farooq Rahman was obviously being self-serving, he reminded me when we met in 1986 how the army had liberated Bangladesh 'when Awami politicians were scared and staying in Calcutta hotels and boozing and womanizing. There was no political leadership. The army fought on its own. Thousands of soldiers died like dogs, weaponless and helpless. I couldn't get them (the Awami leaders in India) even to come to Jessore, even after it was under our control. Even after surrender they didn't want to come. The Awami leaders were sitting pretty in India in comfortable surroundings. Let the Mukti Bahini fight, let India fight—that was their thinking. The Awami League always considered the armed forces to be against the state.'

Farooq may have thought he spoke for the army, but there were several in the army who were wary of him. Niloufer Huda, whose husband Najmul was an officer close to Khaled Mosharraf, remembers an incident from the time when they were posted in Jessore. Farooq had joined the war towards its end. He was a young officer who was often seen dressed in tweed jackets, when army officers could barely afford thin blankets. He had spent time abroad.

She told me: 'We all found him extremely arrogant, expensively dressed up all the time which was not at all the case for many freedom fighters. On the other hand Maj. Dalim who was in Comilla with us was a brave and happy-go-lucky officer who had lost his finger during the war.[181] One day his wife was teased by an Awami League politician's son at the Dacca Club and Dalim thrashed the young man. But this would cost him his position in the armed forces and he was dismissed.'

Shariful Haque Dalim was deeply upset over his dismissal. He appealed for reinstatement, but the army chief had said the decision was final.

While other officers didn't have views as radical as Farooq's, nor had they been slighted personally as Dalim felt he had been, there was growing resentment against the civilian leadership. Sultana Kamal reflected on this when we met: 'Mujib returned from Pakistan on 10 January, and for the four weeks after Pakistan's surrender on 16 December, the country was under the control of sector commanders. But once Mujib returned, the commanders were no longer visible. I don't think Mujib planned it that way, but that is how it happened. He was the dream leader for the people. He was the hero, even though he hadn't fought the war physically; he was the hero, even in his absence. So there was tension about who deserved to lead the country—army or Mujib—and who had done more to win freedom. From day one, there was a feeling of competition between the two. It intensified because the nation swayed with him, forgetting the army, but it is not to be denied that the army too had lost soldiers and suffered in the battles. And now they were not in control of the nation. After the elections in 1973, the country was completely under Mujib's control. It became a totally civilian country, like India. And I heard comments from many army friends—he wasn't there; he was happily in a jail, now he comes and takes over; we actually fought; our brothers died; we actually did things. When sector commanders' forum was formed, Mir Shawkat Ali[182] explicitly said that—we fought the war, but politicians took it over. They had become corrupt; they were in Calcutta; they did nothing; we fought on the field—that was their view.'

Besides officers loyal to Mujib and skeptical of civilians in general, there were some officers who were aligned to a radical left political party, Jatiyo Samajtantrik Dal (National Socialist Party), which believed in officers elected to the post, to make the army truly democratic. The JSD was suspicious of India and the Soviet Union but was not necessarily pro-China. The JSD was popular among freedom fighters, and Mujib saw it as a potential threat. Col.

Abu Taher[183], a popular radical officer, had long believed in bringing about a people's revolution. Together with Sirajuddul Hussain and Maj. Jalil, Taher had kept urging Mujib to be a 'true' people's leader. These officers had gained enormous popularity among students, even splitting the Chhatra League.

While Mujib was left-leaning and committed to socialist ideals, the Bangladeshi left had always seen the Awami League as a bourgeois party, and as such, in Bangladesh's political landscape he was even considered right-wing, a view that circulated more widely after he consolidated power and undermined institutions. The view was also shared by some of the officers who would later plot to assassinate him, as well as by some sympathizers of the JSD. To counter their influence, Mujib created the Jatiyo Rakkhi Bahini (National Defence Force) which, in effect, became Mujib's private militia, as its members swore personal allegiance to Mujib. Unsurprisingly, joining the JRB was a good career move for some young men, as it ensured them access to commodities which were hard to get in the open market, and they got privileges which set JRB members apart from others.

This became all the more glaring during the period of food shortages. With the new nation unable to provide food across the country, it turned to friendly nations for help, and India and the Soviet Union were among the first countries to provide food aid. Upon independence, Bangladesh had promptly joined the Non-Aligned Movement. Bangladesh had begun exporting jute— its main cash crop—to Cuba, but that meant the United States, a country awash with giant food surpluses would not offer food aid to Bangladesh at a time when it needed it most, because of the US's long-held opposition to trade with Cuba. America imposed trade restrictions on Bangladesh, and that, unfortunately for Bangladeshi people, included food aid.

Meanwhile, Mujib declared 'war' on traders who hoarded food or smuggled it to India, but some of those hoarders and smugglers were members of the Awami League, and once arrested, they would make a few phone calls and were released, to the dismay of an increasingly demoralized officialdom. Nothing seemed to be going right. When Mujib took the guard of honour at the parade on Bangladesh's first anniversary, the plan was for a 31-gun salute. But after the fifth gun was fired, the other guns didn't work, and soldiers had to hastily fire rifles in the air.[184]

◆

In 1973 Mujib gave a speech at Paltan Bazar where he talked about smuggling.

He asked people to catch smugglers and he said he would deal with them. But the audience was skeptical and dismayed—leading Awami politicians were known to be smugglers and Mujib was fast losing credibility. Realizing this, in an attempt to capitalize on his popularity, Mujib held nationwide elections in 1973. The Awami League did spectacularly well, winning 282 of the 289 directly contested seats. But while the elections cast a warm, happy glow around him, his political fortunes suffered after that. Social and economic conditions continued to deteriorate. Food shortages escalated, most economists and agriculture experts characterize the food shortages of 1974 as the equivalent of a man-made famine. By October 1974, Tajuddin left Mujib's government, being unable to influence him to change his ways, and being unwilling to be part of a government that was no longer acting in the interests of the people. Tajuddin had enormous credibility because even though he was in Calcutta during the war, he was free to mobilize the political processes that gave legitimacy to the freedom movement, unlike Mujib, who was in a Pakistani prison, and unable to lead his people during the nine months of conflict. Tajuddin was personally immensely popular, and some analysts viewed his resignation as a way to protect his reputation, so that some day in future he may be able to take over the country's leadership, through legitimate democratic means.

The famine had taken a severe toll on Mujib's popularity. Bangladeshis had vivid memory of the famine of 1940s. It had been easy to pin the blame at that time—the villain was British imperialism—but now Bangladesh had its own government, led by a man elected by popular mandate. How could he not deliver? Irene Khan remembers poor people from the countryside flocking to the city, going from house to house seeking food. 'They were so thin you could see their ribs,' she told me. Others mentioned seeing dead bodies lying on the streets as pedestrians walked past, not because they did not care, but because they lacked the means to do anything. Industrial production continued to fall, as did food production, and some people began feeling nostalgic about the time when the country was part of Pakistan.

The mood had turned distinctly sharp against Mujib. The American journalist Lawrence Lifschultz, who has the unique distinction of being expelled at various times from India, Pakistan, and Bangladesh, who had noted how many Bangladeshis had cheered when Zulfikar Ali Bhutto made his first visit to Bangladesh as Pakistan's prime minister, told me there were conflicted feelings among some Bangladeshis who in 1974 were living through the first stages of a severe famine. Clearly, some believed their hopes had been belied, but to him, the cheering of Bhutto seemed particularly perverse, given the circumstances of Bangladesh's emergence and Bhutto's role in it. Mahfuz Anam too said he was shocked to see the ovation Bhutto received when he visited Bangladesh. 'The man was singularly responsible for the tragedy,' he said. 'Mujib was unnerved by seeing the reception and welcome Bhutto received.' After a pause, he told me: 'It should have been an early warning signal for Mujib about his leadership.'

Some of the civilian stalwarts of the freedom struggle began leaving the establishment. Among the many intellectuals to part company with the Awami League was the economist Anisur Rahman. He was a professor at the university. He had been a neighbour of the Guhathakurta family, and he had seen violence during the war first-hand. He was a radical economist, deeply suspicious of foreign capital, and believed in Bangladeshi self-reliance. He expected Mujib to usher in an egalitarian society but he was increasingly dismayed by what he saw. When I met him at his home in a quiet street in Dhaka near the Liberation War Museum, he told me: 'The war and its aftermath were painful not only because of what happened, but because of the dream that has been shattered. So many things were promised and so much we have lost. And we lost that dream to a great extent because of the betrayal of the so-called nationalist elites.'

The liberation struggle had brought the elite and the ordinary people together in a united fight. 'We ate together, starved together, suffered together and shared our lives. The basic premise was egalitarianism to fight disparities. We had seen the disparity with West Pakistan, and we wanted the east to be different,' he said. But after independence, the elite and the people separated. 'The elite rejected the people. A gap was created between the elite and ordinary people, and fundamentalists used it to go after the people. The elite wanted to get rich quickly and we are now paying for their greed,' he said ruefully. After one of his visits to India, Anisur Rahman noticed more luxury cars in his hometown than in Delhi or Calcutta and he found that jarring.

During the war, with Mujib in jail, Tajuddin Ahmed had been the prime minister of Bangladesh's government-in-exile, and he had decided that Bangladesh would not take assistance from any government that was hostile to the idea of Bangladesh. That meant refusing American aid after independence. With egalitarianism as its goal, the new government had appointed Anisur Rahman to formulate the country's income policy. He decided that the highest salary in the country should be 750 taka per month. Government servants' residents would be small and cars would be withdrawn as a perk. But when Mujib was released and went to London, he announced that Bangladesh would accept aid from everyone, undercutting Tajuddin's socialist ideal. 'Mujib brought America with him to Dhaka. Such policies would create an affluent class in the country, creating a market for American goods and consultants, while the rest would be deprived and we'd solve problems of poverty only over a much longer time. That was the great American design and it came with Mujib,' Anisur Rahman said.

Mujib was still an excellent rabble-rouser—he was a powerful speaker who could sway masses. But he was not an economist. By any conventional yardstick, the policies he pursued had a distinct, pro-Soviet, socialist tinge. Drawing inspiration from the Soviet Union and Indira Gandhi's India, he decided on nationalising vast sectors of the economy. Mujib had come to power during an era when the left was a powerful force in international politics. By taking such measures Mujib was also partly trying to blunt the influence of and criticism from the left. Mujib's nationalization affected many manufacturing companies and trading enterprises were also taken over.

At the same time, his sacrifices were recognized and his personal popularity had not yet dimmed. But in the chattering classes of the capital, there were some who began to ask if Mujib had played his cards wisely. Did he really want an independent Bangladesh, or was he always playing for a bigger role within Pakistan, such as being its prime minister (which he should have been in 1971, by right)? If he was keen on an independent Bangladesh, why did he not make an explicit call for independence in his famous speech on 7 March? Why did he wait till Pakistan launched Operation Searchlight, whose consequences were catastrophic for Bangladesh at a human level, while for Pakistan, only politically so? Asif Munier, whose father was among the intellectuals taken away during the last days of the war and never seen again, told me how his mother was angry with Mujib. Asif recalled: 'She said the Liberation War was a national movement, but why could he not have prepared the country better? Why did we have to wait for the blow on 25 March?'

Mujib was genuinely compassionate—he deeply respected those who had suffered, such as birangonas and widows. Once, Basanti Guhathakurta, the widow of professor Jyotirmoy went to meet Mujib to discuss some problems about her school. As she entered the room she saw that Mujib was surrounded by political associates and bureaucrats. But as soon as Mujib saw her enter, he immediately stood up to greet her. He was the only one to do so at first, but later everyone else followed. 'My mother seemed to feel the respect he had for her as a war widow, and it had left an indelible impact on her till the last days of her life,' her daughter Meghna told me.

Mujib also attempted being a peacemaker within families. He came to know the case of an officer who suspected his wife's fidelity during the war, when he was away fighting while she was at home. The officer was thinking of leaving her. Mujib advised him not to do so, saying that it would set a horrible precedent. If everyone did so, millions of families would get broken in the new nation, he is supposed to have said, and prevailed upon the officer against leaving his wife.

And yet, he found it increasingly hard to meet collective expectations. In 1972 when Indira Gandhi visited Dacca, a group of women whose husbands, sons or brothers were still missing, picketed in front of his house. Mujib was in a great rush but paused to speak to them, agitatedly saying: 'I hear you, I understand you would like your loved ones back. Believe me, I am trying. But you are not the only ones. I have thousands of other cases to deal with, and you will have to wait.' No doubt what he said was sincere, accurate and true, but it is not what the women wanted to hear.

Slowly, disenchantment began to grow. Anisur Rahman and other like-minded intellectuals and economists began talking to one another—who would challenge Mujib first—the left or the right? The left was upset because he wasn't delivering. The right wanted to capture the state.

Mujib felt powerless to tame inflation. He found administration difficult. He was probably concerned about the growing corruption. He could not have been unaware of the hooliganism that Rakkhi Bahini was being accused of. The resignation of Tajuddin Ahmed from his government and the departure of advisers like Anisur Rahman had troubled him deeply and personally. He was getting isolated, and he had been unable to convince people that they were better off being independent than being part of Pakistan. Alarmed by many of these concerns, in January 1975 Mujib amended the Constitution to become president for a five-year term. He gave himself full executive powers. In February, he abolished all opposition parties, declaring Bangladesh a one-party state, destroying the parliamentary system. He renamed his party the Bangladesh Krishak Sramik Awami League (BAKSAL). As in a communist or fascist state, he required all civilian government officials to join the party.

Fundamental rights, which were painstakingly enumerated in the Constitution, now stood suspended and Bangladesh began to resemble a tinpot dictatorship, albeit ruled by a civilian. There was a new slogan: Ek Neta, Ek Desh; Sheikh Mujib, Bangladesh. There was also personal hubris—if Gaddafi had his green book, Kim Il-Sung had his ideology of juche, and Mao had his little red book, Mujib created an ideology called Mujibism, which he expected Bangladeshis to adhere to. Mujibism was 'nationalism, socialism, secularism, and democracy', all broad subjects, sometimes clashing with one another, and no thought was given to reconcile them.

The BAKSAL format was flawed, and many liberals felt embarrassed. Sultana Kamal felt that had Mujib tried something similar in 1972, immediately in the glow of Independence, it might even have worked, provided Mujib gave the ownership of the revolution to the people. 'In 1975, it estranged and distanced everyone,' she said. But BAKSAL's aim seemed to be preserving his own power, at the time of growing unpopularity. Anisur Rahman said: 'By creating BAKSAL Mujib showed his true colours that he was not a genuine socialist.' That is a semantic criticism, since some of the steps Mujib took, such as nationalising industries and closing down all but a few newspapers, were in line with the Soviet approach to communism—and to that extent, closer to socialism than capitalism. The timing of the creation of BAKSAL was inept. Mahfuz Anam says: 'If the aim of BAKSAL was to bring about national unity then Mujib should have done something about developing national consensus in 1971 itself. This was the wrong time, the wrong format. Instead, he should have invited opposition parties in a coalition. But he wanted to create one party.' Mujib also banned all newspapers, except two each in English and Bengali—feeling demoralized, Mahfuz Anam left the newspaper he was working with because it had been nationalised. Anam calls the formation of BAKSAL Mujib's greatest blunder. 'It is still a mystery to me what led him to do that. He had it all. There was nothing, nobody in Parliament opposed to his policies, except for a few voices. He was the tallest man in the country. Why did he do it? It was in total contrast to his political heritage. It was a dramatic transformation from a multiparty system to a one party state.'

Many stalwarts of the freedom struggle began disengaging from Mujib after BAKSAL was formed. Tajuddin Ahmed had already left the cabinet in 1974. Kamal Hossain left the government and went to Oxford. A few weeks later, Mujib sent word to him saying he should return, but Hossain

said he had started working on his research. However, in March he got a
sealed letter insisting he return, and Hossain did the very next day; it was
an emotional meeting. Mujib took Hossain to the terrace of his house and
said: 'You can't go off to write books. I need you; I don't have the luxury
of working without you.' He also hinted that he was concerned about
restlessness in the army.

Hossain told him he did not have to be in such a situation. He could have
done things differently.

But that was not possible; that was water that had flown through the
Buriganga. Mujib said he now needed Hossain by his side. He asked him to
become the foreign minister and go to the Commonwealth meeting which
was to take place in Jamaica in June.

Hossain rejoined the government. As foreign minister, Hossain's travels
continued. He wished to tackle the issue of 'stranded Pakistanis' or Biharis
the Urdu-speaking Muslims who had migrated from Bihar in India to East
Pakistan; many of whom had sided with Pakistan during the Bangladesh
liberation war—but Pakistan was reluctant to discuss their fate.

In 1974, India, Pakistan and Bangladesh signed a tripartite agreement
under which three categories of Biharis were to be taken to Pakistan: those
born in Pakistan before or during 1971 and who were now 'stranded'; central
government employees but not including those working for railways; and
25,000 from the camps on humanitarian grounds. The rest would be offered
Bangladesh nationality.

One reason Pakistan did not want the Biharis was Bhutto's own political
preference. If hundreds of thousands of Biharis came to Pakistan, it would
create another ethnic enclave, complicating Pakistan's own ethnic patchwork
quilt further. After having taken 25,000 Biharis from Bangladesh, Pakistan said
it had no further responsibility, which meant they had become Bangladesh's
responsibility, and remained in camps.

Hossain confronted Pakistanis at a meeting of the Organisation of Islamic
Conference (OIC), but the Pakistanis said they did not have full instructions
to carry on the negotiations. They asked for time till 1 September. The Saudi
foreign minister, too, requested that Bangladesh give Pakistan the desired time.

Hossain agreed, since 1 September was only six weeks away.

◆

Mujib had been receiving warnings. One late night in April, Tajuddin went to meet Mujib, who welcomed him but asked why he had come to visit so late. Tajuddin told Mujib he wanted to speak to him face to face, and because Mujib was always surrounded by people, he had decided to come when everyone left. He advised Mujib to leave his house in Dhanmondi. It is not safe for you anymore; the army might turn against you, he warned the President. Mujib promised to look into it.

At the Commonwealth meeting in Jamaica, Hossain met Indira Gandhi and she told him that she was hearing worrying intelligence reports about plots against the government. 'I sat on the edge when I heard this,' he told me.

When Hossain relayed Indira Gandhi's concerns to Mujib, he confidently said: 'No Bengali will ever shoot me. If anyone objects to me, I will go to my village with my chador on my shoulder. I am not attached to this office.'

Then on 10 August, Mujib called Hossain aside and told him that he felt he could not keep Khondaker Mostaq Ahmad, a cabinet minister, in the ministry for much longer.

◆

Kader Siddiqui's mother had been unwell. On 14 August he went to see her at the hospital. By the time he left, he saw tanks on the road. He asked the director of Rakkhi Bahini why there were tanks on the road. He was told that Mujib was going to the Dacca University the next day and the army was going to provide protection. There had been a grenade explosion on campus to protest his arrival, and the Bahini did not want to take any chances.

But Siddiqui was not so sure. He went to Dhanmondi to meet Mujib. It was late at night, but Mujib was often accessible, particularly to people like Siddiqui whom he had known. He came out, wearing a baniyan and lungi, for it was late and he was about to go to sleep. He had to speak the next morning at 8:40 a.m. at the university. Siddiqui told him that he had seen five tanks on the road. Mujib shook his head and said he was wrong, because there were only three tanks, not five. But Siddiqui insisted he had seen five tanks. 'You must have seen the same tank twice; it is night,' Mujib laughed. Siddiqui said: 'I am good with numbers; even if I can't read and write very well, I can count.' But Mujib thought nothing of it and said, 'If you still see five tanks in the morning, tell me.'

◆

At 1 a.m. on 15 August, Farooq Rahman, Khandaker Abdur Rashid and

Shariful Haque Dalim called other junior officers, including Nur Chowdhury, Aziz Pasha, Rashed Chowdhury, Sultan Shahriar Rashid Khan and Bazlul Huda. Farooq commanded the Bengal Lancers, the tank regiment, and Abdur Rashid led the 2nd field artillery. Farooq and Rashid were close—their wives were sisters. In the confessional statement he made later, Farooq said that it was at that time he disclosed the full plan to them, saying there was no way to change the government of Bangladesh except using force, otherwise the country would become subservient to India. The army might get disbanded and we would become India's slaves, he said. Mujib's house had to be attacked, and he was not to escape. He would then have to be brought to the cantonment. In case they met with any resistance, Mujib had to be killed. The artillery would control the Rakkhi Bahini headquarters and the Mirpur Bridge. Bazlul Huda and Nur Chowdhury were to join A.K.M. Mohiuddin for the attack on Mujib's home. Farooq himself would lead the tank force with Shariful Hossain in the last tank.

In 1975, Dhanmondi was not yet the fashionable suburb it has become now. There were flooded foundation trenches and boundary walls of bungalows, on the other side of which lay nothing but dust, waste and grass, and the few large houses 'rose like catafalques above streets which existed only by common consent since they had no surfaces to mark them out from the fields that surrounded them', as Amitav Ghosh describes the place in his novel, *The Shadow Lines*.

Before dawn on 15 August, 700 soldiers left their barracks and headed for the three homes where Mujib and his family lived. As we have seen, they first attacked Mujib's brother-in-law Abdur Rab Seraniabat's house at 27 Minto Road while another group went to Mujib's home, Number 677 on Road 32.

Mujib's personal assistant and receptionist A.F.M. Mohitul Islam, who was barely twenty-two, had finished his night duty at around 1 a.m. and had gone to bed late. At 5 a.m. his phone rang. He picked it up, still feeling sleepy. 'Get the police control room,' Mujib said at the other end of the line. He had heard of the attack on Seraniabat's house.

It was time for the changing of the guards at Mujib's house, and Havildar Mohammed Quddus Sikder was among seven guards hoisting the national flag as the bugle sounded. They were stunned when they heard gunshots from the lakeside. The guards crouched and took positions behind the boundary wall, preparing for an attack. They were shocked when army men in black and khaki uniform stormed through the gate and commanded: 'Put your hands up.'

Meanwhile Mohitul dialled the police control room immediately, but he could not get through. He called the telephone exchange, but the person at the other end of the line would not speak.

Mujib asked again why he hadn't contacted the police yet. Mohitul said he hadn't been able to call anyone.

Mujib had come down and snatched the telephone receiver and said: 'This is President Sheikh Mujib speaking.'

Bullets slammed the room and shattered the windowpanes.

Mujib and Mohitul bent low. Abdul, the house-help, brought Mujib's kurta and pyjamas which he quickly put on and came out.

He shouted at the guards: 'There has been firing all around. What are you doing?' He went up where his family was still in bed.

As he entered his bedroom, his wife Fazilatunnesa, looking very afraid, told him: 'Criminals have attacked Seraniabat's residence.' Mujib already knew.

Rama, another house-help, heard this and rose from his sleep. He ran down and saw the chaos outside. He rushed to Mujib's son Kamal's room and knocked the door hard, telling him and his wife Sultana that the house was under attack.

Kamal got dressed quickly and ran down. Rama took Sultana to the first floor. He also woke up Mujib's second son Jamal, who took his wife Rosy and went to his mother's room.

Downstairs, Mohitul saw Kamal coming down, shouting: 'Army and police members, come with me.' Just at that moment, the killers entered the house. They faced Kamal. Mohitul and a police officer, Nurul Islam, stood behind Kamal, looking in horror. Mohitul recognized Maj. Bazlul Huda, who shot Kamal's leg. Kamal jumped before falling, saying, 'I'm Sheikh Kamal, Sheikh Mujib's son.' Mohitul added: 'Don't shoot him.'

But there was more gunfire, tearing through Kamal's body. Upstairs, Rama could hear someone groaning. It was Kamal, already shot multiple times, breathing his last.

The officers walked through the house, looking for Mujib. Mohitul heard the loud voice of Mujib saying something. He heard gunshots. He didn't know what was going on.

But Havildar Quddus saw. He was ordered to follow the killers as they went in, and he had obeyed.

Huda and Nur were at the landing of the staircase and Major Mohiuddin and his soldiers could be seen at the top. They were with Mujib. They were coming down. Nur said something in English which Quddus did not understand.

'What do you want?' Mujib asked loudly.

They did not answer. Huda and Nur began shooting, their guns aimed at Mujib.

Like a toppled statue, Mujib's body tumbled down, spraying blood everywhere, smearing the wall and staircase. Shivering in a corner, Rama saw Mujib die. The soldiers told Rama to get lost. He crawled into the bathroom of Fazilatunnesa's room. There he saw Sultana, Jamal, Rosy, Russell, and Naser huddled in a corner. Rama informed them that Mujib had just been killed. He could hear footsteps outside the door—the soldiers had returned. They fired at the door, knocking it down. Fazilatunnesa calmly went to the door and opened it, saying; 'If we have to die, let us die together.'

The soldiers took Naser, Russell, Fazilatunnesa and Rama towards the stairs. When Fazilatunnesa saw Mujib's dead body lying in a pool of blood, she broke down and said: 'I won't go further. Kill me here.'

The soldiers took her back to her room. Major Aziz Pasha and Risaldar Muslemuddin started firing—Fazilatunnesa, Jamal, Rosy, and Sultana. All collapsed and died.

Other soldiers had taken Naser, Russell, and Rama to the ground floor. Naser pleaded: 'I am not a politician; I do business.' An officer told him: 'We won't hurt you. Take your seat in that room.' Then he took Naser into the bathroom and opened fire. Mohitul heard Naser beg for water. An army man winked at another and said: 'Go and give him some water.'

The other soldier went inside the bathroom and shot Naser again.

Russell, who was not yet ten, was shocked and devastated. He clung to Rama and Mohitul.

'Bhaiya, Will they kill me too?' he asked Mohitul.

'No, bhaiya, they won't kill you,' Mohitul said.

Just then a soldier took Russell away. Russell pleaded; he said he wanted to go to his mother.

'Take him to his mother,' Major Pasha told a soldier.

The soldier smiled and took Russell to the first floor. Russell was howling. There was another burst of gunshots.

Huda came out of the house and walked around. Their mission had been accomplished. Just then, a jeep pulled over in front of the house and Major[185] Farooq Rahman stepped out.

'All are finished,' Huda calmly told him.

◆

An air force helicopter took Mujib's body to his village Tungipara, where the local imam was told to bury him quickly. But the imam refused; he said a proper Muslim burial was not possible unless the body had been washed. The officer told him to bathe the body in ten minutes and bury it in another ten.

Mujib's last bath was with a cheap locally-made detergent bar. A poor villager donated a sari to cover his body. While washing the body the imam noticed one bullet that had entered from the left side of his back. On the right side he counted nine more bullets. The main veins were slit, and his index finger, which he raised in his speeches was missing.

There was no memorial, no stone placed at the time, at the grave. Mujib may have liked that. Abdul Gaffar Chowdhury, a journalist who wrote poems during the language movement, once wrote an essay called 'Lenin and Mujib'. It seems Gaffar had gone with Mujib to Moscow and they were taken to see Lenin's tomb. There they saw an embalmed Lenin. Mujib told Gaffar that when he died he did not want to be remembered in this manner. 'It would be as if I have died permanently from the minds of the people,' he told Gaffar. 'I want to die such that I am constantly remembered in the imagination of the people,' he said.[186]

◆

Mohitul was in a hospital to get his injuries treated. Thereafter he escaped to his village, Jhikargacha in Jessore, but the army tracked him down and took him to the cantonment. There, they kept asking him who the assassins were. They said he had to give the names because they wanted to arrest them. But Mohitul had been warned by someone during the detention to pretend that he did not know anything, otherwise they would kill him instantly, so he did just that. They tortured him, but he kept saying he was a mere receptionist and could not recognize any of the killers.

M.R. Siddiqi, the prominent Awami League politician from Chittagong to whom Mujib had sent the crucial message containing the Independence declaration in 1971, was living in Dhanmondi with his wife Latifa and their children at the time. They lived on Road 28, close enough to Mujib's house on Road 32. 'Early morning we heard blasts,' Latifa told me. 'We got very scared because the sounds were really loud. We thought some kind of war had begun again. I felt very jittery.' Her son told her to get under the bed.

Siddiqi tended to wake up early and turn on the radio to listen to the news. Suddenly they heard the voice of Brigadier Dalim making the announcement that he had the city of Dacca under his control. He remembered Dalim; he was known in Dacca's elite circles. He was known to have little regard for Awami League politicians, who he saw as pleasure seekers who had suffered far less than soldiers during the war.

Tajuddin Ahmed's daughter Simeen Hossain Rimi also heard loud sounds that morning at 5:30 a.m. Tajuddin tried calling Mujib, but nobody picked up the phone. He then turned on the radio and heard Dalim announce that Mujib had been killed. His wife sensed trouble for Tajuddin too, and told him to go to the neighbour's house. But he refused, saying if he did, and if Mujib survived, he would think Tajuddin was involved in the plot. In that atmosphere Mujib may no longer have understood who was his friend and who an enemy.

Shortly, the army arrived at Tajuddin's house and he was placed under house arrest. They cut his phone line. Armed guards surrounded his house. Tajuddin asked the officers if his daughters could go to school. He told Rimi to keep her eyes open and tell him whatever she saw. When she left for school a car followed her. She saw a tank at the radio station, another at the main hospital, more tanks at busy junctions, and when she entered her classroom, everyone was shocked to see her. They thought even Tajuddin's family had been murdered.

A week later a police officer came to their house and told Tajuddin they were taking him out. He asked if he should take his clothes. Yes, they said, and he understood he was being taken to jail.

'How long will you be gone?' his wife, Zohra, asked him.

'Take it as forever,' he told her.

Rimi remembered: 'Then we saw a police jeep and we saw a foreigner standing across the road. He was a white man. He was in front of the jeep, he crossed the road running, and he talked with my father for a few seconds.' Thirty years later her sister who was in Washington DC found out that the man was Lawrence Lifschultz, correspondent of *Far Eastern Economic Review,* the Hong Kong-based magazine. Lifschultz had asked him: 'Are you being taken to join the cabinet?' Tajuddin had replied: 'No, I don't think so.'

◆

When Dalim said on the radio that Mujib had died, initially some thought it was some kind of a joke. But they listened to the announcement carefully. It didn't seem as though Dalim was being funny. Soon phones started ringing and people were asking each other the same question—was it true? Everyone stayed indoors. There were no soldiers on the street, but no pedestrians either, which was unusual for Dacca.

A day later, Zulfikar Ali Bhutto announced that Pakistan was going to immediately offer Bangladesh a gift of 50,000 tonnes of rice.

◆

The men who killed most of Mujib's family were junior officers in the Bangladesh army. Several of them had personal scores to settle with Mujib—some had been sidelined and others had been dismissed from positions in the army. The disaffected officers and the troops loyal to them personified the grievances many army professionals felt over the slights the army faced at the hands of Mujib's supporters, in particular the wayward fighters of the Rakkhi Bahini. Later, they also claimed they were concerned about growing corruption, and as Farooq would tell me a decade after the assassination, they were concerned about Mujib aggrandising all power to himself and effectively destroying parliamentary democracy.

Rashid and Farooq were unabashed about what they did. Both later spoke to Anthony Mascarenhas in revealing interviews on ITV. In 1986, the first time I went to Bangladesh, Farooq spoke to me extensively about his role in the killings as well as his contempt for everything Mujib stood for.

In his television interview with Mascarenhas, Farooq said he had been thinking of how Mujib must go since 1974. He hadn't figured out what might follow, but he was determined to prepare to remove Mujib. Rashid told him he was too junior to tell Mujib what he should do. When Mascarenhas asked him why they had not simply arrested him, Rashid said: 'He [Mujib] is not an administrator, the only thing that he has got [is] a very good quality to agitate the general mass. So [had] he remained alive it would have been very difficult for us to conclude (*sic*) the situation—he is more experienced on the political side. Just to stay in power he would have done any sort of mischievous act at the cost of even the country.'

'So you had to kill him,' Mascarenhas asked.

'Yes, I had to,' said Rashid.

Farooq added that the ideal person to replace Mujib was Ziaur Rahman, who was at that time, deputy chief of staff and a major general. He had the cleanest image and he was known because he had made the radio announcement from Chittagong declaring Bangladesh's independence. Farooq had met Zia on 20 March 1975. He said they strolled in the lawns and Farooq told Zia that the country was going to the dogs. 'We have to change it. We junior officers have already worked it out. We want your support and leadership.' But Farooq said that Zia told him: 'I am a senior officer. I cannot be involved in such things. If you junior officers want to do it, go ahead.'

At this, Mascarenhas asked: 'Did you specifically tell General Zia that your intention was to overthrow Mujib?'

Farooq replied: 'Remember that I was meeting the Deputy Chief of Army Staff, a Major General, and if I bluntly put it that I wanted to overthrow the President of the country straightway like that, there was a very good chance that he would arrest me with his own guards there and then and put me into jail. I had to go about it in a roundabout way. Actually, we came around it by saying that (there is) a lot of corruption, everything is going wrong, the country requires a change ... Yes, yes let us go outside and talk in the lawns.'

Mascarenhas pushed him further, asking him what Zia said.

Farooq continued: 'Then we go up to the lawn and I told him that we are professional soldiers, we serve the country, we do not serve any individual. The army, the civil (service), the government, everybody is going down the drain. We have to change it, we the junior officers, have already worked it out. We want your support and your leadership; and he said, I am sorry, would not like to get involved in anything like that. If you want to do something, the junior officers should do it themselves.' Farooq said Zia then told his aide-de-camp that Farooq was not to be given any appointment in future if he asked.

Zia himself was assassinated a few years later, and Farooq was known to embellish stories, so it is impossible to verify if Zia actually gave Farooq his blessings.

Farooq took Zia's ambivalent remarks as a sign that the junior officers had Zia's tacit approval. They needed someone to be the titular head, and they found him in Khondaker Mostaq Ahmad, who was the commerce minister. They spoke to him in the first week of August and had several meetings with him between 12-14 August.

In the same TV interview, Rashid told Mascarenhas: 'He (Mostaq) said, well, if somebody has that courage [to kill Mujib] and guts to do it, well, that's a good thing probably for future leaders. We wanted to know that he (Mostaq) had no programme of immediately going outside the country anywhere.'

Farooq and Rashid began training their troops from March. They decided to train at night because they wanted their training to appear as part of a routine, so that when the actual troop movements occurred nobody would suspect anything. When the night-time training occurred on 14 August, nobody thought it was out of ordinary. They had eighteen 105mm guns and twenty-eight tanks, and 700 men under their command. The only possible danger was from about 3,000 members of the Rakkhi Bahini who were armed with light weapons and personally loyal to Mujib.

Farooq was also bluffing. They had twenty-eight tanks, but the tanks did not have any shells. As the tanks rode the streets, they did confront a Rakkhi Bahini unit. But Farooq decided to continue to ride the tank forward and brought the tank within six inches of the troops. The Bahini did nothing and let them go.

One of the first steps the killers took was to immediately arrest Awami politicians close to Mujib—Syed Nazrul Islam, who was vice president during the wartime cabinet of the Mujibnagar government, Quamaruzzaman, minister of interior, relief and rehabilitation, and Capt. Mansur Ali, who had been finance minister, who had been part of Mujib's cabinet, and had refused to join the new one, besides Tajuddin, who had left the government because of differences with Mujib.

Khondakar Mostaq Ahmad was declared president. At the end of his first broadcast to the nation, he said: 'Bangladesh Zindabad.' The choice of an Urdu declaration, and not the Bengali 'Joy Bangla' was a strong indicator of the way the government would now act. Pakistan immediately offered food aid; a few Islamic states soon recognized Bangladesh.

One of Mostaq's first acts was to rename BAKSAL as Awami League and restore old political parties. He was known to be pro-West and sceptical of Bangladesh's close ties with India. But he wasn't alone at Bangabhaban. The majors who had plotted and carried out Mujib's execution were also ensconsed there, living out any junta's fantasy—power without responsibility.

Mostaq promised to restore parliamentary democracy within 18 months, and pledged to restore public confidence in the government. In a move popular with many Bangladeshis, he announced the dissolution of the Rakkhi Bahini, transferring its weapons and assets to the army. While he promised to undo Mujib's authoritarian steps, Mostaq nonetheless became the chief martial law administrator, as chaos continued in the country. In September, Khondaker gave the killers immunity through an ordinance, because, it said, it was 'expedient to restrict the taking of any legal or other proceedings in respect of certain acts or things done in connection with, or in preparation or execution of any plan for, or steps necessitating, the historical change and the proclamation of martial law on the morning of 15 August 1975'.

◆

In August 2005 *The Daily Star* and *Prothom Alo* commemorated the thirtieth anniversary of the coup d'état that killed Mujib and much of his family by publishing a series of articles investigating the massacres. Lifschultz wrote the series where he revealed that one of his principal sources, which alleged CIA links with the political leadership of the coup, was in fact the US Ambassador to Bangladesh, Eugene Boster.

While Boster sought anonymity during his lifetime, Lifschultz disclosed after Boster's death that the ambassador had in 1977 informed him and his colleague, the American writer, Kai Bird, that the US Embassy had contacts with the Khondaker group six months before the coup, and that the ambassador had himself ordered that all links with Khondaker and his entourage be severed. Boster claimed he learned later that behind his back the contacts continued with Khondaker's associates until the actual day of the coup.

In the book, *Bangladesh: The Unfinished Revolution,*[187] Lifschultz and Bird document Khondaker's prior links to a failed Kissinger initiative during the 1971 war. Khondaker's colleagues in Bangladesh's government-in-exile had discovered his covert contacts with Kissinger, and it ended with him being placed under house arrest in Calcutta. Four years later, Khondaker—who was in Mujib's cabinet—became president after the military coup, and once in office, he granted immunity to the assassins.

It would take thirty-four years before the cases against Mujib's killers could be heard properly and those found guilty, sentenced. It took so long because between 1975 and 2009, the Awami League was in power only once, from 1996 to 2001, and even then, it fell short of majority, winning

146 of 300 seats, and it was dependent on allies. Other political parties and governments had little interest in pursuing those cases.

Not only was investigating the conspiracy no longer a priority for the governments that followed, but successive governments gave several of the men accused of the assassinations diplomatic postings.[188] Six of the men remain abroad. Their whereabouts are not public, but until the collapse of the Gaddafi regime in Libya, at various times several of them spent time in, or lived in Tripoli. They are also often believed to have spent time in Pakistan. Some have reportedly managed to get Pakistani or Kenyan passports, making it easier for them to travel, and offering them consular protection, should they ever get detained in a third country. Reports in the Bangladeshi media suggest that some may be in Canada or the United States, although there is no confirmation.

Khandaker Abdul Rashid's daughter, Mehnaz said Ziaur Rahman rehabilitated many of Mujib's killers. She told me her family's hotel expenses in Bangkok were picked up by the Bangladesh government in Zia's time. She also claimed that her duplex family home in Gulshan, a posh area in Dhaka, was a gift from Zia.

It was not easy to meet Mehnaz Rashid. Rashid's daughter is wary of meeting strangers, particularly when the conversation is going to be about her father's role in Mujib's killing. A mutual contact asked me if I would like to meet her and I said yes. The contact spoke to Mehnaz who agreed to meet me, but only at a restaurant of her choice. She would pick me up from my hotel and drop me off somewhere else, from where I'd have to make my own subsequent arrangements. I was not to call her; she would not call me. Messages between her and me were to be exchanged through the contact, via SMS. She also took other precautionary measures.

Mehnaz's caution seemed a bit exaggerated to me, until I heard her story. Mehnaz's father was a graduate of the Pakistan Military Academy. In 1972 he was sent to India, for military training at Deolali. He returned to Bangladesh in 1975. He was shocked by the state of the country. The public distribution system's flour had sawdust in it and sugar contained pieces of glass, she said.

Rashid and his brother-in-law Farooq were enraged by what they saw. They were very close to each other; 'attached like brothers', Mehnaz said. They could never have plotted Mujib's assassination, she insisted. 'They were so close. They sometimes bought shirts of the same colour. They never competed with one another. They were like Ram-Kishan ki jodi', she said, using a Hindu metaphor. Later in our conversation she revealed she was deeply religious.

Mehnaz insists her father never intended to kill Mujib. Their plan was to arrest him and bring him to the Race Course where he would have been tried. But she alleged that officers close to Taher had infiltrated their group and they had other ideas. Taher wanted to wipe out the Awami League and its leadership. She claims that Mujib's sons unwisely started shooting at the soldiers when they entered Mujib's house, and the soldiers affiliated to Taher shot everyone dead.

Mehnaz had been arrested in 2009 and been in jail for seven months over allegations of involvement in a bomb blast against Awami League politician Fazle Noor Taposh, a nephew of Hasina Wajed, an Awami League leader. She was then released on bail, and the case remains pending.

◆

'You have to ask the question: why is Mujib so popular, if he was so bad,' Sultana Kamal told me at her home in Dhaka. 'I agree Awami League did not do well in the last two years of Mujib's government. But from 1975 to 1990 all that people heard was how bad the Awami League was; what a failure its rule was. All kinds of failures were exaggerated and amplified and laid at Awami League's door. People who were part of the Liberation War were taken out of the scene. My mother's poems were no longer in textbooks. A new set of people who were pro-Zia took charge of cultural institutions. The country was constantly told how Zia salvaged the country from disaster and restored democracy. How the military had saved the country, and how the politicians were useless. Nobody could sing songs from the Liberation War movement because many songs mentioned Mujib's name as a leader. The Liberation War began to disappear from radio and television. So you had a generation that was born and brought up believing that Awami League is a troublemaker. There was massive propaganda that turned a large part of the country into anti-Mujib. And yet, take the last elections, and how well the party did. Clearly, people remembered what it meant to fight for a Bengali nation; what Sheikh Mujib meant for that struggle.'

Much has been made about the lack of public grieving over Mujib's death. To be sure, Mujib's personal popularity had fallen significantly by that time—the famine-like conditions had severely undermined public confidence in Mujib and jobs were scarce. Inflation was rampant and the mood was sullen among the people who were aghast that Mujib had turned the democratic nation they had all fought so hard to build into a one-party state so effortlessly. Nevertheless, many revered and loved Mujib and he was admired deeply for his leadership. Kamal Hossain puts it in perspective: 'Some of Mujib's opponents seize on the lack of an emotional response as though it justifies the assassination. But the assassinations were unjustified. You have to remember that the killings occurred in a way that can only be described as extreme terror—the killing of everyone, including the wives of the two sons, and of the ten-year-old boy. The coup leaders who wanted to seize power and knew they were in a minority could get acceptance only by striking terror. They succeeded in shocking everyone into a state of paralysis. When you learnt what they had done, you also knew that they would stop at nothing. They were worried about how people would react, and they correctly guessed that the more horrific their act, the more afraid the people would be. Striking terror immobilizes the population. Besides, since some cabinet ministers continued to serve under the new leader, Khondaker Mostaq Ahmed, the Awami League members were confused. Should they mourn Mujib, or accept the new leaders? Khondaker in fact referred to the assassins as shurjo shontan or 'sons of the sun'.

But even in such a climate of fear, people privately grieved. Mahfuz Anam, who was deeply disappointed when Mujib created BAKSAL, said that those feelings were overtaken by the sense of desolation and devastation he felt when Mujib was murdered. 'I cried; many cried when Mujib died. To say that nobody grieved is rubbish,' he said. But for many, their grief had to remain private.

◆

Kamal Hossain was abroad the day Mujib was assassinated. He met a disconsolate Hasina in Bonn. She told Kamal how Khondaker used to look after them. 'How could he be applauding the killers?' she asked. And then she turned to Hossain and asked: 'You won't abandon me?'

Kamal Hossain told me: 'I said I wouldn't. I told her I would make sure of her return to Bangladesh with honour. I handed back my diplomatic passport and took an ordinary passport so that I could go to Oxford, where I could continue to do my work.'[189]

In May 2014 she made a tearful speech which was heard in stunned silence, in which she recalled her years in exile, which had ended on

17 May 1981. 'It was a Sunday and it was raining heavily', she remembered in her speech. Thousands had come out on the streets to greet her. 'I am amidst you after losing everything', she told them. She had vivid memories of leaving Dhaka before the killings. Her little brother Russell had come to see her off at the airport. When she arrived in Delhi in her exile, she had heard rumours that her mother and brother Russell were still alive, but Indira Gandhi confirmed to her that they had all died. They were all gone now, lying in a graveyard.

In her speech[190] this May, she recalled a dream in which her father told her that the Awami League would stay united and she need not worry.

◆

'It was to the shame of the Awami League that Mujib was murdered but the same cabinet essentially got revived,' Mahfuz Anam said. 'It was disappointing and disgusting.' It is possible that many cabinet ministers continued in the government because martial law was in effect and some may even have been afraid. They would have noted that the leader most loyal to Mujib—Tajuddin—and three others who declined to join the cabinet—Quamaruzzaman, Mansur Ali, and Nazrul Islam—were promptly arrested.

The legality of Khondaker's government has never been properly examined in Bangladesh. It was effectively put together by the assassins, who were relatively junior officers. And they were ordering instructions not from the cantonment but from the presidential palace.

Pakistan's prompt contacts with Bangladesh's new government made many suspect that Pakistan had known about the plot all along, and some in Bangladesh speculate if it even had a role in planning the assassination. There is a news report filed by the French news agency Agence France-Presse on the morning of 15 August which says that Bhutto had called a meeting at 10 a.m. in which he appealed to Muslim states to recognize the Islamic Republic of Bangladesh. (Pakistan had recognized Bangladesh in 1974 and more formal diplomatic ties were established in 1976.) How could the head of state of a country that was, until recently, bitterly opposed to Bangladeshi nationhood come to the conclusion, within five hours of the assassination, that the coup leaders were legitimate?

The Khondaker regime was inclined to cooperate with Pakistan. The government said all unresolved issues between the two countries were no longer important, including sharing of assets and repatriation of Pakistanis who were to face trial in Bangladesh for war crimes. Soon after that, some of the pro-Pakistani people who had fled Bangladesh at its Independence, and against some of whom there were possible charges, began to return to Bangladesh. They clearly felt secure that they would be untouched under the new dispensation.

There was grumbling within the army command. Senior commanders began to wonder why a few majors were running the country. Ziaur Rahman was the chief of staff, but it was unclear who really commanded the loyalty of the armed forces. The government ran the country by issuing decrees, not by passing legislation, nor by announcing policies or by following precedent—there were few in a country that was still only 45 months old. Parliament had stopped meeting. Khondaker himself was a president by decree.

There was simmering discontent in the army—should they really accept this chaotic state of affairs? Khaled Mosharraf was one of the sector commanders during the Liberation War. He asked Zia: if the country is to be run by martial law, why wasn't he running the country? Zia remained non-committal.

On the night of 2nd November Khaled Mosharraf, who was the Chief of General Staff, took steps to arrest the Chief of Army Staff Maj. Gen. Ziaur Rahman, because senior officers felt he had not taken any steps to bring Mujib's killers to justice, nor restored the chain of command destroyed by the junior officers who had conspired to kill Mujib. The increasingly bizarre instructions from the presidential palace had effectively sanctioned the executions of the four imprisoned Awami League leaders, and these can be understood in light of what happened that day. Three officers considered pro-Awami League launched a coup to remove Khondaker and the majors in the presidential palace. Their aim may have been to replace Khondaker and the rebel officers with the four imprisoned leaders, and reinstate civilian government. But the execution of the coup was clumsy, with precious time lost.

Once the coup started, Farooq and Dalim negotiated with Mosharraf to allow them to leave the country. Some accounts suggest that American and Pakistani officials had applied diplomatic pressure to let them go. The killers managed to leave on a special Bangladesh Biman flight late at night. Najmul Huda heard about the escape plan from squadron leader Liaquat, who was a MiG-21 fighter pilot. Huda asked Liaquat if their flight could be delayed, and if he could intercept it in the air the next morning and escort it to Sayedpur airport—or gun it down if the pilot refused to turn. But the aircraft left at night. It was widely expected that the four Awami League leaders in jail might assume power once the Mostaq regime collapsed. But Mosharraf and his officers learned the following morning that they had already been killed. Huda himself was in Rangpur and learned about the killings only when he reached Dacca. He stayed on in Dacca while Huda's wife Niloufer sent him uniforms and extra clothes from Rangpur.

The officers who sided with Khaled Mosharraf included Col. Shafat Jamil, Capt. Kabir, who was Khaled Mosharraf's ADC, Col. Najmul Huda, Lt. Col. A.T.M. Haider, and Gen. Golam Dastagir. Like their adversaries, they too were freedom fighters—Khaled Mosharraf had been wounded severely during the war, and had received the Bir Uttom, one of Bangladesh's highest military honours. These officers were regarded as secular and their sympathies inevitably lay with the Awami League. By implication, that meant they were considered to be pro-India. After removing Khondaker and placing Gen. Zia under house arrest, Khaled Mosharraf became the chief of staff and tanks were sent to the presidential palace.

Then, as if to publicly commemorate Mujib, Khaled Mosharraf's mother and brother led a procession from Kalabagan to Dhanmondi, to Mujib's former residence. That alarmed other officers, who were more aligned to Zia's line of thoughts and suspected that this would increase Indian influence in Bangladeshi affairs.

From the time Mosharraf took over power on 2 November, in spite of repeated warnings from officers who supported him, he made a few crucial strategic misjudgments. Instead of acting firmly and quickly, he entered into protracted negotiations with the junior officers who were in the presidential palace, which proved to be a fatal mistake. He was either unsure of his position and strength, or unable to decide how far he should go. Should he be as ruthless as Mujib's killers and get them killed? Or should he let them fly away? Mosharraf did not want to spill blood in removing Gen. Zia and others. The negotiations for the transfer of power went on. Khondaker was calm—he refused to comply with Mosharraf's demand that he should remove the three services chiefs and he could continue as president. By 5 November, Khondaker agreed to relinquish office and he and Mujib's assassins were going to be allowed to fly to Bangkok.

If Mosharraf's intent was to get the imprisoned Awami leaders released so that they could assume civilian charge of the country, that opportunity had been lost forever.

Things took a nasty turn on 3 November. At about 3 a.m. that night Mohammed Nuruzzaman, who was inspector general of the prison where the four Awami leaders were detained, received a call from Maj. Rashid from the presidential palace, asking if there was any trouble inside the jail. Nuruzzaman reported that everything was fine. Rashid told him that a group of men in uniform might come to the Dhaka jail. They would ask for Tajuddin, Nazrul, Quamaruzzaman, and Manzur Ali, and take them away. Rashid told him to alert the security guards. Another officer called him a few minutes later, asking him to go to the jail himself to check on the security arrangements. Nuruzzaman called the director of the prison and asked him to come immediately to the jail. They arrived around the same time.

Rashid called again, this time at the jail, and told Nuruzzaman that Capt. Mosleuddin would arrive at the jail gate. He should be taken to the cell where the four political prisoners were kept. Nuruzzaman was perplexed by this request and said he wanted to speak to the president. But before he could say anything, Khondaker came on the line and asked him if he clearly understood the instructions. Yes sir, said Nuruzzaman. 'Then carry out the instruction,' he was told.

Within moments, four soldiers led by Capt Mosleuddin arrived in black robes. He ordered the jail officials to take him and his soldiers to the cells of the four prisoners. Nuruzzaman told Mosleuddin that he had instructions from the president that Mosleuddin was to tell him something. Mosleuddin said he was going to shoot them. In his testimony at the trial, Nuruzzaman said: 'We became simply bewildered at his words.' Some reports have suggested that the soldiers were drunk. Nuruzzaman tried getting in touch with the president but could not reach him. Just then another call came through. It was Rashid, who asked if the captain had arrived. Yes, Nuruzzaman said, but he could not understand what was going on. Rashid passed the phone to the president again. Nuruzzaman told Khondaker that the captain had said he was going to kill the four prisoners. Khondaker said, 'Let it be done.'

The captain pointed his gun at them and ordered the senior officials to take his men to the cell. The four prisoners were woken up and separated from other prisoners.

They were not in the same cell. Tajuddin and Nazrul were in one room with six prisoners. Qamaruzzaman was in another cell with seven others. And Mansur Ali was in another cell with seven others. They were taken to another room. The jailor Aminur Rahman was asked to identify them, and he did. Tajuddin realized what was going on. He asked for permission for the prisoners to pray and wash themselves. They were permitted that decency.

The cell was 7 feet wide and it had grilles. The captain and his men entered the room and started firing. The jailor and inspector-general saw this and lay down to avoid being shot. Outside, the sound of the morning azaan pierced the sky. The four Awami leaders collapsed instantly; one of them cried out for water. Tajuddin's daughter Rimi thinks that it was Mansur Ali who didn't die immediately. No procedure was followed—no charges were read out, there was no trial, nor was there any authority that had sanctioned the executions, and there was no scope of an appeal. It was extra-judicial execution, carried out within the prison, witnessed by senior prison officials.

After some time, another team of soldiers came to confirm whether the victims were dead. To make sure, they went straight to the cell and bayoneted the dead bodies.

The assassins had planned their operation well. A few weeks earlier, Dalim had gone to meet senior jail officials, but had not been able to meet them. So he sent them a message to meet him at the presidential palace. When the officials went there, they were asked about security within the prison. The officials said the prison was well-secured. Dalim then asked them what they would do if the army came in and attacked the prison. The officials wondered why they were being asked such questions, but truthfully said they only had rifles and pistols, and could not defend themselves against a formal attack from a superior force. Dalim thanked them and let them go. Simeen Hossain Rimi, who gathered the information while researching how her father died, told me: 'Clearly they were planning the operation for some time, and nobody had an idea of what was being planned.'

The slain politicians' bodies remained in the jail till the evening. At 11:00 p.m. on 4 November, relatives were finally allowed into the jail and the bodies were handed over. The following morning, Abdul Awal, who was the director of the prison, filed a case with the local police station. The Criminal Investigation Department was asked to inquire, but the inquiry was later suspended.[191]

◆

The radical officer Col. Taher was concerned by Khaled Mosharraf's coup. He led Jatiyo Samajtantrik Dol (JSD) a left-wing political party which used the confused state to launch a counter-coup. Taher's aim was to activate all left-leaning troops to take up arms and lead an uprising against the military leaders whom he suspected of being Indian agents, and release Ziaur Rahman. The JSD printed and flooded the cantonment with leaflets exhorting JSD-minded troops to take up arms. While Khaled, Huda, Haider and others were still negotiating the transfer of power at Bangabhaban, Taher's countercoup was already underway. Troops went on streets killing officers or demanding that they take down their ranks. They released Zia and brought him to Two Field Artillery and promised that he would become army chief again. Taher's longer term plan, according to his critics, was to get Zia to restructure the army and then remove him.

Taher spread the word among the troops that the new coup leaders were Indian stooges. Khaled Mosharraf and officers loyal to him had not paid sufficient attention to the left-leaning faction within the army or the JSD. Taher's assumption, naïve in hindsight, was that bringing Gen. Zia to power would facilitate the arrival in Bangladesh of the radical nationalism he believed in. Mosharraf's mistake lay in underestimating Taher's popularity and the JSD's strength. Taher was an astute officer who began rousing his followers, warning them that Mosharraf was doing India's bidding. A rumour emerged that from jail Tajuddin had sent a letter to the Indian envoy, Samar Sen, and India's RAW was assisting the Awami League to return to power. Lifschultz investigated the matter, wrote that the former BBC reporter Atiqal Alam had gone around embassies in Dacca on November 4 and 5, claiming that he had the so-called Tajuddin letter. But when interviewed a few months later, he said he had returned the letter to his source. Other journalists said no such letter existed.[192] (In his memoir, the Indian intelligence officer Raman suggests the reverse—that RAW's failure to predict the crisis in Bangladesh has long been considered one of RAW's biggest blunders). If the conspiracy is to be believed, there was a plot to get the four leaders released from the jail, and they would then return triumphantly and re-establish Awami rule. Mosharraf's mutiny was part of that plan.

Soldiers loyal to Taher, who owed allegiance to Biplobi Sainik Sanstha (Revolutionary Soldiers' Institution) started shouting slogans—Sipahi sipahi bhai bhai, officer-er rokto chai (All soldiers are brothers; they want the blood of some officers). As the mutiny began in the cantonment, Mosharraf and Huda realized they no longer had the control they wanted, and so they left the presidential palace. They decided to fall back on a section of 10 East Bengal Regiment, which was now stationed at the National Assembly.

Meanwhile, Taher and his troops released Zia and brought him out, carrying him on their shoulders. Once Mosharraf and Huda left the presidential palace, their driver told them that Zia was already free and had told the soldiers to kill Mosharraf. But others loyal to Mosharraf had warned him not to trust the driver. Each move they would make could go wrong; there were treacherous turns everywhere. Bangladesh's armed forces at that time were in a complete mess, where soldiers and officers who had fought together no longer knew who to trust, suspecting each move of their rivals. Each of them was ambitious, but had no idea how far they could carry their game forward. It was like chess played by novices in a dark room by candlelight, except that they were playing with the lives of real people, not pawns, and what you saw on the streets was real blood.

Mosharraf, Huda and Haider went to the home of Brig. Nuruzzaman, whom they trusted, and changed from their uniform into civilian clothes. They tried to reach out to other officers loyal to them. They left a safe house in Lalmatia and reached Fatema Nursing Home, which was nearby. But they were betrayed, disarmed, and brought to the Parliament and kept in a room. Officers loyal to JSD made speeches calling them Indian agents. On the morning of 7 November, they were offered breakfast. They couldn't eat anything.

They were taken down to the driveway and humiliated. Huda and Mosharraf were made to stand near haystacks. Mosharraf's last words were, 'Huda, die like a soldier.' Huda shouted to Capt. Siraj of 10 Bengal, 'Ask your bhabi (Niloufer) and children to go back to her father.' They were shot with 7.62mm Chinese-made light machine guns and then bayoneted to ensure that they were dead.

Taher thought his counter-revolution had succeeded; Zia was now in charge. Zia was still very popular as a war hero. Soldiers came out of the barracks and began cheering Zia's return. Officers who feared that they'd get implicated in the Mosharraf coup changed their uniforms and left their posts. Zia immediately made himself deputy martial law administrator. He also took over the portfolios of finance, home affairs, industry, and information, as well as becoming the army chief of staff, and supported Abu Sadat Mohammad Sayem who had been named president and chief martial law administrator.

◆

Niloufer Huda was expecting Najmul to return home on the morning of

7 November, but he hadn't arrived. Niloufer had asked the operator at the cantonment to call her at 7:30 a.m, but when she woke up, it was 8:30 a.m. He hadn't called. She called him and asked why he hadn't woken her up. The operator said that Gen. Zia had been released and 'there is no news of sir' (Najmul). At 9:30, two officers came and told her to get ready, for it was not safe for her to be in the cantonment.

Niloufer hadn't yet heard about Taher's counter-revolt. In the evening, her mother-in-law told her she was not going to leave till Najmul returned, because she didn't want him to come to an empty house. When she reached a house in Rangpur where she was being kept under safety, she saw other officers' wives. They looked at her and stared; some started to cry. The other women knew Najmul had been killed. 'I asked them why they were crying; I told them he is in hiding, that he will return,' she told me. 'But something in my mind told me this was wrong. I said to myself: please show me some light, and closed my eyes. But I could only see darkness, black, jet-black darkness, and there was no light,' she said quietly.

On the 9th morning she was told she'd be taken to Dhaka in an airplane. She told her mother-in-law that Huda and others had been arrested, and they must go to Dacca. She wore some bangles but the other wives had come to see her and they again started crying. She wore a silk sari; she made her children too dress properly. The officer who came to see her at the airport was solemn.

When they landed in Dacca she saw her brothers had come to receive her, along with two officers. They drove to her cousin sister's house. She heard a voice in her mind, saying—*you will not see him; he is dead.* She quietly asked her brother, who had come to pick her up at the airport, what happened? He kept quiet. 'Where are you taking me, at least tell me that?' He said they were going to Gulshan, their elder cousin sister's house.

And then she was told what had happened—that Najmul had been dead since 7 November. 'You have to ask Zia for the body; they won't give it to us,' her brother told her. Her relatives cried when they saw her. She said she wasn't going to cry; she had come there to reclaim his body.

When she spoke to Zia, who knew her husband well, she asked him with the direct tone that is her characteristic style: 'Why was Huda killed when you are here?' Zia kept quiet. Then he said: 'He was killed because he was misguided by Khaled Mosharraf.' Niloufer asked him where the body was. Zia said it was in good care. 'Whatever you want, whatever you need,

I will do it for you,' he assured her.

I want nothing, she said. I only want his body.

Zia said the troops were still agitated, so she could not have it today. 'As long as I am alive, I will do whatever I can for you,' he told her.

She had one request: she wanted the coffin to be draped in the national flag.

Zia kept quiet.

'I was angry because he kept quiet. It meant he wouldn't do it,' she told me. 'But now I have understood. He could not allow the national flag because they were being branded as Indian agents. I so wish we had gone back to Calcutta and stayed there. But my husband told me he would never leave his country. I did not know this but he had left a message for me in a recording which ended saying "Victory is ours." He had left it with Subrata Mitra when he went back to Bangladesh to fight the war. He had also written—"Keep your head held high. I have not done anything wrong." It felt as if he was talking about his death and it became my guidance. Then he left; I was in Calcutta; and while going, he didn't look back. He was going to his country.'

Niloufer collected Huda's body the next day. Her daughter Naheed, who was five, looked at the body, and said: 'They have brought Abbu home but his feet are so white.'

◆

If Taher saw himself as a kingmaker bringing in a socialist revolution, he was about to get a nasty surprise. Within a few days of assuming power, Zia grasped quickly that Taher's views of the people's revolution were too radical, and it was not something he was comfortable with. Zia also realized that while he had the formal power, Taher was getting to be more popular and wielded informal power over the army. Zia considered the long-term consequences and promptly arrested Taher, staging a counter-coup within a counter-coup. He re-established the leadership of the official, orthodox army, so that a new people's army that Taher had dreamed of could not emerge.

Taher's aim was to establish a real 'people's democracy', guided by the radical Left ideas popular at that time, by using the popularity of Zia, a war hero, as a titular, symbolic ruler. To get the entire army behind him, Taher needed Zia on his side. But Zia was shrewd—note how he promptly distanced himself from Farooq's plans to assassinate Mujib, if Farooq's account is accurate—and he understood instinctively that a popular army with elected officers would be impossible to control. He sensed that it was now or never. So before Taher could call the shots, he settled in as the army chief, surrounded himself with his confidants, and within days he arrested Taher. A show trial of Taher followed, after which he was convicted and executed.

Zia took two more decisions to protect himself. He gave immunity to Mujib's killers so that they would not see him as an enemy. And he made sure that they left the country, after which they would not be allowed to return. Connect all the dots, as some conspiracy theorists in Bangladesh tend to do, and you see an extremely clever and convoluted plot in which many rivals eliminate each other, leaving Zia the last man standing. When I met Simeen Hossain Rimi at her home in late 2011, she told me: 'I want that actual story of the conspiracy to get known. If nobody knows the conspiracy, how can you rectify or deal with what happened? How can there be justice?'

If indeed Zia's strategy was to take over without leaving any fingerprints, it seemed to be working perfectly according to his plan. While the Khaled Mosharraf-led mutiny added an element of surprise, Taher came to the rescue by freeing Zia and getting rid of Mosharraf. Once in the saddle, Zia ensured that Mujib's killers left the country. After a sham trial, he had Taher executed. With a nudge, he replaced the elderly Sayem and became the president of Bangladesh. Like all military officers who seize power, he immediately postponed elections for a new president and Parliament. Like all dictators, he promised early elections. And like all strongmen, he made himself the chief martial law administrator. By November 1976, Bangladesh suddenly began to look like a poor imitation of Pakistan.

NINE

GETTING TO KNOW THE GENERALS

After the bodies were buried, broken furniture removed, shattered glass cleaned up, and pools of blood wiped out from the homes and jail cells in Dacca, one man stood tall—Ziaur Rahman. Mujib was gone, and so was most of his family including his likely successors, from within the family or in jail; potentially threatening troublemakers—the junior officers—were sent off to Bangladeshi embassies abroad; the unexpected threat that Khaled Mosharraf had posed had disappeared; the rebellious officer Taher who could have become a real danger in the longer term was gone. The leader of the Z Force during the Liberation War, Ziaur Rahman, could now finally lead the country whose independence he had fought for, whose independence he had declared—in Mujib's name—to the world.

Ziaur Rahman was a dapper man. He liked to choose his clothes well. At his memorial in Chittagong the curators have curiously displayed the clothes he wore, including their labels. The trousers are well-cut and grey, but the shirt is from Harrods, the store in Knightsbridge in London which is a place of pilgrimage for the wealthy from around the world. The briefcase is Samsonite, and other personal effects show the style of a man of certain understated elegance. If Zia did his own shopping, he knew what to buy and where to buy it—if he expected his aides to do it, they had taste and a good budget.

Zia was a military man. Nobody accused him of being an ideologue—he was pragmatic. He had no lofty aims like Mujib who had propagated 'Mujibism'. Zia was a man from the cantonment, used to thinking in terms of military strategy, giving orders, surrounding himself with people loyal to him, and expecting his instructions to be obeyed unquestioningly. While that may make for an efficient administrator, it was not very useful in a noisy democracy, and more so in Bangladesh, where as Abu'l Fazl had noted in Mughal times, the dust of dissension is always rising.

The political party that led the freedom struggle was now orphaned, other parties were tiny and didn't have much influence, and there was confusion about the ideals on which the nation was to be built. Bengali? Muslim? That existential genie was already out of the bottle when Khondaker Mostaq Ahmad ended his speech commending Mujib's killers with 'Bangladesh Zindabad'.

Possibly with a view to create a constituency beyond the cantonment—where he was never sure whom he could trust—Zia started to begin his speeches with the phrase 'Bismillah-ir-Rahman-ir-Rahim (In the name of Allah, the Beneficent, the Merciful)'.

Zia was not an Islamic fundamentalist by any means, but he had been trained in the Pakistan Military Academy, and as such he was greatly influenced by Pakistan's governing ideology, which arose from mistrust of Hindus and Indians; indeed, in the binary way many Muslim League leaders presented the issue to Pakistanis, it meant Hindus were Indians and Indians were Hindus. Zia was not opposed to the Awami League during the war. But those who remained in the Awami League did not trust him, mainly after Mujib's death. As Zia set about creating political space for himself, he realized he would need his own power base. While he had the army—he was still a serving officer—he had seen how mercurial the mood of the army was, and how easy it was to organize a coup. Khaled Mosharraf's coup had succeeded remarkably smoothly, and Taher's counter-coup had also gone through rather easily. That showed unruly anarchism, revealing no controlling authority. That jolted Zia. He wanted to make sure that he would not have to rely only on the army in case of an emergency.

That meant placating the Islamist opinion, because the secular politicians were not able to trust him, and he could not trust all the men in uniform. He did not have much choice except to turn to Islamic parties, and the way to earn their support was by making political gestures. He made some politically inept choices, such as bringing Shah Azizur Rahman in his cabinet, given that Azizur was widely viewed as a collaborator, as he had gone to the UN as a Pakistani delegate in September 1971 to speak against the independence of Bangladesh. 'It was a slap on our face,' Sultana Kamal said, recalling that appointment. He also showed a poor understanding of Bangladesh's diversity—when he spoke of Bangladeshi nationalism, he failed to mention the country's many ethnic minorities—which was surprising, since when he escaped from Chittagong during the Liberation War and wanted to cross the border to India, he was offered sanctuary along the path by the Chakmas in the Chittagong Hill Tracts. But in that, he was not very different from Mujib either, or the post-1972 Awami League or its constitution, which did not refer to them either. And yet, ironically enough, Zia's Bangladeshi nationalism, and recognition of Bangladeshi identity in fact provided potentially more space for recognising 'other ethnicities' and 'other' languages, than the earlier Bengali nationalism position had done.

While he was creating his power base, he also had another goal—to reform and streamline the army. Bangladesh had two types of officers—those who had fought the Liberation War and those who had not. Those who had not were not necessarily traitors. Many of them were part of the armed forces but based in West Pakistan when the conflict began, and they were then kept under detention, as Amena Mohsin's father was (although he was a doctor, and not a fighting soldier, with the army). They could not return to Bangladesh until Bhutto and Indira Gandhi signed the Simla Agreement and Pakistani POWs were repatriated. Only after that exchange of prisoners did Bhutto agree to let Bengali officers and men of the former East Pakistani wing of the Pakistani army return to Bangladesh. Had they been in Bangladesh, quite probably many of them would have fought valiantly for freedom. But in the Mujib era, those with liberation war credentials were given preference and those who had been repatriated were often made juniors to officers who were their juniors before the war. In a hierarchy-conscious organization like the armed forces, this was playing with fire.

Zia restored old ranks and hierarchies and refused to discriminate in favour of one or the other. (If he did discriminate, it was by packing his inner circle with loyalists and discriminating in favour of Islamists). But Zia's move angered freedom fighters who had made rapid advances in the military during Mujib's time. Zia was astute in identifying discontent—whenever he found someone getting restless, he offered him a plum position as a diplomat abroad. The officer became happy and became wealthy. More importantly, his ability to potentially disrupt the Zia rule was minimized. This was similar to Suharto, the Indonesian general who eliminated rivals by making them diplomats abroad, in order to consolidate his rule. One decision Zia made was in appointing Hussain Muhammad Ershad as his deputy chief of staff. Ershad was a repatriated officer with no freedom struggle credentials but he increasingly came to be seen as an important general. Finally on 21 April 1977, Zia made it known to President Sayem in no uncertain terms that his health was poor, and taking the hint, Sayem resigned and Zia took over as president.

A month later, he declared a 19-point programme for political and economic development which focused on agricultural growth and integrated rural development. He followed the advice of international aid agencies and launched a popular food-for-work programme. Confident of his growing popularity, Zia called a referendum. The result was so lop-sided that it would surprise even his genuine supporters. The turnout was 88.5 per cent, and Zia reportedly received the support of 98.9 per cent of the voters, a margin that would embarrass Soviet apparatchiks. But there was no realistic opposition to challenge the result. It was too demoralized.

In an attempt to create the impression that he was demilitarizing the administration, Zia said he would induct more civilians into the cabinet, even though some were retired military officers. He also appointed a Supreme Court judge, Abdul Sattar, as his vice-president.

To create his own power base, Zia realized that being more liberal or secular was not going to be easy. Military officers tend to be conservative and Zia was no exception. The only way to distinguish his rule from the Mujib era was to reduce the emphasis on secularism and socialism. Faith would have to become important, and given the politics of Bangladesh, it would mean language would have to share space with religion. If the worry under the Mujib era was that Bangladesh might look like India's poor cousin, the longer term worry under Zia's rule would be that Bangladesh would look like Pakistan's poor cousin. It created an existential angst—if Bangladesh was not like India, was it like Pakistan? If so, why was the war necessary in 1971? And if not, why was there a Partition in 1947? Or was a third, distinct identity possible, which was neither overwhelmingly Muslim, nor only Bengali?

In any case, Bangladesh was not only a Bengali country—the people in the Chittagong Hills had their own language; the Burmese-influenced Chittagongian dialect was hard even for Bangladeshis from elsewhere to understand; and Garo was spoken in the north near Sylhet in the area contiguous to the Indian state of Meghalaya; and in the east in the Santhal region, other languages and dialects were spoken often. And of course there was Urdu, for there were many Biharis still living in the camps, besides Urdu-speakers in Dacca itself, from old Calcutta and Murshidabad. Religion could perhaps unite this mishmash, Zia thought. At the Pakistani Military Academy Zia probably learned that Islam's unifying power could override the many languages spoken in Pakistan—Urdu of course, but also Punjabi,

Sindhi, Pakhtuni, Baluchi, Bengali, Gujarati, and many others.

And so Zia took the first step towards restoring religion in Bangladeshi political life. He amended the Constitution's preamble, inserting the salutation 'Bismillah-ir-Rahman-ir-Rahim', and in Article 8(1) and 8(1A) a statement was added, calling for 'absolute trust and faith in Almighty Allah', replacing the Mujib-era commitment to secularism. Socialism was replaced with a commitment to economic and social justice. He also began improving relations with Islamic countries. Relations with India were proper but cold. They improved after 1977, when Indira Gandhi lost parliamentary elections and the new prime minister, Morarji Desai, stopped Indian support for some pro-Mujib rebels operating from Indian soil, including Kader Siddiqui and his men, who had escaped to India after Mujib's assassination. Zia was also an early pioneer of the idea of a union of South Asian nations—Bangladesh, Bhutan, India, the Maldives, Nepal, Pakistan, and Sri Lanka—for regional cooperation, which would eventually lead to the creation of the South Asian Association for Regional Cooperation (SAARC) in 1983.

Zia's first major crisis was in September 1977, when Japanese Red Army terrorists hijacked a Japan Air Lines (JAL) plane and brought it to Dacca. While the government was trying to negotiate with the terrorists a mutiny broke out in Bogura. Even as the army tamed that mutiny, another uprising started on 2 October in Dacca. Those mutineers attacked Zia's home in the cantonment (but did not succeed) and temporarily took over the Dacca radio station. They even reached the airport and killed some of the air force officers who were negotiating an end to the hijack drama. The army reasserted its authority but the image of the government suffered hugely. Zia turned the crisis into an opportunity and sacked the top brass of the military intelligence, as well as three senior officers who were in line to become army chief at some point. One of them was Maj. Gen. Muhammad Abul Manzur, who had been a sector commander during the Liberation War.

Suspicious of elements within the army now, Zia took one of his biggest gambles. He insisted that cabinet ministers who were also in the army must give up their military rank. He began to insist on being called president, dropping his military rank. He called for elections in 1978 and lifted the ban on political parties. He even allowed Ghulam Azam, the exiled chief of the Jamaat-e-Islami to return to Bangladesh in July and the party could re-establish itself, initially with a different name.

A national front led by the Jatiyo Gonotantrik Dal (National Democratic

Party) supported Zia. He defeated his rival, Gen. Osmani, who had led the Mukti Bahini during the Liberation War, winning 76.7 per cent of the vote to become president, although there were allegations of widespread rigging. He also created his own party, the Bangladesh Nationalist Party. In the parliamentary elections that followed, the BNP won 44 per cent of the vote and sent 207 of the 300 members to parliament.

On 17 May 1981, Zia finally permitted Hasina Wajed, daughter of Mujib, to return to Bangladesh from her exile in India. The Awami League was significantly weakened at that time. Zohra Tajuddin, the widow of Tajuddin Ahmed, had valiantly kept the party together, and many Awami League leaders had spent time in jail. There were disputes within the party about who should lead the organization. Hasina received an overwhelmingly warm welcome, which must have troubled Zia. Hasina had declared no political ambition, but she was Mujib's daughter, and she could energize Mujib's disheartened supporters and create a political alternative. How to tackle her would have to become a major priority for him.

Later that month Zia decided to go to Chittagong to sort out political differences among local leaders of the BNP. He was to stay in the Circuit House, set on a busy road in the port city. Abul Manzur was the commander of the cantonment in Chittagong. He had been close to Zia—the two had fought the Liberation War together, after all. He trusted Manzur so much that after the coups of 1975, he asked Manzur to return to Bangladesh from his posting in India. Manzur aspired to be the army chief of staff, but Mir Shawkat Ali was his senior. Piqued by their rivalry, Zia appointed Ershad as the army chief in December 1978. Zia also sent Manzur to Chittagong after the intelligence failures that led to the embarrassing episode at the airport.

On the night of 29 May, Zia ate chicken soup, rice and chicken curry, mutton dopiaza, dal, and salad, with pudding to round off a good meal. He had told the cook to prepare a breakfast of tea, bread, fresh fish, roasted chicken, fruit cocktail, and lemon. That would set him off for a good start knocking BNP heads together the next day.

At about 4 a.m. on 30 May, three teams of army officers, allegedly including Manzur, attacked the Circuit House where Ziaur Rahman was still asleep. They had come without their soldiers. They were armed with eleven submachine guns, three rocket launchers and three rifles that could fire grenades. Lt. Col. Fazle Hossain started the attack when he launched two rockets towards the Circuit House which left a gaping hole in the building.

They then entered the Circuit House, looking for Zia. Zia was in a room which had two fine paintings—*Noon* by Chandra Shekhar Dey and *Dusk* by Hasi Chakrabartee.

The officers told Zia that they would like to take him to the cantonment. But just then another team arrived and shot Zia. The president collapsed and died almost immediately. As with Mujib's home in Dhanmondi, darkened bloodstains remain on the carpet and on the wall like a macabre reminder, and when I visited the Circuit House in January 2013, I counted fifteen bullet holes on the walls and on the ground. A guide quietly told me that Zia's body was split in many parts.

The Chittagong Circuit House, which has now been converted into a memorial for Zia, had virtually no visitors when I went there. I had ample time to walk through the ghostly memorial. I looked at the visitors' book, and there had been barely a dozen visitors in the previous two months. The Awami League was in power in Dhaka, and the memorial showed signs of neglect. The caretakers and security guards were extremely curious about the reasons for my visit. Bangladeshi politics has become so binary that they assumed I was writing a book sympathetic to Zia, for otherwise what could be the purpose of my coming to visit this neglected shrine? They also wondered why forty years after the war had ended someone wanted to take the trouble of finding out more about what had happened.

The memorial was intriguing—there were many personal effects of Zia—the clothes he wore, the bags he carried, his pen, and the German china in which guests were served food. There was a glass-encased room, in which there was a Gates Console with a large desk with a black swivel chair from where radio announcers would speak. This one was meant to depict the Kalurghat radio station from where Zia had made the historic announcement declaring Bangladesh's independence. The wall was partly painted white, and it was made of red bricks. There were six knobs on the console and an RCA microphone. But curiously, there was no recording of that speech.

Elsewhere, there were weapons—47cm and 49cm light-machine guns, an old .303 rifle, metal helmets, and another mock-up model of Zia supervising soldiers during the Liberation War. A map which showed the towns where the Z Force operated—Chittagong itself, Rohumari, Chattak and Sylhet.

Finally, there was a room with photographs of Zia with world leaders. Some were spelt innovatively—Shirak for Chirac—and some were misidentified—a photograph of Indian leaders Morarji Desai, Jagjivan Ram and Atal Behari

Vajpayee mentioned the then Indian President Sanjeeva Reddy, who was not even in the photograph.

◆

The enigmatic Ershad, who had no role in the Liberation War, stepped in the vacuum. He ordered the army to suppress the mutiny. The rebels were given an ultimatum to surrender, but the coup's leaders fled towards Chittagong Hill Tracts. A government-led force intercepted them and Col. Matiur Rahman and Lt. Col. Mahbub, who were allegedly among the coup leaders, were shot dead. The army and the police caught Manzur at Fatikchhari, but he surrendered to the police. He was taken to a police station. He requested to be sent to the Chittagong jail and insisted that he should not be handed over to the army. But when he was about to be taken in a truck, an army contingent arrived.

What happened after that remains a mystery. Some accounts say a police constable blindfolded Manzur and pulled him towards the army contingent and handed him to the armed forces. The official government account claims that Manzur was killed by enraged soldiers. Another official report described him as being killed by an angry mob. But the autopsy report showed one gunshot wound at the back of his head. Other conspirators were tried and thirteen of them received death sentences, while five others were given prison sentences.

The mystery surrounding Manzur's killing deepened after Lifschultz got documents that the leading Bengali newspaper *Prothom Alo* had received, which cast Manzur's killing in a different light. Lifschultz wrote about it in *Prothom Alo* and its English sister-daily, *The Daily Star*. The documents provide a somewhat detailed account of Manzur's last moments in the Chittagong Cantonment on 1 June, when he was, 'by all indications assassinated while in army custody', as Lifschultz wrote. The documents comprised affidavits by soldiers at the cantonment, which implicate senior officers in murdering Manzur. The soldiers allege that the senior officers were part of a special operation and were following orders through an identifiable chain of command.

The operation, as the soldiers described it, was in two parts: Manzur had surrendered to the police with his family, and was held at Hathazari police station outside Chittagong. A military unit was meant to remove Manzur from police custody. Following Manzur's plea that he not be handed over to the army, the police officers decided that they would hand him over to the army only if Vice President Sattar insisted upon it. Air Vice Marshall Sadruddin and Inspector General A.B.M.G. Kibria had a meeting with Sattar where they tried to persuade him not to turn Manzur over to the army. Even as those meetings were going on in Dacca, an army unit came to the police station at Hathazari and demanded that Manzur be handed over to them.

The soldiers whose testimonies *Prothom Alo* had received claimed that a superior officer had given the soldiers the mission of collecting Manzur from the Hathazari police station and taking him in military custody after which he was to be eliminated. The order apparently came from the army high command.

The soldiers left to capture Manzur even as Kibria and Sadruddin were arguing with Ershad in Sattar's presence, saying Manzur had to be under police custody. The alternative was to fly Manzur and his family to Dacca under police escort. Senior officials in Chittagong did not know that Kibria was fighting for Manzur's life.

Manzur had warned a colleague in Dacca that Ershad had planned to kill him. Lifschultz writes that Manzur's enemies within the army could not let him survive. And if he survived he might tell the tale about what happened in Chittagong and how Zia was murdered.

Sattar gave in to Ershad's insistence. That, Lifschultz writes, sealed Manzur's fate. Sadruddin reportedly told Sattar: 'Sir, please make sure that nothing happens to Manzur and that he is given a [fair] trial. If anything happens to Manzur, you [Sattar] will be answerable to the nation.' Sattar was confident that Manzur would receive a fair trial, but that evening Manzur was killed in army custody. Lifschultz revealed that Manzur made several phone calls to Gen. Moinul Choudhury and Gen. Mir Shawkat Ali between 30 May and 1 June. None of the calls helped.

◆

Vice President Abdus Sattar took over as president and was elected in a popular vote in November 1981. Sattar tried reasserting civilian authority, but Ershad resisted Sattar's moves. Sattar had to set up a national security council, which included him, the new vice-president, and prime minister and the three chiefs of the armed forces. To limit the military's influence, Sattar tried to get rid of the number of military officers on government duty.

But by now Ershad had set his sights on the presidential office and did not want Sattar to get in the way. In March 1982 Ershad removed Sattar in a coup and assumed full powers under martial law. Like other generals before him in Bangladesh and in other countries, and indeed like Zia, he promised fresh elections and said his move was a temporary one.

At one level, Ershad's position was now secure. While Hasina Wajed had returned to Bangladesh, she was in no position to reshape the Awami League, or pose a serious threat. And Zia's grief-stricken widow Khaleda, who would become a major political figure within a decade, was still distraught and in mourning, and the BNP was not organized enough to mount a challenge. The military too was leaderless—Ershad was a repatriated officer without a track record during the Liberation War, and the generation of commanders and officers who were part of that war had either faded from the scene or ended up killing one another. The cycle of violence, revenge, and reprisals never seemed to end—junior officers had killed Mujib and replaced him with Khondaker Mostaq Ahmad; Khaled Mosharraf removed Mostaq; Taher had Khaled Mosharraf killed and released Zia; Zia had Taher executed in jail after a secret trial; gave immunity to the junior officers but sent them overseas; other officers killed Zia, and Manzur was blamed; army officers then had Manzur killed. This was Ershad's moment.

And yet, Ershad had no power base of his own. A lonely man with power isolated in a palace can be dangerous. Ershad had power but felt insecure. He tried to establish his Bengali credentials by renaming Dacca in 1983, calling it Dhaka. He also renamed the Dhaka airport after Gen. Zia.

But his unpopularity was rising, keeping pace with inflation, and public confidence in him was falling, in keeping with the value of the Bangladeshi taka. He needed a support base, and he too decided to find it in playing politics with religion. All political parties that mattered—the Awami League, BNP, and Jamaat-e-Islami—were opposing him. To deal with that, Ershad decided to make Islam the state religion in the hope of getting Jamaat, and possibly BNP too, on his side. 'What Zia started by abolishing secularism, Ershad completed by bringing in state religion,' says Sultana Kamal.[193] Ershad had legitimized the politics of Jamaat-e-Islami, the conservative, fundamentalist party committed to Islamic practices and determined to bring public life under Shariah or Islamic law. Under Mujib, the Jamaat had no prospects; under Zia, the Jamaat began to regroup. Under Ershad, it realized it could act openly.

To establish his devoutness, Ershad went on Hajj and frequently invoked Allah in his speeches. He attempted to turn a population that was at ease with its culture and religion to focus more on the majority faith. Ershad also continued the Zia-era policy of protecting the immunity Zia had granted to Mujib's killers. Those who were part of the foreign service received promotions. The masterminds of the coup against Mujib, Rashid and Farooq, had left for Libya. They attempted to return to Bangladesh during the Zia years, but were not allowed to enter. In later years, Farooq did manage to enter the country twice, he was immediately arrested.

Ershad sent some of his generals to study alternative models of governance which included a role for the army. His generals went to Thailand and Turkey. In 1983 in India I had interviewed the former police commissioner of Vadodara, Jaspal Singh. He was suspended after a communal riot in his city, but he was very popular among the city's Hindus. Jaspal had earlier been with the Border Security Force of India and he had undergone military training with Ershad and considered Ershad to be his friend. He said he was surprised by Ershad's rise to power. While he didn't call Ershad mediocre, he diplomatically said Ershad had successfully concealed his ambition. He also said that Ershad did not hold any firm views and India could influence him if it played its cards right, and many in Bangladesh say so it did.

Analysts in Bangladesh say Ershad was keen to establish a permanent role for the military in Bangladesh politics, the way Indonesia had managed to do with its dwifungsi or dual-function system, where the army protects the nation but also takes part in governing it. Such an idea is anathema to democracies, including India's, but is quite popular and prevalent in many parts of Asia, as the Thai coup of 2014 reminds us once again.

All dictators crave democratic approval—it is just that they don't like the unpredictability of election results, because there's the possibility of losing.

South Asian leaders who have suspended democracy have invariably promised to hold fresh elections to acquire legitimacy. In 1975, Indira Gandhi declared a nationwide emergency, suspended fundamental rights, and arrested tens of thousands of political activists after a high court invalidated her election to parliament. But seeking legitimacy, in 1977 she called for elections, only to lose. In Pakistan, Gen. Zia-ul Haq, who overthrew Zulfikar Ali Bhutto in 1977 (and later executed him), initially announced that elections would be held within ninety days. (He ruled Pakistan for nearly a decade; his rule ending in a mysterious air crash.) Zia had called himself the Chief Martial Law Administrator, or CMLA, and Pakistani democrats joked that CMLA meant 'cancel my last announcement.' In his poem, 'The Solution,' Bertolt

Brecht offers a simple way out: couldn't the government dissolve the people and elect another?

But elections are not so simple, and losing dictators don't have the option of electing a new electorate. Ershad called for presidential elections in 1986, but he did not want to take any chances. He placed such onerous conditions that all major parties boycotted the elections. That was embarrassing. To give the elections some credibility Ershad encouraged Farooq to stand against him. And Farooq obliged, since he hoped it would give him legitimacy in Bangladeshi politics in a way he had never imagined.[194]

Ershad won the elections overwhelmingly. Many felt those elections were rigged ruthlessly—booths were captured, voters were intimidated and bribed, and ballot boxes had disappeared. Commonwealth observers who had come to Dhaka said they had come to see an election, but instead they had witnessed a tragedy.

Soon after that election I went to Bangladesh for the first time on an assignment from *Debonair* magazine, India's pale imitation of *Playboy*. Like its American counterpart, *Debonair* sold many copies because it published photographs of women wearing little or no clothing, but again, like its American counterpart, it also published fiction, poetry, interviews, and long-form narrative non-fiction. At that time it was the only magazine I knew which would send me to another country for a month with only a vague idea of what the story should say, and then run the story in three parts over three months. And so, I went to Ershad's Bangladesh, and met politicians, human rights lawyers, businessmen, academics, and ordinary people. I travelled to Sylhet and Srimongol in the north and spent the rest of the time in Dhaka. I practiced my Bengali which was admittedly limited and poor, and Bangladeshis indulged me for some time, before responding in Hindi. One afternoon I discovered a long line of people at the Indian High Commission, waiting to collect visas. When I tried taking a photograph, a Bangladeshi policeman came waving a wooden staff, threatening to beat me up. I promptly said I was a shangbadik, a journalist, from Bombay, and that I was an Indian, so I was handed over to Indian officials. (They told me later that they had asked the police not to let anyone take photographs because that week, a newspaper had run articles criticising the Indian High Commission for being slow in issuing visas and making Bangladeshis wait outside without any shelter, regardless of heat or rain, which was quite probably true.)

Almost everyone I met at that time spoke of Bangladesh with pain, not joy. They felt their freedom struggle had been in vain. That was the year Bangladesh was turning fifteen, but they felt the country had nothing to show for it. Its heroes were dead or killed and its villains were walking around the city without shame. That was the time I met Farooq at his home in Banani.

Popular uprising against Ershad, in particular over his corruption, began within two years, and by 1990, Bangladesh had become ungovernable. Ershad had ruled with a stern hand, and to deal with unrest, he imposed emergency. Students and activists were killed in cold blood and civil society leaders were arrested and lawyers were tortured. There had been continued demonstrations for over a year. Nobody seemed to be obeying his orders. Thousands marched against the regime almost daily, and Ershad finally resigned on 6 December after the army chief, Lt. Gen. Nuruddin Khan refused to clamp down on an urban protest that students were leading. Ershad was placed under house arrest.

In the elections that followed in 1991, Zia's widow Khaleda led the BNP to victory.

TEN

TWO WOMEN AND THEIR TROUBLED
INHERITANCE

The two women were born two years apart—Khaleda Zia in 1945 and Hasina Wajed in 1947. They carry two of the most important legacies in Bangladesh. They have both fought together against a dictatorship, then led the government separately, and are now fundamentally unable to work with one another. Their mutual suspicion and dislike has kept Bangladeshi politics in an awkward stalemate, with power shifting from one to another with the regularity of a pendulum until this year, when Hasina Wajed's Awami League was re-elected to office in a parliamentary election that Khaleda Zia's BNP boycotted, because of which nearly 150 MPs were elected uncontested, raising questions about the legitimacy of the election process. But there was a time when they joined hands to lead a movement that removed Ershad from power.

Within a year of her husband's assassination in 1981 in Chittagong, Khaleda had decided to be part of politics and began working to regain power by launching a campaign to restore democracy and challenging General Ershad. Hasina Wajed, who had returned to Bangladesh from exile, joined her in the struggle to establish democracy in Bangladesh. Their collective campaign brought the country to a standstill, but they succeeded in removing Ershad a decade later. But once that job was done, the two women retreated to their corners, and Bangladesh's governance has since then passed from one woman to the other, with brief periods of caretaker governments in between.

Khaleda was keen to get to the bottom of what happened in Chittagong in 1981. In the early months after Zia's death, she had accused Ershad of involvement with Zia's assassination. Aminul Huq, an Awami League-appointed attorney general was asked to continue his investigations. Aminul Huq's credentials were impeccable. He was a Mukti Bahini freedom fighter under Maj. Saifullah and it was the killing of his older brother Sgt. Zahurul Huq in 1969 that sparked the demonstrations which led to the collapse of the Agartala Conspiracy Case against Mujib and several Bengali officers. Aminul had also defended officers who were arrested and court martialled for their alleged involvement in the murder of Zia. The confessions had been made under torture. After Ershad fell, it became possible for these questions to be raised. Lifschultz's articles in February 2014 about Manzur show why those cases need to be reinvestigated, and they can be reopened provided there is political will.

In 1986, Khaleda became the leader of the Opposition, and came to power in 1991. Her first term ended amidst rancour, as Hasina deployed the weapon of repeated hortals or mass general strikes against her. Over the years, too many elections in Bangladesh had been rigged. There was mass clamour for clean elections. Concerned about the temptation for a ruling party to rig elections, Bangladesh came up with a unique solution from 1996, first proposed by the Awami League and championed by Hasina, of the outgoing government leaving when its term ended and the appointment of an unelected caretaker government with the sole job of running the administration and elections. New elections would take place a few months later under the supervision of the caretakers. The experiment produced cleaner elections and the playing field was level—unsurprisingly, results became less predictable.

In 1996, the Awami League emerged with the single-largest number of seats, but fell short of majority by five seats. The politics was still volatile; only a few weeks before parliamentary elections were to take place that year, Lt. Gen. A.S.M. Nasim and other officers were plotting a coup, but they were caught out and dismissed. The Awami League was able to form a government, with Hasina becoming prime minister.

Hasina's ascendance emboldened some people to reignite old cases against Mujib's killers. The complaint regarding the assassinations of Mujibur Rahman and his family was two decades old. Mohitul Islam, who was Mujib's assistant in 1975 had first filed a complaint on 23 October 1976 at the Lalbagh police station. He had been unable to shake off the experience of witnessing the family being killed, in particular, the young boy Russell. But the sub-inspector on duty slapped him and took him out of the premises and warned him that if he took the case, the officials of the entire police station would be killed. Mohitul told a reporter of *The Daily Star* that he felt deeply hurt and cried. He told the journalist: 'In hindsight, I think I would have expressed my gratitude to that sub-inspector for not accepting the case. I think he was right. If that case was filed, the killers would not have spared me.'

Once Hasina was elected, he felt confident enough to file his complaint again. On 2 October 1996 he went to the Dhanmondi police station and filed a First Information Report. In explaining the delay, he wrote: 'Thought about the security of my life, and other various adversities led me to delay filing of the case regarding the incident [Mujib's murder]'. The trial could begin only in November, after Hasina's administration repealed the indemnity ordinance of 1975.[195]

The trial court framed charges and proceedings ended on 8 November 1998, when fifteen of the accused were sentenced to death and four were acquitted. An appeals process was to follow. But the matter dragged because judges were reluctant to take on such a high profile case. It dealt with partisan politics, and could seriously harm a judge's career, once the government changed. Self-protection guided some of the decisions, delaying justice. The judges' concern was understandable: should Hasina lose the 2001 election would the judicial process go forward? Or would the new government stop the trials? What would happen to the judges who had ruled on the case so far? Latifur Rahman, who was Bangladesh's Chief Justice from 1 January 2000 to 28 February 2001, would write in his book: 'When most of the senior judges felt embarrassed to hear the Bangabandhu killing case, it seemed to the [Supreme Judicial] Council that the judges were reluctant to hear the case and avoiding responsibilities.'

One festering sore in Bangladesh was the position of the country's minorities. The Chittagong Hill Tracts (CHT) region lay on Bangladesh's border with Myanmar and India, and the people who lived there professed faiths other than Islam and spoke languages other than Bengali. Rebel movements had taken hold and Dhaka often saw demands for autonomy and respect for local culture and traditions as potentially secessionist moves, and a conflict ensued. During Hasina's first term, one of her achievements was to sign a peace accord to end that internal conflict.

Since 1977, Bangladesh had faced an insurgency in CHT, where the local Chakma community and other indigenous hill people had long resented the impact of decisions made in distant capitals. The resentment went back to the time when Bangladesh was part of Pakistan, and the Kaptai Dam was commissioned in 1960. That had displaced tens of thousands of valley dwellers, particularly Chakmas. Once Bangladesh became independent, the hill people's aspirations were sidelined yet again, as the new nation's leaders embraced Bengali language and Bengali identity. The local worry was that

Bengalis would now settle in the hills on a mass scale, which would erode the identity and integrity of the unique status of the region and its peoples. Their initial conversations with Mujib after he became prime minister didn't go anywhere. Successive governments continued to treat the Chittagong Hill Tracts with neglect, and in 1977 the Chakmas launched an insurgency led by the Shanti Bahini.

The Chakmas have a troubled history in Bangladesh. The Chittagong Hill Tracts region has several ethnic groups, including the Bawm, Chak, Chakma, Khumi, Khyang, Lushai, Marma, Mro, Pangkhua, Tanchangya and Tripuri. The Chak, Chakma, Marma and Mro are Buddhist. The Khyang are Buddhist or Christian. The Tripuri are either Hindu or Christian. Several of them retain their own indigenous beliefs, albeit in conjunction with mainstream religions or faiths. The CHT region shares geographic and cultural characteristics with India's Northeast and adjoining areas of Myanmar. Historically, the hills were terra incognita where the Mughal control had not reached, and the area preserved its unique ethnic and linguist characteristics during the British years, when the region enjoyed a great deal of autonomy due to its remoteness. In the late eighteenth century the Chakmas had fought with the East India Company, and as part of their truce, they had become a British tributary with the understanding that the British would not administer the region directly. In 1860 the British annexed it as part of British India but agreed not to interfere with local administration.

Chakma rulers continued to raise taxes on agriculture and forestry but the division between the people of the hills and the plains sharpened when Bengali zamindars and other tenants refused to pay their taxes to Chakma rulers. Due to rising population pressure the need for land increased and frontiers opened, and with that, conflict began between the indigenous people and settlers. The zamindars lobbied the British authorities who then began taking away the powers of the Chakma rulers. Thus, more and more of the erstwhile swidden lands of the shifting hill cultivators, known as jumias, were occupied by Bengali farmers. The process continued from the eighteenth to the early twentieth century, whereby large chunks of hill territory, formerly the homes of hill peoples, became sedentary settlements of Bengali wet-rice cultivators, and gradually annexed to the 'regulation' districts of Chittagong and greater Noakhali.

In 1947, a section of the Chakmas wanted to be part of India, particularly because they feared persecution in a state based on the concept of nationhood for the Muslims of India. However, they wished to retain the region's autonomy. Some wished to abolish chiefship. Another group sought to maintain a constitutional chiefdom in confederation with the native states of Tripura and Cooch Behar. But in the never-ending negotiations about who would get Calcutta—India or Pakistan—the Chakmas were forgotten. 'From 15-18 August 1947, the Indian flag flew in these hills,' Devasish Roy-Wangza, the traditional ruler of the Chakmas, told me when I met him at his apartment in Dhaka in late 2012.

As a traditional ruler, Roy-Wangza has direct administrative responsibilities as a tribal judge, in land and revenue matters, and an advisory role with the government. Separately, he trained as a barrister in the UK, and is also an advocate in the Bangladesh Supreme Court. He is a member of the UN Permanent Forum on Indigenous Issues, doing his second term. Explaining the Chakmas' allegiance, Roy-Wangza told me: 'Our economic ties were mainly with East Bengal but cultural affinity was with India.' But what determined CHT's fate in 1947 was its economic contiguity with the Chittagong port. According to some accounts, CHT was being traded away because India wanted Gurdaspur in Punjab to be part of India and not see it go to Pakistan.

Chakma leaders went to Delhi to appeal to the Congress party in India. They were assured that the CHT would remain with India, but that did not happen. Roy-Wangza says that documentary and historical accounts of Partition show that the British viceroy Lord Mountbatten did not make the award public because Vallabhbhai Patel, India's first home minister, reportedly wrote to Mountbatten saying it was unacceptable for the CHT to go to Pakistan, and if it did, the Chakma would be justified in resisting it, and if they did resist, they could count on Indian support. The award was formally announced only two or three days after India and Pakistan became independent.

For Pakistan, the hills offered a strategic value. The area offered just the location where the Pakistani intelligence could train Mizo rebels who were hiding in the region and fighting the Indian state.

In the months leading up to Bangladesh's independence, the Chakmas became wary of Bengali nationalism. Amena Mohsin, an international relations expert who has studied the CHT conflict for her doctorate at Cambridge, told me: 'The Chakmas did not fear Punjabi dominance because West Pakistan was so far. But Bengalis were everywhere, taking over more and more land in the plains and threatening their lives in the hills.' In the 1970 election, the Awami League lost only two seats out of 162 in East Pakistan, one of which went to Raja Tridiv Roy (Devasish's father), who was the traditional ruler of the Chakmas. During the Liberation War the Raja took Pakistan's side. In his diaries he explains that he did so because at no point did Mujib attempt to include the Chakmas in the Bengali national narrative. The Chakmas were never included in the language movement or the liberation movement, nor were they seen as part of the six-point demands of the Awami League.

The construction of the Kaptai Dam in 1960 had led to a significant loss of habitat and the water of the Karnaphuli River in Rangmati was to be harnessed to produce power, which would bring industry and jobs to the people in the hills. But this economic activity threatened the local way of life. Many Chakmas left for Arunachal Pradesh in India and over the years some became Indian citizens. Others remain as stateless refugees in the northeastern state. Other promises made to the Chakmas were also not being met: the promised industry did not come, the power that was generated was not distributed locally as a priority nor was it free, and few jobs materialized for many Chakmas. The project was meant for the whole of what was then East Pakistan, which meant it benefited mostly Bengalis. 'For the Chakmas, the 1971 conflict was between Bengalis and West Pakistan; they remained indifferent. As chief of the Chakmas at the time, Tridiv Roy, had to protect Chakma interests,' Amena Mohsin continued.

When Tridiv Roy was elected to Pakistan's National Assembly in the 1970 election, he wanted to revive the special status the tribal communities enjoyed. Mujib had offered him an Awami League ticket, but Roy wanted to fight as an independent so that he could consider his options after the elections.

After the results, Roy saw Mujib as the likely prime minister of all of Pakistan and met him to ask for CHT to be made a special area. Mujib asked him to speak to Kamal Hossain, the party's legal maven; Kamal said the idea was sound but Mujib would have to approve. But before they could conclude any agreement, Operation Searchlight was unleashed.

After 25 March, Roy told the Pakistanis not to shell Rangmati, CHT's capital, and in return he promised support to Pakistan. 'My father was forced to collaborate with Pakistan,' Devasish Roy-Wangza said. 'His view was— we are a small nation. We can't take on Pakistan, but Bengalis can. And yet, we were not part of the Bangladesh plan. The Six-Point Plan was all about Bengalis, and there was nothing about Chakmas in it. In March 1971, who knew the future?'

As the conflict escalated, the ruling families of the Chakma, Mong and Bohmong chiefdoms (called circles) left for India or Burma. Tridiv Roy went to Pakistan and became an envoy to Southeast Asian countries for Yahya Khan. Some of the hill peoples were neutral, some joined the Mukti Bahini: during the war, they offered asylum to many refugees leaving for India. Some refugees stayed in the hills throughout the conflict. Tridiv Roy issued Hindus certificates saying they were Buddhists and protected them. Ziaur Rahman's Z Force operated from near here, and he was in the CHT too; Chakmas carried him to safety across the Feni River when Pakistani troops were pursuing him. Roy's uncles trained with the Mukti Bahini. 'But there was no push among the Bahini commanders to arm us because they still thought we were untrustworthy,' Devasish Roy-Wangza said.

Amena Mohsin added: 'When Bangladesh claims that the war was fought by the Bengalis, I always question that because even the Santhals fought, even the Garos fought. The people here suffered because their leaders went off to support Pakistan. It meant the entire area got stigmatized.' It was wrong to single out Chakmas, she said. 'Even in the plains, there were Bengalis who collaborated with the Pakistanis. But nobody said they [all Bengalis] were collaborators—we say there were *some* Bengalis who were collaborators. But with the CHT we don't say that *a segment of the hill people* collaborated. We have created this "otherness", because we are a modern state. We did not trust the Chakmas because of Tridiv Roy, and Tridiv Roy had good reasons not to trust the Bengalis.'

Roy-Wangza says the conversation within Bangladesh had since got vitiated. He said: 'Some Bengali nationalists even claimed that the Chakmas were migrants from Thailand. I once had to contend with this at a debate with a Bangladeshi minister, who said that the tribals were economic migrants. I found it insulting and I spoke out against it. If and when we came here, at that time there was no Bengal. The writ of Dhaka didn't run here, nor did the Delhi government's writ run in the Northeast at that time.'

'This dichotomy of Muslim vs. Bengali is a false one,' Roy-Wangza added. 'We need a multicultural Bangladesh, which could avert all those dichotomies. Bangladesh refused to recognize our distinctness—and it was not only about us; it affected Garo, Khasi, and Santhal communities too. In India, the Lok Sabha cannot interfere in Mizo and Naga territories on land and on religious and social customs—they have a high degree of protection. But there is a strong denial in Bangladesh for protecting indigenous traditions. So long as

Bangladesh persists in believing in the majoritarian model of democracy, Bengali migration here will continue and tribal authority will get eroded.'

Roy-Wangza finds it perplexing that Bangladeshis don't understand the hill people's desire for regional autonomy. 'One of the things uppermost on our minds is—shouldn't people who suffered from atrocities and discrimination from Pakistan be the first to understand our plight?'

Bangladesh had responded to the agitation in the CHT region by using force and its army fought the Shanti Bahini for nearly two decades. Once Hasina Wajed came to power in 1996, she started negotiations which led to a peace accord. While she was rightly hailed for that, over the years, the pressure on tribal land has remained, with Bangladeshi conglomerates seeking land and displacing more people. While there has been a truce since 1997, Amena Mohsin fears that factions have now multiplied and the region has been militarized. People from the plains are interested in the land. Bengalis are building shops where young Chakma boys and men from the hills take jobs as assistants. The Destiny Group, a powerful Bangladeshi business group, has been acquiring community-owned land that poverty-ridden people are willing to sell. Destiny wants to grow tobacco and develop other plantations. The younger generation doesn't mind selling their share of the land because many among them want to move to cities. That also reduces the incentive for the older generation to hold on to the community-owned land. The hill people believe that the land belongs to everyone and don't have well-formed notions of individual ownership. Meanwhile, the settler population has grown and has been asserting its power and rights. Settlers' organizations recently attacked a convoy of the International CHT Commission comprising human rights experts from Bangladesh and abroad who were visiting the area, injuring several of them.

◆

After elections held under a caretaker government in 2001, the Awami League was voted out and the BNP was back in power, this time with the Jamaat-e-Islami as its coalition partner. The appeals cases of Mujib's assassins were quietly shelved. When Chief Justice Mahmudul Amin Chowdhury suggested to the government that an ad hoc judge be appointed, the government heard him politely but did nothing. Khaleda's second term in office was chaotic, with growing civil unrest and violence.

The BNP's alliance with the Jamaat offered the religious party the legitimacy it simply did not have in Bangladesh's politics. The BNP has always enjoyed a core support of at least 30 percent in Bangladeshi politics. But to ensure a majority it needs a few more seats, and the Jamaat was able to provide that. The Jamaat's influence was disproportionate to its parliamentary strength. It had the ability to bring cities to a standstill as its activists would go about enforcing hortals, and fearing violence, nobody would dare step out. (To be sure, the Awami League also enforced hortals with similar tactics.) When the BNP allied with the Jamaat, its leaders—including some who would later get tried in the International Crimes Tribunal—gained political power, with some becoming cabinet ministers.

The political importance of the Jamaat has been an extraordinary development in Bangladesh in the past two decades, given that its electoral performance has been weak. The Jamaat-e-Islami had been banned after the Liberation War. Zia lifted the ban but did not allow the Jamaat to contest elections; Ershad did. In 1986, the Jamaat won ten seats in Parliament, a figure which rose to eighteen in 1991, its best year. In 1996 it won three seats, seventeen in 2001, and two in 2008. In 2013, a court order ruled that the Jamaat could not be registered as a political party because it refused to change its constitution to align it with the Bangladesh constitution. Besides, many of its leaders were convicted in the war crimes trials and it had limited resources to fight elections. The current Parliament, therefore, does not have Jamaat representation.

For the Jamaat, the Awami League is an anathema, although in the past it has allied with the Awami League to fight the Ershad regime. The Jamaat had opposed Bangladesh's creation, and the Awami League was associated with the independence struggle. Hasina personified everything the Jamaat considered wrong—secular and liberal Bangladeshis supported her; politicians around her frequently raised the prospect of setting up the International Crimes Tribunal, which the Jamaat feared would target its leadership; and she was friendly to India. Jamaat sympathizers argue that the 1971 war was a civil war between two halves of a country and one of them seceded; the Liberation War narrative paints Pakistan as an occupying army from whose yoke Bangladesh emerged free. Jamaat sees the conflict as more nuanced than a simple question of West Pakistan attacking Bengalis. To argue that all Bengalis were for Bangladesh from March 1971 onwards was ridiculous. Jamaat lawyers and sympathizers I had met were Bengalis, and the lawyers were representing politicians who had opposed independence. It was Awami

League's assertion, and the belief of many, that some of the Jamaat leaders had committed war crimes, but the Jamaat consistently denied those charges.

Although Jamaat's electoral strength has been weak, it is undeniable that the influence of a more austere, hard Islam has spread within Bangladesh. To use the Indonesian analogy, if Bangladesh's aristocratic elite were like Java's priyayi and the bulk of its population abangan (that is, syncretic in beliefs and nominally Muslim), there was a visible and increasing number of people who began to look like senteri or devout Muslims. While at Independence Bangladesh professed secularism, over the years many of its young men, it found, were turning fundamentalist. *Runway*, the film by Catherine Masud and her late husband Tareque, offers a microcosm of Bangladeshi reality, with a hard-working mother toiling alone at home, selling milk yielded by a cow she had bought with a Grameen Bank loan; her husband working as a migrant labourer in the Middle East; her daughter working as a seamstress in a garment factory; and her son looking for jobs, including in a computer shop, not finding them, and turning fundamentalist. Indeed, with more and more young Bangladeshis going abroad to work, usually in austere Islamic countries of the Middle East, they have come under the spell of fundamentalist preachers. Upon return, they sometimes insist that their wives give up wearing saris and instead wear the hijab or even the jilbab with niqab, and they have stopped sending their daughters to schools and send their sons to madrasas, which are growing at an alarming rate in rural Bangladesh. New mosques are being built with money from the Gulf, and the government is powerless to do anything about it. Tahmima Anam's 2011 novel *The Good Muslim* traces the trajectory of a freedom fighter who embraces religion. Hiranmay Karlekar, former editor of the *Indian Express* and the *Hindustan Times* who had reported the Liberation War four decades ago, told me when we met in Delhi that the rise of fundamentalism is the single biggest threat Bangladesh faces. The book he has written on Bangladesh presents an apocalyptic vision of the future[196] but the society I saw during my visits did not match that dystopic vision.

One concern many in Bangladesh express quietly is the Jamaat's rising influence in the army. Bangladeshi journalists have spoken of incidents where soldiers have gone from house to house to check whether officers are saying their prayers at the right time. They also check if the wives and daughters of army officers are wearing proper, modest clothes. Some army officers' wives increasingly wear the salwar-kameez, and not the sari; they greet each other with salam alaikum and pepper their conversation with words like inshallah, alhamdunillah, and mashallah. Whether these are sartorial or cultural preferences or a sign of creeping Islamisation depends on the viewer's own preferences and prejudices, and those changes are not unique to the army, but also visible in the broader society.

One afternoon looking reflectively out of his window at his office at *The Daily Star*, Mahfuz Anam said: 'The rationale for the demand for a separate state for the Muslims of India was that such a state structure would help to preserve their religious identity and create an enabling environment for their future prosperity. The Muslims of Bengal accepted this argument and massively supported the Muslim League, making Pakistan a reality. But soon after 1947 the Bengali Muslims realized that while the new state protected their Islamic heritage it was not protecting their Bengali heritage. On the contrary it was threatening it. This threat was most dramatically brought home when Jinnah declared during his only visit to Dhaka in 1948, that Urdu will be the sole national language of Pakistan though Urdu was spoken by only 6 per cent of population compared to 56 per cent speaking Bengali.'

Anam continued: 'This shocked us and unleashed our nationalistic aspiration that lay dormant or was somehow side stepped within the all-India debate over the future of Muslims after India's independence. Thus from 1948 to 1971 the total energy of the Muslims here was devoted to preserving and promoting their Bengali identity leading to the birth of our language movement which ultimately transformed itself to our Liberation War of 1971.

So where are we now? Bangladesh was the outcome of our nationalistic aspiration, but it has not resolved the issue of what is the place of our Muslim heritage within the context of secular Bangladesh. To the secularists it is a non-issue. They say we are all Bengalis with some of us being Muslims while others are Hindus, Christian, Buddhists, and so on. To the Islamists we are Muslim first and Bengali later.

The revival of religion-based politics in independent Bangladesh and the fact that one of our two leading political parties, the BNP, propagates religion as a source of our identity, continuously gets a minimum of 30 per cent votes in all free elections, convinces me that the "Muslim-first or Bengali-first" is not a question as light as the secularists would like to believe. Maybe the issue can be better understood if we approach it from a cultural heritage point of view rather than religion. A Bengali Muslim is the inheritor of Buddhist, Hindu and Muslim civilisations with all their cultural, literary and other heritage. A Bengali Hindu also has Buddhist and Hindu heritage but has not been touched by the influence of Islam. So what does this additional heritage of the Bengali Muslim mean? Does it make them a separate nation, as the proponents of Pakistan had us believe in 1947? Or does it have no serious cultural impact as the secularists would want us to believe?'

He reflected on that point and added thoughtfully: 'I do not have an answer. But I believe that there is a serious question that lies unanswered here. It is this "unanswered" question that those who want to revive religion-based politics in Bangladesh constantly exploit. It is one of the incompleteness of our nationalist narrative and weakness of the theoretical basis of nationalistic thinking that we have not been able to build an over-arching intellectual framework that brings our Bengali and Islamic heritage together within a secular state of Bangladesh.'

The dilemma Mahfuz Anam articulates may seem existential to some— but the pulls Bangladesh has experienced, between secularism and Islam, between the madrasas and the regular schools, the debates about the position of women in the society, and the role of Hindus in the society—all these go to the heart of the question of the kind of nation Bangladesh wishes to be. And that includes the linguistic, ethnic, and religious minorities—Chakmas, Santhals, Garos, and indeed Biharis—all of that makes Bangladesh a rich cultural mix. And it is by turning to the tolerant strains of Islam, the inclusive and syncretic aspects of Hinduism, through the music of the Bauls, and the enlightened poetry of Tagore and Nazrul that Bangladesh can redeem the pledge and make Bangladesh truly Sonar Bangla.

◆

While the creative response to the churning within Bangladesh is still evolving, the Jamaat's monolithic worldview does not have much room for minorities. Among the first to feel the pain of Islamisation were the country's Hindus. Aroma Dutta discovered in 1983 that her ancestral home in Brahmanbaria on the Indian border in Comilla district was declared 'enemy property'. A rarely-used Pakistan-era law was prevalent in Bangladesh, under which property left behind by Hindus who had migrated to India in 1947 could be taken over by the state. Such property was declared 'enemy property'. In Dutta's case that provision was invoked and she was on the verge of losing her family home. So she rushed to Brahmanbaria and went to the court. The judge looked at the state's case and said that the home was indeed enemy property, as nobody lived there. When her lawyer asked the basis of his conclusion, the judge said that Dhirendranath Datta, in whose name the property was registered, had fled to India. But the lawyer said that wasn't true; Datta was a martyr of 1971.

The judge asked: 'If you say Dhirendranath Datta has not fled but that he has died, where is the death certificate? Produce it.'

At this, Aroma howled. Nightmarish visions of that night when her dadu was taken away returned. But the law was the law and she lost the case. Recalling that incident, Aroma told me: 'Then I realized: if this happens to me, to Dhirendranath Datta's granddaughter, and if I can't protect it, what would happen to the rest of the country? I told myself—no more crying, no more sitting at home doing nothing. I will do something more difficult. I will fight to change it.'

So she began researching cases of expropriation of property by looking at data going back to 1947 until 1971, and then from 1971 to 1983. And she began to catalogue how much was taken away from people under the law. It was a serious issue at the best of times, and she could not have chosen a more difficult moment to raise it. An economist from Dhaka University, Abul Barkat, joined hands with her. They scoured through data from the land registry and looked at a few sample districts where major parcels of property were taken. In 2000, Dutta's NGO, called PRIP, which was born out of the Private Rural Initiatives Program, a capacity-building development programme targeted at disadvantaged groups, published *An Inquiry into Causes and Consequences of Deprivation of Hindu Minorities in Bangladesh through the Vested Property Act*. The government had changed the name of the law from 'enemy property' to 'vested property', but the rest of the law had not been changed. 'Abandoned' property related to that left behind by people who went to Pakistan after '71, while property which was left by Hindus and other minorities and some Muslims was called 'vested'.

Their research found that in the 1990s through this Act some two million acres of land, property and other resources were confiscated and that 'the total loss of assets by Hindus (was estimated at) Taka 1,505,204 million', which was about 88 per cent of the prevailing GDP of Bangladesh. As many as 40 per cent of Bangladeshi Hindu families were affected by that law. Hindus lost 1.64 million acres of land, which is nearly half of the total land Hindus had owned and nearly 5 per cent of total land area of the country. Abul Barkat's analysis showed that the beneficiaries cut across party lines: 44 per cent of the beneficiaries were from the Awami League, 31.7 per cent from the BNP, 5.8 per cent from the Jatiyo Party, and 4.8 per cent from the Jamaat.

When the study was published, the BNP was in power, and it began to investigate PRIP. Dutta feared imminent arrest, so she took anticipatory bail. There have been more studies since Barkat's, but the important thing Barkat's book achieved was that it focused the attention of Parliament and they moved and amended the law. 'What we have lost cannot now be retrieved,' she said, 'but so many people have now got relief because of the changes.' There is a downside though, and Dutta said: 'The Jamaat is furious with me and has taken personal vendetta against me.'

She found another disturbing pattern: a rise in rape cases in villages where Hindus formed a sizeable minority, and the subsequent departure of Hindus from those villages, which enabled others to take over their property. Dutta told me: 'I didn't think much of it in the beginning. But then I saw that it wasn't sporadic. I tried to convince myself it can't be a pattern, but the evidence was hard to ignore.'

One day, a man came with three or four women and left them in front of her office. The women cried and banged the door. They asked her to help them. They were from Bhola, an island in southwestern Bangladesh. Many women were raped there, they said. They did not know why and they wanted help.

She called Mahfuz Anam at *The Daily Star* and asked if he and his reporters could spend some time listening to their stories. Anam invited them to his office and the journalists listened as the women narrated their tales. Anam was stunned; he shut his eyes and looked down, resting his head on the desk and asked plaintively: 'What do I do? What can I do?'

The newspaper then sent its reporters to the area and their research found that in 132 constituencies which had minority enclaves, there had been attacks on minorities. There was a clear pattern. Dutta says: 'The Jamaat was trying to scare minorities so that they did not come to vote.' Awami League votes were concentrated in those areas because most Hindus tended to vote for the Awami League.

The Daily Star published the stories and Dutta began lobbying to international human rights organizations and the Election Commission to ensure protection for Hindu voters. Amnesty International took up the matter, researched the cases and published a report. Many other human rights groups joined the campaign. Foreign embassies began pressuring the Bangladesh government to investigate these rights abuses.

Once the BNP had come to power in 2001 in a four-party alliance which included the Jamaat, things had taken a nasty turn for Dutta. 'My office was surrounded,' she said. They filed cases against her. She sought anticipatory bail. The government cut off her sources of funding and she could not send her daughter Esha to school for three years, nor organize medication for her ailing mother. Intelligence officials would visit her office, and the government tried to stop her organization from receiving foreign funds. In 2004 she went to the United States to provide testimony at a public hearing on minority rights in Bangladesh and she was told that she would be arrested upon return, so the US Ambassador came to the airport to receive her. He had informed other embassies too, so the government was unable to arrest her. Finally the European Union took up her case with the government. When the BNP's second term in office ended in 2006, one of the first things the caretaker government did was to restore the status of Aroma's institution and she began receiving funding legally again.

Did she ever feel she should leave Bangladesh and make her home elsewhere, I asked. She stared back as though I had asked something preposterous. 'Never,' she said. 'I don't wish even for a moment that I had lived in another country. This is home. Dadu lives here, so I am here. He had chosen not to leave. How can I leave now?' she said, as she broke down. 'I have no religion except this soil. It is soaked with the blood of my grandfather and my kaku. I don't want to leave this. I cannot part from it. After all the suffering, all the humiliation, this is still home. Living as a second-rate citizen is disrespectful and I don't like it. But this is my home. Ei amar bari achhe.'

While there are proportionately more Hindus in Bangladesh than in Pakistan, one undeniable statistical fact is that the Hindu population is shrinking. According to some demographic projections, by 2051, in absolute terms the Hindu population in Bangladesh would be the same as it was in 1974. Dipen Bhattacharya, an astrophysicist who teaches at a college in California, and writes on the Bangladesh-focused blog Alal o Dulal, blames the legacy of the 1947 partition and the failure of the state to safeguard the rights of religious minorities. He points out that while the Muslim population in India grew from 10 per cent in 1951 to 13.8 per cent in 2011, the proportion of minorities in both Pakistan and Bangladesh has gone down. In Bangladesh, the Hindu population fell from 22 per cent to 8.5 per cent in that period; in erstwhile West Pakistan, from 20-25 per cent in 1947 to below 2 per cent today. In absolute terms, the Hindu population has grown from 9.22 million in 1951 to 12.99 million in 2011 in Bangladesh, but in proportionate terms, the decline is steep—from 22 per cent to 8.5 per cent, because the Muslim population has grown far more rapidly (at 4.4 per cent, whereas the Hindu population growth is 0.7 per cent).

Another professor, Mohammed A. Hossain, is troubled by these developments. In a pained and sarcastic article that he wrote in early 2014 after another burst of violence against Hindus, he says: 'The ease with which Hindus suffer at the hands of the Muslims shows that after a few sanctimonious op-eds and weepy speeches, we get ready for more to do to them. Bangladesh suffers from a self-inflicted fantasy that we treat all equally...(but) we loot their property, burn their homes and try to drive them out, (and) we are really saying that this country can't be shared with everyone...Hindu repression will go on till nothing is left to be taken from them.'

If the position of Hindus in Bangladesh is one of the legacies of the war that the nation is continuing to come to terms with, another is the fate of the Urdu-speaking people in Bangladesh. Variously called 'Biharis' and 'stranded Pakistanis', they number in tens of thousands, and many live in congested shanties and are denied some fundamental rights. During the lead up to the country's liberation, the Biharis had sided with Pakistan—after all, they had migrated to East Bengal from Bihar because it was closer, and because it was going to be part of Pakistan. When the language movement rose against Pakistani and Urdu dominance, Biharis saw no future for them—they spoke Urdu, and the nationalism was Bengali. During the war many supported or became Razakars or joined the militia groups—Al-Badr and Al-Shams—and many perpetrated atrocities themselves, or collaborated with Pakistani troops which then committed atrocities, including massacres, mass rapes, and taking women into sexual slavery. As they spoke Urdu fluently, many of them felt closer to Pakistan than even to some of the Razakars, because many Razakars were Bengali.

As with any community, while there were those who had collaborated with the Pakistani troops and possibly committed or contributed to unspeakable acts, there were others who had done nothing and had even integrated with Bengalis, according to Safina Lohani. Many have inter-married, they speak Bengali, and see themselves as Bangladeshi. There were also Biharis who bravely offered refuge to frightened Hindus. The thought-provoking short film made by Tareque and Catherine Masud, *Naro Shundor* (The Barbershop) tells the story of a young Mukti Bahini activist trying to stay a step ahead of Pakistani forces who are looking for him, entering a Bihari barbershop to get his beard shaved, so that he would not be identified. The troops beat up his parents and ransack their home. They then enter the barbershop, where the barber is shaving his beard. When the Pakistani soldier asks if there is any 'Mukti' in the shop, the shop's manager calmly replies, in Urdu, that there are none.[197]

♦

Today, the majority of Biharis live in slums that have grown out of the camps that the International Committee for the Red Cross (ICRC) established in different parts of the country immediately after the war. There were 116 camps in Syedpur, Dinajpur, Rangpur, Bogra, Chittagong, Dhaka, and Narayanganj. These were meant to be temporary shelters and the ICRC and the UNHCR had taken the responsibility to resolve the issue. They prepared an options paper, offering options such as staying in Bangladesh, going to India, or going to Pakistan.

Based on that, the ICRC and the UNHCR appealed to the Pakistan government to take them back. Pakistan's priority was to get the 93,000 POWs back safely. Pakistan said identifying genuine Biharis would be difficult. Bangladesh too wanted Pakistan to take them back. The Biharis also wanted to go to Pakistan—they had chosen to be part of an Islamic nation, not a secular mishmash of Bengali nationalism. But Pakistan did not want them back, and the Biharis had neither the option nor the desire to return to India. Most of them continue to live in camps which are congested slums. They were called 'stranded Pakistanis'.

I went to two such camps. In 2012, I went to Geneva Camp, the largest such camp in Dhaka, with Khalid Hussain, an activist for the Bihari community, and in 2013, with the human rights lawyer Sara Hossain and her colleagues Showvik Das and Ishita Dutta at another camp in Mirpur. Geneva Camp has 25,000 people living cheek-by-jowl in an area of 135,000 square feet. Khalid has been campaigning for equal treatment and rights for Biharis or 'Urdu-speakers' who have chosen to remain in Bangladesh. Filmmaker Tanvir Mokammel has made a bold film, *Swapnabhumi* (The Promised Land) about the Bihari community, in which Khalid features.[198]

Geneva Camp looked like any large slum sprawling over land that builders covet. Its lanes are narrow and there is no proper drainage, so garbage floats through the sides of the lanes. The stench of human waste is overpowering. There are only 250 toilets for 25,000 people, I was told. The surface of the narrow lanes was uneven, and the homes were pressed close to one another. Most homes had only one room. The doors were kept open to let in the breeze and you could peek in, for the poor had no privacy. A group of children, some without clothes, started following us as we walked through the camp. Young schoolgirls, their heads covered, walked to their school; they smiled as I took photographs. A woman and her daughter were haggling over rickshaw fare with a driver who was also poor and wanted 20 takas for a journey that the two women insisted was worth only 15 takas. I overheard conversations in Bihari dialects and the sound of Bollywood songs coming from some homes. Vast amounts of biryani was being cooked in a giant pot, next to which on a big tawa puris were being fried. Meat was sold in large quantities. In small workshops saris were being woven, lungis stitched, and shawls knitted. Children were washing aluminum utensils in stagnant water—it was easy to see how quickly disease would spread. Mosquitoes hovered over us. Barbershops and cobblers, tinsmiths and mills grinding wheat into flour—this was a village of its own, humming with activity.

A generation had grown up in this slum, and another is doing so. Their citizenship status remains unclear. Bangladeshi officials say the Biharis have continued to remain in camps four decades after the war for their own security. There has been some progress in integrating them with the society outside the camps. On 18 May 2008 the High Court Division of the Supreme Court of Bangladesh approved citizenship and voting rights for about 150,000 people who were minors during the 1971 war. But full citizenship is still not easy to acquire. Khalid told me: 'We are all Bangladeshis and have national identity cards, however there is discrimination when people apply for passports in some places.' He runs a paralegal programme in the camps where paralegals help the camp residents to get birth certificates and passports, in Mymensingh, Syedpur and Khulna. In the bigger cities people with addresses in camps still find it difficult to get passports. 'But there is no doubt that we are Bangladeshis according to the Constitution and the citizenship law.'

'We are victims of 1971 because we speak the wrong language,' Khalid told me at a restaurant where we adjourned after the walk through Geneva Camp. 'We spoke Urdu, and so did the Pakistani state and the army, so Biharis were privileged when Pakistan was united. It is true that a large section of Urdu speakers didn't want Pakistan to break. They had lost everything in 1947 and they were told that India was only for Hindus, and so they clung to the idea of Pakistan. When they saw their dream breaking, they were hurt. Pakistani politicians also motivated them, saying Bengalis were like Hindus, and their culture is similar, and they are not very good people. Biharis lived in the cities and the Pakistani government also tried not to integrate them with Bengalis. Even today, if you ask the people in the camp here, or elsewhere in Mohammedpur, the interaction of Bengalis and Biharis is minimal.'

Today, about 300,000 Biharis live in camps all over the country. There may probably be as many more outside the camps. But Khalid told me that the moment even a well-integrated Bihari who has chosen Bangladesh as his home and tries to reclaim his property, he is warned—forget about your property, otherwise we will call you a war criminal. Bengali politicians of all parties issue false affidavits to take over Bihari property, he alleges. In this, the Bihari situation is not vastly different from that faced by Bangladesh's Hindus.

Khalid is sometimes taken aback by the insensitive remarks he hears even from people claiming to fight for human rights. The assistant of one of the activists who has worked hard to get the war crimes tribunals established once called Khalid a war criminal because they disagreed over an issue. 'I was born in 1981,' he protested. 'Then your father was a war criminal, and so are you,' he was told. 'After we do the trials of Bengali Razakars, we will go after you Biharis,' the same man told Khalid. Khalid agrees some Biharis committed horrendous acts in the war. As a result, he feels he and his generation have to bear the burden of the past.

◆

When the BNP's term ended in 2006, political instability and civil unrest had risen. And as per rules, a caretaker government was to have called fresh elections that year. There had been months of political standoff between Hasina and Khaleda over rules governing the elections and the army chief Lt. Gen. Moeen Ahmad compelled President Ijajuddin Ahmed to declare an Emergency and delay the election. The situation was volatile and violence was rising. There was growing disenchantment with political parties. Elections could not be held, and until 2008 Bangladesh was run by caretaker governments. There was also crisis with voters' lists, with enumerators haphazardly dropping the names of anyone who wasn't home when they came calling. A technocratic government was installed as caretakers, in a pattern similar to Thailand in the 1990s. Elections were finally called in late 2008 and Hasina was elected with a thumping majority, the scale of the win surprising even some Awami League leaders. The electoral support for the Jamaat had fallen to an all-time low, and the BNP was stunned by its electoral reverses. Winning 49 per cent of the popular vote and riding on a nine per cent swing, Sheikh Hasina's party increased its tally from 62 to 230 seats, giving it a handsome majority on a scale the party had not known since Mujib's era. Khaleda Zia saw her support fall by 8 per cent to 33.2 per cent, and her party returned only thirty MPs, down from 200. Former president Ershad, now out of jail, gained thirteen seats for his Jatiyo Party, whose parliamentary strength rose to twenty-seven.

Slowly, the appeals process of Mujib's assassins began to move. The appeals were heard in October 2009, and verdicts were awaited in late November.

In the campaign, former freedom fighters and an organization representing former sector commanders campaigned vigorously, saying 'crime wounds, justice heals', asking voters not to support candidates who they described as juddhoparadhi or war criminals. Popular songs condemning them were circulated widely among the voters. Freedom's orphans—the group of Bangladeshis who had lost their parents in the war, and had formed the organization Projonmo Ekattor—kept reminding the people of the past.

Asif Munier, whose father was among the intellectuals taken away by Al-Badr on 14 December 1971 and later killed at Rayer Bazar, said that Projonmo's rationale was to keep the memories of the martyrs alive, because it was not yet time for closure. There were too many answers not given, explanations not received, questions that were unresolved. 'Within the group we don't all think alike; we have our differences,' he told me. 'We are also perceived differently. Some look at us as unspoilt victims. We see ourselves as activists. We also see ourselves as catalysts. In the early 1990s when we were students we found that nobody really knew our stories, so we decided to organize the families of the martyred. In those days, we'd meet regularly and every day someone new would come to us with a heart-rending story about losing a father or a mother.'

The Awami League found that of its many campaign promises, the one that resonated with the new generation of voters was the promise to set up an international crimes tribunal. With its majority, it had the political capital to launch prosecutions. It had received massive support from the young. Many of those who voted for the Awami League weren't even born in 1971; they learned about the conflict only from hushed whispers—through memories of their parents or grandparents, rekindled when an anniversary came, and a promising young student's photograph on the wall reminded the family of what was lost.

By the time the elections were held in 2008, a generation of voters had grown which had known only an independent Bangladesh, with no real memory of Mujib or the politics that led to the creation of Bangladesh. These young people had studied textbooks prepared during the BNP years, and those textbooks often underplayed Mujib's role and emphasized Zia's contribution to the freedom struggle.

Immediately upon assuming power, Sheikh Hasina demanded that the unfinished business of her father's killers' trials be completed. The verdicts came swiftly. The accused were sentenced to death. The punishments were carried out immediately.

Many secular Bangladeshis had hoped that the party would use its majority to revive the country's commitment to its secular roots. But they were surprised by the peculiar compromise Hasina Wajed struck. Bangladesh was a secular country again, but it would also maintain Islam as a state religion, however mutually contradictory that might seem. Awami League's secular urban supporters thought that the party would do away with the religious parts in the Constitution. But some of its leaders thought that doing so would antagonize a large section of the people. Sultana Kamal, who admits that she is not political, was perplexed and said: 'The Awami League knows that we (secular Bangladeshis) have no option but them, so they take advantage of that. Why do all the politicians who get power think that people of Bangladesh want Islam to be the state religion? What do they read or learn from the people's attitude, the way they dress, the way they move, and the festivals they celebrate? And so now we have brought back secularism but we also have a state religion. How they can go together is anyone's guess.'

The government then established tribunals to prosecute international crimes, examined in more detail in the next chapter. The tribunal would polarize the population between those who wanted to let bygones be bygones and those who sought justice; those who wanted accountability and those who sought revenge; and those who believed in a secular Bangladesh and those who wanted religion to be predominant. The prosecutions meandered their way through the tribunal and at the end of five years, all the accused—all but two who were Jamaat-e-Islami politicians—were found guilty, and four have been executed so far.

The fundamental change the Awami League brought about towards the end of its term was to end the practice of caretaker governments administering the country between elections. The party had a large majority which allowed it to change the law so that it would not have to resign and let a caretaker government[199] take over. The Awami League's rationale was that Bangladesh was now a mature democracy, and its politicians could be trusted to hold fair elections. The BNP clearly disagreed and said it would boycott the elections. The Jamaat had been disqualified because it had declined to amend its charter to make it consistent with the new secular principles of the Bangladesh Constitution.

A BNP boycott would erode the credibility of the elections, so in 2013 Hasina proposed an all-party government in which she was willing to invite Khaleda to join. But Khaleda declined—she insisted that a caretaker government must be set up. Khaleda's argument was sound but it did not prevail. Her dilemma was acute. The Jamaat was its ally and had street strength, but it was now deregistered as a political party, and the BNP needed the Jamaat's street support. Without the Jamaat, Khaleda felt if she agreed to participate in elections, she would legitimize the Awami League, and might even lose, if the elections were not free and fair.

Senior politicians in both parties attempted to get Khaleda and Hasina to speak, hoping that they would settle their differences. The two women were to talk on the phone. The call took place, but it was a disaster. The 37-minute conversation offers a fascinating insight into the dysfunctional relationship between the two women.

Over the years, their differences have ranged from the profound (whether Mujib was the father of the nation) to the symbolic (Khaleda claims her birthday is on 15 August, although her marriage certificate and school leaving certificate show different dates, and wry observers in Dhaka say she has chosen to celebrate her birthday on the 15th because it was the day Mujib was assassinated, so as to spite the Awami League leadership), the personal (Khaleda's sons have been in jail on corruption charges), and the petty (Hasina forced Khaleda to move from her large house in the Dhaka Cantonment which was sold to her for a token amount after Zia's assassination. Hasina and her family had earlier been allocated the prime ministerial residence in perpetuity under one of her tenures; this was later annulled by Khaleda Zia's government). Both have severely hurt Bangladesh's economic competitiveness by frequently calling hortals which stall all industrial activity.

Their conversation quickly turned into an infantile exercise of finger-pointing. Several newspapers published[200] a leaked transcript, which makes for fascinating but depressing reading. After a brief, polite exchange, their conversation quickly degenerates into the sort of accusations and counter-accusations that sound like a quarrel between teenagers and not two individuals close to their seventies who have been heads of government.

Hasina: I called you around noon, you didn't pick up.

Khaleda: This is not correct.

Hasina: I want to inform you that...

Khaleda: You have to listen to me first. You said you called me, but I didn't get any call around the time you mentioned.

Hasina: I called your red phone.

Khaleda: My red phone has been dead for years. You run the government, you should know that. And if you intended to call, you should have sent people to fix the phone yesterday. They should at least check whether the phone is working or not.

Hasina: The red phones always work.

Khaleda: Send people over now and to see whether the phone is working.

Hasina: You were prime minister yourself. You know that the red phones always work.

Khaleda: They always work? But mine is not working at all.

Hasina: It is working perfectly. At least, it was working when I called.

Khaleda: I checked it just recently. You just can't tell the truth.

Hasina: There is no reason for me not to tell the truth. I have called several times.

Khaleda: How can a dead phone come to life all of a sudden? Is your phone so powerful that it will bring life to my dead telephone?

And it got worse, reading like an extract from the script of an absurd drama. They then turned to the main topic—the negotiations for an all-party government and the next elections. Hasina invited Khaleda to a meeting on 28 October. Khaleda first said she would come with her colleagues, but when Hasina agreed, Khaleda suddenly said she would not come. Hasina requested Khaleda to stop the strikes, arson and violence. Khaleda shot back: 'Killing people, throwing fires is in your habit. Not ours. We are not in the habit of doing things like that. You torch people, kill people.... Therefore the hortal will be on. It will end at 6 p.m. on the 29th. We can talk afterwards.'

Hasina reminded her of past wrongs she had suffered—a grenade attack at her rally in 2004. Khaleda said her party wasn't involved, and claimed that the Awami League had engineered it.

Hasina: You are only one doing the talking. You are not allowing me to talk.

Khaleda: Why would I do that? You are asking questions, I am replying.

Hasina: I am not getting a chance to speak.

Khaleda: You are only talking about the hortal. The hortal will not be revoked. After our programme is over...

Hasina: Will you keep killing people in the name of hortal?

Khaleda: I don't kill people. You kill people. You killed nine people yesterday...

Hasina: We don't do the politics of murder; on the contrary I see...

Khaleda: This is an old habit of yours. Since after independence in '71, you have been killing people. You killed so many people, did you forget that?

Hasina: We killed people in '71?

Khaleda: Yes of course, after '71.

Later, Hasina brought up the killing of her parents and Khaleda celebrating her birthday on 15 August.

Hasina: When you cut cakes on August 15...

Khaleda: It is my birthday, I will cut a cake.

Hasina: When you encourage the killers of Bangabandhu and cut a cake on August 15...

Khaleda: If anyone is born on August 15, can that person not celebrate his birthday? You make these accusations all the time. Stop this. Ziaur Rahman gave you a new life. [He was] a gentleman and that was why you could do politics as Awami League, otherwise it would have been impossible.

Hasina: You have come to our Dhanmondi 32 residence on many occasions. You have seen Russell in that house.

Khaleda: Drop this topic. I do not want to talk about this. I have made my statement, leave this, we can start something new. If you agree, we can hold a dialogue. If you want to talk, it has to be after the hortal.

Hasina: You will not withdraw the strike?

Khaleda: No, we cannot do that. This is not just my decision, this is a decision of my alliance. How can I change it on my own?

Hasina: Call others in your party and tell them.

Khaleda: No, there is no time for that now. The manner in which you unleashed police on our men, everybody is on the run.

Hasina: Why would we do that?

Khaleda: Who else could have done it? Do [the police] act on my command? You are making [the police] raid the houses of our men. Police are taking them away.

Hasina: It is natural that the police will raid houses of bombers.

Khaleda: You are the bombers. You blast the bombs and put the blame on us. This is an old tradition of yours. Do not come back to the same old discussion. I want to say: if you can talk after October 29, we are interested.

[Both leaders talked at once and the voices were garbled]

Hasina: It seems like you are making a speech in front of the camera.

Khaleda: I do not have any camera in front of me, I am alone.

Hasina: Same with me, there is no camera at my end either.

And it went on. There was another five-minute exchange about her phone, with Khaleda insisting it was dead and Hasina saying it wasn't.

Hasina: Drop your weapons, come to talks… Withdraw your hortal. I am inviting you.

Khaleda: It is not possible. But for that to happen, you have to say that you have accepted our demand for a caretaker. Only then can the hortal be withdrawn.

Hasina: Then what is left there to talk about?

Khaleda: No. There are many processes of a dialogue.

Hasina: Though I have 90 per cent seats, I have asked you for an all-party government.

Khaleda: An all-party government is not possible. We will not participate in an all-party government. Tell me, do you agree on the caretaker? If yes, then we will withdraw hortal.

Hasina would not agree to a caretaker government, and Khaleda would not attend the meeting.[201]

Eventually, the BNP boycotted the elections and the Awami League won the elections with 150 candidates elected unopposed, and with virtually no significant opposition (except Ershad's Jatiyo Party). But by all accounts, Hasina's was a pyrrhic victory.

◆

Dhaka's intellectual elite had been wishing for what is called the 'minus-two' solution—that is, a political future without either of the two women at the helm. It is unlikely to happen. This isn't because of any shortage of talented people in Bangladesh: as the popular joke goes, the country runs because of its NGOs and in spite of its government. Bangladesh has made significant strides in improving its development indicators, leaving India, and indeed Pakistan, behind on some counts. But Bangladesh's army of NGOs deserves much credit for that. NGO leaders have proved themselves to be capable administrators, but they cannot win an election unless they join one of the parties and run from a constituency where their victory is assured. The Nobel Laureate Muhammad Yunus was once expected to take the political plunge—a prospect which rattled both major parties. Yunus did explore a political role in 2007 during the caretaker era, but gave up the idea. But the Awami League attacked him after it came to power. It removed him from the managing directorship of the Grameen Bank, the microfinance institution he had established, on the pretext of his being ten years over the age of retirement and launched investigations concerning financial impropriety. Later, when the World Bank's presidency opened up, Hasina proposed Yunus as a possible candidate, apparently sarcastically, as if to placate Yunus's supporters abroad and make him irrelevant in Bangladesh.

The type of breakdown in relationship between Hasina and Khaleda would matter less if it were a tiff among two neighbours over a social faux pas. But Bangladesh is a country facing a plethora of internal and external challenges. And yet the two women who have ruled the nation for more than two decades now appear fundamentally incapable of rising above their narrow interests. Old hatreds are still remembered as though they occurred yesterday, as though the bloodshed is fresh, and in some ways it is—for neither Mujib's house in Dhanmondi nor Zia's memorial in Chittagong has wiped away the bloodstains from the walls and carpets. Both sides want some atonement from the other, some way to get even, but both are tone-deaf about each other's needs and continue to try and humiliate the other.

Think of the crises the country faces: Bangladesh is one of the countries most likely to get affected by climate change. If Himalayan glaciers melt, vast parts of the country will go under water. Char islands would disappear and many low-lying areas would be lost forever. The country's huge population needs jobs, and its men increasingly find that the only places where they can get those jobs are in Southeast Asia or West Asia, where they must do back-breaking work building roads, airports, stadiums, and office towers. Bangladesh's army is reluctant to take over the country not only because of international repercussions, but because, as Zafar Sobhan, executive editor at *The Dhaka Tribune* puts it: 'The principal source of financial security for [the army's] military personnel is UN peace keeping missions. No Bangladesh army chief will break the consensus of the international community and risk isolating his regime. To act in contravention of international public opinion or international law would not only run the risk of incurring crippling economic sanctions, but of the Bangladesh army losing its lucrative UN peace keeping missions.'[202] International peacekeeping duty is often straightforward and tightly mandated. It becomes a neat little earner for the army, and easier work than managing a country.

With the army less willing to step in than in the past, with no other party or individual able to capture the imagination of the nation, and with the two women turning political dialogue into a soap opera, Bangladesh is stuck in a political quagmire. The future will reveal more of the same: both Hasina and Khaleda have sons who are considered likely heirs to their mothers. The rivalry will then go on to the next generation, taking on an operatic dimension: of an epic where the outcome is known, the chorus keeps warning but the players keep repeating the follies of the past as they go through their motions, and the show goes on, chronicling a disaster foretold.

ELEVEN

JUDGEMENT DAY

'The struggle of man against power is the struggle of memory against forgetting', Milan Kundera has written in his memorable novel, *The Book of Laughter and Forgetting.*[203] Kundera was writing about the need for the people who lived on the periphery of the Soviet Union to hold dear the memories of a past being obliterated as Soviet tanks marched into Prague in 1968 (as they had in Budapest in 1956).

In Bangladesh, men like Mofidul Hoque, founder-trustee of the Muktijoddha Jadughor, the Liberation War Museum in Dhaka, tried doing precisely that: the museum displayed war posters and memorabilia, maintained a library, archived documents, recorded oral histories, sent buses with material to schools in remote parts of the country, held seminars, and encouraged children to ask their grandparents to tell them stories of the war and share stories with each other, draw art, and ensure that nobody would forget.

Hoque told me that the museum was meant to create a permanent record of the cruelties. He took me to see mass graves on a Sunday. As we drove to Dhaka's outskirts one day, he told me, 'The tragedy of Pakistan is that they have imposed there today what they could not impose here in 1971. We have to look at Pakistan today to realize what we could have become. Bangladesh was never meant to be like that.' Months later when I met Peter Kann at his home in New Jersey, he would say something similar: 'Pakistan has turned logically into the direction it would have taken anyway, and to that extent Bangladesh was lucky to leave that train.'

We reached a small park set between two buildings which had garment factories. The plot was about 2,800 square feet. It was neat and clean. There was a garden, and along the walls death camps of other wars and places where mass atrocities had occurred were listed: Armenia, Nazi Germany, Buchenwald, Treblinka, Dachau, Auschwitz, Ravensbruck, Mauthausen-Gusen, Bergen-Belsen, and Terezin. And then there were numbers—estimates of people who died in various genocides—Indonesia, 1.2 million; Vietnam,

3 million; Bangladesh, 3 million; Cambodia, 1.7 million; Yugoslavia, 225,000; Rwanda, 1 million; Afghanistan, 2 million; Guatemala, 200,000; East Timor, 200,000; Sudan, 2 million.

This was a mass grave. It was called the Jalladkhana Memorial.

Hoque was in a philosophical mood that morning. Reflecting on the idea of nationhood, he said: 'Pakistan was Ben Anderson's imagined community but Bangladesh was always a real nation', referring to the academic's seminal concept that nation-states are imagined communities—they are social constructs imagined by people who perceive themselves as being part of a group. Bangladesh, he argued, was a more cohesive idea than Pakistan was.

I saw a poem inscribed on the wall:

Sakkhi Banglar rokto bheja mati
Sakkhi akasher chondro tara
Bhuli nai shohider kono smriti
Bhulbo na kichhui amra

This blood-stained soil is our witness
So is the sky and so are the stars
We will not forget the memories of martyrs
We will not forget anything.

Hoque said that when they decided to consecrate this grave, initially the neighbourhood was concerned about crowding. But they have now accepted their new neighbours. Visitor arrivals varied between a few dozen to a few hundred. The day before my visit, 256 visitors had come to the grave. A song from a Hindi film played in the background as we walked. A river ran alongside. Hoque pointed out the river and said one reason there were many graves near the water was that the Pakistani army often killed people along the river because it made it easier to dispose off the bodies.

There is a bell you can ring to enter the mass grave as if it were a sacred place. 'One has to enter without shoes, like people do in a temple or mosque. The idea of ringing the bell has been drawn from the famous lines of John Donne,' Mofidul Hoque told me, referring to Donne's 'Meditation XVII'. Hoque consulted the records and said that seventy skulls and 5,392 bones and belongings had been found at this mass grave. The museum authorities are now trying to identify the remains and associate them with the stories of the people who died. 'We would like to link the families and recreate the bonds,' he said. Inside, there are some personal effects—purses and gamchhas. A copy of the Genocide Convention, which the UN adopted on 9 December 1948, judgments of the Nuremberg and Tokyo tribunals which prosecuted Nazi and Imperial Japanese Army war criminals, the Rome Statute which set up the International Criminal Court, and a copy of Bangladesh's 1973 law setting up its tribunal are displayed.

Staying true to Kundera's call—to remember and to repel the tendency to forget—wasn't going to be easy in Bangladesh. For decades the country was ruled by leaders who did not want to dwell too much in the past, or that part of the past which did not conveniently fit their own narratives. Collective amnesia spreads quickly, like a virulent infection, and its power can be seductive when there are other distractions. It numbs the senses. In Bangladesh, it spread through the country like the mist rising from the Padma, making familiar landmarks disappear in the fog. Hoque was busy fighting that fog.

◆

The path to justice is not simple. Too often after armed conflict the interests of victims have had to make way for political expediency. Memorialisation is important but it isn't enough. Victims need closure. Establishing the mechanism for administering justice requires strong public and political will, as well as substantial resources. It also requires a secure context, where witnesses can testify, judges can operate, lawyers can argue, and the process is transparent and accountable.

The idea of prosecuting mass atrocities after armed conflict goes back to the 1940s. Soon after World War II ended, the victorious allies set up tribunals in Nuremberg and Tokyo to prosecute Nazi and Japanese war criminals. Those trials were swift and so were the verdicts, even though there was philosophical criticism. Radhabinod Pal,[204] an Indian judge who was appointed to the Tokyo Tribunal in 1946, called the trial process 'an exercise in victors' justice', and dissented from the majority verdicts, in which Japanese defendants were found guilty.

While those two tribunals established the principle that grave abuses would not go unpunished, it had been difficult to pursue justice for wartime atrocities until the end of the Cold War. Securing justice for international crimes requires international agreement about what constitutes a crime and whether the accused should be tried. In the divisive mood during the Cold

War, when an enemy's enemy became a friend regardless of his own record, prosecutions were impossible, and indeed, there was no international court.

Ending conflict often required all sorts of compromises, including granting immunity to commanders or political leaders who had, quite literally, blood on their hands. There have been breaches of the laws of war, which date back to the Hague conventions of 1899 and 1907 and later the Geneva conventions, in most cases of armed conflict. Political exigencies have usually overridden the justice and accountability imperative, and people who should have faced prosecution have often gone unpunished. Some truce agreements even allowed perpetrators of grave abuses to office in power-sharing arrangements; sometimes they are given immunity and allowed to leave the country and live in exile.

The end of the Cold War created conditions in which the Rome Statute was adopted in 1998, leading to the establishment of the International Criminal Court (ICC) in 2002. For a case to be tried at the ICC, the UN Security Council can refer a specific conflict or situation to the ICC. Besides, the ICC can on its own try international crimes if these are committed since the Court was set up or after a country ratified the statute. Those provisions are unlikely to change, which is one procedural reason the ICC cannot take up cases of the 1971 war.

There is the concern of politicisation of the ICC. The United States withdrew from the ICC soon after President George W. Bush took office, saying the US had its own robust judicial procedures to deal with war crimes, and could take care of itself. It was also concerned that US troops operating abroad could get prosecuted. The US however supports time-bound, conflict-specific courts, and recently supported the French-sponsored resolution to refer the situation in Syria to the ICC.

The United Nations has set up several ad hoc tribunals to deal with specific conflicts. The International Criminal Tribunal for Yugoslavia was set up in 1993 in The Hague; the International Criminal Tribunal for Rwanda came into being in 1994 in Arusha, Tanzania; and the Special Court for Sierra Leone was established in 1996 in Freetown, Sierra Leone. In 2003, the Extraordinary Chambers in the Courts of Cambodia was set up, although with limited international support.

Why those conflicts, and why not others? The selectiveness in seeking justice is also problematic. These courts are not without controversy. African heads of government have rightly pointed out the disproportionate amount of prosecutions launched against African leaders at a time when conflicts in Sri Lanka, Syria, Israel-Palestine, and indeed, Afghanistan and Iraq have not been investigated. Thabo Mbeki, former South African president, and Mahmood Mamdani, a Columbia University professor, wrote recently: 'A growing number of countries in the African Union advocated withdrawal from the International Criminal Court. Instead, the debate has focused on the motives of African leaders, not on the inadequacy of court trials as a response to politically driven mass violence. The ICC is built on the model of Nuremberg. But mass violence is more a political than a criminal matter. Unlike criminal violence, political violence has a constituency and is driven by issues, not just perpetrators.'[205] Ignoring politics, and focusing only on the crime does not serve the purpose of justice, they argue; it might even create conditions for the crimes to recur.

The Bangladeshi case was complicated because the Pakistani POWs were never in Bangladeshi custody. They were taken to India, and India and Pakistan agreed on an exchange of POWs which led to the return of thousands of Pakistani POWs, including 195 officers and men against whom Bangladesh claimed to have credible evidence of war crimes. Bangladesh went along with the compromise because Pakistan assured Bangladesh it would try the 195 — but it never did.

Pakistan did set up a commission of inquiry under Justice Hamoodur Rahman. It estimated that around 26,000 civilians had died during the war. The commission presented its first report in July 1972. In 1974 the commission was reopened to allow the released POWs to testify. Seventy-two people recorded evidence, including Lt. Gen. A.A.K. Niazi, who commanded the Pakistani forces in the east, Maj. Gen. Rao Farman Ali and Maj. Gen. Jamshed and others who held command of various divisions, including senior naval and air force commanders. Senior civilian personnel also testified.

Hamoodur Rahman submitted the report to Prime Minister Bhutto on 23 October 1974, who promptly classified it, fearing that the report would demoralize the army and may even prompt an ambitious general to stage a coup. When a year later Hamoodur Rahman asked Bhutto about what was being done about the report, Bhutto reportedly said that the report was missing. It was lost, or stolen and could not be found anywhere. Hamoodur Rahman then asked the chief of staff, Gen. Zia-ul-Haq, but he too said the report was lost.

In 2000, Pakistani media claimed that the report was at the military headquarters. The Indian magazine *India Today* got a copy and released its contents. The Pakistani newspaper *Dawn* published the supplementary report, which was critical of Yahya Khan (who had died in 1980), the following day. Later that year Pakistan formally declassified the full report and made it public. Nobody was prosecuted. Gen. Pervez Musharraf, who ruled Pakistan at the time, said the story of 1971 was not only one of a military defeat but also a political debacle, and singling out generals alone, as the report did, was not fair.

The report accused the army of carrying out wanton arson, mass killings, the killing of intellectuals and burying them in mass graves, and selectively killing Bengali officers, civilians, businessmen and industrialists, raping a large number of women, and targeting and killing Hindus. The report also accused the military commanders for surrendering too soon and blamed the military for its role in running the country since Ayub Khan's coup in 1958 which it said had eroded the combat readiness of the army. It criticized military tactics, dismissing some attacks on India as militarily unsound. The report remarked: 'Even responsible service officers have asserted before us that because of corruption resulting from such involvement, the lust for wine and women and greed for lands and houses, a large number of senior army officers, particularly those occupying the highest positions, had lost not only their will to fight but also their professional competence.' The report called for a public trial of Yahya Khan and other senior military officers, including Gen. Abdul Hamid Khan, Lt. Gen. S.G.M.M. Pirzada, Lt. Gen. Gul Hasan, Maj. Gen. Umar and Maj. Gen. Mitha; five other lieutenant generals and three brigadier generals were to be tried for willful neglect of duty—these included Niazi, Jamshed, M. Rahim Khan, Irshad Ahmad Khan, B.M. Mustafa, and others.

Niazi, who bore much of the blame, used his interview with *India Abroad* newspaper to challenge the commission for exonerating Gen. Tikka Khan, Shahibzada Yaqoob Ali Khan, and Rao Farman Ali. He blamed Yaqoob for aggravating the crisis in East Pakistan and marvelled over the fact that after 'having messed up everything, Yaqoob deemed it fit to desert his post and resign, while taking cover behind his conscience. He should have been sent to the gallows for betraying the nation. However Bhutto restored his rank and sent him as ambassador to the USA', he complained. He added: 'Bhutto was afraid of making it [the report] public given the fact that he was equally responsible for the circumstances that finally led to the dismemberment of Pakistan.' He also named Tikka's action of 25 March 'barbaric', because of which Tikka earned 'the name of butcher'. He praised his forces for being 'a small, tired and ill-equipped garrison' which somehow completed all given tasks 'under the worst possible conditions against overwhelming odds', as against the western garrison which surprised India with an attack and yet capitulated within ten days and lost 8,800 sq. km. of territory.

Niazi was livid that he was being made the scapegoat. He quoted the Indian brigadier Shahbeg Singh telling him: 'Your goose is cooked, sir. They have decided to put the whole blame on you and your command.'

Bangladesh's hopes to make the Pakistani army accountable were dashed when Bhutto claimed that the report was lost, and those expectations vanished entirely after Mujib was assassinated and Khondaker Mostaq Ahmad praised the assassins. The Awami League was weakened, and neither Zia, nor Ershad, nor the others who ruled Bangladesh for brief periods, showed any interest in pursuing those cases. But victims and survivors clung to hopes. As time passed, many died; witnesses moved on with their lives; some perpetrators disappeared in Pakistan; a few became prominent politicians in Bangladesh.

◆

Justice is slow in Bangladesh. According to the inspector-general of prisons, some 47,000 people are still awaiting trial. And the prisons are overcrowded. According to GIZ, the German development agency which is funding a prison reform programme in Bangladesh, the country has some 66,000 prisoners, although its prisons can hold only about half those numbers.[206] There is shortage of judges and the poor are not guaranteed legal aid.

As I travelled through the country, I heard the demand for justice from all strata of society. Fishermen whom I met on riverboats, rickshaw-pullers in Dhaka, birangonas in Kushtia, lawyers in the high court, bankers in Motijheel, Dhaka's commercial district, pacifists in Noakhali, and academics in Cox's Bazaar—they all wanted justice, and they were not necessarily Awami League supporters. Late one December night in a room in a hut without any lights in the Chars, the villages on riverine islands mired in extreme poverty, I sat surrounded by twenty farmers huddled together shivering in cold. They told me they were waiting for justice. All of them had tragic stories to share—women they knew who were raped, young brothers dragged away, tortured and killed, homes burnt, crops razed, and those who had boats had to surrender those to the Pakistani army. They blamed Punjabi soldiers and Bihari Razakars; they lamented the forced departures of Hindu neighbours and young women taken away into sexual slavery. They wanted those collaborators tried.

Earlier in Chuknagar, I had walked with Ershad Ali Morel towards the tree where he had found the infant girl Sundari and saved her life. He had seen his father die when a Pakistani soldier had shot him in their field. His humane impulse prevailed even at such an emotional moment—he thought of someone less fortunate than him and gave Sundari a new lease of life, as she lay, an infant, crying at the breast of her murdered mother.

I asked Ershad Ali: 'If you were to meet that soldier again, what would you do?'

'I would behead him,' he said immediately. 'Then I would cut his body into pieces and throw it for the dogs.'

Many such voters, from all parts of the country, had voted for the Awami League for a range of reasons. But the promise to end the culture of impunity resonated with many voters, including the young. There were risks. Reopening old wounds can lead to further violence and divide the nation. Given the bitterly partisan nature of Bangladeshi politics, some wondered if the real reason for the trials was to cause permanent damage to the BNP's alliance with the Jamaat, so that the Jamaat would disappear and the BNP would find it impossible to get elected on its own without the Jamaat's street power.

The Awami League was taking a calculated risk when it announced that it would set up the tribunals: political support for the Jamaat was at an all-time low—in the elections it had won only two seats—and the BNP was on the ropes, its strength having been decimated. In 2009, the timing for establishing the tribunals seemed right—in two years, Bangladesh would celebrate the 40th anniversary of its independence. The accused, the alleged perpetrators, the victims and survivors, and the witnesses, were growing old; the evidence against them was increasingly reliant on people's memories. There wasn't much time left.

As a step to end the culture of impunity, Bangladesh's decision to set up the tribunals was commendable. And doing this in a home-grown court where there was no possibility of an international process, was even more so.

The Awami League government set up the Bangladesh International Crimes Tribunal in 2010. The Bangladesh tribunal is different from other international courts and tribunals. It is established to prosecute international crimes, but it is not an international tribunal—that distinction is important.

It means unlike at the UN-appointed tribunals, all judges and lawyers are Bangladeshi, and not necessarily experts in laws covering international crimes. And they operate under national law, whether made by statute or through judgments of the higher courts. And while they draw on the interpretations of international courts related to international crimes, they are not bound by these, and while they draw on laws related to international crimes, the punishment is as per Bangladeshi law.

Its biggest impact is when the death penalty is awarded. Neither the ICC nor the UN-assisted international tribunals set up for other conflicts have provision for the death penalty. Indeed, the trend worldwide is to abolish the death penalty, but Bangladesh retains it, which is one reason why countries that have abolished the death penalty will not extradite men accused of Mujib's assassination to Bangladesh. Likewise, the United Kingdom is unlikely to extradite one of the men the tribunal has convicted after a trial in absentia — Chowdhury Mueenuddin, a British citizen of Bangladeshi origin — given the death penalty provision, as well as concerns his lawyers have expressed about the trial process. (During the early stages of the trial, Bangladesh said it would seek his extradition, but no formal request was made to Britain).

Bangladesh's decision to impose the death penalty has placed the human rights community in a major dilemma. Groups like Amnesty International and Human Rights Watch have campaigned for years against impunity and would normally be expected to laud Bangladesh's efforts to end the immunity enjoyed by people accused of war crimes. But both human rights groups are also campaigning to abolish the death penalty, and Bangladesh's use of death penalty in such cases makes it harder for them to support the process of justice.

I asked human rights lawyers in Bangladesh why the country awards the death penalty. After all, the men accused of war crimes are now in their seventies, and when I saw some of them at the tribunals, they looked frail and old. A banker told me: 'I can understand the human rights concern. But why is the concern raised only in these cases? Many criminals are awarded the death penalty for murders they commit. Why doesn't Amnesty International or Human Rights Watch get involved to protect those individuals?'(Actually they often do, but that work doesn't get noticed).

Whenever people perceive double standards, they start believing in conspiracies. And in Bangladesh the growing perception is that the tribunal's critics are influenced by Saudi Arabian money and lobbying. The Bangladesh law minister claimed that lobbyists have spent $25 million to influence international opinion, although no evidence has been offered. Bangladesh has also since appointed an international firm to present its views.

The reference to 'Saudi money' is instructive. Many Bangladeshis have been going to Saudi Arabia for work and are returning influenced by Wahhabi Islam. The Saudi leadership would presumably not want the Jamaat leadership to disappear. Jamaat's critics in Bangladesh argue that by defending the Jamaat leaders, international human rights groups are serving the Saudi agenda. That may be coincidental, and unfair to the international human rights groups. But while these groups say their response is principle-driven, their critics from within Bangladesh's human rights community say that the international human rights groups have got it wrong. They are ending up uncritically allying with the Jamaat, and they should question how the Jamaat itself detracts from and denies human rights. International human rights groups are rightly concerned about procedures because they always uphold the principle of fair trials. But by not stressing the importance of ending impunity sufficiently loudly, they do not see the point secular groups in Bangladesh are making— that the fundamentalists, whose rights the international human rights groups are defending, respect human rights only when it suits them, and forget all about protecting the rights of others when they are in power.

The question of domestic political considerations is unavoidable. Observers in Bangladesh and outside, including Jamaat and BNP supporters have speculated that the Awami League has set up the tribunal as an elaborate ruse to eliminate the Jamaat as a political force, and by doing so, permanently weakened the BNP. Jamaat supporters have said that the tribunal is an assault by atheists and secular Bangladeshis aimed at delegitimizing the role of religion in Bangladesh. (All but two of the accused are from the Jamaat.) At the same time, during my travels through the country, I have met dozens of people, not connected with one another and not necessarily politically active, who support the tribunal.

In several villages we drove through, we would see lists of names on the walls of schools or near the village square. The lists were of two types. One listed the names of people who had died during the war. They were the martyrs. The other list named people accused of being Razakars. There was a sense of vigilante justice at work here—the individuals named as Razakars had no way to get their names erased, whether or not they were guilty. Gouranga

Nandy, a journalist in Khulna told me that what the villagers knew earlier by word of mouth is now getting known publicly because of these boards. A social activist I met in a village along the Khulna-Jessore road explained to me: 'We are listing only bad people. We are naming them. Their names are now going to get spoiled.' True, but how was he certain that those were, indeed, bad people? What if they were innocent? 'Everybody knows,' he said, dismissing my question. At a meeting at the House of Lords in London a Bangladeshi activist confidently asserted 'We have all the evidence', when a senior executive of the Human Rights Watch was explaining why it was so important for the evidence to be clear and proper. Bangladesh needs real justice, not mob justice, nor trials by media or hearsay. It is entirely in the interest of Bangladesh to ensure that the trial process is exemplary, that evidence is gathered scrupulously, and there are no doubts about the verdict. For the sake of the victims, Bangladesh must ensure that the trials are fair.

◆

Then there is the question of numbers. If the Hamoodur Rahman Commission's estimate of 26,000 deaths is too low, there are questions about the number of deaths that the Bangladesh government has claimed—three million. Bangladeshis also describe what happened in 1971 as genocide.

Genocide has a specific meaning in international law, which categorizes mass atrocities during armed conflict as *war crimes, crimes against humanity,* and *genocide. War crimes* include the murder of civilians in times of war, the expulsion of people from their homes and communities, the running of forced labour camps and the indiscriminate destruction of cities or villages not justified by military necessity. *Crimes against humanity* are defined as widespread or systematic attacks against civilians—not always during a war—and these include murders, deportations or forced transfers of populations, and attempts to exterminate through deprivation of food and other essentials. The gravest of all crimes is *genocide*, which is the deliberate and systematic destruction of an ethnic, racial, religious, or national group in whole or part.

Getting the numbers right is not easy. In the confusing and chaotic days after a failed coup in 1965 in Indonesia, when President Sukarno handed over power to General Suharto by signing the Supersemar Decree, a brutal crackdown against communists followed, and many people died. How many? There have been dozens of estimates, ranging from 78,500 (the army's guess) to the two million that communist sympathizers claim. The Indonesia expert

Benedict Anderson thinks the figure was between 500,000 to one million dead. That's a very wide range.

Four decades later, the British medical journal *Lancet* used modern statistical sampling techniques and claimed that perhaps 650,000 'excess deaths' occurred in Iraq since the Allied invasion. The *Lancet* study is controversial—the website Iraq Body Count, some academics, and statisticians, have all questioned *Lancet's* methodology, which other academics and statisticians support.

In 1971, the population of East Pakistan was about 70 million people. If three million people died in the war, then that accounts for nearly 4 per cent of the population. The killings took place between 25 March, when Pakistani forces launched Operation Searchlight, and ended in mid-December, when Dhaka fell to the Indian army and the Mukti Bahini forces. Bangladesh calls this *gonohotta*, or genocide.

What complicates any rational discussion about the number is that it was Mujib who first used the figure three million. Challenging that figure, in a sense, is like *lèse majesté*. On 18 January 1972, the British journalist David Frost interviewed Mujib, where he said: 'Three million people have been killed, including children, women, intellectuals, peasants, workers, students.' Frost asked him how he knew that the number was so high. Mujib said his people had been gathering information, and he had received messages from many parts of the country. While final calculations were not complete, the figure, he was certain, was not less than three million.

There were some who doubted it. One theory helpfully tried to explain that Mujib meant to say three lakh (300,000) but like many people in South Asia, he confused 'lakh' (100,000) with a 'million' (1,000,000). In fact, Serajur Rahman, former deputy head of BBC Bengali Service publicly said so.[207] Another senior bureaucrat at that time tried to go to the source, and said that the figure had been reported in *Pravda,* the newspaper of the Communist Party of the Soviet Union. But there was no substantial basis to the claim in *Pravda.*[208] (It also gave an exaggerated figure of the number of intellectuals killed).

The late Rudolph Rummel, a political scientist at the University of Hawaii, who studied mass killings and coined the term 'democide' to describe murders by elected governments, has written:

> The human death toll over only 267 days was incredible. Just to give
> for five out of the eighteen districts some incomplete statistics published

in Bangladesh newspapers or by an Inquiry Committee, the Pakistani army killed 100,000 Bengalis in Dacca, 150,000 in Khulna, 75,000 in Jessore, 95,000 in Comilla, and 100,000 in Chittagong. For eighteen districts the total is 1,247,000 killed. This was an incomplete toll, and to this day no one really knows the final toll. Some estimates of the democide are much lower—one is of 300,000 dead—but most range from 1 million to 3 million. The Pakistani army and allied paramilitary groups killed about one out of every sixty-one people in Pakistan overall; one out of every twenty-five Bengalis, Hindus, and others in East Pakistan. If the rate of killing for all of Pakistan is annualized over the years the Yahya martial law regime was in power (March 1969 to December 1971), then this one regime was more lethal than that of the Soviet Union, China under the communists, or Japan under the military (even through World War II).[209]

Bangladesh did establish a committee to investigate the number of deaths but its report was never made public. As the British journalist David Bergman, who was the main investigative reporter for the path-breaking film, *War Crimes File,* writes: 'It has been suggested that this was because the details of only 57,000 people could be identified. Of course, this was only months after the end of the war, and the low number could have been due to the practical difficulties of undertaking a systematic national survey in the immediate post-war period.'[210]

Bergman writes that the only scientific study has been by the then Cholera Hospital (now called International Centre for Diarrhoeal Disease Research) in a place called Matlab, where 120,000 people lived. In an article in 1976, researchers wrote of the army coming to the area in April and in June the army raided the headquarters and conducted counter-insurgency operations. This led to people leaving the area. Hostilities increased, and by November insurgents controlled the entire area. Their study revealed 868 excess deaths due to all causes. On that basis they attempted to extrapolate the figure to understand the overall demographic impact. Acknowledging that there were different impacts in different areas, and that Matlab Bazar could not represent the entire country, the authors concluded that the excess death rate in Matlab implies an overall excess number of nearly 500,000. Other subsequent studies point out a range of 125,000 to 505,000. And indeed, among news reports of that time, Kann in the *Wall Street Journal* has consistently mentioned the figure of deaths at 'half a million deaths' over the nine months.

All assessments are, essentially, speculative, including Pakistan's Hamoodur Rahman Commission, which claims 26,000 died based on 'situation reports.' Sarmila Bose's estimate, much criticized by war crimes activists, is of between 50,000 and 100,000 deaths. Richard Sisson and Leo E. Rose cite Indian officials saying that the figure was about 300,000.[211] Gary Bass uses the figure 200,000, citing a range of estimates including from the State Department and the CIA, and Lt. Gen. Jacob, who commanded Indian troops in the war, gives the figure of 'several hundred thousand'.[212]

Clearly, if the figure many Bangladeshis accept as accurate—three million—is believed, then those deaths amount to 11,235 deaths a day. That would make it one of the most lethal conflicts of all time. Put another way, consider this: one of the most brutal conflicts in recent years is the civil war waged in the Democratic Republic of Congo, where the international community increased military presence after the International Rescue Committee reported that 5.4 million people died between 1998 and 2008. A more thorough Canadian analysis now concludes that the actual figure is about half. At 5.4 million deaths, the daily death toll would be 1,500; at 2.7 million, 750 per day. Was the 1971 war up to fifteen times more lethal than the Congolese conflict?

We simply don't know. But it is an important question. Many Bangladeshis feel that raising such a doubt undermines their suffering and belittles their identity. But a thorough, unbiased study, going as far as facts can take the analysis, would be an important contribution to a serious understanding of the subcontinent's recent history. It is also extremely unlikely that such an analysis is now possible, given the absence of records, the passage of time, and the passing of many witnesses.

Peter Kann explains it another way: 'At a given time there were some 70,000 Pakistani troops there (the figure rose to 90,000 towards the end of the war). There were some killings by the Biharis and some internecine killing among Bengalis. Try dividing 3 million by 70,000 (about 43)—it doesn't make sense. That suggests a lot of killings per soldier—and all the soldiers were not out in the field shooting. In any normal army, a quarter to a third of the men are in actual combat; others offer logistical support. The three million figure makes no sense.'

◆

Regardless of the number of people who died, it is important that the victims reach closure and justice is served. Bangladesh had sought justice early—soon after Independence, Bangladesh had passed the International Crimes (Tribunal) Act, 1973, and the 2010 tribunals essentially follow that law. The act authorizes the prosecution of people living in the country who were members of the armed forces or paramilitary groups. Its main targets are the collaborators but also some perpetrators. Mofidul Hoque of the Liberation War Museum told me: 'From a legal point of view, our law was a very historic act. When the international community was not acting, when many countries were not recognising us, and nobody was prepared to address international crimes here, a small nation had initiated the process on its own.'

In 2009 Bangladesh introduced new rules of procedure and evidence. Critics said that the law needed many more amendments to bring it up to the current international standards.[213] It is no doubt true that Bangladesh's 1973 law was an improvement upon the standards used in earlier war crimes trials, such as the Nuremberg and Tokyo tribunals after World War II. Bangladesh's logic of using the law of 1973 is that it wants to ensure that the trial does not impose standards of another time on crimes committed at a particular point of time. That sounds fair, but it raises complications. In 1971, crimes against humanity were defined narrowly—these could occur in the context of an international armed conflict. Was the Liberation War a civil war or an anti-colonial struggle? Then there is the question of genocide. In describing the conflict as genocide, prosecutors extend the definition beyond what the Genocide Convention says. The Convention does not cover 'extermination of a political group.' That may be a limitation of the Convention, but such is the law.

Whether the number of deaths was 26,000, as the Pakistani commission claims, or three million, as Bangladesh government and many Bangladeshis continue to assert, this we know: that many Bengali students and intellectuals and others of different faiths, and Bengali Hindus, were targeted, and killed in genocidal acts; that many Bengali women were raped, impregnated, or forced into sexual slavery; that more Bengali intellectuals were abducted and murdered two days before surrender; that not all Pakistani commanders were brutal, nor all Pakistani soldiers were evil, and certainly not all Pakistani citizens approved their military's conduct; that in the conflict scenario Bengalis also did terrible things to Pakistanis and Biharis, which may not qualify as genocide, but was tragic in every sense.

Remembering that past and holding people accountable is the way Bangladesh wants to bring this tragedy to a closure. Irene Khan told me: 'You can have debates about whether particular acts constitute war crimes or genocide. You can debate whether what happened was a war or an internal conflict. But they were crimes against humanity. There was obviously culpability and collusion of some locals with the Pakistani army. There was that whole list of intellectuals who were picked up and killed. These were not fighters, these were civilians. Those crimes have remained uninvestigated; it is extremely important that there is a commission of inquiry, if Bangladesh is to put a closure to this chapter of its history. Even if you will have only a limited number of prosecutions, you need a full record of what happened.'

◆

Initially, the UN (and some states) had offered technical assistance and international advisors. But Bangladesh reportedly declined such offers of assistance. The United Nations Development Programme offered financial assistance and the UN itself was willing to give support for the planning. The European Union too passed resolutions supporting the tribunal. The US Ambassador-at-Large on War Crimes Issues, Stephen Rapp, promised US support so that Bangladesh can 'hold an open and transparent war crimes trial with the rights of defence for the accused'. The International Bar Association said that the 1973 Legislation, together with the 2009 amending text, 'provides a system which is broadly compatible with current international standards'.[214] (The IBA also made recommendations, which critics say Bangladesh ignored). The International Center for Transitional Justice, a New York-based organization pursuing accountability in cases involving mass atrocities, initially assisted by taking the tribunal judges to The Hague to observe proceedings at the tribunals prosecuting war crimes in Yugoslavia and at the ICC itself. But later they withdrew support.

But some academics raised questions about the tribunal's impartiality.[215] Among the amendments that governed the tribunal's conduct were provisions that a political party that had worked against the liberation of Bangladesh could be tried on the same charges as individuals, which clearly seemed to target the Jamaat.

After its first round of investigations, the War Crimes Fact Finding Committee identified over 1,500 suspects. In 2010, the government announced a three-member judges' tribunal (Mohammed Nizamul Huq as chairman, with

A.T.M. Fazle Kabir and A.K.M. Zahir Ahmed), a seven-member investigation agency, and a 12-member prosecution team. By 2012, the first indictments were announced, which included nine leaders of the Jamaat-e-Islami— Ghulam Azam who headed the party in 1971; Matiur Rahman Nizami, the current party chief; deputy chief Delwar Hossain Sayeedi; secretary-general Ali Ahsan Mohammad Mojahid; and other leaders Muhammad Kamaruzzaman and Abdul Quader Mollah, media tycoon Mir Quasem Ali (who owns pro-Jamaat news organizations, including a television station), and Abul Kalam Azad (Bachchu), a former cleric. Two BNP leaders were also indicted, both being former ministers—Salahuddin Quader Chowdhury and Abdul Alim. Wartime hero Kader Siddique cautioned early that some of the indicted leaders had few responsibilities and were not leaders. According to him, of the first lot of indicted leaders, only one—Ghulam Azam—was a leader. The rest were followers, he said.

The Bangladeshi tribunal handed out its first sentence in January 2013. Abul Kalam Azad (Bachchu), a preacher associated with the Jamaat, was sentenced to death. He had however left the country and been tried in absentia. More dramatic was the verdict on 5 February 2013, when the tribunal ruled in the case of Abdul Quader Mollah, a rotund man who looked affable and disinterested when I had attended his trial a few weeks earlier in January. That day Mollah sat quietly in his seat, not paying attention to the prosecutors building the case against him, nor listening to the judge who occasionally admonished the lawyers for not preparing their cases properly. The gallery was full of people listening to the arguments intently. They were all Bangladeshis; I was told later that many of them were Jamaat supporters.

Many stared at me because I stood out, looking like a foreigner. Besides, I was not a regular visitor. Before getting my pass to attend the tribunal I had to satisfy the court officers of the purpose of my interest, since foreigners were generally not allowed. Bangladesh was being extra careful those days, because a group of Turkish legislators had attended the trial, not revealing who they were, and then issued a public statement calling for the trials to be suspended. Bangladesh reacted angrily, seeing the legislators' visit as interference in its internal affairs.

I was writing notes in my diary and trying to listen to the arguments and I could only see the lawyers' backs. They spoke in a mixture of Bengali and English, and I had to struggle to keep pace with the arguments because the case was already at an advanced stage. There was no place to sit, and the room was stuffy. Abdul Quader Mollah, wearing thick glasses with an old-style translucent plastic frame, looked at me, wondering who I was. When I looked back, he nodded and smiled. I nodded back.

Mollah was 65 years old at that time. The charges against him were formidable: He was alleged to have killed 344 civilians as part of the Al-Badr militia, which worked closely with the Pakistani army. He denied the charges, and his lawyers said that Jamaat leaders were singled out as part of a political vendetta. He looked like an old preacher, and he was a science graduate who had twice stood for parliamentary elections unsuccessfully. He was also a teacher, and during the Zia years he was vice-president of the Dhaka Journalists' Union.

He had joined Al Badr because he felt that opposing the unity of an Islamic nation (Pakistan) was an un-Islamic act. For his acts during the war, he was called 'the butcher of Mirpur'. The charges he faced were grim: the killing of a student; ordering aides to murder a pro-liberation poet; killing of other men, including families; leading a group of seventy Al Badr militia to Khanbari and Ghotan Char and abducting freedom fighters, torturing and killing them; and leading another group of militia to kill hundreds of people in Alubdi village.

The judge found him guilty on five counts and sentenced Abdul Quader Mollah to life imprisonment under Section 20(3) of the 1973 Act, and an additional 15 years. In effect, he would remain in jail for the rest of his life. His supporters were deeply dismayed, but Mollah smiled. Dozens of policemen escorted him to the van after the verdict, and just as he was being ushered in, he triumphantly looked at his supporters, grinned, and flashed the 'V for victory' sign.

His supporters erupted and applauded him. They were also extremely angry. Until the verdict, they had thought of the tribunal as politics by other means—the quaint, kabuki-like rituals that the two warring women of Bangladeshi politics practised time and again, pushing and hurting one another but knowing when they must stop.

It was early 2013; within a year elections were to be announced. His lawyers would drag the appeals process until it would be time for elections. There would be a caretaker government and Mollah probably thought that Hasina would not risk trying to rush the judges to come out with more judgments, particularly when the date of elections would be so close. At that time, Hasina's victory was no way certain. Inflation had been rising.

Electricity outages were common. There was simmering anger against the Awami League's youth wing after its activists had brutally assaulted a young Hindu man on the streets, on the pretext of their believing him to be an opposition activist, causing his death (just one and the worst of many such killings reported in the year). And people were getting sick of corruption. Indeed, the World Bank had just cancelled a major loan to build a bridge on Padma River, citing corruption at a high level of the government. Voters would surely support the BNP, the assumption went, and that could bring BNP back to power. Jamaat supporters assumed that in such circumstances Khaleda would set the Jamaat leaders free. And so would end another act in the never-ending drama of Bangladesh politics. But in 2011 the Supreme Court had declared the 13th Amendment void, which meant a caretaker government between elections was no longer required.

When Mollah flashed the victory sign it had an unintended effect. It was seen not only by his supporters surrounding the police van in which he was being taken away, but it was captured on camera by press photographers and television networks. Relatives of victims and young people who had fought for the trials were incensed when they saw a smiling Mollah on their television screens. It brought back memories of immunity that the leaders had enjoyed and the impunity with which they acted. The V sign was an arrogant snub, a brash and foolish gesture, meant to insult all those who were fighting for justice. The reaction was swift; the spark was ignited.

◆

The tribunal meets in the Supreme Court complex in Dhaka, which sits along the Suharawardy Park, off Maulana Bhashani Road. At the other end is Shahbagh, a busy square near the national museum. That square became the unlikely location of protests following the Mollah verdict. After seeing the 'V sign' on television and in newspaper photographs, one by one the people came, unannounced, spreading the message through word of mouth, through social media, and through text messages on cell phones. The message got amplified by activists who allied with the movement, and later, many more ordinary people came, and stalls emerged offering snacks, drinks and water. The media arrived and politicians turned up to make speeches. Students and teachers, middle-aged men and women, the elderly and the children, the devout and the unbelievers, women in jeans and in saris, women in jilbab or with their heads covered; men with beards and skull caps, but also men in jeans and T-shirts. They had all congregated at Shahbagh, carrying posters and shouting slogans. They were angry because they felt Mollah had got off too lightly.

Many narratives were intertwined in this mass of humanity. There was the narrative of the family that lost a loved one in 1971 and which had not been able to find out what happened to that father, or brother, or sister, and had sought justice in vain for four decades. There was the narrative of those who saw their loved ones killed, and had sought an answer from Bangladesh's ruling class: Why us? Why had nobody been punished? There was also the narrative of the unconsoled, who wanted nothing less than revenge, and who would like to see those responsible for the bloodshed in the country die at the hands of the state. And there was another important narrative: of Bangladeshis who wanted to reclaim the promise of liberation, of a secular Muslim-majority country united by a language.

A small girl rose from the crowd, her eyes brimming with anger, her face red under the warm winter sun, and she kept screaming: phaanshi chai! (I want hanging). Children were encouraged to shout phaanshi chai. Boys sat around at night and day with nooses chanting phaanshi chai. Billboards had pictures of nooses. In the popular conception of justice, evil deeds do not go unpunished. But when cases are delayed, or never come to trial at all, and when the accused walk around freely and some even get rewarded, people lose faith in the system. The desire for revenge had hardened in the absence of remorse from the perpetrators and the lack of any sign of justice from the authorities for nearly four decades. The people of Shahbagh were tired of waiting.

Hawkers and small businesses saw an opportunity. There were chotpoti stands, and puchka and jhaalmuri were sold everywhere. There was even singing and dancing in the carnival atmosphere, and films like *Muktir Gaan* and *War Crime Files* were shown. Amidst all that, the battlecry to end the culture of immunity: phaanshi chai.

The girl who screamed 'phaanshi chai' was clearly speaking for many, even though she had had no experience of the war. She wanted blood. Abdul Quader Mollah had been given a fair trial. Now it was time to hang him. The crowds kept rising by the hour. It was impossible to walk through the crowd; people were standing cheek-by-jowl, and they shouted their hearts out, demanding what increasingly sounded like vengeance, and not justice.

Those crowds did not move. If they went home, another lot came to replace them. For Dhaka's drivers, a prominent part of the city's road network had disappeared from the map. People created space for the devout who fell to their knees at the appointed hour and bowed for prayers. The sight of the praying men and women added another complicated dimension to the Bangladesh story—here were religious Muslims praying for justice, and their idea of justice was that men who fought on behalf of their religion and had killed others, including Muslims, in the name of Islam, should now be executed. Ironies multiplied.

As per the law, the demand the crowd was making was absurd and impossible. Under the prevailing law, while an accused had the right to seek leniency, the prosecutor could not appeal seeking harsher sentence. But the crowd now wanted that law to change. A minister addressed the crowd. Speaking through a loudspeaker he challenged the court to increase the sentence to death penalty, even though the law did not permit that. Soon, the parliament obliged, permitting the prosecutor to appeal.

Later, the demonstrations turned violent: the death sentence given to one of the accused tried in absentia had already led to widespread rioting and martyrs' memorials in several towns had been vandalized. Police opened fire and many people died. Troops were placed on alert. Ahmed Rajib Haider, a blogger who was among the many who had pioneered the Shahbagh protests had been found murdered. The Jamaat had characterized the conflict as that between the religious and the atheists, and they called the so-called atheist bloggers blasphemers. Adding to the ironies, a government professing secularism now prosecuted four bloggers, accusing them of hurting religious sentiment. The idea of laws preventing the hurting of religious sentiment in a secular democracy was itself another paradox. You can't be secular by half-measures; Sultana Kamal's warning about the implications of retaining certain religious provisions in the constitution rang true.

Hortals returned with a vengeance. During my six trips to Bangladesh for the purpose of researching this book, I have spent over a hundred days in the country, and of those, I lost at least ten days to hortals. The BNP (whose leader Salahuddin Quader Chowdhury of Chittagong has since been found guilty of torture, murder and genocide by the tribunal) called for a strike that book-ended the three-day visit of India's Bengali-speaking president, Pranab Mukherjee, to Dhaka. Khaleda Zia refused to see him, saying that the strike (which her party had called) sometimes turned violent so she could not step out to meet the Indian president.

◆

One day I saw a few young men lift a large portrait at Shahbagh Square and I heard a collective gasp. It was a seminal, emotionally charged moment, as though the crowd was waiting for the woman whose photograph they now held aloft to emerge from somewhere, as if she was going to say—now I can sleep. The photograph was of Jahanara Imam, who Bangladeshis knew as shaheed janani, 'the mother of martyrs'.

Jahanara Imam was born in 1929 in Murshidabad in India. She grew up all over Bengal as her father was in the civil service and was transferred periodically. She graduated with an arts degree from Lady Brabourne College in Calcutta and moved to Mymensingh in East Pakistan after the Partition. She married a classmate of hers and settled in Dhaka, where she taught at a school. In 1960 she gave up her job as headmistress to look after her sons Rumi and Jami, who were eight and six.

She was a writer who became a political activist. After Operation Searchlight, her son Rumi decided to join the Mukti Bahini. He became a freedom fighter. She began writing a diary about the time—*Ekattorer Dinguli* (Days of '71)[216]—which is one of the most direct and vivid memoirs of that year. Rumi was a brave warrior who took part in many daredevil missions against the Pakistani army.

Jahanara Imam's memoir was extraordinarily powerful and poignant, recreating the horrors of the nine months through her acute daily observations, combining the grand political themes with concerns of pure domesticity. Her house gets filled with freedom fighters who want to hide for the night. Her concern is not about them getting caught, but how she is going to feed them. She is worried that her servants might squeal and reveal what's happening in her home. We don't see the violence; we feel it. Visitors come and brag about the Mukti Bahini's achievements, but she wants to know where her son is and how he is doing. If they knew, they wouldn't tell her. He returns, a war-weary man with a beard. She is thrilled seeing him all grown up and wants him photographed; he hates the sight of himself in the mirror and doesn't let her.

He leaves again and carries out a spectacular attack on Pakistanis and the whole of Dhanmondi celebrates. But his whereabouts are betrayed, and a Pakistani officer turns up at their home and takes away the two boys and their father. Her husband and Jami return; Rumi doesn't. Her husband has been tortured and dies three days before Bangladesh's freedom. Rumi is never seen again.

When Jahanara Imam saw Ghulam Azam allowed back into the country and permitted to participate in elections, she was livid. She formed the Ghatak-Dalal Nirmul Committee (The Committee to Exterminate the Killers and Collaborators) and became its mascot. The committee began gathering evidence against the perpetrators of war crimes and their collaborators and demanded trials. Inevitably, the Razakars and other alleged war criminals became her focus, because trying Pakistani soldiers or officers was now impossible. In 1992 the activists set up gono-adalats (people's courts) in Dhaka and tried and sentenced people they accused of war crimes. Bizarrely, the Khaleda Government charged her and others, including actors, teachers, and poets, with sedition—the charge was dropped only after her death.

Jahanara Imam was diagnosed with mouth cancer in 1981, but she continued to press for war crimes trials, reminding all Bangladesh governments to live up to the spirit of the revolution. She fought for justice for all those who perished. Her struggle was tireless, as she kept reminding the politicians of what the country had lost and how it was important to account for what happened before the nation could become normal again. She died abroad in 1994; when her body was brought to Dhaka for burial, thousands of people lined the streets to pay their respects. Seeing her face held aloft in that large poster revived the stalled wheel of history; her unfinished work was continuing, and a new generation of Bangladeshis, some young enough to be Rumi's children, had picked up the banner and were seeking the justice she had fought for.

◆

In the end, the government changed laws to permit the prosecutors to appeal the verdict against Mollah. Human rights lawyers around the world who had been following the process became alarmed. The international community was getting increasingly concerned over the shortcuts the tribunal seemed to be taking. While prosecution lawyers would get more time to prepare themselves, defence lawyers said they were being denied additional time. Defence lawyers were not allowed to bring laptops or other electronic devices to the court, whereas one prosecutor was able to use an iPad during the trial. Defence requests to call foreign experts as witnesses were not granted. Defence lawyers also said they were sometimes not allowed to cross-examine witnesses. Foreign observers found it hard to get the permission to witness the trials, as did many local nationals. Visitors too could not bring laptops or any recording devices to the proceedings. There were deeper concerns too. After the Quader Mollah verdict, Sam Zarifi, the head of Asia for the International Commission of Jurists warned that the flawed nature of the trials could deepen divisions within the country which had resulted from the 1971 war, rather than heal them.[217]

A team of British lawyers represented some of the defendants to mobilize international opinion on behalf of their clients. Steven Kay Q.C. criticized several provisions of the 2009 law, but the tribunal then accused him of violating the British Bar's code of conduct. I met Toby Cadman, another British lawyer from the same team, representing the Jamaat defendants. We met at a coffee shop near his chambers in London when he explained that his criticism of the tribunal was about the manner in which it had operated and its legal framework. If not done properly, it wouldn't bring justice to the victims, he said, and the international community had the responsibility towards Bangladesh to ensure that justice was delivered.

Cadman has long experience in dealing with war crimes. He has been the head of the Prosecution Section for War Crimes at the Bosnian War Crimes Chamber; in Syria he has represented victims of human rights abuses. Since January 2011 he has represented the Jamaat defenders and advised Salahuddin Quader Chowdhury. When we first spoke, the Shahbagh protests were going on, and the Jamaat had been demonstrating against the protesters.

Cadman agrees that Bangladesh has the right to hold the trials and in principle it is always preferable for trials to take place where the crimes occur. But he thinks the Bangladesh experience has demonstrated that the country is neither prepared nor able to hold the trials properly. 'I am now actively campaigning for the trials to be moved out of Bangladesh and placed under international supervision,' he told me.

Cadman was not allowed to represent his clients at the tribunal, but in that Bangladesh isn't unique; foreign lawyers can't appear before courts in England and Wales either, unless they have appropriate local qualifications. He had visited Bangladesh five times previously but in August 2011 he was held at the Dhaka airport for ten hours and finally refused entry. He said: 'These are complex trials with evidence that dates back to forty years and the trials deal with concepts with which very few people are fully familiar.' Cadman pointed out that he was not alone in criticising the procedures—

Human Rights Watch, International Centre for Transitional Justice, Amnesty International, the UN Working Group on Arbitrary Detention, the UN Special Rapporteur on Summary Executions, and the US ambassador-at-large Rapp have all at various times criticized the tribunal. Recommendations made by international organizations have remained largely ignored. Awami League supporters have called Cadman a Razakar.

While the Rome Statute (which Bangladesh signed in 2010) does not apply retroactively, making it impossible to try the 1971 cases using the Statute, as a state which has signed the convention, Bangladesh has certain obligations. Cadman says that holding a trial that breaches fair trial principles is incompatible with being a state party (that is, a party that has signed a convention).

The government has vigorously challenged its critics. It says that the process has been fair. But critics have contended that some defendants have been interrogated without the presence of their lawyers; international advisers who could help provide the best defence are not allowed; the accused have been detained for long periods before the trials have begun; and often the lengthy charge-sheets are given to the defence team fairly late. Defence lawyers I spoke to also said that limitations were placed on their ability to cross-examine witnesses and the number of witnesses they could call.

On 5 November 2012, Shukho Ranjan Bali, a defence witness from Pirojpur who had come to the court to testify in the trial of Delwar Hossain Sayeedi, disappeared from the gates of the courthouse.[218] Human Rights Watch quoted eyewitnesses who said Bali was abducted from the gates and some said he was then seen in police custody. Bali was originally a prosecution witness, but he later changed his view and had agreed to testify for the defence. Within moments of Bali's disappearance, the defence team raised the matter in the tribunal, which asked the prosecution to investigate. The prosecution responded a few hours later that the episode was fabricated.

The defence team said Bali had met them at their offices in the morning on 5 November. They drove together to the court. At the gate, they were ordered out of the car and had to identify themselves. Defence lawyers said 10-12 uniformed police were present at that time. When Bali was identified by name, the police detectives insisted on taking Bali with them. The defence lawyers as well as Bali argued that he was a witness and they had to get to the court. A white van marked 'Police' drove up from inside the court premises. Bali was reportedly slapped several times and forced into the van, which then drove off. He had not been seen since. Bali's relatives hadn't heard from him either. When Human Rights Watch asked Justice Nizamul Huq, he agreed it was not normal practice to ask the prosecution to investigate the defence witness's disappearance, but gave no reason why he had asked the prosecution to investigate. He denied any bias.

Bali disappeared after the prosecution claimed that it was not able to produce certain witnesses, including Bali. Prosecution lawyers were then allowed to present his written testimony which could no longer be challenged, nor could Bali be cross-examined. When defence lawyers challenged that, their plea was dismissed.

A few months later, in a remarkable turn of events, Bali was found in an Indian jail. He alleged that police had abducted him and officials later told him that both he and Sayeedi (the accused) were going to die.[219] Bali told the *New Age* newspaper that he was detained for about six weeks in Dhaka before he was driven to the Indian border and handed over to the Indian Border Security Force towards the end of December 2012. After that, he had been detained in different Indian jails, before being taken to the Dum Dum Correction Home. He pleaded guilty for illegal entry into India and was imprisoned for 105 days under India's Foreigners Act of 1946. In late 2013, the tribunal sentenced Sayeedi to death for crimes, including the murder of Bali's brother.

In September 2014, the Appellate Division of the Bangladesh Supreme Court reduced Sayeedi's death sentence to life imprisonment.

But there are concerns about what the accused might do to witnesses, too. In some cases, people remain scared of testifying against certain defendants. One man in Chittagong, who has testified in the trial of Salahuddin Quader Chowdhury, feels his life is in danger (which is why he remains anonymous) because he testified how he had seen Chowdhury giving orders to kill innocent people. When he testified, Chowdhury glared at him and another witness who provided a similar testimony, and shouted at them, saying they should watch out, because one day he would be free and 'look after them'. Another Chittagong resident testified that in 1971 a family near Chowdhury's house regularly heard screams and cries from his house, suggesting that at night they tortured people. Such witnesses told me they were afraid of the defendants being acquitted.

Perhaps the most sensational case has been the so-called Skypegate. In December 2012, the *Economist* published an article drawing on transcripts of alleged conversations involving the chief justice of the tribunal, Nizamul Huq, and Ahmed Ziauddin, a Bangladeshi legal academic in Brussels who directs the Bangladesh Centre for Genocide Studies there. Rayhan Rashid, a student at Oxford, was also involved. Huq ordered the bureau chief of the *Economist* to reveal how he obtained the transcripts. The publication said it had neither solicited the material, nor paid for it, and had made no commitment to publish it. But the idea of a tribunal judge talking about the case with someone not connected with the process was damaging and Huq resigned soon after that.[220] Later, a report in the *Wall Street Journal* showed that Ziauddin had also played a role in the proceedings, including discussing how verdicts should be written. It also quoted Huq saying he was under pressure from a government official to move quickly.[221]

I spoke about Skypegate to a leading Bangladeshi jurist with wide international experience. He saw nothing fundamentally wrong with a judge discussing a case with recognized experts—judges are not hermits, he told me. Judges need to challenge their logic and thinking and sometimes that is possible by talking to experts not connected with the court, including international experts. But he agreed that there has to be transparency and disclosure. Defense lawyers too said that judges have the right to consult experts, but that they should do so by bringing in amicus curiae, or reveal who they are consulting with. The process has to be transparent—in this case it was not, and the presiding judge eventually had to step aside. No action was taken against those who had spoken to him, however.

As soon as the story appeared in the *Economist,* the Jamaat lawyers demanded a retrial, saying the entire process was tainted. The new presiding judge refused to do so, saying the evidence was obtained illegally. But it created the peculiar situation in the Sayeedi case, where the judges who finally ruled on the case had not heard the full case—the chief judge had resigned, and another judge had quit earlier because he had been unwell.

Concurrently, the government changed the law to allow the prosecution to seek a harsher sentence, and Quader Mollah's sentence was increased to the death penalty. He was executed on 12 December. On 28 February, Delwar Hossain Sayeedi was sentenced to death for genocide, rape and religious persecution; on appeal, his sentence has been converted to life imprisonment. Muhammad Kamaruzzaman was given the death penalty on 9 May for mass killings, rape, torture and kidnapping. Ghulam Azam was sentenced to 90 years' imprisonment on 15 July for incitement to violence, conspiracy, planning, abatement and failure to prevent murder. Two days later, Ali Ahsan Mohammad Mojaheed was given the death penalty. Chowdhury Mueenuddin was handed the death penalty on 3 November for crimes against humanity and for being part of Al-Badr. He was also accused of the murder of intellectuals at Rayer Bazar between 14–16 December, although he has denied all these charges and refused to appear before the tribunal. He lives in the UK, which is unlikely to extradite him, given the risk of death penalty or torture. On 2 February 2014, A.K.M. Yusuf, founder of the pro-Pakistan Peace Committees and leader of the Razakars in Khulna, who was in prison awaiting his trial, died.

◆

International experience with tribunals has been mixed. While the procedures are followed scrupulously, their conviction rate has been low. Verdicts take long—in some cases, victims or survivors have died, the political context has changed, and in two recent cases, the accused has died. Slobodan Milosevic was brought to trial before the ICTY but died the day before he was to be sentenced. More recently, former Khmer Rouge leader Ieng Sary died in Phnom Penh even as the trial against him was on at the Extraordinary Chambers in the Courts of Cambodia. In August 2014, two elderly Khmer Rouge leaders, Nuon Chea (88) and Khieu Samphan (83) were found guilty of murder, persecution, forced transfers, enforced abductions, and attacks against human dignity, and given life imprisonment. But public confidence in the process is weakening because the proceedings have gone on for more than nine years now, at a cost of over $200 million, and there have been only a handful of convictions.

The ICTY in the Netherlands hasn't reconciled communities in the Balkans. During the Bosnian civil war of 1992–1995, many Muslims were killed at camps in Manjaca and in the town of Prijedor in what is now Republika Srpska, and some of the bodies were dumped in unmarked graves in or near the iron ore mine in Ljubija. Over the years, Muslims have wanted a memorial shrine near the mine, commemorating the buried. The Serbs don't want such a memorial. They have threatened to blow it up if it gets built.

I was once at a coffee shop in Sanski Most, interviewing Muslim survivors who were telling me about a mass grave near the iron ore mine. Suddenly they stopped talking and one of them kicked me under the table when I continued to talk. Two men had entered the coffee shop. One of the men sitting next to me told me in a hushed tone that the two were former Serb soldiers. I turned to look at them. They were staring at us. 'Do you want to go home safely?' my interpreter whispered to me. 'Then talk about Indian films.' A surreal conversation about Amitabh Bachchan movies followed, as we tried to pretend that I was an Indian tourist in these parts.

The ICTR was established to prosecute crimes committed during the Rwandan conflict of 1994. During that war, Hutus killed close to 800,000 Tutsis and moderate Hutus in a hundred days between April and June 1994. That conflict ended only after Paul Kagame's Rwandan Patriotic Front vanquished the Hutu forces. Kagame has since brought prosperity to the nation but his autocratic rule is intolerant of criticism; it has shielded him from accusations of his own role during the war. The ICTR met in Arusha, Tanzania. When I was there in 2010, it had convicted 54 people and acquitted 8. But hundreds of thousands were involved in the violence, and some 10,000 died in prison before their trials could even begin. In 2001, Rwanda set up a community justice system, called gacaca courts, for crimes that are considered less grave. These courts were drawn from Rwandan traditions, which sought conciliation at a personal level. By treating the two types of crimes—grave and not so grave—differently, the Rwandan experience showed two legal principles in action: retributive justice and restorative justice.

Most international tribunals are built on the premise of what legal scholars call *retributive* justice: you deal with crime with proportionate punishment. The prosecutor represents the state and the defence represents the accused; the dialogue is between them and an impartial judge presides. The victims do not have a role. The tribunal in Arusha was based on the principle of retributive justice. The gacaca courts come closer in their approach to *restorative* justice, where the focus is on the needs of the victims and offenders and involves the community, instead of the more adversarial approach of retributive justice. Victims get a sense of closure. As the French journalist Jean Hatzfeld describes in his trilogy *The Antelope's Strategy*, *Life Laid Bare* and *Machete Season*, the approach of the gacaca courts did appear to work in some local cases.[222] In Rwanda, following the gacaca process, former perpetrators are slowly returning to villages where they had killed people, and relatives of victims are beginning to realize that revenge is not an option.

The range of responses from different societies to similar crimes reveals the complexity of dealing with the past. Cambodia has commemorated the victims of Pol Pot's regime (1975–1979) at Tuol Sleng, the school famously turned into a prison and torture chamber by the Khmer Rouge, which is now a museum in Phnom Penh. The guides here are former inmates—some selling their books, some willing to be photographed with tourists. Socheata Poeuv, a US-based Cambodian-American film maker who has documented survivors' testimonies in Cambodia, once told me the story of a woman whose neighbour had turned in her father to the Khmer Rouge. Her father was murdered in the killing fields. When Socheata asked her how she felt, the woman spoke in an unnaturally calm tone, saying maybe her father had done some bad deeds in his previous life. And what if he hadn't, Socheata asked her. 'Then he,' she said, pointing out the neighbour's hut, 'will return in his next life as a frog.'

One experiment many cite as particularly effective is the Truth and Reconciliation Commission (TRC) of South Africa. Set up in 1994 after apartheid ended, here, victims could come and speak of the human rights violations they had endured, sometimes in public hearings.[223] Championed by the Anglican archbishop Desmond Tutu, the Commission had the specific purpose of preventing further bloodshed that a process of settling scores would have entailed. The Commission was not meant to heal personal tragedies. Those who had committed abuses—security forces, police officers, politicians who had given orders, and government officials who had followed orders—gave testimony; in return they received amnesty from civil and criminal prosecution. It allowed many to escape punishment, as the novelist Gillian Slovo was to discover. She was born in South Africa and now lives in London. Her father, Joe, led the South African Communist Party. During the apartheid he and her mother, Ruth First, lived in exile in Mozambique, from where they carried on their anti-apartheid activism. They were among the few whites to take on the South African regime. First had been detained without trial in 1963 and the couple fled South Africa after the African National Congress leadership was rounded up. Tragedy struck in Mozambique, when apartheid agents sent First a letter bomb, which exploded, killing her.

Slovo ended up confronting the man responsible for sending that lethal parcel to her mother. She discovered that a copy of her book, which she had autographed, had ended up with that man. I met Slovo in late 2008, soon after the terrorist attacks in Mumbai, and I asked her if it was possible for her to forgive. After all, South Africa had astounded the world with the TRC, which offered a non-violent way in which the oppressor and victim could resolve differences face to face. Slovo told me, 'Lots of countries like truth commissions because they look at South Africa and think of the miracle. But I am not sure if it was entirely miraculous; it had its flaws, too. The commission was a compromise to stop people from fighting. People need to see if the two sides want to stop fighting first. It is impossible otherwise to start a process that goes so deep. There is a difference between individual and collective responses. South Africa's experience reflected the thinking of an archbishop [Desmond Tutu] whose church believed in forgiveness.'

Forgiveness can help the victim, liberating the individual from the instinct seeking revenge. It can sometimes ease the pain and heal the wound, Slovo said. She believes that forgiveness is complicated at the individual level, even if it might be easy at the collective level.

Each trauma is individual; each closure is unique. A system cannot fine-tune the delivery of justice such that each victim is satisfied. Some nightmares never end; some wounds never heal. But the formal acknowledgement that crimes were committed is essential, so that nobody can deny that something terrible had happened. The realization that it can happen again and the resolve that it must not—these are important building blocks to create a world where impunity has no place. It is not an easy prospect.

◆

The idea of forgiveness is steeped in religious beliefs. Guhathakurta had studied at a convent, and Christian ideas of mercy were ingrained in her. She told me: 'I remember the first thing I did was to say: I forgive those who killed my father. But in a multicultural system it doesn't always work. Not all religions are about forgiveness. Revenge is permitted in many religions. Human beings have a primordial urge to take revenge.'

Many years later, Guhathakurta was interviewing victims of 1971 for a film. She was talking to those who escaped from killing fields, and families of people who were victims. That's when it occurred to her: trauma never really ends. Her nightmares will always stay. She acknowledged her anger. She did not want revenge; she wanted justice. She said: 'For me, justice would be when the Pakistani government realizes what it did. But they have not even recognized the genocide. For me, justice means something like Berlin's Holocaust Museum is constructed in Islamabad. I want to see signs where they say that such an event took place, and it was our fault, because we did it, and we are sorry. You can't ask the daughter to forgive the murderer of her father. Revenge doesn't make sense, either. Just because my father died doesn't mean yours has to die. But recognition, that something took place, and the fact that it should not take place again—that's justice. '

Bangladesh abounds with victims—each family has a horror story of its own, where a loved one has been hurt grievously, and the ones who have committed those atrocities have not faced justice, nor expressed remorse. It is impossible to heal everyone. But honest accounting of what happened would be a good start. Trying Mujib's killers, seeking the extradition of those living abroad and solving the mystery of the jail killings are useful steps in making sense of their warped politics, where individuals bragging about killing defenceless people were being rewarded. Trying war criminals is also an important step. Many have enjoyed impunity for too long. But Bangladesh's politicians—of the left and the right, of the religious or the secular strain—have to ask themselves: till when do they want the cycle of blood-letting and revenge to go on? Ultimately, Bangladesh's devout Muslims who want their daughters to cover themselves in the purdah have to live in a society where millions of women would not only be wearing saris, but some of them would also sing and dance. Many would like to have Bengali names drawn from the Sanskrit tradition which has nothing to do with Arabic or Islamic sounds. And there will be the Chakmas, with their Buddhist faith; the Santhals, and the Garos; the Hindus in their temples; and the Biharis, who must leave those dreadful camps and be able to live elsewhere in the country. In the end, as Mbeki and Mamdani wrote, Hutus and Tutsis would have to live together in Rwanda, and blacks and whites in South Africa. 'There is a time and a place for courts, as in Germany after Nazism, but it is not in the midst of conflict or a nonfunctioning political system. Courts are ill-suited to inaugurating a new political order after civil wars; they can only come into the picture after such a new order is already in place,' they concluded.

Mbeki and Mamdani are right up to a point. But the Bangladeshi tribunal is not taking place soon after the war. The wounds haven't healed but they aren't fresh. Mamdani has long championed regional responses to regional crises, and Mbeki was closely involved with the South African TRC. And yet, prosecution of perpetrators has a salutary effect. University of Minnesota academic Kathryn Sikkink believes in the importance of prosecutions because she says that holding former leaders legally accountable strengthens the prospects for successful transitions to democracy. More importantly, there is a cascade effect:[224] as such trials become more common all over the world, violators find that they can run but they cannot hide. The trial of high-ranking violators in fact acts as a deterrent against future crimes.

Human rights are universal, but human wounds are particular. To heal those wounds is not a simple matter—it means understanding what caused the violence, and moving beyond simplistic notions of victims and perpetrators. It means trying to create conditions in which desires, dreams, and rights conflict, the resolution is through negotiation, and not through violence. It means respecting the dignity of the other. The identities of 'perpetrators' and 'victims' are fluid, just as one person's terrorist is another person's freedom fighter. When these identities are fluid, we must remember that not all Bengalis were victims, nor all Biharis perpetrators or collaborators, and nor all Punjabis killers. Instead of living in the past, it is time to leave the past.

Towards the end of the Pakistani writer Kamila Shamsie's novel *Kartography*, Maheen tells her niece Raheen, 'Bangladesh made us see what we were capable of. No one should ever know what they are capable of. But worse, even worse, is to see it and then pretend you didn't. The truths we conceal don't disappear, Raheen, they appear in different forms.'

After the war was over, Pakistan's civil society reached out to Bangladeshis. Ahmad Salim edited a volume of poignant essays, *We Owe an Apology to Bangladesh*[225], in which prominent Pakistani writers, human rights activists, and poets wrote about 1971, challenging the official version of truth, and fought for justice for Bangladeshis. It was a brave thing to do, and it was commendable.

Kindness is part of human nature. Recall Ershad Ali Morel, who found an infant Sundari and lifted her and brought her to his Hindu friends because he noticed that her dead mother had applied vermillion through the parting of her hair, which meant she was a Hindu. The day I met Ershad Ali, I also met Sundari. She remembered nothing of the massacre at Chuknagar—how would she, she was barely a few days old at that time. Over the years she had heard the story of how Ershad Ali had picked her up and taken her to a friend's house. 'Ershad is a Muslim but he did not take me to a Muslim home. He took me to a Hindu home,' she told me, 'I don't know my real mother's name, nor do I know my real father's name. But I know the names of my parents who brought me up. I heard my story from my mother when I turned fifteen. My adoptive parents struggled to raise me and got me married.'

But life hasn't been kind to her. Her husband has been chronically sick and she has had to work hard every day. She has weak kidneys and her parents have died. Her son works as a casual labourer. Her other son helps out at a barber's shop. She works as a housemaid. 'It is very hard,' she said and broke down.

We shared a simple lunch of dal and rice with fish, vegetables, pickles, and onions. I asked her how she felt when she found out about how Ershad Ali found her. 'What can I say,' she said. She had tears in her eyes and yet she smiled. Ershad Ali, sitting next to me, also had tears in his eyes.

'I have survived,' she said.

Later, we drove to the spot where Ershad Ali had first found Sundari. I took their photographs there. They did not have much to say. She had covered her head with the pallu of her sari. He stood straight. After I had taken the photographs I thanked them for sharing their stories with me. They smiled. I shook hands with Ershad Ali and folded my hands saying nomoshkar to Sundari. She nodded, bowing her head briefly. Then they turned away and walked across the field along separate paths—they lived at different ends of the same village. One man, one woman; one Hindu, one Muslim; they trusted one another, respected each other's identity and faith. Neither was rich financially, but in a country torn apart by vicious bloodshed, Ershad Ali gave the most precious gift—of life—to an infant who would not have survived, and with that singular act he had revealed the wealth of kindness within him. They weren't only survivors; in their own way, they had become an inspiration. Their existence celebrated life. They personified the spirit of this land, about which Nazrul and Tagore wrote poems, whose spirit Lalon captured in his songs, which Satyajit Ray and Ritwik Ghatak there, and Tareque and Catherine Masud here, had filmed, and through which rivers from the mighty Himalaya flowed, blending in the Bay of Bengal. They made this land golden Bengal.

In December 2011, I had gone to the Bangla Academy to see the photographs of Raghu Rai from the Bangladesh war. When the war ended, Rai had stored his images away, forgetting about their existence, until 2011, when he called his old friend, the Bangladeshi photographer Shahidul Alam, with great excitement: he had found the old negatives. That was a huge discovery; Bangladesh was turning forty that year, and the generation that fought for its freedom was growing old and would soon fade away. Alam had made it the mission of his life to document the Bangladeshi saga in all its manifestations by promoting visual culture through his agency, Drik. He was himself compiling the works of photographers from Bangladesh and abroad for the book he published in 2011, *The Birth Pangs of A Nation*[226] which included some of Rai's photographs. The book went on to win an Asia Publishing Award in 2012. Rai published his own collection as well, in which Alam wrote the introduction.

Rai's exhibition exposed a new generation of Bangladeshis to the pain their parents' generation had endured. Many young Bangladeshis paused for a long time in front of some images, some taking pictures on their cellphones.

One of Rai's most telling images is of a mother unable to feed her child from her emaciated breasts. Her body is so skeletal you can count her ribs. Looking at that photograph, two teenage boys started sniggering, as if they had never seen nipples before. Seeing them leer as though the image was vulgar revealed why Bangladesh needed to reclaim its history. Among those teenagers, the image had evoked what could be only be seen as bibhatsa (disgust) rasa, and not karuna (compassion) or krodha (anger). And this is why Rai's photographs and Alam's work mattered.

That evening, as I walked through the gallery with a Bangladeshi friend I saw other images that left a deep imprint in my mind: of a woman with her head covered, her gnarled fingers resting on her knees, over which she places her chin. A woman carrying her sole surviving pot in her right hand and a breastfeeding infant in the left, a gamchha covering her torso. Another woman, older, sitting in a tattered palki, is being carried by two men with taut muscles. An old woman, her back bent at a right angle, a stick guiding her forward and her feet bare, walks along a windswept rice field with a coconut tree in the background. Another girl, not yet a woman, bare-chested, stirs a pot, her hair wet. A naked child lying on the ground, between the large pipes in which families have taken shelter. And that image, of the mother holding her child tight, realizing she can't feed it. Pathos has rarely been captured so movingly; and yet, responses varied—my friend had tears in her eyes; those young boys continued to giggle.

◆

What to make of the past—how to understand it, and how to move forward are exceptional challenges for individuals, and far more so at the collective level. With all its flaws, the tribunal has provided one teaching moment—that Bangladeshis do care about their past. How far back that past goes, and what to make of it, are issues on which there does not have to be an immediate consensus. But the founding principle of Bangladesh was plurality and diversity, united by language—with space and respect for other languages—and dominated by one faith—with space and respect for other faiths. When I saw the crowd at Shahbagh, with men in lungis and beards and in jeans and T-shirts, women in burkha and women in saris, it looked like what the nation wanted to be. The spirit of Shahbagh was a collective desire to become the kind of Bangladesh the freedom fighters died for. But can that spirit be upheld by a state that makes one religion official, and which prosecutes writers and bloggers who think differently? Can it be true to the original dream if it leaves no room for compromise?

The history of that war had lain buried all these years because it was inconvenient to wake up those ghosts. The young want that sepulchral enforced silence no more. That past was unquiet. They want to dig open graves, and they seek answers. The truth that emerges may be uncomfortable, but it has to be faced.

Pakistan too has to face its truth. Some remain in denial. Abulkalam Shamsuddin had grown up surrounded by Hindu neighbours, and he was particularly fond of a Hindu woman he called his aunt, who made delicious sandesh. He had been a doctor for the Mukti Bahini in Agartala and treated scores of freedom fighters. After the war he moved to the United States and settled in Baltimore where he told me his story,[227] his eyes frequently welling up with tears. He had grown up in a society where the Hindu was an Indian, supposed to be an enemy; a Pakistani Muslim was supposed to be his brother. And yet, it was a Pakistani man at a pizza shop who reminded him what 1971 was all about. When Abulkalam told him he was Bangladeshi, the pizza shop owner said, 'Bangladesh? What's that? There is only Pakistan.' Abulkalam never returned to that shop.

Mofidul Hoque remembers a young Pakistani woman who visited the Liberation War Museum. She later prepared a video which she concluded with a message for her parents' generation:

Tumne chhupa ke rakha
Meri kaum ne chhupa ke rakha
Hamne chhupa ke rakha

You kept it hidden.
My community kept it hidden.
I kept it hidden.

On 14 December 1971, two days before the Pakistani army surrendered, the Al-Badr killed dozens of civilians—who would have formed the intellectual backbone of the new nation—as if to cripple it at birth. Over at Rayer Bazar in Dhaka, Projonmo 71 has left a plaque which carries a verse from Asad Chowdhury's poem. Until there is closure, the question it poses will continue to resound across the bleeding rivers and sighing valleys of this land, awaiting an answer: 'Tomader ja bolar chhilo bolchhey ki ta Bangladesh? (Does Bangladesh speak what you wanted to say?)'

ACKNOWLEDGEMENTS

This book's origin lies in 1986 when I had returned to India after graduate studies in the United States. Bangladesh had turned 15. I was curious about what had gone wrong with its politics—coups and assassinations had damaged its early promise and dream of creating Sonar Bangla or Golden Bengal. It had just had a pathetically rigged presidential election in which Gen. Ershad had duly got himself declared victorious. Ershad's rival was Farooq Rahman, the colonel who would not repent when we talked about his role in planning and executing the conspiracy that led to the assassination of Sheikh Mujib and most of his family in 1975. In other countries, he would have been in jail. In Dhaka, he went about openly. I thought that was bizarre.

The editor of *Debonair* magazine at that time, Anil Dharker, was willing to let me loose in Bangladesh for a month and see what I'd come back with. I interviewed Farooq and many others and wrote three long articles for *Debonair.*

In 2010, justice caught up with Farooq. Sheikh Mujib's daughter Sheikh Hasina Wajed was the prime minister. The interminably long trial against Farooq had reached its conclusion; Farooq and five other conspirators were executed that January. I wrote a long piece of the kind that only Anant Nath and Vinod Jose at the *Caravan* would publish. Jonathan Shainin steered the story with Adam Matthews and David Besseling questioning me constantly and helping shape it to improve it.

One afternoon in London Jeet Thayil introduced me to David Godwin who read the story from the *Caravan* and immediately said—this is a book, not only an article. And he encouraged me to develop the idea. I couldn't have had a better agent and ally. David Davidar at Aleph saw the potential and from the forest of ideas, helped draw a straight line, keeping me focused.

Some parts of this book have appeared in other forms in *Debonair* and the *Caravan,* and I wrote about the photography of the refugees and the war in an essay in *The Birth Pangs of a Nation,* the book Drik published in 2011, supported by the UN High Commissioner for Refugees.

I built a small library of books about Bangladesh and made several trips to the country, and neither would have been possible without the generous support of the Swiss Ministry of Foreign Affairs, in particular Gabriele Derighetti and Caroline Trautweiler. Their support without seeking any editorial control helped me understand Bangladesh better and gave me the freedom to explore the story in depth and write what I saw.

Many people have contributed to this book in a range of ways, but the conclusions are mine. My heartfelt thanks to:

Sanjoy Hazarika in Delhi, Naeem Mohaiemen in New York, and Ansar Ahmed Ullah and Leesa Gazi in London, for opening doors in Bangladesh;

Afsan Chowdhury, Farhad Ghuznavi, Hameeda Hossain, Imtiaz Ahmed, Irene Khan, Kamal Hossain, Mahfuz Anam, Meghna Guhathakurta, Mofidul Hoque, Ruby Ghuznavi, Sara Hossain, and Shahpar Selim in Dhaka; Devangshu Datta and Nilanjana Roy in Delhi; Pragya Tiwari in Bombay; Aamer Husscin, Fawzia Mahmood, Gita Sahgal, Leesa Gazi, Mushtaq Khan and S.N. Vasuki in London; Nayanika Mookherjee in Durham; Bina D'Costa in Geneva; and Lawrence Lifschultz in New Haven; for discussing Bangladesh, its history, society, and culture with great passion, sharpening my understanding, and indulging my ignorant questions with good humour, pointing out the pitfalls I should watch out for, and reading, at various times, part or whole drafts of the book;

Chowdhury Abrar, Akku Chowdhury, Amena Mohsin, K. Anis Ahmed, Anisur Rahman, Anisuzzaman, Aroma Dutta, Asif Munier, Bibi Russell, Catherine Masud, David Bergman, Devasish Roy-Wangza, Fakrul Alam, Ferdousi Priyobhasini, Kader Siddiqui, Khalid Hussain, Khushi Kabir, Latifa Siddiqi, Masud Karim, Mahrukh Moinuddin, Mehnaz Khondaker, Misha Hussain, Mohammed Zamir, M.A. Hasan, Muntasir Mamoon, Niaz Zaman, Nilufer Huda, Rehman Sobhan, Rimi Hossain Simeen, Rokeya Kabir, Sarwar Ali, Shaheen Akhtar, Shahidul Alam, Shehryar Kabir, Sonia Amin, Sultana Kamal, Tahmina Saleh, Tanvir Mokammel, and Zafar Sobhan in Dhaka; Kamal Sengupta, Khurshid Alam, Mahfuzur Rahman, and Mushtari Shafi in Chittagong; Gouranga Nandy in Khulna, Jharna Dhara Choudhury and Naba Kumar Raha in Noakhali; Sikha Saha and anonymous birangonas in Kushtia; Raunaq Mahal Dilruba Begum in Bogura; Safina Lohani and anonymous birangonas in Sirajganj; and Achintya Biswas, Ershad Ali Morel, Nitai Chandra Gayen, and Sundari in Chuknagar; Hiranmany Karlekar in New Delhi, Wolfgang-Peter Zingel in Heidelberg; Abulkalam Shamsuddin in Baltimore; Peter Kann in Princeton, and James P. Sterba in New York, for sharing experiences and insights about the horrors of 1971 and the nuances of contemporary Bangladesh;

Mainul Islam Rahat all across the country, Farhana Begum and Shamuza Mizan in Bogura, Ishita Datta, Mostafabhai, Nadira Farhat, Russellbhai, and Showvik Das in Dhaka, and Gouranga Nandy in Khulna, for accompanying me on my travels in the country and where necessary, translating interviews for me;

Abdur Razzaq, Shamsul Bari, and Tajul Islam in Dhaka; Brad Adams and Toby Cadman in London; and Anita Ramasastry in Seattle, for explaining to me the intricacies of international law and its applicability;

Anika Rabbani, Asif Saleh, Chulie de Silva, Doris Voorbraak, Eeshita Azad, Ehtesham Huda, Farah Ghuznavi, Faustina Pereira, Miriam Otto, and Sadaf Saaz Siddiqi in Dhaka; Ahsan Akbar, Faisal Gazi, Ian Martin, Runi Khan, Simona Sultana, Sohini Alam, Tahmima Anam in London; and Raju Narisetti in New York, for support and encouragement;

And Suraya Khan, Faisal Sharif, Rahnuma Ahmed, Shahidul Alam, and Shahpar Selim in Dhaka; Ruchir Joshi in Kolkata; Devangshu Datta, Murali, Nilanjana Roy, and Usha Ramanathan in Delhi; and my brothers Pranav and Utpal Tripathi in Bombay, for generous hospitality at their homes.

Simar Puneet edited the text with her deft touch. Aienla Ozukum made the process smooth and was remarkably patient; and Bena Sareen designed just the right cover for the Indian edition that tells the complex story eloquently.

After the book's release in South Asia, Philippa Sitters at David Godwin Associates took it to a wider stage. I thank Jaya Aninda Chatterjee at Yale University Press for believing in the book and giving it wings. I also thank Meredith Phillips at Yale University Press for helping to guide the book to an international readership and Shahidul Alam at Drik for identifying the photograph of Rashid Talukder that told the story of the tragedy.

I dedicate this book to my sons who are my friends—Udayan and Ameya in New York. They were keen to read the book and kept reminding me to get off the internet and get on with my writing. Here it is.

I am grateful to the following sources, which have granted me permission to reproduce materials in this book:

The Caravan: A Journal of Politics and Culture, for permission to reproduce extracts and part of three articles "Bangladesh's Quest for Closure," "The Year of Living Dangerously," and "Delayed and Denied."

Debonair magazine, for permission to reproduce parts of my interview with the late Col. Farooq Rahman, published in *Debonair* in 1986.

Tarfia Faizullah, for permission to reproduce an extract from her poem, published in her collection *Seam* (2014).

Amitav Ghosh, for permission to quote an extract from his novel *The Shadow Lines* (Ravi Dayal, 1988).

Sultana Kamal, for permission to reproduce extracts from poems by the late Sufia Kamal.

Sudipto Chatterjee, for permission to reproduce his translation of the song "What's Lalon's Faith?"

The University of Southampton Library, for permission to reproduce a letter that Lord Mountbatten wrote to Mahatma Gandhi in 1947.

Taslima Nasrin, for permission to reproduce part of her poem, which appeared in *The Bangladesh Reader*, edited by Meghna Guhathakurta and Willem van Schendel.

The Nazrul Institute, for permission to quote from an extract from the poem at the monument near the shirishtola tree at the Dhaka University campus.

Rabindra Bhavan, Visva-bharati University, for permission to quote from Rabindranath Tagore's verse at the monument near the shirishtola tree at the Dhaka University campus.

Quotation from 'September on Jessore Road' by Allen Ginsberg. Copyright © Allen Ginsberg 1956, 1961, used by permission of The Wylie Agency (UK) Limited.

CHANGING TERMS OF TRADE BETWEEN EAST AND WEST PAKISTAN

	West Pakistan	East Pakistan	Total
1948–49 to 1960–61:			
Export earnings	8,962	12,488	21,450
Imports (-)	20,060	8,913	28,973
Foreign trade	–11,098	3,575	–7,523
Net capital import	5,015	2,508	7,523
Foreign exchange	–6,083	6,083	0
Net Inter-wing trade	2,994	–2,994	0
Exports/imports	5,460	–5,460	0
Imports/exports	–2,466	2,466	0
Net resources	3,089	–3,089	0
1961–62 to 1969–70			
Export earnings	15,043	15,402	30,445
Imports (-)	33,578	17,157	50,735
Foreign trade (-)	18,535	1,755	20,290
Net capital import	13,527	6,763	20,290
Foreign exchange	5,008	–5,008	0
Net inter-wing trade	4,508	–4,508	0
Exports/imports	10,400	–10,400	0
Imports/exports	–5,892	5,892	0
Net resources	500	–500	0

	West Pakistan	East Pakistan	Total
1969–70			
Export earnings	2,220	2,111	4,331
Imports (-)	4,081	2,369	6,450
Foreign trade (-)	1,861	0,258	2,119
Net capital import	1,165	0,954	2,119
Foreign exchange	-0,696	0,696	0
Net inter-wing trade	0,743	-0,743	0
Exports/imports	1,666	-1,666	0
Imports/exports	-0,923	0,923	0
Net resources	0,047	-0,047	0

All figures in billion Pakistani Rupees.
Courtesy: Dr Wolfgang-Peter Zingel– South Asia Institute of Heidelberg University, Department of Development Economics.

INTERVIEWS WITH BIRANGONAS

'They cut her breasts and destroyed her. She died.'

M was fourteen at the time of the war; the military came one night. Her uncle fled with his daughters and her to a jungle. They stayed safe that night, but the next morning a Razakar saw them. They slowly returned to their house, but the Razakar had already informed the soldiers.

There were eight of them. They raped M and her cousin, SO. They took another girl, who was called Beauty, to the army camp. She was sixteen. They raped her for three days. 'They cut her breasts and destroyed her. She died,' M said.

Later, M got married and her husband did not know about this incident. She could not have children because she was severely injured. When her husband found out about what had happened, he left her.

◆

'I don't remember what the three men did to me.'

HK hid behind the haystacks when the soldiers came. They had been hiding for a few days; her husband told her to go home and bring some rice and water. They went crawling to the house. But the soldiers found her husband and shot him in the thigh. She tied his leg up when they saw her.

They came to take her. One of her children tried to intervene but they hit the child hard with the rifle. Her three-year-old girl died.

'I don't remember what the three men did to me. Meanwhile, my husband regained senses. He realized they had taken me away. He went to my son, who was a teenager, and told him what had happened. The son said he'd go and kill the soldiers. But the father said he cannot fight them. The only thing is to protect yourself,' HK said.

The son came to the house and found her, got her water. That's when HK realized she was still alive. Her husband died soon, as his wound remained untreated.

◆

'I dreamt of a Bangladesh where I could live safely. Today I don't have food to eat.'

K used to cook for freedom fighters in a village called K'pur—three meals a day for thirty people. She did this quietly and stealthily, but one day a Razakar found out and told the army that she was cooking for the freedom fighters. He brought the army with him.

The freedom fighters figured out the army was coming so they fled. She left with them. When she was on her way to the new camp with four other women, a group of soldiers found them. They raped them and took K's two-and-a-half-year-old daughter to the camp. But a kind Bihari man called H, who supported the liberation movement, got her daughter back. He then warned her not to work with freedom fighters again.

Towards the end of the war, the army found out where H's sympathies lay. They took him away to kill him, but the village rose as one and rescued him.

◆

'My husband always brought up my rape because he thought he was violated and it was my fault.'

NJ was at her parents' home; they had already left because the Pakistani army was expected any moment. She left carrying a rice bag on her head and her child on her waist. The troops saw her. They surrounded her, held her and threw the child. They took her behind a school and raped her. 'I could not even get up,' she said. She could barely walk. Her parents took her to a doctor who treated her.

She spent three years at the rehabilitation centre. She recalled: 'Bongobondhu told us that he would accept us, even if no one else accepts us. You are like my daughters, he told us.'

When her husband returned, initially he did not know what had happened to her. When he did, he left her and remarried. Sixteen years later, he came back to live with her. 'He died in my home,' she told me.

'Why did you take him back?' I asked.

'People around him had told him that he should go back to me. I wanted my children back. Having their father around was important for them, so I let him come back. He never apologized. I used to work as a weaver and he would still insult me. He never understood—he always brought up my rape because he thought he was violated and it was my fault,' she explained.

◆

'I was very young.'

S was recently married when the war started. 'I was very young—15 or so,' she said. The Pakistani army was randomly attacking villages. One day they came to her village and burned her house down. Her husband was away at work in T'gaon. S lived with her mother then, but Razakars came there and told them it was safe to return. They were deliberately misinformed. The army had been waiting for them.

S hid in a pond besides a brick factory. But the army found them and ordered them to come out. The women were raped on the bank of the pond.

When her husband found out about that, he left her, returned to T'gaon and remarried. She now lives with her three sons—one is a rickshaw puller, while the others do odd jobs. S works as domestic help in different houses.

◆

'When I cross the road, people call me the wife of Pakistani military.'

AS's house was near a bridge; they used to store Mukti Bahini's weapons in their home. One day the freedom fighters blew the bridge; AS was with them passing the weapons. Those fighters told government officials that she was a freedom fighter too. But her neighbours continue to pass bad comments. 'When I cross the road, people call me the wife of Pakistani military. They tell us that when I die nobody will bury me,' she said. She told me that some of the Razakars manipulated records to obtain certificates denoting them as freedom fighters. They are getting benefits from the government. She cooked rice for the young boys and men fighting for freedom. She spied on the Pakistani military, found information on the location of their weapons from attendants at the hospital. She fed the boys who came from India, and hid their weapons safely. But she is not called a freedom fighter; those Razakars are.

'I'm tired of telling my story time and again. Nobody has done anything. We have no certificates but the Razakars do. I have nothing to show what

I did. Death would be much better than living like this,' she said.

◆

'I felt helpless; nobody was around. My husband did not want me back.'

R. spoke in a low voice. Her husband had gone to D'pur. She had no money; she could not run away. She saw people being killed in front of her. When the shooting started, she hid in a haystack. Razakars were walking around, looking for women. They came to her house. They picked up her child, so she came out running. They threw away the child. 'They violated me,' she said calmly.

People she knew had gone away and there was nobody to save her. They wanted to take her to the Pakistani army unit. She cried. They told her to go to the camp, where she would get everything—food and medicines. But R denied. She would rather die, than go.

'I felt helpless; nobody was around. The army had raped me; the Razakars had brought them to me. I had three children at that time. Two of the children were with my brothers; the youngest was with me; I was breastfeeding him. I decided to die with him. If need be. I was breastfeeding the child,' she said.

After that, she left for A'pur. She knocked on many doors and begged for help. She walked to her brother's home in another village.

She paused for some time, sobbing softly.

After the war, her husband returned. Her neighbours started to gossip and told him what had happened. 'He did not want me back,' she said. She went to the women's rehabilitation centre. Once it was closed down she worked as domestic help.

◆

'They only raped the poor.'

H made a hole in the ground and hid there when the soldiers came and set her home to fire. She was married and had a child, but they found her and raped her. 'They only raped the poor,' she said.

One day a train with Pakistani soldiers was coming to her village. Mukti Bahini set that train afire. 'I saw that and felt some satisfaction. All my sacrifices had not been worthless. I felt at peace,' she said.

◆

'I pleaded with them to leave me alone, but they raped me.'

AI's father was reading the Quran when the soldiers entered her home. They killed him and burned her house. She and her husband fled through the jungle and managed to reach her parents' place. When calm seemed to have returned, they came back to their home. But the army returned again.

AI held her nose and jumped in the water. She spent a long time in the pond, raising her head momentarily to breathe. The Razakar from their village found her and told her not to worry; that she would be safe at home. 'I trusted him and came out. I was scared because I saw soldiers passing by my home,' she said.

One day six men came. They were big and burly and carried guns. They asked her husband and father-in-law to leave. 'I pleaded with them to leave me alone, but they raped me,' she said. Five of the men raped her repeatedly. Her husband had been hit hard in the chest; he died later.

◆

'You are like my father, so please don't do this to me.'

AY lived with her daughter near the riverbank. Soldiers came to her home one day. One of the soldiers caught her hand. She told him: 'You are like my father, so please don't do this to me,' but he still raped her. Her husband fled to their farm. The soldiers burned their house. When he came back, the husband told her to leave but the village elders intervened and he took her back.

◆

'I never told my children what had happened but they found out from other people, who told them that their mother wasn't a good person.'

SU remembers seeing two Pakistani soldiers entering her house—one stayed at the door and one placed a gun on her husband's neck. They asked him to leave. He tried to leave with their children, but the children refused to leave. The soldier hit SU with his gun. She fell down and fainted. 'They may have raped me; I don't remember what happened,' she said, wiping her eyes.

Her husband brought her and the children to her father's home. Her father angrily asked: 'why have you brought her here?'

People in the village started saying bad things about her. She received no support from the state, only from private NGOs. 'I never told my children what had happened but they found out from other people, who told them that their mother wasn't a good person,' she added.

◆

'Sometimes people called me a prostitute.'

MO was 18 and married when the war started. She stayed at her parents' house for a week after her brother's death.

The army came to her father's village. Her father took her to the forest, hoping to find cover, but the army found them. The tried to snatch MO away from her father. 'My father held my hand tight, but so did the army. They started kicking my father, and he left me,' she said.

Three soldiers and a Razakar attacked her and she fainted. Her mother was in a state of shock. They sent word to her husband to come and collect her, but her father-in-law told her husband not to take her back. But he did take her back after six months. 'Sometimes people called me a prostitute—even now. The society did not accept us,' she said.

After the war the men in the village killed the Razakar.

◆

'Local politicians and NGOs have given us only words, but we have received nothing.'

AK was 14 or 15 and grew up in H'pur, and was married to a man from D'pur village. The army came to her village in October that year. She was at her in-laws' house. Many neighbours were Hindus and they had left for India. AK did not have money so they could not go to India. Besides, the military controlled the roads. 'We are small people, we did not want to take risks,' she said.

One day her husband went to Padma River to catch fish. She saw the weavers gather their wives and sisters and tried leaving with them; but they did not take her as she was not from their community. So she went to a poor villager's home to hide as she saw the army coming.

The soldiers told all women to come out. The women ran, and AK joined them, but the soldiers caught up. They told her: 'If you move, we will shoot you.'

Two soldiers raped her. Afterwards her mother-in-law came and took her away. They crossed the river and she cleaned her. Her husband got angry with her but a local Awami League leader and school teacher told him that it wasn't her fault. He then agreed to take her back.

'Even my daughters were treated badly by their husbands because of what happened to me. This is common knowledge, so people know. Journalists come and write stories, so our stories are known. Our need is a small plot of land and a monthly pension. Local politicians and NGOs have given us only words; we have received nothing.'

◆

'My husband was understanding. He knew I was alone, I was not protected, and I was violated. I had to save myself.'

J could hear the train coming to her village at 3 a.m. Her husband was hard of hearing, so she woke him up thinking the army was coming. She thought the soldiers would come and kill all of them. Reluctantly, her husband agreed to flee.

They hid in ponds and in the fields of sugarcane. They heard gunshots. They left quietly in the darkness and reached a village where the whole village was hiding. But the army reached there the next day and set the school on fire. They fled but the soldiers caught up with them. There was a woman with them who had just had a baby. She was still bleeding. They killed her child and cut her into pieces.

J kept running through the field as four soldiers were chasing her; she managed to swim away. Her husband could not find her for three days. He found her at another village. They lived there for six months.

It was later that she told her husband that the soldiers had raped her before she jumped into the water. They had restrained her while raping her. When she screamed, they slapped her hard. 'My husband was understanding. He knew I was alone and unprotected; and was violated. I had to save myself,' she said. 'He never insulted me, or brought it up. I never talked about it willingly.' But nobody was willing to employ her.

APPENDIX III

INSTRUMENT OF SURRENDER

The Pakistan Eastern Command agree to surrender all Pakistan Armed Forces in Bangla Desh to Lieutenant-General Jagjit Singh Aurora, General Officer Commanding in Chief of Indian and Bangla Desh forces in the Eastern Theater. This surrender includes all Pakistan land, air and naval forces as also all para-military forces and civil armed forces. These forces will lay down their arms and surrender at the places where they are currently located to the nearest regular troops under the command of Lieutenant-General Jagjit Singh Aurora.

The Pakistan Eastern Command shall come under the orders of Lieutenant-General Jagjit Singh Aurora as soon as the instrument has been signed. Disobedience of orders will be regarded as a breach of the surrender terms and will be dealt with in accordance with the accepted laws and usages of war. The decision of Lieutenant-General Jagjit Singh Aurora will be final, should any doubt arise as to the meaning or interpretation of the surrender terms.

Lieutenant Jagjit Singh Aurora gives a solemn assurance that personnel who surrender shall be treated with dignity and respect that soldiers are entitled to in accordance with provisions of the Geneva Convention and guarantees the safety and well-being of all Pakistan military and para-military forces who surrender. Protection will be provided to foreign nationals, ethnic minorities and personnel of West Pakistan origin by the forces under the command of Lieutenant-General Jagjit Singh Aurora.

BIBLIOGRAPHY

Afroz, Tuheen (ed.), *Genocide, War Crimes and Crimes against Humanity in Bangladesh: Trial under International Crimes (Tribunals) Act, 1973*, (Forum for Secular Bangladesh, 2010).

Ahmed, Imtiaz, *Historicizing 1971 Genocide: State versus Person*, (University Press Limited, 2009).

Ahmed, K Anis, *Goodnight, Mr Kissinger*, (University Press Limited, 2012).

———, *The World in My Hands*, (Random House India, 2013).

Ahmed, Maj Akhter, *Advance to Contact: A Soldier's Account of Bangladesh Liberation War*, (University Press Limited, 2000).

Akbar, M.J., *India: The Siege Within*, (Penguin, 1989).

Akhtar, Shaheen, *The Search*, (Zubaan, 2011).

Akhtar, Shaheen; Begum, Suraiya; Guhathakurta, Meghna; Hossain, Hameeda and Kamal, Sultana, *Rising from the Ashes: Women's Narratives of 1971*, (University Press Limited, 2012).

Alam, Habibul, *Brave of Heart*, (Academic Press and Publishers Library, 2008).

Alam, Shahidul, *The Birth Pangs of a Nation*, (Drik, 2011).

Ali, Rao Farman, *How Pakistan Got Divided*, (Jang, 1992).

Ali, S Mahmud, *Understanding Bangladesh*, (Hurst, 2010).

Anam, Tahmima, *A Golden Age*, (John Murray, 2007).

———, *The Good Muslim*, (Canongate, 2011).

Barkat, Abul, *An Inquiry into Causes and Consequences of Deprivation of Hindu Minorities in Bangladesh through the vested Property Act*, (PRIP Trust, 2000).

Bass, Gary J, *The Blood Telegram*, (Alfred A. Knopf, 2013).

Blood, Archer K, *The Cruel Birth of Bangladesh: Memoirs of an American Diplomat*, (University Press Limited, 2002).

Bose, Sarmila, *Dead Reckoning: Memories of the 1971 Bangladesh War*, (Hurst, 2011).

Butalia, Urvashi, *The Other Side of Silence: Voices from the Partition of India*, (Duke University Press, 2000).

Chatterji, Joya, *Bengal Divided: Hindu Communalism and Partition, 1932-1947*, (Cambridge University Press, 1994).

Chatterji, P.K., *Struggle and Strife in Urban Bengal: 1937-1947*, (Dasgupta, 1993).

Chaudhuri, Nirad, *The Autobiography of an Unknown Indian*, (University of California Press, 1951).

Chowdhury, G.W., *The Last Days of United Pakistan*, (University Press Limited, 2011).

Collins, Larry and Lapierre, Dominique, *Freedom at Midnight*, (Simon and Schuster, 1975).

Das, S, *Communal Riots in Bengal: 1905-1947*, (Oxford University Press, 1991).

D'Costa, Bina, *Nation-Building, Gender and War Crimes in South Asia*, (Routledge, 2011).

Eaton, Richard M, *The Rise of Islam and the Bengal Frontier: 1204-1760*, (University of California Press, 1993).

Elliot ,John; Imhasly, Bernard; and Denyer, Simon (ed.), *Foreign Correspondent: Fifty Years of Reporting in South Asia*, (Viking Penguin, 2008).

Faizullah, Tarfia, *Seam*, (Crab Orchard Review, 2014).

Faruqui, A, 'A Failure of Command: Lessons from Pakistan's India Wars 1947-1999', *Defense and Security Analysis*, Vol 17, 1, 2001.

Firdousi, Ishrat, *The Year That Was*, (Bastu Prakashan, 1996).

Ghatak, Ritwik, *Rows and Rows of Fences*, (Seagull, 2000).

Ghosh, Amitav, *The Shadow Lines*, (Ravi Dayal, 1988).

Goradia, Nayana, *Lord Curzon: The Last of the British Moghuls*, (Oxford University Press, 1993).

Gordon, Leonard, *Brothers Against the Raj*, (Columbia University Press, 1990).

Guhathakurta, Meghna, and van Schendel, Willem, *The Bangladesh Reader: History, Culture, Politics*, (Duke University Press, 2013).

Hasan, M.A., *Why Genocide and How to Prevent Genocide*, presented at South Asia Institute, Heidelberg University, 2013.

Hatch-Barnwell, Stephen, *The Last Guardian: Memoirs of Hatch-Barnwell*, (University Press Limited, 2011).

Hensher, Philip, *Scenes from Early Life*, (4th Estate, 2012).

Hoque, Mofidul, *Bangladesh Genocide and Quest for Justice*, (American Institute of Bangladesh Studies, 2011).

Hossain, Kamal, *Bangladesh: The Road to Independence*, (University Press Limited, 2012).

Hossain, Mokkorom, *From Protest to Freedom: The Birth of Bangladesh*, (Shahitya Prakash, 2011).

Hussain, Delwar, *Boundaries Undermined: The Ruins of Progress on the Bangladesh-India Border*, (C Hurst, 2013).

Hyder, Qurratulain, *Fireflies in the Mist*, (New Directions, 1994)

Imam, Jahanara, *Of Blood and Fire: The Untold Story of Bangladesh's War of Independence*, (University Press Limited, 1990)

Imam, Neamat, *The Black Coat*, (Penguin, 2013)

Islam, Manzu, *Song of our Swampland*, (Shahitya Prakash, 2010).

Islam, Nurul, *Making of a Nation: An Economist's Tale*, (University Press Limited, 2003).

Islam, Rafiqul, *A Tale of Millions*, (Ananya, 1974).

Jacob, Lt Gen J.F.R., *Surrender at Dacca: Birth of a Nation*, (Manohar, 1997)

Jalal, Ayesha, *The Sole Spokesman: Jinnah, the Muslim League, and the Demand for Pakistan*, (Cambridge University Press, 1985).

Kabir, Ananya Jahanara, *Partition's Post-Amnesias,* (Women Unlimited, 2013).

Kabir, Shahriar, *The Intolerable Sufferings of Seventy One*, (Forum for Secular Bangladesh, 2009).

———, *Tormenting Seventy One*, (Dana Printers, 1999).

Kann, Peter R, *A Reporter at Large: Selected Writings of Peter R Kann*, (Dow Jones & Company, 2007).

Karlekar, Hiranmay, *Bangladesh: The Next Afghanistan?* (Sage, 2005).

Khan, Adib, *Seasonal Adjustments*, (Allen & Unwin, 1994).

Khan, Asghar, *Generals in Politics: Pakistan 1958-1982*, (Vikas, 1983).

Khusru, B.Z., *Myths and Facts: Bangladesh Liberation War*, (Rupa, 2010).

Kissinger, Henry, *The White House Years*, (Phoenix Press, 1979).

Lalon Giti, (Aftar brothers, undated).

Lifschultz, Lawrence, *Bangladesh: The Unfinished Revolution*, (Zed, 1979).

Mahmud, Sezan, *Operation Jackpot,* (Mehedi Hasan, 2009).

Malik, Amita, *The Year of the Vulture*, (Orient Longmans, 1972).

Mamoon, Muntassir, *1971: Chuknagar Genocide*, (International Centre for Bengal Studies, 2011).

Mascarenhas, Anthony, *A Legacy of Blood*, (Hodder and Stoughton, 1986).

———, *The Rape of Bangladesh*, (Vikas 1971)

Minow, Martha, *Between Vengeance and Forgiveness: Facing History After Genocide and Mass Violence*, (Beacon Press, 1998).

Mohaiemen, Naeem (ed.), *Between Ashes and Hope: Chittagong Hill Tracts and the Blind Spot of Bangladesh Nationalism*, (Drishtipat Writers' Collective, 2010).

Mohsin, Amena, *The Politics of Nationalism: The Case of the Chittagong Hill Tracts*, (University Press Limited, 1997).

——— and Ahmed, Imtiaz, *Women and Militancy: South Asian Complexities*, (University Press Limited, 2011).

Mookherjee, Nayanika, 'Available motherhood: Legal technologies, 'state of exception' and the dekinning of 'war babies' in Bangladesh', *The state and children's fate: reproduction in traumatic times,* (2007).

———, 'Remembering to Forget: Public Secrecy and Memory of Sexual Violence in Bangladesh War of 1971', *Journal of the Royal Anthropological Institute*, 12: 433-450, (2006).

Muhith, A.M.A., *Bangladesh: Emergence of a Nation*, (University Press Limited, 1992).

Nabi, Nurul, *Bullets of '71: A Freedom Fighter's Story*, (Shahitya Prakash, 2012).

Noorozzaman, Quazi, *A Sector Commander Remembers: Bangladesh Liberation War 1971*, (University Press Limited, 2011).

Oldenburg, Philip, 'A Place Insufficiently Imagined', *Journal of Asian Studies*, Vol 44, 4, 1985.

Parekh, Kishor, *Bangladesh: A Brutal Birth*, (Image Photographic Services, 1972).

Payne, Robert, *The Tortured and the Damned*, (Vigward Limited, 1979).

People's Committee, *Report of People's Inquiry Commission on the Activities of War Criminals and Collaborators*, Ekattorer Ghatak Dalal Nirmul Committee, 1994.

Raghavan, Srinath, *1971: A Global History of the Creation of Bangladesh*, (Harvard University Press, 2013).

Rahman, Anisur, *Through Moments in History*, (Pathak Shamabesh Books, 2007).

Rahman, Mahmud, *Killing the Water*, (Penguin, 2010).

Rahman, Sheikh Mujibur. Alam, Fakrul (trans.), *The Unfinished Memoirs*, (Viking, 2013).

Rai, Raghu, *The Price of Freedom*, (Niyogi Books, 2013).

Raja, Maj. Gen. Khadim Hussain, *A Stranger In My Own Country: East Pakistan 1969-1971*, (Oxford University Press, 2012).

Raman, B, *The Kaoboys of R&AW: Down Memory Lane*, (Lancer, 2007).

Reza, C.M. Tarek, *Ekattor: Bijoyer Shei Khon*, (Nymphea, 2008).

Rosenbaum, Peter, *Payback: The Case for Revenge, (* The University of Chicago Press, 2013).

Sahgal, Nayantara, *Indira Gandhi: Tryst With Power*, (Penguin, 2012).

Saikia, Yasmin, *Women, War, and the Making of Bangladesh*, (Women Unlimited, 2011).

Salik, Siddiq, *Witness to Surrender*, (University Press Limited, 1997).

Salim, Ahmad, *We Owe an Apology to Bangladesh*, (Shahitya Prakash, 2012).

Schanberg, Sydney, *Beyond the Killing Fields: War Writings*, (Potomac Books, 2010).

Shafi, Mushtari, *Days of My Bleeding Heart*, (Mowla Brothers, 2010).

Shamsuddin, Abul Kalam, *Confession of a Terrorist! Musings on Bangladesh Liberation War*, (IP-6 Research Inc, 2011).

Sikkink, Kathryn, *The Justice Cascade: How Human Rights Prosecutions are Changing World Politics*, (WW Norton, 2011).

Singh, Lt Gen Depinder, *Field Marshal Sam Manekshaw: Soldiering with Dignity*, (Nataraj, 2002).

Sisson, Richard and Rose, Leo E, *War and Secession: Pakistan, India, and the Creation of Bangladesh*, (University of California Press, 1990).

Sobhan, Rehman, *A Memoir of My Role in Bangladesh War*, (Centre for Policy Dialogue, 2013).

———, 'East and West Pakistan: Economic Divergence'. Asian Survey, Vol 2, 5, 1962.

Sumro, Durdana, and Ghazala, Hameed, *Bengal Raag*, (University Press Limited, 2006).

Talbot, Ian, 'Jinnah and the Making of Pakistan', *History Today*, Vol 34, 2, 1984.

Talbot, Phillips, *An American Witness to India's Partition*, (Sage, 2007).

van Schendel, Willem, *A History of Bangladesh*, (Cambridge University Press, 2009).

Zaheer, Hasan, *The Separation of East Pakistan: The Rise and Realisation of Bengali Muslim Nationalism*, (University Press Limited, 1994).

Zaman, Niaz, *A Different Sita*, (Writers Ink, 2011).

——— and Farrukhi, Asif, *Fault Lines: Stories of 1971*, (University Press Limited, 2008).

ENDNOTES

PROLOGUE

1. In the years after Independence, several bahinis or forces that had been formed during or towards the end of the war had continued to operate, keeping control of areas where they had fought, acting as de facto militia meting out instant justice because the civilian administration was still trying to cope after the catastrophic war and the famine that had followed. The Rokkhi Bahini was loyal to Mujibur Rahman and was created after the war. It had gained notoriety because it had become a law unto itself, making increasingly absurd demands on a harassed citizenry, souring the mood of the public, and was allegedly involved in serious human rights violations, including torture and extra-judicial killings.
2. Her interview with bdnews24.com
3. 'Six Killers Still Out of Reach', *The Daily Star*, 15 August 2012 (http://archive. thedailystar.net/newDesign/news-details.php?nid=246248).
4. 'House of Aziz Pasha's Brother Torched', *The Daily Star*, 1 February 2010 (http:// archive.thedailystar.net/newDesign/news-details.php?nid=124318).
5. Hossain, Kamal, *Bangladesh: The Road to Independence,* (University Press Ltd, Dhaka, 2012).
6. According to bdnews24.com.

ONE: THE LAND THAT WASN'T EASY TO CARVE

7. The term 'Bangla' is derived from Vangala, which refers to the region and the language.
8. Mahasthan Brahmi Inscription, *Banglapedia: National Encyclopedia of Bangladesh*, Vol 6(2003), p350.
9. Guhathakurta, Meghna and van Schendel, Willem, *The Bangladesh Reader: History, Culture and Politics* (Duke University Press, 2013), p 37.
10. He is also believed to have attacked the Nalanda University in 1193 leading to its destruction.
11. University of California Press, Berkeley (1993).
12. There is also the joke in Bangladesh that Zia International Airport was so named because its acronym spelt ZIA. Not to be outdone, the new name for the airport

is Hazrat Shahjalal International Airport, which can be read—creatively—as HASINA, if the "a" after H and "n" after I are capitalized.

13. Khan, Shamsuzzaman and van Schendel, Willem (trans.), *The Bangladesh Reader*.

14. Macaulay, Thomas Babington, *Minute on Indian Education* (1835).

15. A digital version of the novel can be found here: http://digital.library.upenn.edu/women/sultana/dream/dream.html.

16. Chaudhuri, Nirad, *The Autobiography of an Unknown Indian*, (University of California Press, 1951).

17. Goradia, Nayana, *Lord Curzon: The Last of the British Moghuls*, (Oxford University Press, 1993), p 212.

18. Including Punjab's Lala Lajpatrai, Maharashtra's Bal Gangadhar Tilak, and Bengal's Bipin Chandra Pal.

19. Chatterji, Joya, *Bengal Divided: Hindu Communalism and Partition: 1932-1947*, (Cambridge University Press, 1994).

20. 'India: I and my Government', *Time* magazine, 8 February 1932.

21. Chatterji, op.cit..

22. Chatterjee, Partha, 'Transferring a Political Theory—Early Nationalist Thought in India', *Economic and Political Weekly*, Vol 21, 3, (18 January 1986).

23. Huq had presented the Lahore Resolution at the session of the Muslim League in 1940, which called for 'independent states' for Muslims in Northwest and Eastern India.

24. Jalal, Ayesha, *The Sole Spokesman: Jinnah, the Muslim League and the Demand for Pakistan*, (Cambridge University Press, 1985).

25. Anchor Books, 1999.

26. Mukerjee, Madhusree, *Churchill's Secret War*, (Basic Books, 2010).

27. Knowles, Daniel, 'Time to scotch the myth of Winston Churchill's infallibility, http://blogs.telegraph.co.uk/news/danielknowles/100169841/time-to-scotch-the-myth-of-winston-churchills-infallibility/

28. Herman, Arthur, 'Without Churchill, India's Famine Would Have Been Worse', http://www.winstonchurchill.org/learn/in-the-media/churchill-in-the-news/966-without-churchill-indias-famine-would-have-been-worse.

29. http://www.bbc.co.uk/blogs/thereporters/soutikbiswas/2010/10/how_churchill_starved_india.html

30. *The Bengal Tragedy*, (Hero Publication, Lahore, 1944), pp 101–2.

31. Markovits, Claude, *The Calcutta Riots of 1946*, Online Encyclopedia of Mass Violence, published 5 November 2007 (http://www.massviolence.org/The-Calcutta-Riots-of-1946) accessed 3 February 2014), ISSN 1961-9898.

32. Chatterji, P. K., *Struggle and Strife in Urban Bengal, 1937-1947*, (Das Gupta, Calcutta, 1991).

33. Das, S., *Communal Riots in Bengal 1905-1947*, (Oxford University Press, Delhi, 1991).

34. While India's Supreme Justice, Sir Patrick Spens's official report was not made public, one Indian historian did use the document in recounting the violence.

See Ibid. Also see Tuker, F., *While Memory Serves*, (Cassell & Co, London, 1950); the memoir of Sir Francis Tuker, who was the lieutenant-general in command of the army in the eastern command.

35. Butalia, Urvashi, *The Other Side of Silence: Voices from the Partition of India,* (Duke University Press, 2000).

36. Talbot, Phillip, *An American Witness to India's Partition,* (Sage, 2007).

37. Because of the famine.

38. Dandavate, Madhu, '*Gandhi's Human Touch*', annual lecture presented at the Gandhi Foundation, London (1997)(http://www.mkgandhi.org/humantouch.htm).

39. Ibid.

40. Sylhet was a Bengali-majority district which was administratively treated as a part of Assam. At the time of Partition, the district was offered a choice to go with Bengali-speaking East Pakistan or stay with Assam. Sylhet was a Muslim majority region but the Bengali factor was equally important. A famous Sylheti Muslim League partition-era slogan in Sylheti dialect went: *Sylhet Loilam Gono Votay Assam Loibo Lathir Zooray* (We took Sylhet via the people's vote, we'll take Assam by the strength of our lathis).

41. Translated by Meghna Guhathakurta.

42. Ghatak, Ritwik, *Rows and Rows of Fences,* (Seagull Books, 2000), p 50.

TWO: THE GIRL WHO NO LONGER FELT PAKISTANI

43. Translated by Leesa Gazi at author's request.

44. Translated by Devangshu Datta at author's request.

45. 55 per cent.

46. *The Pakistani Gazetteer,* 25 February 1948.

47. Ibid.

48. Zaheer, Hasan, *The Separation of East Pakistan: The Rise and Realisation of Bengali Muslim Nationalism,* (Oxford University Press, Karachi and University Press Ltd, Dhaka, 1994), p 21.

49. Jahan, Rounaq, *Pakistan: Failure in National Integration,* (Columbia University Press, New York, 1972).

50. Muhammad Ali Jinnah's first presidential address at Pakistan's Constituent Assembly on 11 August 1947 cited in G. Allana, *Pakistan Movement Historical Documents,* (Department of International Relations, University of Karachi, nd [1969]), pp 407–411   (http://www.columbia.edu/itc/mealac/pritchett/00islamlinks/txt_jinnah_assembly_1947.html).

51. Later in life Nurul Amin went on to become Pakistan's titular Prime Minister during the Liberation War; he was later the vice-president under Zulfikar Ali Bhutto.

52. The letter's text can be found at: http://en.wikisource.org/wiki/Resignation_letter_of_Jogendra_Nath_Mandal

53. Oldenburg, Philip, 'A Place Insufficiently Imagined in Language, Belief and Pakistan Crisis of 1971', *Journal of Asian Studies,* Vol 44, 4, (1985), pp 711–733.

54. Hossain, Kamal, *Bangladesh: The Road to Independence,* (University Press Ltd, Dhaka, 2013).

55. van Schendel, Willem (op.cit.), p 112.

56. 'Interview with Hasan Azizul Huq by Md Mahabubar Rahman', van Schendel, Willem (trans.), *The Bangladesh Reader,* p 169.

57. van Schendel, Willem, 'Intaz: the Five-fold Citizen', *A History of Bangladesh* (Cambridge University Press, 2009), pp 102-103.

58. Many such laws were changed after the War of Independence in 1971, but the Enemy Property Act remained on the books. Awami politicians took over the property left behind by the Hindus who had sought refuge in India during the war, according to Dutta.

59. Talbot, Ian, 'Jinnah and the Making of Pakistan', *History Today,* Vol 34, 2(1984) (http://www.historytoday.com/ian-talbot/jinnah-and-making-pakistan).

60. Author interview with Sultana Kamal; Hoque, Mofidul, 'Sufia Kamal: Her Journey towards Freedom', *The Daily Star,* 7 July 2012 (http://archive.thedailystar.net/forum/2012/July/sufia.htm).

61. Sobhan, Rehman, 'East and West Pakistan: Economic Divergence from The Problems of Regional Imbalance in Economic Development of Pakistan', *Asian Survey,* Vol 2, 5 (1962), cited in *The Bangladesh Reader.*

62. Khan S.U., 'A Measure of Economic Growth in East and West Pakistan', *Pakistan Development Review,* (Autumn, 1961).

63. Reports of the Advisory Panels for the Fourth Five Year Plan 1970–75, Vol I, published by the Planning Commission of Pakistan.

64. For detailed statistical analysis, see Appendix I.

65. CBS News clip with Walter Cronkite: https://www.youtube.com/watch?v=YUCMCXfscgc#t=24.

THREE: THE MAKING OF A SAINT

66. In the Constituent Assembly Mujib said, 'Sir [President of the Constituent Assembly], you will see that they want to place the word "East Pakistan" instead of "East Bengal". We had demanded so many times that you should use Bengal instead of Pakistan. The word "Bengal" has a history, has a tradition of its own. You can change it only after the people have been consulted. So far as the question of One Unit is concerned it can come in the constitution. Why do you want it to be taken up just now? What about the state language, Bengali? We will be prepared to consider One Unit with all these things. So I appeal to my friends on that side to allow the people to give their verdict in any way, in the form of referendum or in the form of plebiscite.'

67. Blood, Archer K., *The Cruel Birth of Bangladesh,* (University Press Ltd, Dhaka,

2002) p 41.

68. van Schendel, Willem, *A History of Bangladesh*, (Cambridge University Press, 2009), p 124.

69. Interview with Gen. A.A.K. Niazi, *India Abroad*, February 2004 (http://www.rediff.com/news/2004/feb/02inter1.htm).

70. Khan, Asghar, *Generals in Politics: Pakistan 1958-1982*, (Vikas Publishing House, 1983), p 28, cited in van Schendel (op.cit.)

71. Blood, op.cit., p 181.

72. According to Mahfuz Anam's recollection.

73. Anonymous source.

FOUR: THE NIGHT THE KILLINGS BEGAN

74. Basanti Guhathakurta wrote a memoir of the war in Bengali in 1991, called *Ekattorer Sriti* (Memories of 1971). I have drawn my narrative primarily on interviews and conversations with Meghna Guhathakurta including a visit to the apartment complex where she graciously took me, as well as Professor Anisur Rahman's memoir *My Story of 1971: Through the Holocaust that Created Bangladesh* (1991).

75. The three main rivers of the country.

76. Interview with Irene Khan, 2011.

77. The video can be seen here: https://www.youtube.com/watch?v=CUD9sNkt2RI

78. Malik, Amita, *The Year of the Vulture*, (Orient Longmans, New Delhi, 1972), pp 79–83.

79. The film can be seen here: https://www.youtube.com/watch?v=lvbotYo-6rI

80. In the case of Rokeya Hall, there are some accounts which claim dozens of women were raped and taken away to cantonments. They were rescued months later by the Red Cross. One of the problems with the Bangladesh war of liberation, as with many other conflicts, is that few records are kept making it hard to get confirmed figures of the number of dead or wounded. Critics sympathetic to Pakistan have blamed Bangladeshis for exaggerating their suffering; writers sympathetic to Bangladesh have accused Pakistan of understating the army's brutality and cruelty. Rather than relying on those accounts, I have discussed the issue of rape separately in a stand-alone chapter, drawing on personal testimonies of women I interviewed in Bogura, Sirajganj, Kushtia, and Dhaka in 2011 and 2012. More testimonies can be found in Appendix II.

81. Blood, op.cit., p 207.

82. Sheel, Kaliranjan, *Jagannath Hall-ei chhilam* (I was in Jagannath Hall), Haider, Rashid (ed.), *1971: Bhoyaboho Obiggota*, (Sahitya Prakash, Dhaka, 1996).

83. These figures have been discussed elaborately later.

84. Blood, op.cit.

85. Ibid., p 201.

86. Mascarenhas, Anthony, '*Genocide*', *The Sunday Times*, 13 June 1971.

87. The headline in *The Pakistan Times* on March 27, 1971 read: 'Political Activities Banned: Awami League is Outlawed—Defiance of Law Act of Treason—A.L. Insulted National Flag and Quaid—Transfer of Power Pledge Retreated—President's Address to Nation.'

88. According to most accounts, it read: '*This may be my last message to you. From today Bangladesh is an independent country. I am calling you, wherever any of you are and with whatever you have in your hands to build resistance against the occupation army until your last breath. Carry your struggle until the day when the last soldier of the occupation army is driven out from the land of Bangladesh and final victory is won.*' (cited in Anisur Rahman's memoir, cited earlier).

89. I have based this account from extended interviews with Mushtari Shafi, Latifa Siddiqi, and others in Chittagong. Bangladesh's politics is now so vitiated by the bitter rivalry among the two major parties—Awami League and the Bangladesh Nationalist Party—that there is a dispute over the exact words Ziaur Rahman used while making the independence declaration; in particular, whether he made the announcement in the name of Mujibur Rahman or not. Awami supporters insist he said so, as they go about minimising Zia's role in the Liberation War. BNP supporters argue that Zia did not invoke Mujib's name; and that he made the announcement in his own name. At root is not only the conflict over who was the greater freedom fighter and greater patriot—Zia or Mujib—but also, who played a bigger role in winning Bangladesh's freedom: civilian Awami politicians or East Pakistani soldiers who rebelled under the command of various sector commanders.

But it is a puerile controversy. In *Muktir Gaan* (Freedom Song), the documentary of film-makers Tareque and Catherine Masud, there is a recording of Zia's announcement, which clearly states that he was speaking on behalf of Sheikh Mujib. And yet, the issue has become so divisive in Bangladesh now, that it is impossible for anyone to express a view about what may really have happened, for fear of being accused of partisanship. While the Zia Memorial in Chittagong has recreated the radio console from where Zia made the announcement, no recording of the announcement is played at the memorial. The truth is that there were several announcements made by several people, of whom Zia was the most prominent. In some announcements, Mujib's name may not have been invoked, but in others, it was. Regardless, both sides want to claim victory, and in the current political mood, neither party is willing to concede its position.

90. Kamal, Sufia, *Benibinnash shomoy to ar nei,* Ahmad, Abrar (trans.), *Under the Krishnachura: Fifty Years of Bangladeshi Writing,* (University Press Limited, 2003), cited in van Schendel, Willem, *A History of Bangladesh,* (Cambridge, 2009).

91. Blood, op.cit., p 155.

92. Ibid., p 215.

93. http://www2.gwu.edu/~nsarchiv/NSAEBB/NSAEBB79/BEBB8.pdf

94. Raghavan, Srinath, *1971: A Global History of the Creation of Bangladesh,* (Harvard, 2013).

95. Bass, Gary, *The Blood Telegram: Nixon, Kissinger, and A Forgotten Genocide,* (Knopf, New York, 2013).

96. Ibid.

97. Kissinger, Henry. *White House Years,* p 848.

98. Mascarenhas, op.cit.

99. Al-Badr and Al-Shams, like the Jamaat-e-Islami, opposed Bangladesh's independence. Some of its leaders took part in what they described as the civil war of 1971 through the militia—Al-Badr and Al-Shams and Razakars as well as through Peace Committees that the Pakistani army had set up. The Jamaat owes its origins to 1941, when Syed Abul Ala Maududi founded the party in Lahore. It did not support the creation of Pakistan, believing instead that India would one day get converted to Islam. After 1947, Maududi moved to Pakistan, and what is today the Bangladeshi Jamaat became its East Pakistan wing. Ironically, not enthusiastic about the creation of Pakistan in 1947, Jamaat by 1971 also did not support its break up.

100. Rai, Raghu, *Bangladesh: The Price of Freedom,* (Niyogi Books, 2013).

101. An undated video shows some of the panic in Dacca as refugees prepare to leave (http://www.youtube.com/watch?v=t8FqfHcvr0c).

102. UN High Commissioner for Refugees, 'Chapter 3: Rupture in South Asia', *The State of the World's Refugees: Fifty Years of Humanitarian Action,* (Geneva, 2000) , pp 59–77 (http://www.unhcr.org/3ebf9bab0.html).

103. Joan Baez's song can be seen here: http://www.youtube.com/watch?v=KUcgzphu850

104. There was huge support for the Bangladesh freedom movement in India at that time, in particular in Calcutta, from where the Bangladesh government-in-exile operated. The writer and film-maker Ruchir Joshi who grew up in Calcutta was a schoolboy at that time and he remembers elders around him referring to 'genocide'. Salil Chowdhury, the composer in Bombay's film industry, created a series of songs that were to form part of an opera dedicated to Bangladesh's freedom struggle, but the project did not materialize. The recordings were digitally restored and are now available through the Internet.

105. The film can be seen here: https://www.youtube.com/watch?v=vFHlPID-eSk

106. A few accounts, including Bose's book, refer to three trucks. The witnesses I spoke to all mentioned two, so I have chosen the figure two.

107. Film synopsis here: http://observerbd.com/details.php?id=4804.

108. Mamoon, Muntassir (ed.), *1971: Chuknagar Genocide,* (International Centre for Bengal Studies,Dhaka, 2011).

109. A crore is 10 million, not one million, as the *Guardian* reports.

110. Bose, Sarmila, *Dead Reckoning: Memories of the 1971 Bangladesh War,* (Hurst, London, 2011).

111. Gordon, Leonard, *Brothers Against the Raj,* (Columbia University Press, 1990).

112. Bose, op.cit., p. 124.

113. Ibid.

114. Bose, op.cit. 125

FIVE: THE FREEDOM FIGHTERS

115. Kann, Peter R, 'A Flickering Cause', The Wall Street Journal, 21 April 1971, (Reproduced in A Reporter At Large: Selected Writings of Peter R Kann (Dow Jones & Co, for private circulation).
116. Bhutto, Benazir Daughter of the East (Hamilton, 1988)
117. Coggins, Dan, 'The Battle of Kushtia', Time magazine, 19 April 1971 (http:// content.time.com/time/magazine/article/0,9171,905021,00.html).
118. Akbar, M.J., India: The Siege Within (Penguin, 1989), p 74.
119. Jacob, Lt Gen J.F.R., Surrender at Dacca: Birth of a Nation, (Manohar, Delhi, 1997), p 44.
120. Raman B. The Kaoboys of R&AW (Lancer Publishers, Delhi, 2007), p 7-8.
121. Field Marshal KM Cariappa Memorial Lectures 1995-2000 (Lancer Publishers, Delhi, 2001). http://indianeconomy.org/2007/10/12/when-manekshaw-confronted-indiras-cabinet. While this anecdote is colourful and characteristic of Manekshaw's style, there are no other records of the conversation, except his speech, as reported. Even if parts of it are apocryphal, the spirit of the conversation is consistent with the aura Manekshaw exuded.
122. Mascarenhas, op.cit.
123. Ibid.
124. Kann left Dow Jones & Co before it was acquired by News Corp.
125. Kann, Peter, 'Grieving Multitudes Flee East Pakistan; Add to Area's Turmoil', The Wall Street Journal, April 28, 1971.
126. Sisson, Richard and Rose, Leo E., War and Secession: Pakistan, India and the Creation of Bangladesh, (University of California Press, 1991)
127. Jacob, op.cit., p 91.
128. Salik, Siddiq, Witness to Surrender, (University Press Ltd, Dhaka, 1997—first published 1977), p 104
129. Ibid., p 97–106.
130. Greenway, David, Mujib's Secret Trial, Time magazine, 23 August 1971.
131. Bass, op.cit.
132. Gofran, Abdul, Foy's Lake Gonohotta (Massacre at Foy's Lake), in Haider, Rashid (ed.), 1971: Terrible Experiences., Nazneen, Sohela (trans.) Totten, Samuel, S Parsons, William, W Charney, Israel (ed.), Century of Genocide: Critical Essays and Eyewitness Accounts (Routledge, 2004, pp 274–275).
133. One of them, Pervaiz Mehdi Qureshi, later became the chief of Pakistan's Air Force (1997–2000).
134. Salik, op.cit., p 128.
135. D'Costa, Jerome, A Tribute to My Father (Bangladesh Genocide Archive, http:// bangladeshcanadaandbeyond.blogspot.co.uk/2009/03/bangladesh-war-of-

independence-tribute.html)

136. Faruqui, A, *Failure in Command: Lessons from Pakistan's Indian Wars, 1947-1999,* Defense and Security Analysis, Vol 17, 1 April 2001, pp 31–40 (Routledge).

SIX: A FRIEND IN NEED: IN WHICH INDIA JOINS THE WAR

137. Operation Focus was the opening airstrike by Israel at the start of the Six-Day War in 1967. At 7:45 on June 5, 1967, the Israeli Air Force launched a massive airstrike that destroyed the majority of the Egyptian Air Force on the ground. By noon, the Egyptian, Jordanian and Syrian Air Forces, with about 450 aircraft, were destroyed. Israel also disabled 18 airfields in Egypt. It remains one of the most successful air attack campaigns in military history.

138. A report about the speech can be found at: http://www.bharat-rakshak.com/1971/Dec03/Art02.htm

139. Kann, Peter, 'From a Dacca Hotel, Indo-Pakistani Conflict Resembles a War Movie', *The Wall Street Journal,* December 7, 1971 ibid. Kann.

140. Sontag, Susan, *On Photography,* (Picador, 1977).

141. Behr, Edward, *Anyone Here Been Raped and Speaks English?,* (New English Library, 1978).

142. Parekh, Kishor, *Bangladesh: A Brutal Birth,* (Image Photographic Services, Hong Kong 1972).

143. Salik, op.cit., p 193–194.

144. Raghavan, Srinath, op. cit.

145. For the Surrender Instrument, see Appendix III.

146. Assuming for a moment that the 1971 war was 'a conflict not of international character', Common Article 3 of the Geneva Conventions applies in this case. The Article states: 'In the case of armed conflict not of an international character occurring in the territory of one of the High Contracting Parties, each Party to the conflict shall be bound to apply, as a minimum, the following provisions:

(1) Persons taking no active part in the hostilities, including members of armed forces who have laid down their arms and those placed 'hors de combat' by sickness, wounds, detention, or any other cause, shall in all circumstances be treated humanely, without any adverse distinction founded on race, colour, religion or faith, sex, birth or wealth, or any other similar criteria. To this end, the following acts are and shall remain prohibited at any time and in any place whatsoever with respect to the above-mentioned persons:

    (a) violence to life and person, in particular murder of all kinds, mutilation, cruel treatment and torture;

    (b) taking of hostages;

    (c) outrages upon personal dignity, in particular humiliating and degrading treatment;

    (d) the passing of sentences and the carrying out of executions without previous judgment pronounced by a regularly constituted court, affording all the judicial guarantees which are recognized as indispensable by civilized peoples.

(2)   The wounded and sick shall be collected and cared for. An impartial humanitarian body, such as the International Committee of the Red Cross, may offer its services to the Parties to the conflict. The Parties to the conflict should further endeavour to bring into force, by means of special agreements, all or part of the other provisions of the present Convention. The application of the preceding provisions shall not affect the legal status of the Parties to the conflict.'(http://www.icrc.org/ihl.nsf/WebART/375-590006).

147. May, Brian, *The Times,* December 21, 1971, p 4. Also see Stanhope, H, *Mukti Bahini Bayonet Prisoners After Prayers, The Times, 20* December 1971, p 4.

148. Lifschultz, Lawrence, *Bangladesh: The Unfinished Revolution,* (Zed Press, 1979), p 64.

149. Saikia, Yasmin, *Women, War and Making Bangladesh: Remembering 1971,* (Duke University Press, 2011), p. 257.

150. http://www.lrb.co.uk/v29/n19/tariq-ali/pakistan-at-sixty

151. Mamoon, Muntassir, *The Vanquished Generals and the Liberation War of Bangladesh,* Ibrahim, Kushal (trans.), (Somoy Prakashan, 2000), p 29.

152. An interview with Col. Tara can be found here: http://www.youtube.com/watch?v=U6leipErpKg

153. http://uddari.wordpress.com/2011/03/30/liberation-war-historicizing-a-personal-narrative-by-col-nadir-ali/

154. The month of shraban, the period of rains.

155. In 1974, Faiz visited Bangladesh and was grieved by what he saw and felt enormous guilt over what Pakistan had done to the nation. He wrote a memorable ghazal, later translated by the gifted Kashmiri poet, Agha Shahid Ali.

156. https://www.youtube.com/watch?v=tIu5jZjaHA0

157. Kann, Peter, 'Dacca Diary II: A Reporter Chronicles Long Week of Waiting for Sordid War to End' (*The Wall Street Journal,* December 21, 1971).

SEVEN: THE BRAVE ONES

158. Anam, Tahmima, *The Good Muslim,* (Harper Collins, 2011).

159. I thank the actor Leesa Gazi and the academic Nayanika Mookherjee for pointing out this reference to me. Many in Bangladesh have credited Mujibur Rahman with coining the term. But Gazi used the clipping in her play, *Birangona,* drawing on Mookherjee's research which reveals a long-forgotten news report from December 1971 which said: 'It was reported on 22nd December 1971, 6 days after the war ended, the Interim Government of Bangladesh, announced that all young girls and women who have been subjected to inhuman torture and rape by the occupying Pakistani army in the last nine months will all be accorded full

respect as Birangonas of the Bangladesh liberation struggle.'

160. Malcolm, Janet, *The Journalist and the Murderer,* (Alfred A. Knopf, 1990).

161. Mookherjee, Nayanika, *The Spectral Wound: Sexual Violence, Public Memories and the Bangladesh War of 1971,* (Duke University Press—forthcoming).

162. Mondol, M Akhtaruzzaman, *Amader Ma-Bon* (Our Mother and Sisters), in Rashid Haider (ed.) *1971: Terrible Experiences,* p 197.

163. Saikia, Yasmin *Women, War, and the Making of Bangladesh: Remembering 1971,* (Duke University Press, 2011).

164. One important exception is Afsan Chowdhury's monumental four-volume work, *Bangladesh 1971* (Mowla Brothers, 2007) which succeeds to a great extent in providing a truly complete account of the experiences of all communities affected by the war.

165. My visits to Bihari camps would have been impossible without the support of BLAST.

166. Review of *Women, War, and the Making of Bangladesh: Remembering 1971*, Bina D'Costa, Journal of Genocide Research, Vol 14, 1, 2012 (http://www.tandfonline.com/doi/abs/10.1080/14623528.2012.656994).

167. Ferdousi Priyobhasini has narrated her story on the Bangla website, www.gunijan.com.

168. The Women's International War Crimes Tribunal on Japan's Military Sexual Slavery (the Women's Tribunal) was a people's tribunal organized by Asian women's rights and human rights organizations and supported by international NGOs. It was set up to adjudicate Japan's military sexual violence, in particular the enslavement of 'comfort women,' to bring those responsible for it to justice, and to end the ongoing cycle of impunity for wartime sexual violence against women. http://www1.jca.apc.org/vaww-net-japan/english/womenstribunal2000/whatstribunal.html

169. D'Costa, Bina, *Nationbuilding, Gender and War Crimes in South Asia,* (Routledge, London, 2011) (second edition 2013). Also D'Costa, Bina, *Children as Political Subjects-Babies as Political Objects* in *Children and Violence: Politics of Conflict in South Asia* (ed. D'Costa, Bina) (Cambridge University Press, London, forthcoming).

170. Raja, Khadim Hussain, *A Stranger in my Own Country: East Pakistan 1969-1971,* (Oxford University Press, 2012).

171. Farman Ali, Rao, *How Pakistan Got Divided,* (Jang Publications, Lahore, 1992).

172. *Ami Birangona Bolchhi* (I, a Brave Woman, am Speaking) is a collection of stories that Ibrahim wrote based on her work as a member of the women's rehabilitation centre that looked after many of the raped women. Some of the women had been taken away and they resettled in Europe after they underwent abortion. Some chose to accompany the soldiers back to their homes, where the soldier was already married. These were vivid and believable stories, written as first person narratives. And they added another complex layer to the narrative about women

during the war, besides saying a great deal about how they were stigmatized by Bangladeshis and family members after the war.

173. Although M, a social worker, told D'Costa in an interview: 'Nobody wanted Pakistani babies. Nobody! Neither the parents, nor the government, and nor the women.'

174. In an interview given just before his death in Sydney, Australia, on 13 October 2008, Dr Davis commented on his work in Bangladesh immediately after the War: http://archive.thedailystar.net/suppliments/2009/december/victorydayspecial/page02.htm

175. Mookherjee, Nayanika, Available motherhood: Legal technologies, 'state of exception' and the dekinning of 'war babies' in Bangladesh.' Childhood: a journal of global child research. Special issue, *The state and children's fate: reproduction in traumatic times* 14(3): 339-354. (2007)

176. See Appendix II.

EIGHT: THE ASSASSINATION OF A FAILED REVOLUTIONARY

177. Anderson, Benedict, *Imagined Communities,* (Verso, 1991).

178. A Bangla phrase, meaning 'boys abandoned by their mothers and thrashed by their fathers.'

179. As reported to author.

180. Lifschultz, Lawrence, *Bangladesh: The Unfinished Revolution,* (Zed Press, 1979).

181. He was honoured with Bir Uttom, Bangladesh's second-highest military honour.

182. Shawkat Ali had been sector commander for Sylhet.

183. Taher was appointed sector commander for Mymensingh / Tangail in October when Ziaur Rahman was moved to Sylhet, but he was grievously injured and lost part of his leg. He was sent to India for treatment in November.

184. Mascarenhas, Anthony, *Bangladesh: A Legacy of Blood* (Hodder and Stoughton, 1986).

185. He was promoted to lieutenant-colonel after the coup.

186. Meghna Guhathakurta's recollection.

187. Lifschultz, op.cit.

188. A formal trial of the assassins was only going to be possible if the Awami League came to power. That happened in 1996, and Mujib's daughter, Sheikh Hasina, became prime minister. The cases began and the court found all 12 defendants guilty. But Hasina lost the 2001 elections, and the process stopped, resuming only after her victory in the elections of December 2008. The Bangladesh government wants to bring the surviving officers back to Bangladesh to face trial. But bringing all of them back may not be easy, because under Bangladeshi law they are likely to face executions. Two of the countries where these men are allegedly hiding are Canada and South Africa and both have abolished the death penalty. Kenya has also temporarily suspended the death penalty, making

it harder for those governments to extradite them to Bangladesh.

189. During his lifetime Sheikh Mujib was close to Kamal Hossain. He even got him to return to his cabinet after old colleagues like Tajuddin had left him. But Hasina and Kamal parted ways in early 1990s and in 1992 Kamal formed his own political party, Gono Forum.

190. http://bdnews24.com/bangladesh/2014/05/17/pm-s-poignant-recollection

191. In August 1996, when the Awami League came to power, the case was revived. In October, the investigative officer charge-sheeted 21 officers. Mostaq had died by then. On 20 October 2004, the court ruled, sentencing three fugitive former army personnel to death, 12 former army personnel were sentenced to life imprisonment, and acquitting five others, including four senior politicians of the then ruling Bangladesh Nationalist Party, were acquitted. On 28 August 2008, the Supreme Court acquitted some more of them.

192. Lifschultz, op.cit., p 66.

NINE: GETTING TO KNOW THE GENERALS

193. Hasina would continue the trend when she rejected the views of several experts and parliamentarians who argued that as a secular republic, Bangladesh should repeal the constitutional provision that made Islam its state religion.

194. Later Farooq formed the Freedom Party which participated in the sham elections of 1988, and one of the officers who shot Mujib, Bazlul Huda, got elected to parliament on its ticket.

TEN: TWO WOMEN AND THEIR TROUBLED INHERITANCE

195. Similarly, it should be noted that soldiers who knew who had killed Manzur were willing to testify only after Hasina came to power.

196. Karlekar, Hiranmay, *Bangladesh: The Next Afghanistan?*, (Sage, 2006).

197. http://tarequemasud.org/films/naroshundor/

198. Swapnabhoomi. See http://www.swapnabhumi.com/index.html

199. The Awami League had campaigned for what became the 13th amendment which enabled the caretaker governments, and such a rule was established in 1996. The Supreme Court in 2011 ruled the amendment 'void', making the requirement of caretaker government unnecessary.

200. The conversation can be heard on this link. http://www.dhakatribune.com/politics/2013/oct/29/partial-transcript-hasina-khaleda-conversation.

201. A partial transcript of the conversation in Bengali can be read here: http://www.dhakatribune.com/politics/2013/oct/29/partial-transcript-hasina-khaleda-conversation

202. Sobhan, Zafar, 'Bangladesh: In the Aftermath of 1/11', *Seminar,* Issue 611, 2010. http://www.india-seminar.com/2010/611/611_zafar_sobhan.htm

ELEVEN: JUDGEMENT DAY

203. Kundera, Milan, *Kniha smíchu a zapomnění (The Book of Laughter and Forgetting)*, (Harper Perennial, 1979).
204. Coincidentally, Pal was born in Kushtia in what was then East Bengal.
205. Mbeki, Thabo, and Mamdani, Mahmoon, *Courts Can't End Civil Wars, The New York Times*, 5 Feb 2014) http://www.nytimes.com/2014/02/06/opinion/courts-cant-end-civil-wars.html?
206. https://www.giz.de/en/mediacenter/10964.html
207. Rahman, Serajur, '*Mujib's Confusion on Bangladeshi Deaths*', *The Guardian*, 23 May 2011) (http://www.theguardian.com/world/2011/may/24/mujib-confusion-on-bangladeshi-deaths).
208. The choice of *Pravda* as a source should raise doubts. A joke in the Cold War era went thus: there were two major newspapers in the Soviet Union—*Pravda* (truth) and *Izvestia* (news). And Russians knew that there was no news in *Pravda* and no truth in *Izvestia*.
209. Rummel, Rudolph, *Death by Government*, (Transaction Publishers, 1997), p 334.
210. Bergman, David, '*Questioning an Iconic Number*', *The Hindu*, 24 April 2014: (http://www.thehindu.com/opinion/lead/questioning-an-iconic-number/article5940833.ece).
211. Sisson and Rose, op.cit.
212. Jacob op.cit.
213. Karim, Bianca, Theunissen, Tirza (29). Shelton, Dinah (ed), *International Law and Domestic Legal Systems: Incorporation, Transformation, and Persuasion* (Oxford University Press), p 114.
214. Amir-Ul Islam, M. (2012). Morten Bergsmo, Cheah Wui Ling, ed. *Old Evidence and Core International Crimes*. Torkel Opsahl. p 254.
215. See, for example Karim, Theunissen, op.cit.
216. Imam, Jahanara, *Of Blood and Fire: The Untold Story of Bangladesh's War of Independence*, (Advent Books, 1989).
217. Syed, Zain Al-Mahmood, '*Bangladesh War Crimes Court Sentences Islamist Leader to Life*', *The Wall Street Journal*, 5 February 2013. (http://online.wsj.com/news/articles/SB10001424127887324445904578285253762636258?mg=reno64-wsj).
218. Human Rights Watch: *Bangladesh: Find Abducted Witness* (http://www.hrw.org/news/2013/01/16/bangladesh-find-abducted-witness, Jan 16, 2013).
219. Bergman, David, *Witness Alleges State Abduction*, (New Age, Dhaka, 16 May 2013) (http://www.newagebd.com/detail.php?date=2013-05-16&nid=49319#.UZSr-KLFXO_).
220. 'The Trial of the Birth of a Nation', *The Economist,* 15 December 2012 (http://www.economist.com/news/briefing/21568349-week-chairman-bangladeshs-international-crimes-tribunal-resigned-we-explain)
221. Wright, Tom, '*Bangladesh War Crimes Tribunal Bogs Down*', *The Wall Street Journal*, 20 December 2012 (http://online.wsj.com/news/articles/SB1000142412788732

377720457818915391859230 8?mg=reno64-wsj)

222. Hatzfeld, Jean, *Machete Season: The Killers of Rwanda Speak* (Picador, 2006), *Life Laid Bare: The Survivors in Rwanda Speak* (Other Press, 2007), and *The Antelope's Strategy: Living in Rwanda After the Genocide* (Picador, 2010).

223. Krog, Antjie, *Country of my Skull,* (Random House, 1999).

224. Sikkink, Kathryn, *The Justice Cascade: How Human Rights Prosecutions Are Changing World Politics* (Norton, 2011).

225. Salim, Ahmad, *We Owe an Apology to Bangladesh,* (Shahitya Prakash, 2012)

EPILOGUE

226. I have written the opening essay about the war and refugees in that book.

227. Shamsuddin, Abulkalam, *Confession of a Terrorist* (ip-6 Research, 2010).

INDEX

THE COLONEL WHO WOULD NOT REPENT